For Reference

Not to be taken from this room

A Concise Glossary of Feminist Theory

A Concise Glossary
of Feminist Theory

Sonya Andermahr
Nene College, Northampton

Terry Lovell   Carol Wolkowitz
University of Warwick

A member of the Hodder Headline Group
LONDON • NEW YORK • SYDNEY • AUCKLAND

First published in Great Britain in 1997 by
Arnold, a member of the Hodder Headline Group
338 Euston Road, London NW1 3BH
175 Fifth Avenue, New York, NY 10010

Distributed exclusively in the USA by
St Martin's Press, Inc.,
175 Fifth Avenue, New York, NY 10010

British Library Cataloguing in Publication Data
A catalogue record for this book is available from the British Library

Library of Congress Cataloging in Publication Data
A catalog record for this book is available from the Library of Congress

ISBN 0 340 59663 5

Printed and bound in Great Britain by JW Arrowsmith, Bristol.

Acknowledgements

We would like to thank our friends, families and colleagues for their help and support. A special thank you is due to Pauline Wilson for her work on the manuscript.

Introduction

Concepts and Theory in Feminism

> Dictionaries are produced and, with a show of authority no less confident because it is usually so limited in place and time, what is called a proper meaning is attached...when we go beyond these to the historical dictionaries, and to essays in historical and contemporary semantics, we are quite beyond the range of 'proper meanings'. We find a history and complexity of meanings; conscious changes or consciously different uses; innovation, obsolescence, specialization, extension, overlap, transfer; or changes that are masked by a nominal continuity (Williams, *Keywords* 1983: 16-17).

Raymond Williams's *Keywords* was to be a different kind of dictionary, one which aimed to capture concepts on the move in history, in order to reveal '...not concepts but problems...' (Williams 1977a: 11). This seems to us to be exactly what is required in a glossary of contemporary feminist theory, since contemporary feminism draws so heavily on what Edward Said (1983) has named 'travelling theory'. 'Like people and schools of criticism, ideas and theories travel – from person to person, from situation to situation, from one period to another', and as theory travels, so it is 'transformed by its new uses, its new position in a new time and place' (226–7).

Feminist theory has grown exponentially since the late 1960s. Its first impetus came from the emergent women's movements in the USA and Europe, and it became entrenched in contemporary intellectual life as feminist courses began to appear on the curriculum in higher education and in other educational settings. It is tied, then, to the fortunes of Western 'academic feminism' – courses in women's studies and gender studies which may be taught as part of degree programmes within orthodox disciplines or in specialist interdisciplinary centres. It is further reinforced by the publishing industry. There is scarcely a publishing house in the 1990s that does not have its women's studies/gender studies list.

This development was partly the result of the coincidence, variably in different national contexts, of the expansion of higher education, the increasing participation-rates of women as part of that expansion, and the emergence of the 'second wave' of the women's movement. The disciplines in which feminist theory and scholarship first appeared were those which attracted a high proportion of these new women students, and which attracted women who defined themselves as feminists.

In the USA, it was above all in literary criticism that feminism began to flourish, not without considerable resistance. In Europe, including Britain, it is probably true to say that on balance the social sciences provided the main sites for feminist theory. Sociology, a major beneficiary of the expansion in higher education (in Britain 17 new departments of sociology were set up between 1960 and 1970, and the number of degrees in sociology attained between 1962 and 1967 had increased by 389%), and the new field of cultural studies which dated only from the mid-1960s, were of particular significance.

The terms of feminism were drawn from the new feminist language that began to be produced by radical feminists in the USA, which involved reworking and reclaiming terms that had been used to demean women ('crone', 'dyke', and more fundamentally, 'woman'), and inventing new terms. But the concepts that began to inform feminist theorizing tended to be created through the critique and appro-priation of sociological theory, for example 'patriarchy', 'ideology', 'socialization', 'sex-roles'.

The radicalism of the 1960s was marked in sociology by a shift away from the dominant paradigm of the 1950s, sociological structural-functionalism, in favour of twentieth-century Marxism and sociological phenomenology, the dominant sources of 'travelling theory' at that time. Twentieth-century Marxism was a Marxism of the superstructure which was concerned to avoid the most discredited forms of economic reductionism. The 'keyword' at this time was 'ideology', and it was this concept above all which was appropriated for feminist theory to conceptualize 'patriarchy'.

'Ideology' was used as the organizing concept in discussions of sexual divisions and hierarchies, and for the analysis of culture, including literature and the visual arts. It was therefore placed under intense pressure, made to cover a great deal of ground, inside and outside of feminism. However, the term represented one of the weaker links in the conceptual repertoire of Marxism, and it became evident very early on that additional theoretical resources were required to tackle the work it was being asked to do. Literary and cultural studies required a more adequate account of language than was generally available within the Marxist frame, and feminists in all fields of study urgently required a more plausible theory of sexuality than Marxism could offer.

All the new resources for feminist theory were centred upon language. The 'linguistic turn' had affected all the disciplines of the humanities and social sciences between the mid-1960s and the mid-1970s, and the theories which 'travelled' from this period included structuralist linguistics and semiology, sociological and anthropological structuralism, Lacanian psychoanalysis, deconstructionism, and poststructuralism. This swathe of theory was centred in philosophy and critical theory rather than in sociology, and so the undertow for those who travelled with travelling theory pulled away from sociology and history to some degree.

The same drift from sociology and history to philosophy and cultural and literary studies may be detected during the 1980s and 1990s in feminist theory. Feminist philosophy was a relatively late development, but one which has rapidly made ground since the mid-1980s, with an important boost coming from Australian feminist philosophy as well as from France and Germany.

The Aims of the Glossary

The main aim of the glossary is to identify the concepts that have structured feminist theory in the period of the second wave, from about 1968, indicating their provenance in travelling theory from this time (although this time-frame is not strictly adhered to. There are some references to earlier feminisms, from the eighteenth and nineteenth centuries, and from the first half of the twentieth century – notably the work of Simone de Beauvoir and Virginia Woolf). The glossary aims to trace the variety of ways in which these concepts have been transformed as they were critiqued and appropriated. There are few 'keywords' in feminist theory that are not contentious, and we aim to show *what is at stake* in the disputes and debates of contemporary feminism rather than to provide neat definitions.

Travelling theory does not stop travelling when it is appropriated. The concepts of feminist theory have been in turn critiqued and appropriated by categories of women who were marginalized by a movement largely dominated by the concerns of white, Western and middle-class heterosexual women. Many of those who helped to develop that theory were deeply dismayed to discover that the charge of 'symbolic violence' which we had laid against male-dominated theory and politics might be extended to feminist appropriations as well. Lesbian feminism, Black feminism, anti-imperialist, and 'post-colonial' feminism have provided potent sources of further critique and appropriation in the 1980s and 1990s. Indeed it is no longer possible to speak in the singular of 'feminist theory'. Nor has this been a one-way process. Women have developed and conceptualized traditions of resistance in every part of the globe, throughout their history.

This brings us to consider a second concept which Said has made his own, that of 'cultural imperialism' (Said 1993). Travelling theory is itself deeply implicated in cultural imperialism. Travelling theory in the second half of the twentieth century is Western theory, but the encounter with subjugated non-Western traditions of thought and practice has produced hybrid, plural forms which in turn now circulate within transformed travelling theory. 'Partly because of empire, all cultures are involved in one another; none is single and pure, all are hybrid, heterogeneous, extraordinarily differentiated, and unmonolithic' (Said 1993: xxix). The traveller returns, travels again, and never returns unchanged.

Travelling theory is notoriously arcane. It makes of study hard work, and this has provoked more than a little hostility within 'grassroots' feminisms outside the academy. Academic feminism has been accused of elitism and an unnecessary obscurantism: of perpetrating 'symbolic violence' against the feminist project to which it owes its very existence. It has to be admitted that these charges are not entirely without foundation, and indeed students who are obliged to engage with such theory frequently make similar complaints. Therefore it is important to be clear about the purposes of this glossary. It does not aim to provide an introduction to feminist theory, nor yet a substitute for reading widely within such theory. Rather the aim is to provide a guide and companion for those who find themselves embarked, for whatever reason, on an engagement with this body of theory and perhaps struggling in its more obscure reaches. While we have tried as far as we are able to be accessible and clear, complex concepts in use across a wide range of fields, as travelling theory pursues its wayward journeying across the disciplines, cannot be rendered instantly transparent and painless. The book is for use upon the journey and not a substitute for travelling.

This glossary differs from Jeremy Hawthorn's in that it is not single-authored. Each of us is situated intellectually in particular ways which overlap but are not identical. Our backgrounds are in literary studies, cultural studies and sociology, and sociology respectively. The reader may therefore expect to find that the work is polyvocal. We discussed the possibility of initialling all the major entries, but decided that since we do not aim at authoritative definitions, it was entirely consistent with the project to let these differences stand. Equally, however, our joint competences and interests are far from comprehensive. The knowledge produced in glossary form is, like all knowledge, socially, intellectually and culturally situated.

Other Useful Dictionaries and Reference Books

Maggie Humm (1996). *The Dictionary of Feminist Theory* Second Edition. New York and London: Harvester Wheatsheaf.

Cheris Kramarae and Paula A. Treichler (1985). *A Feminist Dictionary*. Boston, London and Henley: Pandora.

Two valuable dictionaries which are broader in scope than this glossary, and serve a rather different purpose. They cover a broad range of terms, across different levels of abstraction and a wide range of discourses, specialized and 'common sense'. Kramarae and Treichler include entries under 'psychoanalysis' as well as 'humourless' and 'boarding school'. Humm includes short entries for individual theorists such as Germaine Greer and Willhelm Reich. Inevitably the broad coverage means that none of the entries is very lengthy, and the complexity of some of the more theoretical terms is sometimes lost as a result.

Mention should also be made here of:

Mary Daly, with Jane Caputi (1987). *Webster's First Intergalactic Wickedary of the English Language*. Austin, Mass: Beacon Press.

This is a glossary of 'new feminist language', a project to which Mary Daly herself has been the foremost contributor.

William Outhwaite and Tom Bottomore (eds) (1993). *The Blackwell Dictionary of Twentieth-Century Social Thought*. Oxford: Blackwell.

J.O. Urmson and Jonathan Rée (eds) (1989). *The Concise Encyclopaedia of Western Philosophy and Philosophers*. London: Unwin Hyman.
A useful survey, but with little engagement with feminist philosophy.

Dictionaries which are not specifically feminist are uneven in their coverage of feminist usages of the terms included. Typically, as in Outhwaite and Bottomore, there is some attempt to include feminist usage. But using this valuable source in particular, it has often been sobering to discover the extent to which feminism has simply been ignored in many of the entries. This is particularly true of those in the areas of philosophy and political theory. In some cases a comparison between the entries in this glossary and in the *Blackwell Dictionary* will show that while the former usually takes cognizance of the concerns of the latter, and although many of the *Blackwell* entries engage with feminist usage, many remain which are written as though we live in a genderless world, and as though feminists had never addressed the concept in question. This is true even in areas where feminists have made major contributions, such as political philosophy and theory.

In addition, while the number of women contributing entries to these compilation dictionaries is no necessary indication of the degree of engagement with feminist thought, it is nevertheless a cause for concern that so few are represented. Feminist thought and scholarship is still, on this evidence, largely contained, cordoned off from the mainstream/malestream.

Elizabeth Wright (ed.) (1992). *Feminism and Psychoanalysis: A Critical Dictionary*. Oxford: Blackwell.

A multi-authored, critical dictionary. The many contributors come from across the field, and include both academics and clinicians. The input is therefore much broader than is the case with a glossary written by three people in dialogue with each other. However, its critical commentary on key terms serves a similar purpose to our own and we are indebted to this dictionary for our entries on psychoanalysis. Like our own guide, the dictionary engages with contemporary critical theory, but owing to its psychoanalytic frame, it does not have the social science agenda that we have included.

Jeremy Hawthorn (1992). *A Glossary of Contemporary Literary Theory*. London: Edward Arnold.

Hawthorn's glossary was the model for our own. Rather than repeat material he covers, we have referred the reader to his excellent entries. His glossary is an honourable exception to the comments above on 'the main/malestream'. There is a systematic engagement with feminism, and we have frequently picked up issues which, for lack of space, he treats only briefly.

Using the Glossary

We have followed Hawthorn in the practice of using longer 'keyword' entries to group together related concepts which are cross-referred, to avoid too much repetition, and in the use of small capitals within entries to point towards related entries. We also follow Hawthorn in capitalizing cognate terms where they occur, for entries which are not identical; for example DECONSTRUCT when the actual entry is DECONSTRUCTION.

Bracketed references refer the reader to the bibliography. Our experience in compiling this glossary has been that good indexes and bibliographies are as rare as gold dust, and we have departed from Hawthorn in adopting an inclusive rather than more limited bibliography which includes all references cited with author and date in the text, and not only those we have actually quoted. We have entered each item in the edition in which it is most readily available, but indicated where possible the date when it was first published.

Terms of foreign origin are italicized, and italics are retained even where they are in general use outside the language of origin, for example Roland Barthes's distinction between *plaisir* and *jouissance*.

This glossary is also available in a longer, hardback edition. This version is a shorter, student edition, which omits some of the more general entries and abridges certain others.

A

Abject   A psychoanalytic term used in the work of Julia Kristeva. Literally meaning 'cast out', according to Kristeva the abject is that which 'disturbs identity, system, order' (1982: 4). Significantly, she associates abjection with the maternal body in so far as the latter symbolizes a disturbing generative power and repulsive fecundity within phallocentric systems of thought. Abjection is the horror of physical engulfment; of not recognizing the boundaries between self and other, hence its repression from the patriarchal symbolic order. The term has been taken up in cultural studies by feminist critics, for example by film critic Barbara Creed (1993) in her work on the MONSTROUS FEMININE.

Absence   See METAPHYSICS OF PRESENCE.

Abuse   See VIOLENCE AGAINST WOMEN.

Academic feminism   There is little systematic, theoretically and politically informed study of FEMINISM in the academy. Empirical studies grounded in an EQUAL OPPORTUNITIES perspective document women's disadvantage in changing conditions of academic practice. They register gendered differences in access to degree courses and to posts; to promotion, and remuneration; vertical and horizontal segregation is uncovered – the continued concentration of women in relatively low-status areas, on short-term contracts (Morley and Walsh [eds] 1995).

    RADICAL FEMINIST interventions have emphasized the built-in MASCULINITY of mainstream scholarly practices and institutions – competitive, hierarchical, authoritarian – to argue that unless this changes, then the success or failure of women competing within them is of little moment for feminism. In an influential essay Adrienne Rich argues for a 'woman-centred university', aiming not simply for insertion and integration, but at challenging existing practices (Rich 1980b), and this approach is echoed in the work of feminist EPISTEMOLOGY which began in the early 1970s to adumbrate protocols for the conduct of feminist research.

Pierre Bourdieu's sociology of academic practice provides concepts that might prove useful (Bourdieu 1988). He analyses the deep unease of those cultural 'nouveaux riches' whose early socialization leaves them wanting in terms of the working cultural capital of intellectual life. Early exposure and familiarity is compounded and consolidated through (the right) schools and universities. Those who do not build upon such a base may never feel full confidence that they really belong. Some never gain this ease, however much recognition is bestowed and won.

While, all things being equal, academic women may suffer this unease to a greater degree than academic men, CLASS and 'RACE' cut across GENDER as ever, and quite critically in this case. Amongst those women who have gained academic success we may certainly distinguish between those who are relatively well endowed with this working cultural capital of the academy and those from sections of the community brought up to understand that such things are, in Bourdieu's phrase, 'not for the likes of us'.

Debates over feminism within the academy recur over the alternative strategies of inserting feminism within the 'mainstream' DISCIPLINES, or striking out for an independent, INTERDISCIPLINARY base where new, women-friendly and non-hierarchical practices may be instituted (Gunew [ed.] 1991). Both strategies have been followed. But assessing the differences that feminist interventions have made is complicated by the fact that the history of feminist presence within the academy is coterminous with radical changes at both the intellectual and institutional level in higher education.

We are beginning to see, all over the globe, the emergence of high profile, successful feminist academics, who carry some considerable influence, whether in traditional disciplines or in interdisciplinary studies of women and gender. Women and feminists are increasingly found in 'gatekeeper' roles within the institutions of scholarship, disciplinary and interdisciplinary. A more or less defined sub-field has emerged, with its own publishing houses, departments and centres, its own badges of DISTINCTION. We are now in a better position to examine the various ways in which the competing demands of feminist politics and of academic success have been negotiated, and the extent to which practices obtaining in this emergent complex differ or converge with those elsewhere, under the conditions of the late twentieth century in a profession which has undergone great change.

See also BACKLASH.

Aesthetics Throughout its history, aesthetic theory has been shot through with assumptions about women and gender (Battersby 1989). Four related issues have dominated feminist aesthetic theory in relation to most of the major aesthetic forms: the MARGINALIZATION of women; the 'female aesthetic'; the 'FEMININE' in art; and the nature of the filtering process which determines inclusion or exclusion from the CANON.

Anglo-American 'GYNOCRITICISM' locates women in the margins (Gilbert and Gubar 1979; Showalter 1978). Gynocriticism points to the disabling effects upon women writers of 'man-made language' but suffers, claims Moi (1985), from having no theory of language comparable to that of the post-Lacanian FRENCH FEMINISTS. Women are not, of course, the only occupants of the margins. There is a long history of exclusions along the lines of class and 'race'. BLACK FEMINIST criticism has encompassed the marginalization of Black writers (Christian 1985). But because these differences intersect, the gynocritical project of identifying the characteristics of 'women's writing' becomes more problematic.

Do women write/paint etc. 'as women'? Does the cultural product bear distinct traces of the embodied, sexed self of its producer? Gynocriticism has usually answered these questions in the affirmative. Feminist aesthetic theory from a number of different perspectives has entered reservations (Battersby 1989; Felski 1989a; Moi 1985; Parker and Pollock 1981; Wolff 1983). But French feminist aesthetics as well as Anglo-American gynocriticism engage in this issue. It is Irigaray who has enjoined women to 'write with the body', to develop what she termed *PARLER FEMME* (Irigaray 1991), and who has been in consequence accused alongside gynocriticism of essentialism (Moi 1985; Whitford 1991)

FRENCH FEMINISM proffers a different marginalization thesis: not the marginalization of women in cultural production but of 'the feminine' in LANGUAGE itself. The margins of language are, however, places of great privilege and creativity within contemporary POSTSTRUCTURALIST philosophy. It might be expected therefore that this approach would be particularly favourable to women artists and writers. However it is, notoriously, the male avant-garde that reaps the benefit of this celebration of femininity, which Battersby (1989) brands as 'femininism' rather than feminism.

The fourth issue arises because of the revaluation of forms and GENRES which women have developed, or work within extensively. Often these are of low status, and in many cases do not secure the distinction of the label 'art'. Feminism has led to an interest in not only the history of the novel, in which women played a major part (Spender 1986; Spencer 1986; Lovell 1987) but also personal writings, diaries, letters, and genre fiction (Felski 1989a; Radway 1984). In film and media studies, it has lead to renewed interest in television soap operas, film melodrama and 'women's pictures' (Ang 1985; Brunsdon [ed.] 1986; Geraghty 1991; Gledhill [ed.] 1987; Modleski 1982; Modleski 1991). In the fine arts, the distinction between 'art' and 'crafts' has been interrogated in work on such forms as embroidery and quilting (Parker 1984).

Feminists agree that there is a marked gender division of labour in the production, consumption and transmission of art. Historical research on women's art and its reception has qualified gynocriticism's more radical thesis: 'women artists have not acted outside cultural history, as many commentators seem to believe, but rather have been compelled to act within it from a place other than that occupied by men' (Parker and Pollock 1981: 14). The focus, then, shifts from marginalization and exclusion, to a more positive mapping of the places from which women have produced, and the nature of the attractions and compulsions which channel them into these places, and into particular forms and genres. Sexual difference in cultural production, on this reading, is historically variable and socially produced (Armstrong 1987; Felski 1989a; Lovell 1987).

See also *ÉCRITURE FEMININE*; WOMEN'S CULTURE.

Affidamento See ITALIAN FEMINISM.

Ageism Discrimination/prejudice against older people. Franco Moretti argues that eighteenth-century Europe witnessed a change associated with the self-consciousness of MODERNITY, in which youth became identified as the most significant period of life. Modern cultures do not place high premium on age, and late 1960s women's movements rode the crest of a counter-cultural wave which celebrated youth and was deeply anti-authoritarian. Feminist unwillingness to cede authority to age was compounded by the reserve of this GENERATION of the late 1960s towards the maternal GENERATION. The heroic 'grandmother' generation was honoured for having fought valiantly to win the vote. Their daughters, the generation that came to maturity in the 1940s and 1950s were seen as having frittered away this heritage – a 'traitor generation' (Stacey 1989: 141).

As the dominant generation of second-wave FEMINISM has advanced through the life-cycle, so its preoccupations have changed, and, because of the position this generation has gained within feminist scholarship, its changing concerns usually secure a hearing. We have moved from the daughter's complaint, through the trials of caring for dependants at both extremes of age, to the dawning recognition that caring is a relationship and that we are even more likely to find ourselves on the receiving than the giving end, due to the greater longevity of women (Graham 1993). Moreover, as second-wave feminists have found themselves in positions of (relative) power and authority, there has been perhaps a little less reluctance to recognize relationships of empowerment: what ITALIAN FEMINISM calls *affidamento* or entrustment.

Ageing may be viewed as a gender-differentiated process, not least because of demographic differences, but also because the meaning of advancing age, in a highly sex-differentiated culture, is necessarily sex-specific to some degree. Some feminists have argued that the post-menopausal period of women's lives is one in which the obligations incurred by younger women, not least the obligation to be sexually attractive to men, are lessened. De Beauvoir is deeply equivocal: 'It is in the autumn and winter of her life that woman is freed from her chains... Rid of her duties, she finds freedom at last...at the very time when she can make no use of it' (de Beauvoir 1953: 595).

Greer is more positive. In a full-length study of the menopause she writes: 'As long as they like themselves [women over fifty] will not be an oppressed minority' (1991: 2). She takes up the RADICAL FEMINIST defiant reclamation of the older woman as 'crone', 'wise woman', 'witch' (Daly 1991) and is sharply critical of attempts to defer the ageing process through hormone replacement therapy and other means.

Agency A crucial term in the theory and practice of feminist, as indeed of any POLITICS. Its history in feminist theory is complicated and beset by contradictions. Feminism's founding gesture involves the identification of women's lack of agency and their construction as victims of PATRIARCHY; as Wollstonecraft writes: 'Was not the world a vast prison and women born slaves?' (1987: 79). The goal of feminism has repeatedly been formulated as women's self-determination; i.e. that women become actors in the world on their own terms. While both these formulations have proved effective in mobilizing the WOMEN'S MOVEMENT, there are a number of well-rehearsed problems with them. Firstly, the designation of women as victims serves to compound women's OPPRESSION under patriarchy and threatens to erase what agency they do manage to exercise. Secondly, the goal of self-determination is dependent upon the HUMANIST belief that it is indeed possible to determine the SELF. Various theories of SUBJECTIVITY – including PSYCHOANALYSIS, POSTSTRUCTURALISM and MARXISM – deny that it is possible in any straightforward way.

In addition, feminist theorists of women's agency working within a CULTURAL STUDIES paradigm have inherited two distinct models, namely 'culturalism' and 'STRUCTURALISM', which conceive of agency in contrasting ways. Culturalism, with its roots in British Marxism, seeks the historical and ethnographic retrieval of working–class consciousness and emphasizes possibilities for agency. E.P. Thompson's *The Making of the English Working Class*, for example, sets out to demonstrate that 'the working class was present at its own history' (1968: 8).

In contrast, structuralism, originating in French linguistic philosophy, highlights the determination of the SUBJECT by various structures, rejecting as humanist fallacies culturalist notions of agency. While male exponents of both models have in practice tended to ignore the question of women's agency, feminist theorists have necessarily engaged and confronted the problems of each. The structuralist model carries a risk of political inaction in that the concept of agency dissolves in the determining POWER of discursive structures or processes. In contrast, the culturalist model runs a risk of overstating the degree of social agency of oppressed groups, seeing signs of resistance everywhere in POPULAR CULTURE. Reading Mills and Boon fiction as subversive of the patriarchal Symbolic is one example (cf. ROMANCE).

Contemporary interest in POSTMODERNISM can be seen as indicative of a desire to move beyond a dichotomous model of agency. Yet its effects are contradictory: the postmodern fragmentation of IDENTITY implies the unviability of individual/collective action; the postmodern multiplication of identity suggests the possibility of 'agency' through consumer choice or discursive play. However, notwithstanding such DECONSTRUCTIVE moves, the notion of agency reappears in altered form in many postmodern discourses, such as in Rorty's (1989) concept of localized agency.

A refinement of the culturalist model was introduced in the notion of NEGOTIATION by which subcultural groups attempt to negotiate a space in relation to the dominant CULTURE. The concept has given rise to a number of interesting analyses (e.g. Gledhill 1992), but it inevitably carries with it an inappropriate connotation of (capitalist) contract negotiation supposedly between social equals. Working-class girls obviously do not 'negotiate' their social reality with the same resources or advantages as do middle-class girls. The ways in which women's different and differing social locations in relation to RACE, CLASS, SEXUALITY and other vectors of difference affect the degree of agency available to them is a central issue in recent theorizations of the politics of DIFFERENCE.

Notwithstanding such problems and the fact that women's agency remains poorly theorized within feminist theory, feminists agree that it is politically imperative to hold on to the notion of women's agency (Mani 1992).

See also MASCULINITY; VIOLENCE AGAINST WOMEN.

Androgyny See BISEXUALITY.

Anti-foundationalism See FOUNDATIONALISM.

Anti-humanism See HUMANISM.

Anti-imperialist critique See COLONIAL DISCOURSE; IMPERIALISM.

Aporia A figure of speech, from the Greek, for an apparently irresolvable logical difficulty, in which a speaker appears to be in doubt about a question. The most famous example is Hamlet's soliloquy 'To be or not to be'.

Jacques Derrida uses the term to signify a certain excess in language; a point at which a text's self-contradictory meanings cannot be resolved, or when the text undermines its own fundamental grounding principles. As such, identifying moments of aporia becomes an important move in DECONSTRUCTIVE criticism.

Appropriation In Marxist theory, a key term denoting the relationship of the capitalist to the product of the labour-power of the worker. Feminists exploring the ways in which Marxist theory might be used to analyse the OPPRESSION of women, pointed to the appropriation of women's bodies and their labour, including their capacity to reproduce, by men as well as by capital (Sargent [ed.] 1981).

The term is also applied to POSTMODERNIST 'raids' upon theory. Feminist postmodernists borrow from sources that may be entirely innocent of any engagement with issues of gender, reworking and transforming them for the purpose of developing feminist theory. Leslie Dick (1989) cites plundering as a fruitful strategy for feminist cultural workers whom she encourages to raid the dominant CULTURE and rework its produce in new, subversive ways.

However Moi (1991) warns that feminist appropriations must be linked to CRITIQUE, drawing on Kate Soper's definition of the latter as 'explaining the source in reality of the cognitive shortcomings of the theory under attack' and calling for 'changes in the reality itself' (Soper 1989: 93). Appropriation may thus be a principled and political element in feminist strategy and no mere play with words.

Archaeology In *The Archaeology of Knowledge* (1972) Foucault rejects the postulates and procedures of the history of ideas, which he argues usually seek in discourse 'the slow emergence of truth from error' (Sheridan 1980: 104). Although for Foucault DISCOURSE bears some relation to its extra-discursive 'conditions of existence', he is not interested in looking behind it for something hidden; rather, it is 'all surface'. As Maureen Cain (1993) explains, archaeology looks for rules which govern the relationship beween 'items' which are constituted and deployed by the discourse itself. She illustrates this with examples from her own field of feminist criminology. Items constituted by the rules of the discourse include the objects of discourse (for example crimes, convicted people, defences, mitigating circumstances); the subjects of discourse (for example the law); enunciators of the discourse (judges, attorneys) and sites of discourse (courts and so forth). However, Foucault's later work focuses less on abstract and general methodological principles and more on detailed GENEALOGIES of particular concepts and PRACTICES.

See also KNOWLEDGE; POWER.

Archaic mother See MATERNAL BODY.

Archetypal criticism Archetypal criticism originated in J.G. Frazer's comparative study of mythologies, *The Golden Bough* (1963), and C.G. Jung's psychoanalysis. Jung argued that certain myths and symbols represent primitive forms and memories which survive in the collective unconscious. Examples of archetypal patterns include death, rebirth, love and conflict.

More recently, critics have been alert to the dangers of reductionism and ESSENTIALISM attendant on the application of universal models to particular cultural texts, and have sought to specify cultural differences.

A feminist variant of archetypal criticism emerged in the 1970s which, while sharing an interest in the structural analysis of MYTH, rejects the existing mythical REPRESENTATION of women and gender, and seeks to elaborate alternative archetypal figures and patterns. In her *Archetypal Patterns in Women's Fiction*, Annis Pratt (1982) employs categories of male and female drawn from Jungian archetypes to examine women's fiction. Pratt sees certain patterns as signalling a buried FEMININE tradition that is at odds with cultural norms.

Recent reworkings of archetype and myth by feminist writers such as Alice Walker (1984b) and Angela Carter (1978) have gone some way to challenging the patriarchal character of inherited cultural narratives.

Articulation   According to Stuart Hall (1980) there is no necessary connection between IDEOLOGY and social formations: such connections always need to be *articulated* in terms of a relation between cultural and material parts.

See also IDEOLOGY; MATERIALIST FEMINISM.

Authenticity   A concept which has permeated modern Western thought since the early modern period, part of a family of terms including SELF and SUBJECTIVITY, all currently under erasure in the climate of anti-HUMANISM and 'the linguistic turn' in modern theory.

Within feminism the idea of authenticity is articulated in concepts such as WOMEN'S CULTURE. The 1980s saw the HEGEMONY of IDENTITY POLITICS in feminism. But as the parameters of IDENTITY expanded, so the categories of self-identification proliferated to the point which is difficult to distinguish from INDIVIDUALISM.

A thorough exploration of authenticity and related concepts, and a defence of them in the light of POSTMODERNISM and POSTSTRUCTURALISM, may be found in the work of Charles Taylor (1989; 1991).

Authority   Roughly, the legitimate exercise of POWER. Different types of authority are recognized within social theory. Max Weber distinguished traditional, legal-rational, and charismatic, and located the first in terms of a development from the quasi-natural authority of the head of the PATRIARCHAL household. But there has been little interest within the discourses of social theory in the gendering of power and authority.

The concept of power has had wider circulation within feminist theory than that of 'authority', partly because women's exercise of power is denied legitimacy (Rosaldo and Lamphere [eds] 1974). While the initial focus has usually been on the power which men exercise over women in a wide variety of contexts, women's power, especially their ability to empower other women through COMMUNITIES OF WOMEN and WOMEN'S CULTURE, was given early recognition in RADICAL FEMINIST writings, and another, alternative source of authority was identified in women's EXPERIENCE. With the exception of ITALIAN FEMINISM, there has been less willingness to recognize the forms in which women exercise authority over others, except insofar as it has occurred in domains which have previously been exclusively or predominantly male, and the interest is in how women deal with male refusals to recognize their authority, and in the question of whether women exercise it in a distinctive manner (Wajcman 1996).

The reluctance to recognize women's legitimate power in certain areas of social life is perhaps because its domain is female and familial. Women most often have authority over other women and children. Ellen Moers's pioneering *Literary Women* signalled this relationship in her concept of the 'educating heroine' (1977), and it is primarily in this field of feminist studies of education that this form of female authority has been discussed (Miller 1996). Nancy Armstrong, drawing on Foucault, has insisted that 'domestic woman', who emerged as the consort of 'economic man' in early modern Europe, was a powerholder, one moreover who was defining and exercising new forms of (domestic) authority (Armstrong 1987). But the Foucauldian feminist literature on the disciplinary regimes which produce 'docile bodies' (Foucault 1977) has overwhelmingly concentrated attention on girls' and women's bodies as objects of disciplinary regimes of diet, exercise, etc. (Bordo 1993) but not on women's longstanding role in many cultures as designers, initiators and executors of these regimes.

Authorship   A concept which has received much critical and theoretical attention in recent years from a variety of sources. Firstly, feminist critics have challenged the long-standing equation of authorship and MASCULINITY (Battersby 1989; Gilbert and Gubar 1979; 1988). In a brilliantly witty exposé of the sexual politics of authorship Gilbert and Gubar ask the question 'Is the pen a metaphorical penis?', and trace the gendering of textual production through imagery in the work of male writers from the Renaissance to the present day (1988: 227).

In addition to undertaking critiques of male authorship, feminist criticism has produced theories of the specificity of female authorship (Cixous 1976b; Gilbert and Gubar 1988; Showalter 1978) which, while diverse in approach, share a focus on the gendered aspects of textual production. Elaine Showalter gave this woman-centred criticism the name GYNOCRITICISM, its aim being the recovery and re-evaluation of women's writing in terms of women's EXPERIENCE and CULTURE. In contrast, feminist critics of a more sociological bent have drawn attention to the social and historical contexts in which women have undertaken authorship (Felski 1989a).

Secondly, in an independent move, the notion of the author has come under attack from poststructuralist critics, most notably Roland Barthes whose 1968 'The death of the author' (1977a) argued that TEXTUALITY or writing presaged the end of author-oriented literary criticism. For their part, feminist critics have been less cavalier about doing away with the concept, particularly at a time in history when women have begun to author texts in unprecedented numbers. Some have pointed to the irony of a situation in which women find a voice at the moment when male intellectuals declare the author to be an irrelevance.

See also AESTHETICS.

Autobiography   See PERSONAL NARRATIVES.

B

Backlash   Susan Faludi's *Backlash: The Undeclared War against Women* (1992) coined the term for the anti-feminist rebound of the 1980s and 1990s. Backlash signals attempts to limit women's advances in employment, family law and reproductive rights or to narrow feminism to issues of equity (for example, Sommers 1994). Backlash in academia – an aspect of the so-called 'culture wars' (Ferguson *et al.* 1996) – sees feminist studies, Black studies and gay and lesbian studies as limiting free speech through their insistence on so-called 'political correctness', but ignores the 'intellectual harassment' of feminists and others (Clark *et al.* 1996). One problem with 'backlash' as an explanation of the rightward pro-family drift in the cultural landscape, however, is that it tends to highlight the machinations of organized anti-feminist campaigns; some research suggests that people's feelings of material and psychological vulnerability play an important role in nostalgia for traditional families and the rise of Christian fundamentalism (Stacey 1987; 1990).

See also ACADEMIC FEMINISM; POSTFEMINISM.

Becoming woman   The concept is central to the philosophical thought of Gilles Deleuze, where it represents the departure from PHALLOCENTRIC modes of thinking. His notion of becoming is adapted from Nietzsche's anti-Hegelian philosophy which affirms the positivity of DIFFERENCE conceived of as a multiple and continual process of transformation. In *A Thousand Plateaus*, Deleuze and Guattari elaborate on this process:

> For us...there are as many sexes as there are terms in symbiosis, as many differences as elements contributing to a process of contagion. We know that many beings pass between a man and a woman; they come from different worlds, are born on the wind, form rhizomes around roots; they cannot be understood in terms of production, only in terms of becoming (1992: 242).

Rosi Braidotti (1994b) argues that Deleuze's emphasis on process, dynamic interaction and fluid BOUNDARIES makes his thought highly relevant to the feminist analysis of late industrial PATRIARCHAL culture. However, Braidotti also points to the discrepancy between his theory of becoming woman and feminist theories of women as sexed subjects. She argues that it is the relationship between the two that is crucial for feminists for whom the deconstruction of phallogocentrism cannot be 'disconnected from the concrete changes taking place in women's lives' (1994b: 115).

Binary/binarism   An either/or distinction common to a variety of human systems of COMMUNICATION. LANGUAGE provides good examples of organization of reality into oppositions, as in night/day; black/white; nature/culture; male/female.

Binarism constitutes the basis of STRUCTURALISM. In linguistics, the Saussurian sign is made up of two halves, the signifier and the signified (cf. SIGNIFICATION); and in anthropology, Lévi-Strauss (1968) analyses CULTURE in terms of sets of paired oppositions such as the 'raw' and the 'cooked'.

The concept of binary opposition is also central to DECONSTRUCTION. According to Derrida, the terms of the opposition do not possess an equivalent value; one term is privileged over the other, so that they form a hierarchy. Deconstruction offers a method of unpicking such oppositions by exposing their construction and mutual implication.

It is in this regard that binary oppositions have a particular resonance for feminist critics as it is the subordinated term that is so often aligned with FEMININITY. Sherry Ortner, in 'Is female to male as nature is to culture?', argues that in patriarchal cultures women are organized into polarized categories which results in their being seen as 'sometimes utterly exalted, sometimes utterly debased, rarely within the normal range of human possibilities' (1974: 505). A similar theme is explored by Hélène Cixous who in 'The laugh of the Medusa' (1976a) identifies some of the dominant binary oppositions in Western culture and whose *ÉCRITURE FEMININE* seeks to deconstruct them. The deconstruction of sexual binarism is, in effect, what the work of French feminists has been primarily concerned with. In her influential essay 'Women's time' (1989), Julia Kristeva advocates moving beyond a binary model of gender difference altogether.

Bioethics   See BODY; MORAL REASONING.

Bisexuality   In Darwinian thought bisexuality represents a biological concept, referring to the presence of male and female sexual characteristics in an organism. Secondly, it refers to the co-existence in the human psyche of feminine and masculine psychological characteristics. Thirdly, it describes an individual's love of or desire for persons of both sexes. Freud (1905) emphasizes the primal polymorphousness of human DESIRE and argues that all human beings have an original bisexual constitution in respect of both SEX and SEXUALITY.

In the last 20 years debates have raged over the inclusion of the term 'bisexual' in lesbian and gay organizations, institutions and conferences. Clearly, on one level bisexuality represents a challenge to the normative or COMPULSORY HETEROSEXUALITY identified by RADICAL FEMINISTS among others. It would also appear to demonstrate the mutability of human sexuality. Marjorie Garber (1992; 1996) contends that bisexuality and cross-dressing are historically transgressive practices. Elisabeth Badinter (1989) argues that the 'complementary model' of the sexes has been replaced by a 'resemblance model', resulting in a sexual indeterminacy which allows for the emergence of new sexual IDENTITIES.

Bisexuality would therefore seem to offer feminists a useful means of destabilizing phallic sexuality and multiplying desire. However, bisexual activists/theorists often overplay this aspect, adopting a version of Freud's concept of constitutional bisexuality in order to present bisexuality as a preferred sexuality. FRENCH FEMINISTS point to the fact that such theories often belie a PHALLOCENTRIC conception of sexuality which denies sexual difference (Cixous 1976a; Irigaray 1985a). Where bisexuality is conceived of as a realm between two polarized sets of characteristics, the result reinforces rather than challenges a repressive binary view of sexuality. In such a monosexual economy, bisexuality is not a real option (Irigaray 1985a). As the lesbian protagonist of Sarah Schulman's novel *Empathy* says: 'Don't you dare tell me that all people are basically bisexual. I couldn't take it' (1993: 70).

Implicit in this comment is the view that theories such as Garber's and Badinter's downplay the interface between forms of sexuality and POWER. No more than hetero- or homosexuality can bisexuality escape the implications of sexual power relations. The character of bisexual, lesbian and gay oppressions is historically variable and discontinuous and cannot be deduced in *a priori* fashion. Nevertheless, bisexuality has functioned as a valuable category in UTOPIAN and literary discourses: Virginia Woolf explores the notions of bisexuality and androgyny, most notably in her bisexual comic fantasy *Orlando* (1992, first published 1928) and in her literary theory of the androgynous mind in *A Room of One's Own* (1977, first published 1929). Her ideas connect to more recent speculations by French feminists such as Hélène Cixous who sees writing as inherently bisexual 'otherwise' (1976b), and Julia Kristeva (1989) whose notion of a third stage of feminism beyond EQUALITY and DIFFERENCE is not dissimilar to Woolf's notion of androgyny as deconstructing bipolar gender difference.

Black feminism   Refers to a variety of FEMINISMS which are identified by their opposition to the RACISM and sexism encountered by Black women. In its various forms it undertakes a sustained critique of the racism and ETHNOCENTRISM of white-dominated systems and practices including feminism. As Valerie Smith has argued, its critique is multi-faceted:

> Black feminists seek not only to dismantle the assumptions of dominant cultures, and to recover and reclaim the lives of black women, but also to develop methods of analysis for interpreting the ways in which race and gender are inscribed (1990: 271).

Similarly, Kimberlé Crenshaw identifies the concept of the 'intersectionality' of RACE and GENDER in the lives of black women as central to Black feminism, 'thereby rendering inapplicable ... any single-axis theory about racism and sexism' (cited in Valerie Smith 1990: 272). Historically, Black women's campaigning has reflected this intersectional emphasis, encompassing struggles – such as anti-lynching, civil and education rights – on the fronts of race and gender simultaneously; although for many Black women, from Ida B. Wells to the supporters of O.J. Simpson, the viciousness of racism requires that 'race' frequently be prioritized.

Politically, the term 'Black' is linked primarily with a vision of a Pan-African Black IDENTITY in Africa and in the diaspora. But in Britain it is also used more generally to indicate a political identity that is non-white, and until recently 'Black feminism' functioned as a generic term for non-white feminisms. There has been much debate about which groups the term designates and whether it has been used in too inclusive a manner. For example, does 'Black' include women from the Indian subcontinent and Chinese women? American feminists coined the inclusive term WOMEN OF COLOUR to address this issue. POST-COLONIAL THEORY has usefully pointed to the colonial construction of First and Third World 'ethnic' identities, emphasizing the discontinuities as well as the continuities of 'living colour' in a global context.

One of the founding texts of Black feminism is Barbara Smith's 'Towards a Black feminist criticism' (1985) which named it and set out its agenda. In offering a reading of Toni Morrison's *Sula* as a lesbian novel, the essay also made an important contribution to lesbian criticism. The work of Audre Lorde (1984) and Alice Walker has also been central to Black feminism; and the cross-generic style of both writers – blending fiction, theory and autobiography – has become characteristic of Black feminist writing. Lorde's concepts of the 'sister outsider' and the 'house of difference' and Walker's (1984a) notion of 'WOMANISM' provided Black feminism with a critical vocabulary with which to articulate the specificity of Black femininity.

By the late 1980s critics began to challenge the Black feminist emphasis on identity politics (Aziz 1992; Spillers 1984; Spivak 1987). And recently, a debate concerning the relation of Black feminism to POSTMODERNISM has emerged. bell hooks comments on black women's apparent lack of interest in postmodernism arguing that it has failed to speak to them (1991: 23). In fact there is a postmodern practice amongst Black and post-colonial theorists. For example, the work of the CHICANA feminist Gloria Anzaldúa (1987) displays a postmodern awareness of the multiplicity or 'border crossing' of identity. Certainly, postmodernism has accompanied if not initiated a new anti-ESSENTIALIST emphasis in Black feminist writing and new theorizations of the relation between social location, identity and politics (Boyce Davies 1994). While postmodernism would seem to destabilize certain feminist conceptualizations of Black womanhood, it should be emphasized that the critique of ESSENTIALIST assumptions about gender, sexuality and 'race' is precisely where the politics of Black feminism begin. The transformative effect of Black feminism on feminism in the West and world-wide cannot be underestimated, and women's studies in the 1990s is in the process of being reconceptualized to take seriously 'DIFFERENCE' in all its aspects.

Body   Feminism has a history of deep ambivalence towards the female body, which has figured alternately as the source of women's OPPRESSION and as the locus of a specifically female POWER. Both approaches focus on the REPRODUCTIVE body; on female SEXUALITY, menstruation, pregnancy, lactation, menopause. These corporealities of women may be seen as making us vulnerable to male domination and control, both directly through the exercise of superior physical power, and indirectly through social compulsions and the REPRESENTATION of sexual DIFFERENCE across a variety of discourses (Bordo 1993; de Beauvoir 1953; Firestone 1971; Laqueur 1990; Sayers 1982).

Those who prefer to celebrate the female body as a source of power, affirming women's corporeality positively in its differences from that of men, and valorizing its reproductive capacities have been accused of ESSENTIALISM. In male-dominated socio-cultural worlds, every affirmation of female difference is likely to be used to further disadvantage women (Narayan 1989).

From the 1980s there has been a virtual 'resurrection of the body' in social and philosophical theory. This has its base in those POSTSTRUCTURALIST and PHENOMENOLOGIST philosophies which claim Nietzsche in their GENEALOGIES – Foucault, Lacan, Merleau-Ponty, and many others. The starting point of these 'wayward philosophies' (Grosz 1994) is a refusal of the mind/body dichotomy which has dominated Western thought, and its dissolution in a concept of a subjectivity which is irreducibly corporeal.

These contemporary philosophies of corporeality follow significantly different directions. Foucault's work is more firmly oriented towards the social and the historical, in its institutional sense, rather than the phenomenological and interpersonal contexts explored by Merleau-Ponty. Pierre Bourdieu's work, too, shifts the mind/body distinction through the concept of PRACTICE which is governed by its own 'logic of practice' rather than by conscious mental processes (Bourdieu 1990a). The strikingly original contribution of Elaine Scarry, writing on the body in pain, is also located within the phenomenological tradition but outside the poststructuralist frame. It offers an enormously powerful resource which has as yet remained largely untapped by feminist theory (Scarry 1985).

The body which has been resurrected in this corpus of theory is THE body: implicitly male. The project of developing a 'corporeal feminism' has therefore had to undertake CRITIQUE as well as APPROPRIATION. Corporeal feminism emphasizes fluid BOUNDARIES, connection rather than separation, interdependence rather than autonomy, to develop an alternative model of the lived sexed body. It shares with feminisms of difference the task of affirming a corporeal feminine specificity, while claiming to escape the reification of difference which invites 'othering' and may be charged with ESSENTIALISM.

The work of Luce Irigaray has been central to all those engaged in this feminist project. In her critique of Western philosophy (Irigaray 1974) she argues that this tradition cannot acknowledge or recognize the maternal OTHER in its difference from the male who has monopolized the position of subject. Unless this recognition is won, and the PHALLOCENTRIC foundations of what passes for KNOWLEDGE are undermined, women will never achieve full sex-specific subjectivity, and men will continue to MISRECOGNIZE themselves as they strive to distance themselves from their own bodies.

This project of identifying the sexed corporeal basis of thought and subjectivity has been variously developed by Bordo (1993), Braidotti (1994b), Grosz (1994) and many others, as well as by Irigaray. It has attracted a number of criticisms, chiefly, that it does not escape essentialism; and also, that it privileges GENDER over other axes of difference, particularly those of 'RACE' and CLASS.

Defenders of corporeal feminism (Schor and Weed [eds] 1994; Whitford 1991) have rejected both charges. The difference in question, they claim, is no longer one that is open to reification, for it is difference per se which is being affirmed: an absolute, incommensurable, and in principle infinitely proliferating difference.

However this in itself causes further difficulties. If the bases of possible difference – 'race', class, gender, bodily ability, age, SEXUALITY etc.... (and here we encounter what Elizabeth Spelman [1990] refers to as 'the problem of the ampersand'), are infinite, then there is no stopping point short of the unique embodied individual. We risk 'reduction to infinity': 'the view from everywhere' (Haraway 1991). 'In any case' asks Susan Bordo, 'just how many axes [of difference] can one include and still preserve analytical focus or argument?' (Bordo 1993: 222).

De facto, however, there is a high degree of consensus about which markers of difference are significant. The litanies that usually begin with 'race, class and gender' are remarkably similar. The point is frequently made that these axes of difference are in any case not simply overlaid upon one another, but are mutually constitutive. Again it is simply not possible to specify this process of interconstitutionality with more than a small number of axes of difference, without dissolving into radical individualism.

Borderlands   The term comes from a work of the same name by the US Chicana feminist Gloria Anzaldúa (1987). Coined to describe the multiple and marginal positions of Chicana women in the US, it has been embraced by Black and Third World women more generally to describe their multiple locations.

See also CHICANA THEORY.

Boundaries   The concept of boundaries, signifying the marking off of a delimited space, has recently achieved prominence in POSTMODERN, POST-COLONIAL and feminist discourses as a metaphor for going beyond or exceeding IDENTITIES of various kinds, not least the identities prefixed by the term 'post'. Boundaries between the SELF and its other, between human and animal, between and within genders and, particularly, ethnicities are being explored and contested. Homi Bhabha (1994) speaks of cultural HYBRIDITY as unsettling fixed IDENTIFICATIONS and opening up possibilities for new kinds of symbolic interaction beyond the barrier. Donna Haraway (1991) advocates a feminism of boundary crossing and emphasizes the value of networking in partial connections with others. Gloria Anzaldúa (1987) sees 'border crossing' as the literal and symbolic condition of both the CHICANA SUBJECT'S difference and her survival. Notwithstanding these positive and sometimes utopian formulations of boundary crossing, there is clearly a distinction to be drawn between actual and imaginative border crossings, and between voluntary NOMADISM and, for example, the experience of illegal immigrants whose relation to the border is prescribed by state law. In the latter case, the implications of breaching boundaries point to OPPRESSION rather than to liberation.

See also LIMINALITY.

C

Canon   The term, as Hawthorn states, refers '(i) to WORKS which could indisputably be ascribed to a particular AUTHOR, and (ii) to a list of works set apart from other literature by virtue of their literary quality and importance' (1992: 25). The role of academic institutions in the construction of canons is crucial; the 'Great Tradition' of F.R. Leavis, for example, has been immensely influential.

Feminist literary criticism quickly identified the male-dominated character of the Western canon and proceeded to challenge its selection procedures. As Hawthorn comments, 'this struck at the claim to universality that lay behind the idea of a single canon' (1992: 26). At the same time feminist critics of the male canon began to construct alternatives: Elaine Showalter (1978) identified a tradition within women's writing which included three distinct phases – the feminine, the feminist, and the female; and Patricia Meyer Spacks's full-length study entitled *The Female Imagination* (1976) identified the main exponents of an autonomous female literary tradition.

While this strategy has had important and far-reaching consequences in terms of the recovery of 'lost' women writers, the (re)publication of 'canonical' texts by women, and their inclusion on the syllabus, it does not question the desirability of canons per se. A more radical position is adopted by feminists who criticize the institution of canon formation, whether mainstream or alternative, and argue that any concept of the canon is necessarily exclusive, privileging some texts above others. For example, the female tradition posited by Meyer Spacks is exclusively European and white, and largely middle class. In addition, it can be seen that traditional value judgements about what literature should be like have excluded a vast range of texts including those by Black and working-class writers as well as the middle-class women writers cited by Meyer Spacks. In other words the very criteria of what constitutes 'good writing' worthy of a place in the canon are not gender neutral: the themes, plots, structures, motifs, and NARRATIVE choices of white male writers are those which have been constructed as the universal model of the Western tradition.

See also AESTHETICS; BACKLASH.

Capitalism   A capitalist economy or society is characterized by the pervasive commodification of property, labour and knowledge (Outhwaite and Bottomore [eds] 1993: 60). Classical MARXIST theory predicted that after successive crises brought about by class conflict and capitalism's own internal contradictions, capitalism would be superseded by socialism. Marx saw capitalism as both EXPLOITATIVE and progressive, sweeping away earlier forms of social hierarchy and advancing the capacity of the forces of production.

In Marxist thought capitalism stamps itself on the character of all social relations, including what we now call gender relations. For example, Marx and Engels famously compared the relations between bourgeois husband and wife in the upper classes to the relations between bourgeoisie and proletariat, and later theorists like Herbert Marcuse (1964) went on to analyse other aspects of the relationship between capitalism and the organization of SEXUALITY outside marriage.

Feminists have recognized the positive role capitalism has played in the emergence of feminism, for the replacement of notions of kinship-based rights and obligations by the liberal conception of human rights based in the INDIVIDUAL is central to the early history of Western feminist thought. Although MARXIST FEMINISTS in the 1970s were preoccupied with analysing the role of women's oppression in the wider system of social REPRODUCTION, recent theory approaches the relation between economic organization and gender relations in a less abstract or deterministic fashion. MATERIALIST FEMINISM recognizes that women and men live in societies in which the organization of the economy is of central importance to life chances and social relationships but it sees economic life as itself deeply gendered rather than as a starting point which 'precedes' gender analysis. Among other developments women's relation to CONSUMPTION as well as production is given much more attention. However, feminist APPROPRIATIONS of Foucault specifically reject the idea that POWER relations derive from economic interests and have been more interested in analysing forms of domination related to what Michel Foucault calls 'the will to knowledge'.

Carnival/carnivalesque   The term, derived from Mikhail Bakhtin's account of carnival in early modern Europe, refers to the subversive influence of humour on POPULAR CULTURE and literature. In his study of Rabelais, Bakhtin (1984) identifies three forms of carnival folk CULTURE: ritual SPECTACLE; comic verbal performance; and communal 'marketplace' discourse. For Bakhtin the heterogeneous and anarchic mode of carnival stands in opposition to the liberal individualist cultural forms of MODERNITY and it is carnival's potential to transgress and DECONSTRUCT the modernist body (politic) which appeals to POSTMODERN critics. Mary Russo articulates the contemporary postmodern view that 'the masks and voices of carnival resist, exaggerate, and destabilise the distinctions and boundaries that mask and maintain high culture and organised society' (1994: 62). Postmodern and feminist theories of carnivalesque discourse invoke textual travesty, parody, MASQUERADE, displacement, and verbal tightrope walking. Feminist work on the carnivalesque explores issues of bodily exposure, disguise, gender masquerade, ABJECTION, MARGINALITY, parody and EXCESS. Russo goes so far as to suggest that theory represents a kind of carnival space in the academy (1994: 63), but she also sounds a cautionary note for feminists, pointing out the ambivalence of carnival's anarchic redeployment of taboos around the female BODY and its complicitous place within the dominant culture.

See also GROTESQUE; NORMALIZATION.

Castration complex   A central concept in PSYCHOANALYSIS, the castration complex occurs during the PRE-OEDIPAL stage of infantile development and is closely connected to the OEDIPAL COMPLEX which follows and signals its resolution. According to Freud, 'castration' functions differently for girls and boys: the girl must accept her absolute inferiority because she lacks a penis, while the boy must accept his relative inferiority, the father's castrating injunction against his incestuous DESIRE for the mother, and the possible loss of his organ.

According to Freud, once symbolic castration is accepted and the boy defers to the father, he then becomes heir to patriarchal law. The girl, however, in accepting permanent lack is faced with three paths: (1) she can reject FEMININITY altogether, which according to Freud will lead to neurosis; (2) she can refuse to abandon her pre-oedipal clitoral sexual pleasure and 'masculine' identification; or (3) she can accept the oedipus complex in which she shifts desire from the mother to the father, and substitutes a desire for his baby (= penis) for wanting his phallus.

Feminist writers have challenged various aspects of this theory, notably the notion of 'penis envy' (Millett 1971). Lacan's reformulation of the castration complex shifts the focus from biology to LANGUAGE. In this version castration is connected not with the absence or presence of an organ, but to alienation in language and to subjection to the SYMBOLIC order. In feminist terms, men and women can be seen to occupy different positions in relation to the phallus: for women castration is about *lack*, for men loss. This has been a useful insight in theorizing women's entire relationship to the Symbolic order. One example is the debate on postmodernism in which male contributions tend to emphasize the *loss* of autonomous notions of IDENTITY, whereas female contributions often point out women's historical LACK of a sense of self, demonstrating simultaneously the asymmetry of gender identities and the continuing validity of Freud's original formulation (see Alexander 1987).

Catachresis Defined by the *Oxford English Dictionary* as an incorrect use or a misuse of words or terms, a catachresis is a signifier for which there is no adequate literal referent. Humm (1995) gives the example of the term 'true womanhood' to describe something which does not (literally) exist.

Centre See DECENTRE.

Chicana theory Chicana theory emerged in the Americas in the 1970s and 1980s as a challenge to both the ETHNOCENTRISM of Western feminism and the sexism of male-dominated Black/Chicano culture. Chicana criticism registers the multiple experiences of MIGRATION, regional variation, RACISM and sexism encountered by Chicana women. *This Bridge Called My Back: Writings by Radical Women of Color* (Moraga and Anzaldúa 1981), a key text of Chicana criticism, brings together work which crosses racial and GENRE borders. Gloria Anzaldúa (1987) highlights the importance of the concept of border spaces as locations or sites of contest, change and flux (cf. BORDERLANDS). Borders are places where different cultures, IDENTITIES, sexualities, classes, geographies, races and genders collide or interchange. Anzaldúa represents the consciousness of the 'new Mestiza' – or mixed-race woman – as one involving 'crossing over' and 'perpetual transition', thereby avoiding unitary paradigms and dualistic thought.

 Chicana theory resonates powerfully with so-called FEMINIST MATERIALISM, a name for feminisms concerned to relate (MARXIST-FEMINIST) theories of women's social being to (POSTSTRUCTURALIST) theories of language and ideology. One example is Moraga and Anzaldúa's (1981) notion of a 'theory in the flesh', which self-reflexively articulates discourses of theory and the body together.

 See BORDERLANDS.

Cinematic apparatus See FILM THEORY.

Citizenship Historically, the recognition and enlargement of women's rights as citizens has been an important focus of women's movements. More recently, the marginalization of theories of CLASS has seen economic inequalities addressed as citizens' RIGHTS issues (Coole 1996). However, the recent explosion of feminist interest in concepts of citizenship owes much to current events: conflicts over the rights of migrants and refugees in 'Fortress Europe'; the redrawing of national frontiers and the re-emergence of CIVIL SOCIETY in Eastern Europe; the struggles of Palestinians in the Middle East; moves to draft a republican constitution in Australia (Meekosha and Dowse 1996); the rise of FUNDAMENTALIST regimes; and worries about the erosion of welfare entitlements. As the papers at a recent conference on Women and Citizenship in London demonstrated, the key questions about citizenship look very different from the point of view of, to use Nira Yuval-Davis's (1996) example, a Palestinian woman than from the point of view of the male household head implicit in conventional Western political theory.

Theories of citizenship are theories about the relationship between people, as individuals and collectivities, to the STATE and to the COMMUNITY (Yuval-Davis 1996). Although it could be argued that the gradual expansion of citizenship rights inevitably comes to include women, others argue that as women 'contest white male space' theoretical assumptions about the basis of citizenship rights are necessarily challenged (Meekosha and Dowse 1996). For instance, one well-known challenge to liberal political theory is Carole Pateman's (1988) argument that the foundations of citizenship in the SOCIAL CONTRACT are based on a SEXUAL CONTRACT between men – male fraternity – which privatizes and subordinates women.

One of Yuval-Davis's analyses focuses on problems with the definition of citizenship developed by the British political theorist T.H. Marshall, who saw citizenship in terms of full membership of a community. Interest in Marshall's definition in terms of community has been extensive, partly because it seems to provide scope for defining citizenship quite broadly, making it a useful starting point for legitimizing welfare entitlements, for example. But it runs foul of definitions of the community in moral terms, which can exclude those constructed as ethnic minorities as well as 'immoral OTHERS', such as prostitutes, gay men and lesbians (David Evans 1993). Whereas Marshall's definition takes the community to be coterminous with the members of civil society, in a POST-COLONIAL, sexually heterogeneous world the ideological and material constitution of the boundaries of the community is the very stuff of politics (Mouffe 1993).

Another dimension which theories of citizenship must address is 'whether the citizen is conceptualized as merely a subject of an absolute authority or as an active political agent' (Turner 1990: 209), for example the Greek citizen of the city-state who participated in ruling as well as being ruled (Allen and Macey 1990). If full citizenship rights are seen to rest on particular definitions of active participation, such as participation in paid employment, however, women are likely to be disadvantaged. In this and many other respects, then, the specification of apparently UNIVERSALISTIC criteria as the basis of full citizenship is rarely gender neutral.

See also PUBLIC.

Civil society   This concept, in its modern usage, derives from Hegel, but the most influential development of the term in twentieth-century theory was that of the Italian Marxist Antonio Gramsci, and this is one route through which the term entered Marxist feminist discourse.

The concept of civil society delineates an intermediate sphere between the PUBLIC world of the STATE, and the private world of families and individuals. It included a range of institutions – educational, economic, political, social, cultural – which mediated the two. Jürgen Habermas's development of the CRITICAL THEORY of the Frankfurt School introduced the concept of a 'bourgeois public sphere' occupying the terrain of civil society, which was said to have emerged in the early modern period in such informal public forums as the coffee houses, and in journals such as the *Tatler* and the *Spectator*. In principle, the only condition of participation in this sphere was RATIONALITY, and an interest in and knowledge of public life and morals (Eagleton 1984; Habermas 1989).

Some feminist theorists have drawn on this idea to posit the women's movement as a FEMINIST COUNTER-PUBLIC SPHERE, critical and informed, which provides a public forum within which at various levels the problems and politics of feminist and political action may be aired in unforced, free and equal exchanges (Benhabib and Cornell [eds] 1987; Felski 1989a).

Other feminist philosophers have developed more sceptical analyses to argue that the terms of entry to civil society via the SOCIAL CONTRACT, and the associated concept of CITIZENSHIP, are founded on an ostensibly abstract rational human (propertied) SUBJECT, but that women were outside its terms, and the terms are such that the strategy of EQUAL RIGHTS feminism to extend full membership to women is deeply undermined (Irigaray 1985a; Nye 1988; Pateman 1988).

Feminists more (critically) sympathetic to critical theory argue against the wholesale dismissal of Enlightenment thought characteristic of POSTSTRUCTURALIST and POSTMODERNIST theory:

> those who argue... that the core of present conceptions of justice and equality needs to be retained as the condition of future emancipation, seem to me to have the interests of the vast majority of women more closely at heart than those holding out the promise of a utopia of multiplying difference (Soper 1989: 111).

See also HEGEMONY; INDIVIDUALISM.

Class Feminist theory is divided on the question of class. Whereas POSTMODERNISTS reject class as a macro-analytic MODERNIST category too internally differentiated to be utilized as a significant concept (Walby 1990: 31), many feminists continue to use the concept as a necessary shorthand for structured economic inequality. Feminist theory has also taken issue with the conceptualization of socio-economic categories developed by statistical bodies, such as the Registrar General's classification in Britain, which attempt to locate individuals and households in the class structure.

The Marxist definition of classes as dichotomous, antagonistic social formations created and perpetuated in the process of PRODUCTION (i.e. bourgeoisie and proletariat) was the starting point for many feminist theorists.

Arguing that inequality also derives from the realm of REPRODUCTION, some feminists went on to analyse the relations of men and women as a relationship of SEXUAL CLASSES in which men EXPLOIT women's household work for men and their children. Other feminists have retained a conventional notion of social class, but demonstrate that classes are constructed historically, through processes in which gender IDEOLOGY plays a large part. For example, the domestication of middle-class women, the IDEOLOGY of female passionlessness and the role of marriage arrangements for cementing class alliances were central to class formation, identity and legitimation of class privilege in nineteenth-century England (Cott 1979; Davidoff and Hall 1987; Poovey 1984). However, postmodern feminists would see POST-FORDIST economic and technological developments having fragmented what were once stable social formations, making an example like this of only historical interest. It is ironic that, as Diana Coole (1996) points out, at a time of increasing economic inequality the material differences referenced by class are often theoretically marginalized, because they cannot be accommodated by discourses of difference which focus on culturally diverse voices and flexible identities.

See also MATERIALIST FEMINISM.

Colonial discourse   According to Edward Said (1978), who inaugurated its study, colonial discourse refers to the variety of textual forms in which the West has produced and codified knowledge about non-metropolitan cultures. Colonial discourse analysis draws on Foucauldian POSTSTRUCTURALISM and on Gramscian MARXISM, taking from the former the notion of POWER as discursively disseminated and from the latter the concept of HEGEMONY. In fact, more work has been done on theorizing post-coloniality than in analysing colonial and IMPERIALIST texts.

In *Orientalism* (1978), Said argues that the West, in a 4000-year history, has constructed the East as OTHER through a range of discursive practices which include cultural relations, scientific disciplines and the STEREOTYPES and IDEOLOGIES of ORIENTALISM:

> The relationship between Occident and Orient is a relationship of power, of domination, of varying degrees of a complex hegemony...The Orient was Orientalized not only because it was discovered to be 'Oriental'...but also because it *could be* – that is, submitted to being – *made* Oriental (1978: 4).

Feminist critics have been at the forefront of work on colonial discourse. Gayatri Spivak rereads *Jane Eyre*, a classic text of Anglo-American feminist criticism, as 'an allegory of the general epistemic violence of imperialism' (1989: 185), thereby effecting a radical DECENTRING of Eurocentric perspectives. Similarly, Chandra Mohanty (1993) analyses colonial discourse in the texts of Western feminism, and Lata Mani (1992) examines constructions of Indian women's AGENCY in the legal texts of nineteenth-century colonialism.

See also IMPERIALISM; POST-COLONIAL THEORY.

Colonial subject   The term features in the work of anti-imperialist and POST-COLONIAL theorists to describe the construction of colonial subjectivity through the processes of IMPERIALISM. This work raises a number of important questions concerning the impact of colonialism on the psyches of the colonized; the place of NATIONALISM in political liberation movements; ESSENTIALIST and anti-essentialist views of cultural IDENTITY; and, most importantly of all, as Williams and Chrisman state, whether or not there is 'a colonised subject, and its binary opposite, a coloniser subject, about whom theories can be produced, without regard for the socio-economic class of either party' (1993: 23).

For Homi K. Bhabha (1994), utilizing a psychoanalytic framework, the term encompasses a dual subjectivity of colonizer and colonized. His concept of HYBRIDITY embodies the multiplicity and instability of post-colonial subjectivity which deconstructs both the binaries First World/THIRD WORLD and fixed notions of identity generally.

A closely related term is that of the SUBALTERN which refers to members of the non-elite in colonial cultures. It was introduced by the Subaltern Studies group in India whose aim was to uncover the subaltern voice in colonial history. Gayatri C. Spivak has adopted the term in her work while critiquing the positivist character of its original formulation. Spivak's method is rigorously anti-FOUNDATIONALIST and her work on researching the voices of the oppressed, particularly women, has led her to conclude that 'the subaltern cannot speak' (1993: 104).

Commodities   The twofold nature of the commodity – as use-value and exchange-value – was the centrepiece of Marx's theory of value in *Capital*, and his life's work was devoted to the analysis of capitalist commodity PRODUCTION. The exploration of the world of utopian fantasy and DESIRE which commodities open onto was not explored so readily within the Marxian frame, but has proved more amenable to psychoanalytically informed approaches, and to explorations within the history of art and literature (Bakhtin 1981; Bowlby 1985; Russo 1994; Rosalind Williams 1982), and to SOCIAL HISTORY (Bermingham and Brewer [eds] 1995; Brewer and Porter [eds] 1993; McKendrick, Brewer and Plumb 1982).

The concept of the commodity has touched feminism in a number of ways. Firstly, the recognition that relationships to commodity production and CONSUMPTION under capitalism are gendered. Women's historically variable positioning in relation to commodity production was the first to gain recognition. The organization and DIVISION OF LABOUR within the capitalist MODE OF PRODUCTION are highly differentiated by sex and what Marx saw as a very special commodity, LABOUR-POWER, also requires investigation in terms of the sex of the labourer. Much of women's expenditure of labour occurs outside the world of paid work, and is not subject to Marx's 'law of value' (cf. DOMESTIC LABOUR).

Secondly, it has been observed that the sexual division of labour frequently gives women responsibility for the purchase and processing of many capitalist commodities (by no means all of them) (Bowlby 1985; Nava 1992). Thirdly, the use of women's bodies to sell commodities has attracted repeated comment (Williamson 1978; 1986). And finally the claim made by Claude Lévi-Strauss (1969) that in all societies women circulate in heterosexual economies in exchanges between men which are matched by a counter-flow of goods has stimulated some major contributions to feminist theory (Delphy 1984; Irigaray 1981; Mitchell 1974; Rubin 1975; Wittig 1992).

See also COMMODITY FEMINISM; STRUCTURALISM.

Commodity feminism   All aspects of social and cultural life in modern capitalism are mediated or affected by the commodity form, and feminism is no exception. Feminist CULTURE is increasingly produced and consumed through the purchase and sale of COMMODITIES – books, journals, theatre and cinema performances etc. ACADEMIC FEMINISM is now a staple of the publishing industry.

Marxists of the Frankfurt School (cf. CRITICAL THEORY) regarded the commodity form as dominating all other aspect of the 'culture industry'. The IDEOLOGY of capitalism was carried in the very form and functioning of the commodity. Critics have regarded this approach as unduly pessimistic, and have pointed to the contradictions inherent in the absolute need to sell, to make a profit, which may override otherwise pressing ideological imperatives to be circumspect about what is sold (Campbell 1987; Frith 1981; Lovell 1987; McKendrick, Brewer and Plumb 1982). Discussing 'commodity feminism' Donna Landry and Gerald MacLean argue that instead of either denouncing it or becoming uncritically caught up in its processes we must learn how to 'analyse commodification at work in order to use its contradictions to generate new forms of resistance' (1993: 50).

Commodity fetishism   See COMMODITIES; MARXISM.

Communication   Across the competing PARADIGMS of social theory there is consensus on the significance of communication, and therefore, LANGUAGE, REPRESENTATION, and CULTURE in human sociality.

Jürgen Habermas developed a model and ideal of undistorted speech COMMUNITIES which would be non-coercive and consensual (Habermas 1983), and this model has some resonance with early second wave feminist valorizations of turn-taking, informality, accessibility, and openness in feminist political and social forums (Rowbotham, Segal and Wainwright

1979. But see also Joreen 1974 for an early critique of 'the tyranny of structurelessness').

Models of communication which attenuate this link with human language and culture circulate in other contexts: in the biological sciences, biochemistry, systems theory, ecology, etc. Communication in these contexts is not mediated by language and meaning.

Some POSTMODERNIST and POSTSTRUCTURALIST theorists have reworked this a-cultural concept of communication back into the analysis of social interaction, using the model of a POST-INDUSTRIAL society rooted in microelectronic communications. The postmodernist commitment to boundary-transgression, and to contingency or even chaos rather than any finite DETERMINISM, has encouraged the active seeking out of connections across DIFFERENCES. Donna Haraway has challenged boundary-maintenance between human and animal on the one hand, human and machine on the other (Haraway 1991), arguing that women have much to gain from the dissolution of these BOUNDARIES. Sadie Plant (1995), drawing like Rosi Braidotti (1994b) on the philosophy of Gilles Deleuze, has argued for a conception of knowledge as 'connectionism': the active process of making rather than finding or discovering connections. This approach is one which encourages an alertness to the possibilities of advanced technologies (Marsden 1996) which are frequently viewed with great suspicion within feminism. Networking and multiple interconnections of the kind made possible by the internet may be superimposed on the more traditional feminist images of the web and weaving, although of course it is possible to take a less sanguine view.

See also CYBORGS.

Communities of women   The idea of such communities has been particularly important to separatist elements within RADICAL FEMINISM and LESBIAN FEMINISM. Feminist writers have imagined such communities (Auerbach 1978), most famously Charlotte Perkins Gilman's *Herland* (1979), and going further back, Sarah Scott's *Millennium Hall*, written in 1762, and, in the fifteenth century, Christine de Pisan's *The Book of the City of Ladies* (1983).

It is possible to single out networks of women, shadow communities within 'the community', where responsibility for the creation of community and kinship ties and support systems which secure communal social life are often undertaken (cf. EMOTIONAL LABOUR; KIN WORK), and to associate these with WOMEN'S CULTURE. There has been a growing awareness in addition that all cultures which maintain a sharp division between the sexes, and also some religious traditions, generate all-female groupings, traditionally identified within feminism as sites of female confinement, but also loci of female empowerment and relationship. Feminism has generated studies of the history of convent life (Clear 1987; Lazreg 1992; Luddy and Murphy 1989); of educational establishments for girls, run by women, in which women exercised POWER and AUTHORITY; and of religious and cultural institutions (Mani 1992; Mernissi 1994; Mukta 1994).

Small-scale experiments in all-women communal living have been attempted by second-wave feminists in the wake of the mixed alternative communities of 1960s radicalism, and there are many earlier antecedents. Both mixed and single-sex experiments in communal living are in the tradition of radical UTOPIAN communitarianism which informed movements such as Owenite socialism (Barbara Taylor 1983), Chartism (Schwarzkopf 1992) and the Garden City movement (Greed 1994). Some of the most famous have been short-lived, and patriarchal opinion has been quick to argue that their lesson is that there is no viable alternative to the heterosexual household. It is of enormous importance to the whole political project of feminism to put the lie to such interpretations, and to acknowledge and document the numerous examples of households, small and intimate, or on a larger, more communal scale, which are not structured around the heterosexual couple. Many of these have been created and sustained with quite remarkable success in the face of the enormous pressure of institutionalized and COMPULSORY HETEROSEXUALITY (Bammer 1991).

Community   A term which positively glows in most discursive contexts, but which has no very exact meaning. Raymond Williams notes the links with commonality: 'the common people as distinguished from those of rank... the quality of holding something in common... a sense of common identity and characteristics' (Williams 1983a: 61).

Within sociology the term has been used, since Tönnies, to distinguish small face-to-face groupings (*Gemeinschaft*) from the more inclusive and less 'organically' integrated 'societies' (*Gesellschaft*). Attempts have been made to sharpen the term's analytic usefulness through recognition of its symbolic function in moral and political discourse (Anthony Cohen 1985). It often serves less as a descriptive term than to mobilize a sense of belonging, but also by the same token, to exclude.

In an influential study of NATIONALISM, Benedict Anderson argues that all communities outside the most intimately 'knowable' face-to-face groupings, and possibly even these, depend on their construction and ongoing reconstitution within the imagination. Nations are 'imagined communities' (Anderson 1983). They owe their existence to ritual practices, discourses, sentiments, even to bodily dispositions (Scarry 1985), and the practices of exclusion and inclusion.

Williams's observation that the term seems never to be used unfavourably is well-taken. But feminists have entered reservations in recognition that it is in small face-to-face communities that injurious regimes of GENDER and the OPPRESSION of women are often most difficult to escape. Some celebrate instead the impersonal anonymity of city life (Castle 1986; Wilson 1991) and the 'togetherness of strangers' (Young 1990a: 303).

Feminists cannot, however, entirely distance themselves from 'the community', however equivocally small communities may be regarded. It is the community which provides innumerable sites in which women have exercised POWER and AUTHORITY and which have provided rich opportunities for the development of solidarities between women (Mani 1992; Mukta 1994). The term is powerfully in play in the fight against racism in modern 'multicultural' societies. Familial and community networks provide a first line of defence for vulnerable individuals. And the UTOPIAN concept of 'COMMUNITIES OF WOMEN', celebrated in much RADICAL FEMINIST and LESBIAN FEMINIST thought, immediately triggers a more favourable perspective. 'Communities of women' represent the positive pole of feminist ambiguity over communitarianism (Hartsock 1981; Moraga 1983; Palmer 1989; Rich 1977).

The deep ambivalence must however remain, for small face-to-face communities of various kinds, single- and mixed-sex, may both empower and oppress women. The history books are clear that where women exercise power and authority they have proved as capable as men of abusing that power – as teachers, mothers, matrons in hospitals, senior nuns, mothers-in-law, elder sisters, and so on. We have no shortage of 'iron ladies', and in any context, accountability remains essential.

New forms of communitarianism have emerged from POSTMODERNISM to allow a way forward from INDIVIDUALISM. It offers 'a perspective that grounds our moral and political beliefs in the experience of specific communities and challenges the false abstractions of 'the individual' (Phillips 1992: 14). The solidarities and shared 'lifeworlds' of historically specific communities are the irreducible units of new communitarian thought, which rejects more totalizing MASTER NARRATIVES of unified social formations. But new communitarianism does not address feminist reservations. The 'common values' of community life may be unequally shared within the community. The voices of some members are silenced (Saghal 1989). Drawing on Kymlicka's critique (1989), Phillips asks 'are we so constrained by the shared morality of our own period and community that our assertions on what is wrong only means 'we don't do that sort of thing here'? (1992: 16). She insists on the necessity for feminists to reserve the right to say that this is wrong, although it is precisely what *is* done around here – and is indeed rooted in the myths, symbols and institutions of the community.

See also IDENTITY.

Compulsory heterosexuality   The idea was expressed by Gayle Rubin (1975), who argued that behind the taboo on incest was a prior and more fundamental taboo on same-sex sex. Adrienne Rich gave the term wide circulation in her essay 'Compulsory heterosexuality and lesbian existence' (1980a). The concept overturns the commonsense view of heterosexuality as natural and therefore requiring no explanation. Rich argued that heterosexuality was a social institution backed up by a wide range of powerful sanctions, positive and negative. The emergence, against the floodtide of these sanctions, of 'lesbian existence' evidences, she argues, an even more powerful current which these sanctions seek in vain to repress. She located the source of lesbianism, ultimately, in the fact that girls (and boys) are 'of woman born'. It may therefore be constructed as in some sense more natural for women than is heterosexuality.

Notwithstanding lesbian attempts in the 1970s and 1980s to analyse heterosexuality as an ideological institution implicated in women's OPPRESSION, Celia Kitzinger and Sue Wilkinson (1996) point to the failure of heterosexual feminists to address the issue by acknowledging both the political nature of, and their own psychic investment in, heterosexual IDENTITY. They call for a process aimed at deconstructing heterosexuality, arguing that such a process is essential for heterosexual and lesbian feminists alike in understanding and challenging the GENDER order. Recently, there are signs that heterosexual feminists have begun to engage with this critique (Hollway 1993; 1995; Richardson [ed.] 1996; Segal 1994). Carol Smart (1996), for example, responds from a perspective informed by the POSTSTRUCTURALIST disarticulation of totalities. She argues against totalizing heterosexuality or conflating lifestyles, identities, subjectivities, and practices. Judith Butler's work is usually acknowledged in the context of lesbian and QUEER sexuality, but it is very relevant to feminist theories of heterosexuality. She insists on the necessity to disarticulate heterosexuality and recognize the multiplicity of its forms, and the lack of any necessary connection between sex, gender, and sexuality (Butler 1990). No more than lesbianism does heterosexuality come in a single package.

See also HETEROSEXUAL MATRIX; LESBIAN FEMINISM.

Condensation   See DISPLACEMENT.

Connectionism   See COMMUNICATION.

Connotation and denotation   The terms represent two distinct ways in which language signifies, corresponding to literal and figurative forms of reference. For example, the sign 'cat' literally denotes a feline animal, but beyond this it connotes in sexist cultures a malicious woman. Similarly, while the sign 'mother' literally denotes a female parent, it possesses multiple connotative resonances in a range of cultural, religious, and feminist discourses.

See also SIGNIFICATION.

Consciousness   Feminist conceptualization of women's consciousness was initially (implicitly) modelled on 1960s New Left uses of the concept of class consciousness, especially Marx's distinction between a class-in-itself, an objectively defined category, and a class-for-itself, which realizes its IDENTITY and common interests through struggle. Women's shared objective position, previously obscured through their isolation in nuclear family units, would surface as a political identity through CONSCIOUSNESS-RAISING group discussions of their 'personal' lives. Catherine MacKinnon (1982) saw consciousness-raising as the heart of second-wave feminist practice, its theoretical base and method of organization. Dorothy Smith (1988, first published in another form in 1974) articulated the intellectual excitement of academic women, whose double consciousness – derived from the public world of objective, universal concepts on the one hand and concrete relationships on the other – played such a strong role in developing feminist theory. Sheila Rowbotham explored the historical dimensions of women's consciousness in men's world as a form of subjugated but never fully colonized KNOWLEDGE (Rowbotham 1973a; 1973b). However, by the late 1970s the focus had shifted from group face-to-face consiousness-raising to documenting, through PERSONAL NARRATIVES and other life history writing, the diversity of women's EXPERIENCE.

The concept of consciousness has taken a knocking first from deterministic anti-HUMANIST philosophies which see consciousness and SUBJECTIVITY as determined rather than determining. Secondly, the recognition of women's fragmented subjectivities, differently located in CLASS, ethnic, sexual and age-based hierarchies, has led some theorists to question the notion of women's consciousness as ESSENTIALIST. Finally, because the presumption of a gap between a collective feminist consciousness and individual women's consciousness implies the existence of women's false consciousness, a concept which seems to contradict feminist respect for women's accounts of their own experience, the concept of subjectivity has tended to replace consciousness in feminist writing, without, however, resolving all the difficulties.

Some of the ambiguity in the concept of consciousness (is it produced by a political movement or already there-in-waiting?) was re-played in the development of gay and lesbian political identities (Fuss 1989).

See also PHENOMENOLOGY.

Consciousness-raising An innovation of United States second-wave FEMINISM was the emergence of small groups of women who exchanged experiences and feelings about them in order to raise their consciousness of OPPRESSION. This PRACTICE emerged before the resurgence of feminist PSYCHOANALYSIS, and what was raised in these discussions was not the material of the Freudian UNCONSCIOUS. Rather it was seen as a practice which named and placed under the spotlight KNOWLEDGE that women already had from EXPERIENCE, but which required collective articulation, and the exposure and rejection of an internalized patriarchal IDEOLOGY.

See also CONSCIOUSNESS; RADICAL FEMINISM.

Consumption MARXISM is centred within a PARADIGM of PRODUCTION, and MARXIST FEMINISM in the second wave, in its APPROPRIATION of Marxism, did not seriously challenge this paradigm in spite of the difficulties of thinking

DOMESTIC LABOUR, REPRODUCTION and its social relations, and women's very different patterns of work and leisure within its terms (Nicholson 1987).

However, Marx's starting point in *Capital* is the COMMODITY form, and his theory points towards, although it does not supply, an account of capitalist consumption. For the capitalist

> searches for means to spur workers on to consumption, to give his wares new charms, to inspire them with new needs by constant chatter, etc. It is precisely this side of the relation of capital and labour which is an essential civilising moment and on which the power of capital rests (Marx 1973: 287).

Feminists across the spectrum drew attention to the gendered nature of consumption, and feminist CULTURAL STUDIES in the 1970s and 1980s explored women's positioning in relation to cultures of consumption and leisure. Initially the dominant concept was that of IDEOLOGY, drawing not only on the work of twentieth-century Marxists, especially Gramsci, but also on newer French theories influenced by structural linguistics, in particular the SEMIOLOGY of Roland Barthes (Barthes 1972; 1977a).

The bridge between these approaches was provided by Louis Althusser's Marxist STRUCTURALISM, but it transpired that the bridge led away from the Marxist concept of ideology and on into POSTSTRUCTURALISM, POST-MODERNISM, and theories of SUBJECTIVITY.

The attraction of the postmodernist approach lay partly in its valorization of POPULAR CULTURAL forms, and feminists using this approach drew attention to the active investments made by women in the UTOPIAN pleasures of real or imagined consumption which the concept of ideology was unable to address. A wealth of studies followed: of mass market ROMANCE (Radway 1984; Modleski 1982); women's magazines (Winship 1987); shopping (Bowlby 1985); fashion (Wilson 1985); girls' culture (McRobbie 1987; Nava 1992) and much else besides. Some of these studies held onto the critical concept of ideology, but often this rather dour frame was jettisoned entirely in favour of the idea of a radical making and re-making of subjectivities through display, consumption and participation in cultural play.

A number of feminists have entered reservations (Bordo 1993; Lovibond 1989; Modleski 1991; Soper 1990). While the more traditionally hostile attitude of early second-wave feminism towards cultures of femininity assiduously fed by the mass media failed to recognize the active involvement of women in producing and consuming these cultures, the investments of the SELF made in them, and the utopian and other pleasures yielded, yet a full-blown feminist politics of pleasure – where the assumption may be made that 'if it's pleasurable, then it must be subversive' – is in danger of leaping out of the frying pan and into the fire.

Contingency See DETERMINISM.

Corporeal feminism   See BODY.

Creole/creolization   See COLONIAL SUBJECT; HYBRIDITY.

Critical theory   Indebted to Hegelian Marxism, critical theory is associated with the Frankfurt School (Frankfurt Institute of Social Research) from the 1930s and especially with Max Horkheimer, Theodor Adorno and Herbert Marcuse. It has entered feminist theory not through the work of these earlier exponents of 'negative dialectics', but that of the succeeding generation, especially that of Jürgen Habermas.

Habermas's variant of critical theory was considerably less pessimistic than that of the earlier thinkers of this school, who had posited a monolithic, overarching, bureaucratic modern CAPITALISM, characterized by alienated labour and leisure, of which fascism was simply a variant. The belief in historical progress had been abandoned, along with any faith in the proletariat as the AGENCY for change, and modern critical theory has been concerned to identify alternative agencies.

Like the earlier critical theorists, Habermas characterizes his 'social system' in terms of the destructive 'strategic RATIONALITY' of bureaucratic states and capitalist organizations, but he identified further areas of social life, including what he terms the 'lifeworld' of small COMMUNITIES and interpersonal relations, governed not by instrumental rationality, but, at least in principle, by reciprocity and communicative interaction free from domination. 'Lifeworlds' are integrated and cohere not at the level of 'the system', but socially, through dialogue, patterns of shared norms, and consciously adopted values, in undistorted, idealized speech communities (Habermas 1983). It is among NEW SOCIAL MOVEMENTS, insofar as they avoid an overly narrow particularism, that ideal speech communities have been sought and human emancipatory projects pursued.

A number of feminist theorists look to critical theory as an alternative resource (or occasionally a supplement) to contemporary POSTSTRUCTURALISM and POSTMODERNISM. Its method and its political-emancipatory commitments make it an attractive approach for feminism. The method is reflexive, providing a spotlight under which critical theory may itself be critiqued from a gender perspective before being APPROPRIATED in suitably reworked terms (Benhabib and Cornell [eds] 1987; Fraser 1989).

Some feminist theorists have proposed the conceptualization, indeed the active constitution, of feminism and the various women's movements as a FEMINIST COUNTER-PUBLIC SPHERE, in which the ideal of undistorted communication to achieve consensus might actually be honoured (Felski 1989a). Others are less sanguine about the emancipatory potential of critical theory for feminist projects (Gatens 1991; Irigaray 1974; Pateman 1988), and indeed about the whole ENLIGHTENMENT discourse on which such projects are founded.

See also REASON.

Critique   See CRITICAL THEORY.

Cultural capital   This concept is central to Pierre Bourdieu's theory of intellectual/cultural PRACTICE and the reproduction of CLASS. The dominant class is characterized by Bourdieu in terms of cultural as well as economic capital. With the development of COMMODITY cultures, CULTURE begins to be accumulated relatively independently of economic capital, although the two remain closely linked. Unlike economic capital which may be transmitted across generations directly, 'legitimate' cultural capital (or culture that has been 'sacralized' through the recognition conferred by cultural power-holders), must be acquired first by familiarity through extensive exposure in childhood in the family, and then more formally through education. Family and education are the chief constitutive elements of what Bourdieu terms HABITUS, which conditions the ability to compete successfully in the cultural field, the available strategies of intervention, and the particular areas of cultural specialism in which intervention is chosen. At stake in the field of cultural production and consumption is DISTINCTION, for which players compete, and which permits them to accumulate 'symbolic profit', and sometimes to transpose it into material or economic rewards. The culture thus accumulated is the source of the habitus of the next generation, which secures the reproduction of class and class privilege (Bourdieu 1984a).

Thus far Bourdieu has been drawn upon less frequently within feminist theory than the more familiar figures of POSTSTRUCTURALISM such as Foucault and Derrida. Toril Moi has made strategic use of the concept of cultural capital in her study of Simone de Beauvoir (Moi 1994); Bridget Fowler offers an extended study within feminist sociology of literature that breaks new ground in this respect (Fowler 1997); and Nancy Fraser draws on several of Bourdieu's concepts in her work on political theory (1989; 1995).

See also SYMBOLIC POWER; SYMBOLIC VIOLENCE.

Cultural feminism   A development out of RADICAL FEMINISM, this label has been applied to feminisms which posit the existence of WOMEN'S CULTURE and which privilege CULTURE in their analyses (Segal 1987). Examples of the kinds of things which have attracted this label include mothering (Arcana 1983; Chodorow 1978; Dinnerstein 1977; Rich 1977); SPIRITUALITY (King 1989); language (Daly 1991; Spender 1980); lesbianism and 'woman-relatedness' (Faderman 1981; Jeffreys 1985; Rich 1980a); MORAL REASONING (Gilligan 1982); the Greenham Common women's peace movement (Junor 1996; Roseneil 1995); art (for instance, Judy Chicago's [1993]); male VIOLENCE AGAINST WOMEN (Dworkin 1981; Griffin 1984; Hamner and Maynard [eds] 1987; MacKinnon 1982); PORNOGRAPHY (Dworkin 1981; Echols 1983); UTOPIAN literature (Gearhart 1985).

Early second-wave FEMINISM had shared much in common across the distinctions signalled by labels such as radical, socialist, Marxist, revolutionary, and liberal. The overwhelming consensus was that the differences in nature between the sexes were of small significance, but were magnified and sharpened through assiduous ideological cultivation to produce what Michael Ignatieff, in the context of his discussion of national IDENTITY, calls, following Freud, 'the narcissism of minor difference' (Ignatieff 1994). A commonly reiterated feminist goal was 'the annihilation of all sex-roles' (Koedt, Levine and Rappone [eds] 1974).

SOCIALIST and LIBERAL FEMINISMS have been characterized by some postmodernists and poststructuralists as feminisms of EQUALITY; cultural and RADICAL FEMINISMS as feminisms of DIFFERENCE, because they emphasize the particular characteristics of women (and men), revalorizing women's virtues, confirming men's stereotypical vices (Barrett and Phillips [eds] 1992; Gross 1987; Kristeva 1986; Scott 1990).

Cultural feminism is most often charged with ESSENTIALISM, and/or biological REDUCTIONISM (Segal 1987). However, as the label indicates, the differences in question are held to be cultural and psychic rather than natural and inevitable. Theoretical underpinnings are often sought in OBJECT RELATIONS THEORY, and because biological differences are mediated by psychic processes and the social interactions of baby and mother, they belong, properly, in the realm of culture.

Cultural materialism   The elements of this conjunction of terms often find themselves juxtaposed in various binary pairs. Raymond Williams's point in bringing them together was precisely to deconstruct all thinking which opposes the material world to that of ideas and of CULTURE. He repeatedly distances himself from Marxist models of base/superstructure while remaining committed to the Marxian project of locating cultural texts in social practice (Williams 1977a; 1980b). For Williams, culture, no mere pale reflection of the real business of social life and history, matters.

In this endeavour to break the division between thought and matter, Williams, paradoxically, shares much in common with the POSTSTRUCTURALISM and POSTMODERNISM from which he consciously dissociated himself, in part because of return to the TEXTUALITY he had been at pains to decentre.

Cultural materialism has been seminal within British cultural studies (Sinfield [ed.] 1983), and has proved attractive to feminists, who sometimes describe themselves as 'MATERIALIST FEMINISTS' (Hennessy 1993; Kuhn and Wolpe [eds] 1978; Landry and Maclean 1993). It functions as a 'successor-theory' to Marxist feminism, and provides a bridge between Marxist and some poststructuralist feminisms. Catherine Belsey prefers to speak of 'cultural history', and has engaged in debate with Sinfield and Dollimore on cultural materialism (1989).

In the United States, 'new historicism' in literary theory occupies overlapping territory with cultural materialism, for example, in Stephen Greenblatt's work on Shakespeare and the Renaissance (1980; 1991).

Cultural studies   In 1964 the Centre for Contemporary Cultural Studies (CCCS) was established at the University of Birmingham in the UK under the directorship of Richard Hoggart. A new field of study found a name and an institutional base. Its 'founding texts', all first published between 1957 and 1963, were Hoggart's *Uses of Literacy* (1958), Raymond Williams's *Culture and Society* (1987), and *The Long Revolution* (1961), and Edward P. Thompson's *The Making of the English Working Class* (1968) (Hall 1980; Johnson 1986/7; Turner 1990). Cultural studies took its bearings in relation to English SOCIAL HISTORY, English literature, sociology and anthropology. Its focus was on British working-class culture.

Under the directorship of Hoggart's successor, Stuart Hall, and in the intellectual climate of the NEW LEFT in the 1960s, cultural studies took a more decided turn towards Western continental MARXISM and the newer French theories of STRUCTURALISM and SEMIOLOGY.

The CCCS had for many years an ethos of collective work, and a number of overlapping study groups produced collections of working papers in the areas of YOUTH CULTURE, ethnography, literary studies and women's studies. In 1978, the women's studies subgroup published the influential collection *Women Take Issue* (CCCS 1978). Cultural studies provided an important forum for the development of British feminist thought (Lovell [ed.] 1995).

While there was a degree of tension between feminists and their left comrades within cultural studies, the two mined the same sources in their quest for THEORY. The dominant influence was Althusser's STRUCTURALIST Marxism with its theory of subjectivity drawn from Lacan and then later Foucault's theory of POWER and DISCOURSE. Gramsci, a key figure for the male left at the CCCS, was perhaps less fully assimilated by feminist cultural studies. The impact of Lacan and SEMIOLOGY on British feminism was much greater through FILM STUDIES and the journal *Screen*, although both cultural studies and film studies drew upon the work of Roland Barthes. Feminist cultural studies variously located itself in Britain between the CCCS and what became known as '*Screen* theory'.

Cultural studies has a rather different profile in the US, with rather less emphasis on social class, left politics and POPULAR CULTURE. Here the key influence was perhaps Derrida, as appropriated by the Yale school (dominated by de Man) in literary criticism. In feminism it has emerged in the form of CULTURAL MATERIALISM (Landry and Maclean 1993), and also in the work of POSTMODERNIST and QUEER THEORY (Butler 1990; 1993; de Lauretis 1991b). In the latter the emphasis is perhaps less upon the text in context than on social action and interaction as text.

The early development of British cultural studies paid its dues to POPULISM, and determinedly snubbed the pretensions of 'high CULTURE'. This sympathetic stance towards popular culture found resonance in the concerns of feminists, and immediately problematized the traditional deep hostility of feminism, from Mary Wollstonecraft through Simone de Beauvoir to Germaine Greer, towards cultures of FEMININITY, especially in COMMODITY form. Feminists inside and outside the CCCS began to take seriously those commercial forms produced by or for women: soap opera, ROMANCE fiction, women's magazines, 'women's films', etc. (Dyer *et al.* 1980; Hobson 1982; McRobbie and Nava [eds] 1984; Winship 1987). In the US, the work on romance fiction by Tania Modleski (1982) and Janice Radway (1984) was powerfully influential. A sign of the times, and of the rethinking of feminism's relationship with femininity, was the paper entitled 'Feminism as femininity in the 1950s?' (Birmingham Feminist History Group 1979).

See also IDEOLOGY.

Culturalism See AGENCY; CULTURAL STUDIES.

Culture A portmanteau term whose capaciousness and flexibility at once guarantee its attraction and mark the limits of its usefulness. It is held temporarily in place by binary partners which change promiscuously from one context to another.

'Culture' circulates most widely in the discourses of everyday life, to refer to the works and practices surrounding artistic and intellectual production: 'the best which has been thought and said' (Arnold 1960: 6). It hangs on the walls of art galleries and is performed at the Royal Opera House. Above all, it has residence in the minds of 'the cultivated'. Here the silent conceptual partner refers to those works that, lacking DISTINCTION, fall short of Culture.

Those DISCIPLINES that have made lower-case 'culture' their own – anthropology, sociology, CULTURAL STUDIES – have attempted to make it a more useful concept, but in doing so have added to the problem of its extensive scope. They incorporated artistic and intellectual production within the broader frame of cultural PRACTICE, often stripping away the pretensions of 'high culture' to special status. Anthropologists have been as interested in the material artefacts of everyday life, and in the quotidian social practices and habits of the societies they have studied. Yet there is a strong tidal current which drags attention back to 'the things of the mind', wherever 'culture' holds court. This may be seen in the work of Claude Lévi-Strauss, who mapped the whole gamut of myths, cooking and eating habits, the spatial layout of villages, dress and ornamentation, etc., onto a basic opposition between nature and culture, which, he believed, structured 'the savage mind' (1966). Lévi-Strauss, alongside Jacques Lacan and the STRUCTURALIST theory of language upon which both drew, greatly influenced the feminist theorizing of the 1970s (Mitchell 1974; Rubin 1975).

The key binary opposition which structures much feminist theory is between SEX and GENDER, and there is often a Lévi-Straussean mapping of this pair onto nature/culture (Rosaldo and Lamphere [eds] 1974), and in turn onto the distinction between the material and the non-material. This has made the DECONSTRUCTION of the opposition deceptively simple (Butler 1990; Gatens 1992; Grosz 1994), able to rely heavily on the indubitable fact that the 'natural' BODY is enculturated, and that 'culture' is inscribed in the very dispositions and habits of the flesh.

However, there are traces left in our language of the metaphorical development of the concept of 'culture' which Raymond Williams delineates (1983a): 'horticulture'; 'agriculture'; 'cultivation'. With this very physical origin in mind, it may at once be seen that nature/culture does not align itself neatly with the material and the non-material or mental. Rather it points towards that which is 'man-made' rather than 'found'. Bodies are physically moulded by cultural and social practices from birth.

The idea that gender-divisions are cultural – 'man-made' constructions – has been one of the foundation stones of contemporary feminism, partly on the assumption that what is 'man-made' is more easily transformed than what is natural. That all social worlds are SOCIALLY CONSTRUCTED is merely a truism, yet one whose implications have not always been grasped. When we speak of 'social reality', the second term is qualified by the first and vice-versa. History tells us that what is socially acquired and dependent on continued performance is not necessarily easy to discard, as Judith Butler has pointed out in *Bodies That Matter* (1993), her clarification in of this widespread reading of her earlier *Gender Trouble* (1990).

See also CULTURAL FEMINISM; CULTURAL MATERIALISM; WOMEN'S CULTURE.

Cyborgs Donna Haraway has used the cyborg to figure the POSTMODERN self:

> A cyborg is a cybernetic organism, a hybrid of machine and organism, a creature of social reality as well as science fiction…a kind of disassembled and reassembled, postmodern collective and personal self (Haraway 1991: 149, 163).

The cyborg in social reality references biomedical and other technologies which modify the organism or extend its 'normal' reach: NEW REPRODUCTIVE TECHNOLOGIES, organ transplants within or across species, electronic implants, pace-makers, prostheses. The fictional cyborg – the replicants and robots of science fiction – provides more radical myths, UTOPIAN and dystopian, of the dissolution of IDENTITIES/BOUNDARIES between machine and human (Piercy 1992).

If feminism hesitates before the figure of the cyborg, it is less because of the fears imagined by Mary Wings of a plot to bypass and control women's bodies (1988) than of cyborg manifestations in the form of cosmetic surgery and other body modifications in the direction of a NORMALIZED FEMININITY (Bordo 1993). Haraway, too, recognizes the dangers of 'the informatics of domination' – the intimate connection with the industrial–military complex. But instead of 'othering' the cyborg against an ideal of an organic, bounded and whole female SELF, she invites us to seize, explore and embrace the possibilites it generates for developing 'HYBRID subjectivities' (Braidotti

1994b) that allow the development of affinities across 'race', class, culture: the oppositional possibilities of networking and connection:

> there is no 'place' for women in these networks, only geometries of difference and contradiction crucial to women's cyborg identities. If we learn how to read these webs of power and social life, we might learn new couplings, new coalitions (Haraway 1991: 170).

Marsden (1996) defends Haraway from many of her critics, but argues that in the final analysis, she, too, slips away from the full potential of 'cyberfeminism' into the discourse of 'responsibility' and 'political accountability' which once again reinstates the oppositions between human/animal/machine which she had deconstructed, and an untheorized moral and political AGENCY.

D

Decentre   The binary opposition centre/decentre designates a key concept in POSTSTRUCTURALIST theory. Here, language is conceived of as an unstable and decentred system, one made up of chains of signifiers, without final terms which can guarantee meanings. Derridean DECONSTRUCTION demonstrates how FOUNDATIONALIST discourses attempt and inevitably fail to establish a centre from which to ground themselves. It argues that there is no 'free' point outside the object of analysis, and calls instead for the decentring of systems of knowledge and domination.

The poststructuralist critique of SUBJECTIVITY effects a decentering of the humanist SUBJECT. Lacanian theory rejects the humanist belief in the unified individual who tautologically centres his/her identity in the process of thinking himself/herself – *cogito ergo sum*. It argues that on entering language the subject takes up a position in a relational system. Owing both to the instability of the SIGNIFYING system and our own UNCONSCIOUS processes, we are always as subjects decentred, forever in the process of becoming, rather than being, 'selves'.

See also AGENCY; DECONSTRUCTION.

Decentred subject   See DECENTRE.

Deconstruction   Deconstruction is one of the major strands in POSTSTRUCTURALIST thought. The term originates in the work of Jacques Derrida which is concerned with a critique of the premises of Western philosophy, in particular the hierarchical oppositions which structure metaphysical thought. For Derrida, such thought displays, in Hawthorn's words, 'a LOGOCENTRIC reliance upon a CENTRE or PRESENCE, which reflects the idealist desire to control the play of signifiers by making them subject to some extra-systemic TRANSCENDENTAL SIGNIFIED' (1992: 48). The principal procedure for unravelling the metaphysical oppositions of a text consists of the double gesture of reversal and displacement.

Gayatri Spivak, who translated into English Derrida's *Of Grammatology* (1976), argues that deconstruction is neither a counter-philosophy nor a political programme, but a method. The term is sometimes confused with the Marxist critique of IDEOLOGY, but Spivak insists that 'deconstruction is not ... a new word for ideological demystification' (Spivak, in Williams and Chrisman [eds] 1993: 88). The point here is that such demystification has historically been carried out in the name of a MARXISM which can itself be subjected to deconstructive practice (as indeed deconstruction itself – it is a method which goes all the way round).

Owing no doubt to its preoccupation with TEXTUALITY, deconstruction has had more impact on literary studies than on philosophy and social theory. Literary deconstruction works by what Barbara Johnson calls 'a careful teasing out of warring forces of signification in the text' (cited in Culler 1981: ix); by revealing the hierarchical oppositions within a text and showing how they are 'undone' in the process of establishing themselves. The consequence of deconstruction for interpretation is that it is not possible to posit a final, fixed meaning in a text. Rather, deconstructive readings emphasize the indeterminacy of textual meaning and the ceaseless play of SIGNIFICATION.

Some critics have argued that deconstruction leads to two major problems: firstly, that every text becomes in effect the same text – indeterminate; and secondly, that it implies political relativism or even quietism. While feminists number among its critics, they also feature among its major exponents, demonstrating that it can be turned to political effect in the struggle for the sign. The work of Gayatri Spivak represents a deconstruction of ETHNOCENTRISM in Western, especially feminist, discourses. Spivak argues for its continuing usefulness for 'people outside the First World' by revealing how 'the ethnocentric subject establishes itself by selectively defining an Other' (1993a: 87).

Other feminist practitioners of deconstruction include Barbara Johnson, Shoshana Felman, Luce Irigaray and Julia Kristeva. Johnson's *The Critical Difference* (1980) explores the 'sliding of the signifier beneath the signified' characteristic of literary language; Kristeva's essay 'Women's time' (1989) deconstructs two moments of the WOMEN'S MOVEMENT – based on EQUALITY and DIFFERENCE – and posits a third which undoes the distinction. Luce Irigaray's extraordinary text *Speculum of the Other Woman* (1974) represents a radical deconstruction of a range of Western philosophers including Nietzsche, Freud and Lacan.

Denotation   See CONNOTATION.

Dependency   In societies in which women are POSITIONED as the economic dependants of their husbands, the ideology of dependency has shaped the relationship between family and economy and underwritten state employment and welfare policies. For instance, in the postwar Beveridge settlement in Britain state welfare benefits for families assumed the husband's responsibility for supporting his wife and children. Women's lower wages (and the negligible employment rights attached to part-time work) were seen as justified because married women were seen as only intermittent secondary earners. In the 1970s British feminists concentrated on showing how women's actual experience of economic dependence limited their autonomy and options within the FAMILY household system, by, for instance, making it difficult to leave violent husbands.

However, although women are still disadvantaged by the assumption that they can rely on a husband's income, the sharp increase in single parenthood suggests that at least in Britain and the US women's lives are now less directly governed by an ideology of dependency in the private sphere. Women are increasingly dependent on state benefit or their own low earnings, rather than on an individual man, and neither the state nor men seem to want to support women in their childbearing years (Ehrenreich 1992).

Fraser and Gordon (1994) have challenged the way women's dependence is now stigmatized, for instance in the US workfare programme which forces mothers of young children to seek paid work. They argue that the GENEALOGY of the terms 'dependence' and 'independence' suggests that these terms are defined and deployed in racially specific discourses and carry such strong assumptions about 'human nature, gender roles, the causes of poverty, the nature of citizenship, the sources of entitlement, and what counts as work and as a contribution to society' (1994: 311) that feminists should be wary of reproducing dominant ideology by condemning women's dependence.

For dependency in international relations, see DEVELOPMENT and UNDERDEVELOPMENT.

Desire   Debates about desire – women's and men's – have been central to the history of feminism. Wollstonecraft saw desire as problematic if not dangerous for women, arguing for the necessity of tempering what she saw as (feminine) desiring excess with (masculine) reason. Women have usually featured as desired rather than desiring: Victorian feminists and moral purity campaigners frequently adopted the dominant belief in women's sexlessness in order to resist men's sexual exploitation of women. During the second wave of feminism, revolutionary feminists and political lesbians have suggested that women can and should channel their desires away from men and towards each other. Like feminists before them they have played down female SEXUALITY as part of a political strategy.

What mainstream – and feminist – history clearly demonstrates is that women's desire is nearly always constructed as an adjunct, consequence or reflection of men's. The question of the specificity of women's desire exercises feminists working from a variety of perspectives: is an autonomous female desire possible in a patriarchal, indeed, PHALLOCENTRIC culture? Is it the case that women cannot speak their desire in the SYMBOLIC as currently constituted? Certain discourses – notably ROMANCE – do construct women as desiring SUBJECTS, albeit in ways which are largely recuperable by PATRIARCHY. Nevertheless, it is true that opportunities for women to be the agents of desire are historically severely limited: until recently there was no equivalent for women of men's erotica. As Linda Nochlin puts it:

> There simply exists no art, and certainly no high art ... based upon women's erotic needs, wishes or fantasies ... Those who have no country have no language. Women have no imagery available – no accepted public language to hand – with which to express their [desire] (1989: 138-9).

PSYCHOANALYSIS is *the* analytic discourse of desire and as such it has received much attention from feminist writers. Opinion is divided between those who see psychoanalysis as contributing to women's sexual OPPRESSION within patriarchy and those who see it as one method to explore and understand the psychosexual construction of gendered desire. FRENCH FEMINISTS have been in the forefront of the revision of psychoanalytic models of desire. Cixous and Irigaray criticize both Freud and Lacan for the phallocentricity of their theories, which work to compound the absence of women as sexual subjects in the Symbolic order. Irigaray (1974) claims that woman is constructed in terms of a specular economy according to a phallocentric logic of the same, rendering woman's desire a passive reflection of man's. Cixous (1976a) argues that the male Symbolic is incapable of recognizing feminine JOUISSANCE which women should articulate independently. Both perceive a feminine specificity that cannot be articulated within the male Symbolic order and posit alternative female or feminine economies of desire which are subversive of the dominant order. Kristeva (1989) rejects the idea of a separate feminine economy outside the phallocentric system. She sees the CULTURAL FEMINIST investment in maternal, PRE-OEDIPAL realms as regressive and reactionary. Her view represents a somewhat harsh judgement perhaps of feminists' attempts to construct alternative models of desire. These include Adrienne Rich's (1980a) concept of the lesbian continuum which emphasizes mutuality and female affiliation, and the ITALIAN FEMINIST concept of 'affidamento'.

LESBIAN FEMINIST critiques of psychoanalysis go beyond the challenge to its sexism and misogyny to call into question its reliance on a binary model of sexual desire which reifies rather than destabilizes (normative) heterosexuality (Jackie Stacey 1988). Lesbian theory (Butler 1991; Hamer 1990) has challenged the over-rigid theorizations of the feminist mainstream, which saw some feminists underwriting the ubiquity of women's oppression, and opened a much needed space in which the desire of women of all sexual persuasions might be glimpsed.

Determinism   Late twentieth-century POSTSTRUCTURALISM and POST-
MODERNISM have dealt unkindly with the language of determinism and
causality, along with TRUTH, and the epistemological privileges claimed by
the discourses of science. Louis Althusser, whose work was so influential
upon MARXIST FEMINISM, gave currency to the concepts of 'overdetermination'
and the relative autonomy of all elements of 'social formations' or society (cf.
STRUCTURALISM). Social formations, Althusser held, comprised 'decentred
totalities' in which, in any given historical 'conjuncture', outcomes might be
influenced by a number of factors and did not flow in any single determinable
line of cause and effect (Althusser 1969; Althusser and Balibar 1970).

The post-Althusserians Paul Q. Hirst (1983) and Ernesto Laclau and
Chantal Mouffe (1985) went beyond Althusser to reject all forms of 'totality'
in favour of 'aggregates', of a logic of contingency rather than causality
(Barrett 1991: 65).

Determinism is the doctrine, at its simplest, that everything has a cause,
and the point has been made more than once that this thesis is indeterminable
(Urmson and Rée [eds] 1989: 78). It is very often conflated with the doctrine
of historical inevitability, and even with fatalism and the denial of free will. It
is perhaps more usefully regarded as a heuristic principle or methodological
rule of thumb, which instructs us to look for (complex) causes, using our
preferred theoretical frame of reference to help to indicate where to begin the
search.

It was in this spirit that second-wave feminists, especially in Britain,
turned to Marxism, not in order to persuade it to yield up some iron law of
women's oppression. A brief exploration of the opposed terms (above) may
throw light on the problem.

Contingency is not properly opposed to determinism, but to 'necessity'.
Certainly contingency is incompatible with the limit cases dismissed above, of
fatalism and the operation of iron laws of nature or history, but it does not
mean 'uncaused' – quite the contrary. Tracing contingencies means
uncovering particular complexes of determinations which contributed to a
given outcome. Contingencies are events which need not and may not happen.
The limit case is the unforseeable accident. Unforseeable accidents of course
occur. But the contingencies which have interested feminism have been those
which occur with a certain degree of regularity, and where we may hope to
understand why this is so. They depend on something else, which may be
avoided or may not happen. This approach makes it possible to intervene,
politically, in a manner which would not be possible if all social life were
utterly contingent or accidental, nor if it were completely determined.

In this sense it is absolutely correct to identify feminism with the search
for a 'theory of contingencies'. And indeed this is what the best feminist
scholarship and practice, including MARXIST FEMINISM, has attempted to
develop. A necessitarian feminism is a contradiction in terms. A feminism
which abandons any idea of causal constraint leaps straight over into a
voluntarism which is no less problematic. Rosi Braidotti, following Gilles

Deleuze, offers us the image of ideas as 'projectiles launched into time' that are neither true nor false (Braidotti 1991: 125). We may ask only of their effects, and presumably actions may be understood likewise. But we must be clear about the dazzling irresponsibility (or overwhelming responsibility – it amounts to much the same thing) which this entails. For we can never know what the effects have been if we abandon altogether the concept of causality. If cause and effect cannot be traced with some degree of confidence, then there is simply no point in making any principled interventions in social and intellectual life. If we simply shoot arrows into the air at random, we cannot hope to know where they may land and with what effects. This is why feminism, in all its forms, as Judith Butler argues (1992), must indeed be founded on contingency, but a contingency which is not opposed to modern concepts of causality.

Deterritorialization   See NOMADIC SUBJECT.

Development   How to define development is much contested, in part because the concept carries with it the evolutionary assumptions of its nineteenth-century European antecedents notions like progress and advancement which conveyed invidious distinctions between the more and less developed. Postwar 'development discourse' defined it in terms of economic growth and structural shifts, measured in terms of gross national product (GNP) and other indices of formal economic activity which ignore women's unpaid work. Others argued that development should be defined in terms of material well-being – not simply income but better health, literacy and the enlargement of choice (Young 1993).

'Development planning' refers to consciously planned interventions in the market allocation of scarce resources to promote consciously chosen goals. In the 1970s reformers within the development industry succeeded briefly in turning attention to meeting 'basic NEEDS' through building up the informal economy and alternative technologies, but by the 1990s development planners were again stressing economic growth and market mechanisms, counting better health and education programmes as costs rather than benefits (Young 1993).

It is possible to identify at least three, perhaps four or five, different feminist critiques of development, though they are much less readily categorized than it is sometimes assumed. The earliest, usually characterized as Women in Development (WID), feared that development was leaving women behind. Despite its reformist limitations, WID has had a hard time retaining the resources for women it has managed to claim within the UN, North American and European development agencies in which it is based. However, there has been some success in pushing agencies to identify the gender implications of new development plans and projects.

The Gender and Development (GAD) political economy approach first emerged through links between feminist social scientists in British and

European universities and colleagues in the Third World (Young *et al.* [eds] 1987). Combining SOCIALIST FEMINIST theory with then current Marxist theories of UNDERDEVELOPMENT, it saw gender inequalities in development reflecting the power relations between men and women enmeshed in wider social structures and social processes. A more recently formed network, DAWN (Sen and Grown 1988; see also Braidotti *et al.* 1994), highlights the SOCIAL CONSTRUCTION of gender roles and relations; it is sometimes seen as part of the Gender and Development approach, but others see its focus on women's empowerment as prefiguring later critiques.

The essays in Marchand and Parpart's edited collection (1995) argue that earlier feminist approaches to gender and development have been superseded by a POSTSTRUCTURALIST critique which abhors the 'modernist stereotypes' in all gender and development thinking and the way its language presents women of the South as victims. They argue that earlier postures reflect the binary thinking (development/underdevelopment; First/Third World; North/South) which has been such an important target of feminist theoretical critique. This poststructuralist critique has become associated with the empowerment approach (also termed the Third World Women's approach by Geeta Chowdhry in Marchand and Parpart [eds] 1995: 36), which draws on environmentally concerned holistic perspectives associated with Maria Mies and Vandana Shiva (1993; see also Shiva 1988). This also calls into question the North/South divide and Northern claims to 'know' (Parpart 1995: 237); these theorists are 'determined to develop an approach that is rooted in the experience of women (and men) in the South rather than those of Western women' and call for a 'renewed focus on indigenous grassroots movements' (Chowdhry in Marchard and Parpart 1995: 37). However, the focus on the view from below and the legitimation of local knowledges tends to leave the wider capitalist world system relatively untheorized, while women's current economic vulnerability has led in some cases to a romanticized picture of women's embeddedness in pre-industrial systems of gender relations (Jackson 1995).

Dialogic   Clearly linked to the term 'dialogue', the concept derives from the work of Mikhail Bakhtin and refers to the inherently social character of language. Bakhtin (1981) argues that all linguistic utterances, far from being neutral, carry the traces of social interaction and negotiation. Words are always second-hand and, in engaging in dialogue, individuals struggle to wrest language from its former owners and imbue it with their own usage.

Dialogism applies to literary as well as conversational and interactive forms of discourse. Dialogic theories of the text challenge author-centred perspectives in which meaning is seen to emanate from the AUTHOR, and resonate with POSTSTRUCTURALIST theories of INTERTEXTUALITY. The feminist critic Lynne Pearce (1994) develops dialogic theory to analyse aspects of women's writing such as the orchestration of female voices in the text and the gendering of modes of address. And the film theorist Jackie Stacey (1994) employs it in her analysis of women as SPECTATING subjects.

Diaspora   The term refers to the dispersal across the world of peoples originating in a single geographical location. Examples include the Jewish diaspora resulting from persecution and pogrom, and the Black diaspora owing to the Afro-American slave trade. The term 'diasporic articulations' is used in the context of POST-COLONIAL THEORY to register the nuanced and complex forms taken by post-colonial identities which the binary oppositions Black/white, First World/Third World fail to capture.

Différance   According to Derrida, who coined the term, *différance* defines the operation of language in terms of the two principles of difference and deferral. Saussure demonstrated that signs have meaning because they differ from each other: A is A because it is not B; its significance is a negative rather than a positive one. In addition, Derrida argues that meaning is continually deferred as soon as it is posited owing to the gap between the signifier and the signified (cf. SIGNIFICATION). For example, a dictionary definition of the sign 'woman' produces a potentially infinite number of other signifiers rather than a fixed referent. Derridean *différance* represents a POSTSTRUCTURALIST reworking of Saussurian linguistics; it works deconstructively to point out the way in which meaning is dependent on absence and exclusion.

   Différance and poststructuralism more generally have a number of implications for feminist theory and practice. Firstly, they challenge the traditional basis of feminist politics, women's shared identity, in that there is no fixed presence – a female essence – that can guarantee a project based on women's IDENTITY. Feminists have responded to this challenge in a number of ways. A few have dismissed poststructuralism as having no relevance to feminism. Many have accommodated it as a useful way of guarding against essentialist and universalist statements about women's identity. Others have argued for a strategic ESSENTIALISM (de Lauretis in Schor and Weed [eds] 1994; Fuss 1989; Spivak 1989) which self-reflexively recognizes the essentialism that informs even SOCIAL CONSTRUCTIONIST forms of feminism.

Difference   The difference that has exercised FEMINISM is that between the sexes, and one common strategy has been to minimize those differences crafted by nature/biology and to attribute as much as possible, even many physical differences, to CULTURE or GENDER. The differences between the sexes were SOCIALLY CONSTRUCTED. Feminist political agendas were twofold. On the one hand they aimed at the removal of sex discrimination where sex ought not to matter (for example, in discriminatory labour market policies). On the other they sought the recognition of differences where they were pertinent but ignored (for example, by treating women with domestic responsibilities as though they competed equally when it came to career advancement). The demand for EQUAL RIGHTS was allowed to coexist peacefully with IDENTITY POLITICS. A woman's best interests followed from her sexed IDENTITY, even though this would 'wither away' to insignificance in a future feminist UTOPIA.

However, an alternative feminism founded upon difference, which celebrated familiar but revalorized STEREOTYPES of 'WOMAN' (Kristeva 1986; Segal 1987) has an almost equally lengthy history. If women and men are indeed fundamentally different, however, then a politics of EQUAL RIGHTS is not appropriate. The infamous sex discrimination case in the US in 1979 brought by the Equal Employment Opportunities Commission against Sears hinged on this distinction between EQUALITY and difference, with Sears defending its employment record by arguing that its differential hiring pattern was the result not of discrimination by the company, but of the long-standing cultural differences that divide the sexes and which gave women and men differing employment interests. Two feminists, Alice Kessler-Harris for the EEOC, and Rosalind Rosenberg for Sears, slogged out the issue in court. The EEOC lost its case (Milkman 1986; Scott 1990).

Feminisms of difference are charged by their critics with ESSENTIALISM (Segal 1987). But if so, it is a psychic rather than a biological essentialism, frequently grounded in OBJECT RELATIONS THEORY rather than biology (Chodorow 1978; Gilligan 1982).

Matters were complicated by the critique from diversity mounted by BLACK FEMINISM, which prompted a shift in feminist attention onto the differences between women rather than the differences between the sexes. This critique from diversity has sometimes been fused with the critique from DECONSTRUCTION (cf. *DIFFÉRANCE*) which challenged the very concept of a coherent identity and a SELF from which intellectual and political positions flowed.

It is notable that the one intra-sexual difference that had concerned 1970s feminism, that of CLASS, whilst usually paid lip service, is rarely given much attention in the discourses of difference of contemporary feminism. Focusing particularly on the 'underclass', Diana Coole suggests that material differences rooted in class constitute significant socially constructed differences that cannot be addressed within the terms of these discourses, and which are systematic, and independent of cultural identities. The effect of these discourses of difference has been, Coole argues, to 'silence economic difference as a significant form of differentiation...[and to undermine]...the theories that had previously articulated class and convey an erroneous impression that they have a capacity to accommodate diversities of all kinds' (1996: 4).

Disability   The de-sexing and de-gendering of people with disabilities is nowhere more graphically displayed than in the labelling of public toilets: his, hers, and theirs. In representations of people with disabilities, bodily impairment frequently displaces or is made to override commonly recognized markers of DIFFERENCE and IDENTITY.

The disability rights movement has achieved a high public profile, engaging in a range of forms of political activism, from orthodox forms of lobbying for recognition, resources, and for the removal of the barriers to social participation which transform bodily impairment into disability, to direct action such as chaining wheelchairs to the palings of the House of Commons during protest lobbies. But discussions of the politics and theory of disability have not on the whole placed much emphasis on GENDER (Oliver 1991; Swain *et al.* 1993; Wendell 1992) although the voices of women with disabilities are beginning to be heard (Lonsdale 1990; Morris 1991), and studies of the sexed effects of the built environment have important implications concerning disability (Matrix Group 1984).

The relative lack of emphasis on gender in contemporary theories of disability may be because it is Foucault above all who was most heavily drawn upon in the first instance (Oliver 1991) and Foucault's discussion of the BODY and of processes of NORMALIZATION are notoriously lacking in this respect. Feminist APPROPRIATIONS have had to rework his theory in terms of gender (Bordo 1993; Diamond and Quimby 1988; Hekman 1990; McNay 1992).

Concepts of difference, identity, embodiment, and the OTHER are central to contemporary feminist theory, and Luce Irigaray has been particularly influential in highlighting the morphology of the body in place of the feminist distinction between SEX and gender (Irigaray 1974; 1985a). In this climate of 'corporeal feminism' (Grosz 1994) bodies that are outside or transgress the BOUNDARIES of what is recognized as 'normal' were certain to attract a greater degree of interest; to move, in theory at least, from the margins to the centre (Russo 1994).

But while feminist theories of the body may be drawn on to inform feminist discussions of disability, the gendering of disability cannot be determined by any simple extrapolations from sex/gender systems – for example, along the lines that there is some affinity between the social meaning of femininity and of bodily impairment (Shildrick 1997, forthcoming). It might be more illuminating to consider the whole range of strategies which men and women deploy (Sedgwick 1994) in negotiating rights to basic need satisfaction, and to self-REPRESENTATION of the meanings of particular body morphologies, as these strategies relate to sex and gender. This cannot be done on the basis of theory alone. But contemporary theory offers rich resources for such analysis.

Disciplines   Fields of intellectual enquiry through which KNOWLEDGE is produced and validated. Thomas Kuhn argues that disciplines are regulated by what he terms PARADIGMS (Kuhn, 1970): systematic theoretical and EPISTEMOLOGICAL assumptions, methodological tools, etc. within which, during periods of 'normal science', legitimate research questions are framed and answered. Disciplines are regulated by key gatekeepers who may confer or withhold recognition of DISTINCTION (Bourdieu 1984a).

Periods of normal science were interspersed, in Kuhn's rewriting of the history of science, by revolutionary eruptions during which, the usefulness of the dominant paradigm having waned, new approaches competed for paradigmatic status.

The disciplines of the social sciences are rarely governed by a single paradigm. But it was these disciplines, in their emergent nineteenth-century forms, that particularly interested Michel Foucault: the disciplines of social accounting, directed, according to Foucault, at the systematic monitoring and control of populations and the classification of individuals, such as psychiatry, clinical medicine, statistics, demography, child psychology, pedagogy, criminology, etc. (Donzelot 1979; Foucault 1977).

Feminists have always had an uneasy relationship with both kinds of discipline. In many areas of intellectual inquiry in the social sciences, the humanities, and biological sciences, feminist scholars have deconstructed their disciplines from the perspective of women and gender. INTERDISCIPLINARY women's studies and gender studies have emerged in academe to carve out a new synthesis.

There has been a growing consciousness among feminists of the 'disciplines' in Foucault's second sense – disciplinary practices whose object is the production of the docile 'normal' female body; and we have a growing number of studies of dieting, exercise, beauty regimes, and the schooling of little girls in femininity through the disciplining of their bodies and minds (Bartky 1990; Bordo 1993). These usually position girls and women as the objects of disciplinary practices.

Others have begun to pay attention to women's historical positioning, in addition, as agents of discipline (Armstrong 1987; Moers 1977; Steedman 1982). The disciplinary responsibilities of women are evident from eighteenth- and nineteenth-century conduct literature (Armstrong and Tennenhouse 1987; Vivien Jones [ed.] 1990). The traditional roles of mother, nurse, governess, teacher, moralist, and more recently, beautician, counsellor, dietician, fitness instructor etc. may be understood as disciplinary in this sense.

See also DISCURSIVE FORMATIONS; INTELLECTUALS; THEORY.

Discourse   A central term in contemporary CULTURAL STUDIES which, like IDEOLOGY, is notoriously difficult to define. At its simplest 'discourse' as a noun refers to any utterance or discrete piece of language. It is used primarily in two distinct but overlapping fields of academic study: linguistic discourse analysis and POSTSTRUCTURALIST discourse theory. In pragmatics, a branch of LINGUISTICS concerned with interpretation, discourse designates language in use as opposed to language as an abstract system, thus aligning it with *parole* rather than *langue* (Saussure 1974).

Foucault defines discourse 'as the group of statements that belong to a single system of formation', citing the examples of clinical discourse, economic discourse, the discourse of natural history, and psychiatric discourse

(1972: 107–8). Discursive formations – academic DISCIPLINES and other apparently coherent bodies of knowledge like theology or sexology – construct their own objects of knowledge under the guise of discovery: for instance, sexology invents sex; sociology constructs its own object of knowledge, 'society'; PSYCHOANALYSIS discovers the UNCONSCIOUS. They also create subjects, like 'the homosexual'.

Foucault rejects the Marxist view of the relationship between IDEOLOGY and social systems as one of surface and depth, and substitutes the concept of discursive practice in which KNOWLEDGE/POWER is disseminated at macro- and micro-levels. In practice, critics have retained both concepts and distinguished between them: discourses are seen as language statements produced by particular institutions, through which ideologies circulate.

The concept of discourse is indispensable in 1990s feminist theory, yet historically feminist engagement with the term has been mixed, encompassing enthusiastic APPROPRIATION, rejection and cautious adoption. The former position is exemplified by the feminist journal *m/f* which in the late 1970s to mid 1980s located women's oppression in sexual and gendering discursive practices. The latter positions are represented in the work of Michèle Barrett who in 1980 (Barrett 1988) rejected what she saw as the idealist shift from theories of ideology to 'discursive imperialism', but her 1991 *The Politics of Truth* acknowledges the feminist potential of discourse theory and abandons the concept of ideology. Feminist stylistics and feminist linguistics have also given credence to the study of discourse, showing how the micro-structures of language are related to the macro-contexts of social gender (Sara Mills 1995; Deborah Cameron 1985; Cameron and Coates [eds] 1989).

Discursive formation   See also DISCOURSE.

Displacement   In PSYCHOANALYSIS 'displacement' describes one of the two operations – the other being condensation – of the dream-work (Freud 1900) in which the UNCONSCIOUS displaces the meaning of one object onto another in some way connected to it, or condenses a set of objects into a single image.
    See also METAPHOR.

Distinction   'Distinction' is a keyword in Pierre Bourdieu's theory of CULTURE, as it is developed in his massive study under that title of the sociology of taste (Bourdieu 1984a). Exploiting the ambiguity of the term, he shifts the emphasis away from traditional AESTHETIC questions concerning 'great art', and on to its role in generating and maintaining systematic social discrimination and exclusion. The strong sense of belonging (or not: 'not for the likes of us') is transmitted over generations through markers of taste across a wide range from music and literature to domestic furnishings, hobbies and food preferences.

In any given field of cultural PRACTICE, cultural power-holders confer the recognition of distinction or legitimation, and by the same token, subject those whose taste is found wanting to SYMBOLIC VIOLENCE.

Bourdieu is chiefly concerned with culture in relation to social CLASS, and until recently, has had little to say about GENDER (Bourdieu 1990b), and perhaps for this reason his work has had little impact thus far upon feminism. But as feminism has become more fully embedded within institutions of cultural production such as the university, the potential of Bourdieu's reflexive sociology of culture for the analysis of feminist practice and feminist cultural strategies is beginning to gain wider recognition (Moi 1991; Fowler 1997).

See also CULTURAL CAPITAL; SYMBOLIC POWER.

Division of labour   'The division of labour' refers to the differentiation and distribution of the tasks involved in the PRODUCTION of goods and services (Outhwaite and Bottomore [eds] 1993: 162). In modern industrial societies production is divided into a vast array of separate activities separated in time and place. The division of labour can be a source of interdependence and social solidarity as well as inequality and conflict.

Analyses of the division of labour often distinguish between broad social divisions of labour, such as those between social CLASSES, and the technical division of labour between specialized tasks or roles. The technical division of labour is never neutral or purely technical, however, but organized around socially determined goals. In CAPITALIST society the techniques of material production themselves reflect attempts to reduce labour costs and/or increase productivity. The division of labour is also analysed in spatial terms, as in concepts like the NEW INTERNATIONAL DIVISION OF LABOUR or the GLOBALIZATION of production.

In non-state small-scale societies tasks tend to be allocated on the basis of kinship, with age, gender, descent and marriage providing access to the means of production. Although in capitalist societies the role of gender in the division of labour is less explicit, the broad division between, for instance, paid work and unpaid family labour is usually based on gender, and even where women participate in the labour market women and girls are still responsible for the bulk of unpaid family labour. There is also a gender division of labour within the paid labour force, of course, now usually conceptualized in terms of GENDER SEGREGATION. However, the term 'sexual division of labour' is useful because it encompasses within the same framework both paid work in the labour market and the unpaid, non-marketed family production and caring tasks to which women are recruited through marriage and motherhood.

In terms of what to do about divisions and inequalities in the sexual division of labour, feminists have differed. Some feminists put forward UTOPIAN or communitarian solutions, usually involving the abolition or reduction of the division of labour (everybody does a little of everything); many focus on increasing women's access to better paid 'men's work'; others stress increasing the status and rewards of typical women's occupations and work.

Domestic ideology   Used by feminist historians to identify changes in attitudes to private morality in Britain from the late eighteenth century among the emergent middle classes, the concept names a complex of associated developments which, according to Davidoff and Hall, are rooted in the Evangelical movement (1987). They point to a marked separation of male and female spheres; an attack on the sexual double standard commonplace among the landed classes; and the particular prizing of domestic comfort, home and family life.

This account has been challenged to some extent by feminist critiques of the distinction between PUBLIC and private spheres, whose boundaries were more permeable than the writings of eighteenth- and nineteenth-century conduct literature might suggest, and by the claim that the valorization of domesticity was not unique either to this period or to the middle classes (Berg 1993; Vickery in Brewer and Porter [eds] 1993).

See also SEPARATE SPHERES.

Domestic labour   Formerly neglected by sociologists, who equated work with paid work, the first feminist attempts to theorize domestic work all gave it importance by noting its similarities to or connections with waged work (Benhabib and Cornell 1987). In what became known as the domestic labour debate SOCIALIST FEMINIST theory of the 1970s linked domestic labour to the key concepts of MARXIST analysis, first debating how to understand the contribution made by women's unpaid domestic labour to capitalist profits, but later widening the focus to the functions of domestic labour for the persistence of the CAPITALIST mode of production, including its IDEOLOGICAL foundations. Other feminist sociologists analysed its benefits to men, arguing that through FAMILIAL EXPLOITATION the labour of women-as-wives was exploited and appropriated by male household members. Non-Marxist feminist sociology also analysed domestic work in relation to paid work. For instance, Ann Oakley's path-breaking *The Sociology of Housework* (1974) analysed housework as a low-status, poorly rewarded job with long, unregulated hours of work. Her research was followed by many empirical studies comparing men's and women's contribution to household work. However, other analysts working within the 'women's network' tradition, supported by concepts drawn from Gilligan's (1982) moral theory, focused on household work – especially childcare – as an aspect of nurturing 'care work' which should be valued rather than rejected as a form of OPPRESSION. Yet others stressed the importance of understanding 'caring' labour in the context of the caring relationships within which it is deeply embedded (Graham 1993; Mason 1996).

Although domestic labour was at one time the sole preserve of feminist researchers, it is now finding a place in mainstream economics and sociology.

Some sociologists have adopted rational choice theory to explain women's so-called preference for household work over paid employment (for a review see Bruegel 1995). For others, for example Gershuny (1985) and Pahl (1984), measures of men's, women's and children's household work activities are important to understanding changes in the provision of services to households.

Meanwhile, partly in response to changing demographic profiles, feminist theory and research has gone beyond its original focus on 'home-based-kin-care' (Graham 1991) to incorporate institutional care work and women's responsibilities for adult dependants. Moreover, the growing demand for paid domestic services in Western industrial societies by dual-earner, middle-class households has reinvigorated the tradition of analysing domestic work in terms of EXPLOITATION (Bakan and Stasiulis 1995; Gregson and Lowe 1994). Others are beginning to look at the recruitment of migrant women to domestic work as 'mail order brides' (del Rosario 1995), maids and nannies. All these developments suggest that while focusing on the nuclear-family-housewife's domestic labour underestimated the scope of women's care-related work and the types of social relationships in which it is embedded, 'for love or money' are still key factors in the pressure to care.

Domestic work See DOMESTIC LABOUR.

Dominant ideology The 'dominant ideology thesis' is rooted in Marx and Engels's assertion in *The German Ideology* that 'the ideas of the ruling class are in every epoch the ruling ideas' (Marx and Engels 1965: 64). Western MARXISM since Gramsci has entered reservations, and many have preferred to substitute Gramsci's concept of HEGEMONY for the Marxist model of economic base and ideological superstructure as a more fluid model. Raymond Williams rejected the base/superstructure model (1980a), criticizing it for its separation of the material from the ideational. He proposed instead a classification of cultural PRACTICES (rather than IDEOLOGIES) as 'dominant', 'residual' and 'emergent' formations, with the latter two subdivided into 'alternative' and 'oppositional' forms (Williams 1977a).

The 'dominant ideology thesis' has been challenged in sociology as well as in CULTURAL STUDIES (Abercrombie, Hill and Turner 1980). (For a good discussion of the history of this thesis, see McGuigan 1992.)

Doubleness In general terms 'doubleness' refers to any phenomenon or practice which exhibits a double aspect; for example, the *Doppelganger* in literature, the split subject in psychology.

Doubleness has a strong resonance in women's writing: women's gothic fiction makes use of the motifs of doubles, ghosts and haunting to explore women's sexual and social identities; mirror imagery, in particular, is employed to signify the cultural construction of FEMININITY; and, according to Gilbert and Gubar (1979), nineteenth-century women's texts enact a double gesture of simultaneous conformity to and rebellion against patriarchal MASTER NARRATIVES. More recently, Luce Irigaray (1985a) locates what she sees as the doubleness or multiplicity of female sexuality/textuality in the female body's 'two lips [which] speak together'.

See CONNOTATION; METAPHOR.

Doxa   'Doxa', in Pierre Bourdieu's work, refers to the taken-for-granted, naturalized assumptions and beliefs of a given field of PRACTICE. It bears some resemblance to Gramsci's 'common sense', and differs from IDEOLOGY in that it is largely below the level of consciousness, yet not UNCONSCIOUS (in the Freudian sense) either. It is embedded in the practice itself, and even in the bodily HEXIS of the participants. His approach offers a powerful tool for analysis of the embodiment of gender.

See also BODY; CULTURAL CAPITAL; HABITUS; SYMBOLIC POWER.

Drag   See MASQUERADE; PERFORMANCE; QUEER THEORY.

Dual labour market   The term refers to the division of the labour market into different sectors by barriers which prevent workers from moving to better jobs in another sector. Dual labour market theory in economics was an important stimulus to identifying first racial and later GENDER SEGREGATION in the labour market and explaining them in terms of economically rational employers' strategies rather than in terms of individual prejudices (Barron and Norris 1976; Edwards *et al.* 1975). Later formulations of what is now called segmented labour market theory point to additional factors to explain the persistence of barriers between sectors, including the role of trades unions. More recently, the casualization of previously stable employment seems to be accompanied by a 'feminization of the workplace' (Jenson *et al.* [eds] 1988), in which men's terms and conditions of work have deteriorated along with women's.

Since Beechey (1988) and others highlighted the inadequacy of economistic models for understanding the social processes which shape labour markets, studies of gender segregation have increasingly explored changes and continuities in particular workplaces and occupations, concentrating on identifying the interaction of employers' strategies, technological change, workplace cultures, work identities and the timing constraints presented by DOMESTIC IDEOLOGY (Scott 1994). The influence of POSTSTRUCTURALISM has also highlighted the cultural aspects of job gendering and the multiplicity of power relations in the workplace.

Dual systems theory   Dual systems theory attempts to synthesize MARXIST and RADICAL FEMINIST accounts of women's position in society through positing the ARTICULATION of PATRIARCHY and CAPITALISM without explaining one as an effect of the other. Walby (1990) points out that although some theorists see capitalism and patriarchy as fused (one capitalist-patriarchal system), more usually writers keep them distinct, assigning different levels of the social formation to one system or the other, usually claiming that the economy is best analysed in terms of capitalist social relations but allocating the ideological level, REPRODUCTION and the UNCONSCIOUS to PATRIARCHY.

Whereas the main problem with unitary system explanations is their tendency to reduce different kinds of social inequality to a common cause, dual systems analysis often fails to account for gender disparities that occur within the sphere of production (Nicholson 1987: 28). Attempts to improve the 'unhappy marriage' of Marxism and feminism by rectifying this were fraught with difficulty. For instance Hartmann (1979; 1981) tried to deal with gender hierarchy in production by arguing that while spaces in the labour market of Western occupational structures were determined by capitalist imperatives, patriarchy determined which gender filled them. Men's alliances with each other ensured they were able to keep the better jobs for themselves. However, even this formulation fails to penetrate the apparent gender neutrality of capitalist rationality: employers inevitably devise jobs and divide work between them in a context in which decisions about labour costs, appropriate skills or relevant personality traits are saturated with gender. Walby (1990) attempted to deal with the difficulties of dual systems theory by identifying six distinct sites of patriarchal power, none dependent on the others. However, both unitary and dualist accounts are now challenged by those who argue against overly deterministic STRUCTURALIST accounts of all kinds.

E

Ecofeminism First coined in 1974 by Françoise d'Eaubonne, who called upon women to lead an ecological revolution (Merchant 1992: 184). Although rejecting some elements of 'deep ecology', which rejects reformist piecemeal policies in favour of a new holistic philosophy, ecofeminists share the wider radical ecology preference for revisioning 'interrelationships around humans-in-nature' (Merchant 1992: 86), rather than placing human beings above other living things. Over time ecofeminists have organized important actions against what are seen as ways of organizing PRODUCTION which threaten biological and social REPRODUCTION.

Although Carolyn Merchant, whose books have popularized many of its precepts, sees ecofeminism as coming in different shades – LIBERAL FEMINIST, CULTURAL FEMINIST, SOCIALIST FEMINIST, and 'social feminist' – the ideas associated with cultural feminism have become most closely linked with it. As she says, this often celebrates a prehistoric era, destroyed by PATRIARCHAL scientific culture, in which women were held in high esteem. It 'celebrates the relationship between women and nature through the revival of ancient rituals centred on GODDESS worship, the moon, animals and the female reproductive system' (1992: 191) and women's biology and Nature are celebrated as sources of female power.

In the past few years there has been a reaction against the apparent ESSENTIALISM and irrationality of this posture. Writing in 1992 Merchant suggests substituting an alternative which does not gender nature. She suggests envisioning a partnership ethic that treats humans – men and women – and nonhumans as equals. She suggests that we avoid treating nature as goddess or nurturing mother; the personal or intimate relationship with nature to be fostered is not necessarily a spiritual one. Maria Mies and Vandana Shiva's reformulation recognizes that the new commitment to SPIRITUALITY among Westerners sometimes amounts only to the commodification of fragments of Eastern religions; they suggest redefining spirituality as the 'realization of interconnectedness' (1993: 16). But the image of 'the soil as mother and people as her offspring, not her master' (Mies and Shiva 1993: 104-5) remains a recurrent and powerful motif.

Écriture feminine   The term *écriture feminine* originates in the writing of Hélène Cixous where it designates an experimental and marginal mode of DISCOURSE, characterized as feminine, which is repressed by and subverts the PHALLOCENTRIC Symbolic order. *Écriture feminine* has had many interpreters, not least because Cixous claims it cannot be defined.

Typically, *écriture feminine* deconstructs the opposition between theoretical and literary/poetic modes of writing, blending criticism and polemic with fantasy and wordplay. It foregrounds the SEMIOTIC or material aspects of language. Its often lyrical invocation of the female body has much in common with utopian writing and serves a similarly inspirational and political purpose.

Écriture feminine has been criticized, especially by feminists working in a Marxist tradition (Felski 1989a; Moi 1985), for ESSENTIALIZING women's IDENTITY through the conflation of female biology, psychology and language. However, others have argued that this is a misrepresentation of feminine writing and that French feminists write in the knowledge that REPRESENTATION mediates the relationship between WOMAN and her body and that 'woman' is a construct in language (Grosz 1989; Whitford 1991). The difficulty is partly owing to the more empirical traditions of Anglo-American thought.

An additional challenge to *écriture feminine* comes from feminist LINGUISTICS which maintains that the former's account of feminine modes of discourse is too abstract, primarily concerned with writing rather than speech, and often empirically incorrect (Deborah Cameron 1985; Mills 1995). Some research demonstrates that women take more care than men to avoid imprecision, prolixity and digression – some of the characteristics associated with the French concept of femininity – to achieve the norms of standard language use for the very reason that their speech is less valued than men's (Mills 1995).

Emancipation Historically, feminist discourse identifies the emancipation of women from legal disabilities as its goal. The term is closely associated with the liberal Rights tradition in FEMINISM famously articulated by Mary Wollstonecraft in *A Vindication of the Rights of Woman* (1982). Wollstonecraft formulated the educational and legal basis of emancipation which characterized eighteenth- and nineteenth-century first-wave feminism. By the late nineteenth and early twentieth centuries suffrage campaigning had come to dominate feminist activism. Feminists differed in regarding the gaining of the vote either as one element, albeit important, of women's emancipation or, in some cases, as equivalent to emancipation itself. The advent of second-wave feminism in the 1960s highlighted the failure of the franchise to deliver women's equality and implied the limitations of legislative approaches to emancipation. Socialist feminists pointed to the continuing contradictions of capitalist PATRIARCHY as underpinning women's oppression and called for fundamental changes in socio-economic organization. For RADICAL FEMINISTS, women's liberation, a self-consciously more radical term than emancipation, demanded nothing less than the total dismantling of the SEX/GENDER system.

Embodiment See BODY; IDENTITY; SUBJECT.

Emotional work The active labour of managing feeling, especially in the context of paid employment; also the display of emotional states solely to produce a desired response. Arlie Hochschild (1983) compared the ways in which airline cabin crew (mostly women) are trained to use their appearance, their smile and their empathy to increase passenger comfort and future sales, with the more typically masculine emotional work of debt collectors who act out fear-inducing intimidating gestures and 'face work'. Emotional work is sometimes termed 'selved work' because it involves the alienation of what are conceptualized as facets of the SELF in the course of work. More obviously typical of female than traditional male employment, often the subject of explicit training ('Have a nice day!'), the exhausting performance of emotional work is also a source of stress for healthcare professionals and in other caring occupations.

Empowerment See AGENCY; AUTHORITY; POWER.

Enlightenment The seventeenth- and eighteenth-century European Enlightenment heralded a philosophy which rested on the idea of progress rooted in scientific RATIONALITY and an ordered, law-governed natural world.

The social world, too, was to be subjected to scientific scrutiny with a view to its rational reordering and improvement.

Enlightenment thought has suffered badly at the hands of POSTSTRUCTURALISM and POSTMODERNISM (Irigaray 1974). Poststructuralist theory has generated a critique which is sometimes conjoined with earlier RADICAL FEMINIST dismantling of the categories of 'malestream' thought and masculine UNIVERSALISM (Daly 1991). Other strands of feminism, including that which has located itself in terms of a critical APPROPRIATION of CRITICAL THEORY, along with those who are unwilling entirely to abandon the projects of SOCIALIST FEMINISM, argue that feminism is, historically, a child of the Enlightenment, and that its emancipatory project still offers dividends for women and for feminism. It should not be abandoned lightly or prematurely (Benhabib and Cornell 1987; Felski 1989b; Lovibond 1989; Soper 1986; 1989).

See also MODERNITY.

Enunciation   LINGUISTIC theory distinguishes between two types of enunciation. In French these are *énonciation*, which refers to the act of making an utterance, and *énoncé*, which refers to the verbal statement made. In English, rather confusingly, the former is rendered as 'enunciating', and the latter as 'the enunciation'. As Terry Eagleton (1984) points out, the gap between the two is exploited by POSTSTRUCTURALISTS who see it as an exemplary instance of the sliding of the signifier beneath the signified: the enunciating subject and the subject of the enunciation – the 'I' who speaks and the 'I' who is spoken – can never wholly coincide.

See also SIGNIFICATION.

Epistemology   The branch of philosophy which is concerned with the study of the production of KNOWLEDGE. Epistemological questions are usually cast in more obviously philosophical terms than questions of METHODOLOGY, being concerned with where knowledge comes from and how much confidence we can have in it, rather than questions of strategy, procedure or technique. Alcoff and Potter (eds) (1993) suggest epistemology becomes most important in periods when new PARADIGMS emerge, and INTELLECTUALS have looked for ways to justify the knowledge claims they make as against pre-existing ways of understanding the world.

Feminist epistemology was initially concerned mainly with the way in which the gender and the gender politics of the knower enter into knowledge production. Epistemological questions followed upon new information about women and women's lives, going beyond the development of new methodologies in different DISCIPLINES to consider women as distinct producers of knowledge and not simply as 'objects' about whom knowledge might be produced. Feminists in the 1980s argued that the apparently uninvolved, rational, universal 'objective' standpoint from which the natural and social sciences derived their legitimacy was in reality a male STANDPOINT which denied its own specificity. Objective knowers who assumed themselves to have surmounted their own individual, gendered bodily and emotional specificity projected denied aspects of self onto women, and denied the legitimacy of women's perspectives. Consequently many feminist theorists rejected what Sandra Harding (1987) calls 'feminist empiricism', which tries to eliminate male bias through scrupulous attention to the rules of scientific method.

In the attempt to retrieve and legitimate knowledge from the perspective of women some feminists developed new terminologies and syntax; for instance, Mary Daly's attempt in *Gyn/Ecology* (1991) to substitute terms like 'spin' (and 'spinster') for male-defined processes of knowledge production, or Catharine MacKinnon's (1982) emphasis on CONSCIOUSNESS-RAISING as a form of knowledge production. Others attempted to validate feminist knowledge within the social sciences based on women's specific standpoint, their social location and political engagement. In such cases, Alcoff and Potter suggest, the term 'feminist epistemology' refers to forms of knowledge quite outside traditional philosophy, such as women's 'ways of knowing' or 'women's EXPERIENCE' or 'women's knowledge'.

However, feminist epistemology has increasingly recognized that 'cognitive AUTHORITY is associated not only with gender, but with, for example, race, class, sexuality, culture and age' (Alcoff and Potter [eds] 1993: 3). Although this brings it into closer relationship with the challenges to the ways in which knowledge is conventionally defined coming from other NEW SOCIAL MOVEMENTS, it has also made it harder to privilege women's ways of knowing, women's experience or women's knowledge or to see these as unifying perspectives. Some standpoint theorists have gone on to try to propose ways of legitimating the cognitive authority of feminist COMMUNITIES, or of evaluating the knowledge produced, which go beyond consideration of the gender of the knower and which take more account of differences between women. However, these have in turn been challenged by POSTSTRUCTURALIST feminist epistemologies which reject any attempt to re-establish a FOUNDATIONAL basis of knowledge, however much revised. As Felski (1989b) comments, the rejection of an objective, all-embracing standpoint brought about by a pluralizing of ideological perspectives problematizes simultaneously the absolute authority of any of these (40), including feminism. However, feminist epistemologies of all kinds continue to pay particular attention to the political context and implications of theories of knowledge: necessarily so, since the origins of feminist philosophy in political engagement can scarcely be denied.

Equal opportunities   Refers to efforts to widen the participation of previously under-represented categories, including women. Where equal opportunities entails only the creation of a 'level playing field' by removing directly and indirectly discriminatory employment practices, however, it is unlikely to challenge GENDER SEGREGATION, which is deeply embedded in the occupational structure. Moreover, equal opportunities programmes which seek to enable women to compete with men on equal terms seem to assume the organization of paid work around men's lives or to deny the relevance of sexual DIFFERENCE. Even the recent moves to incorporate difference under the rubric of 'diversity' may do little to equalize differences in men's and women's terms and conditions of work unless they are underwritten by a commitment to gender equality (Liff 1993).

However, because equal opportunities discourse, which identifies the issue as one of 'fairness', is now so widely accepted, it has also been adopted by those with more radical goals, who measure success in terms of outcome rather than intent (Aitkenhead and Liff 1991; Jewson and Mason 1992) or who are concerned to challenge the organization of work on men's terms. Jane Skinner (1988) argues that rather than dismissing equal opportunities because policies so often fail to address structured inequality, the key battle is to redefine and widen the meaning of equal opportunities. Similarly, Cynthia Cockburn (1991) distinguishes between short and long 'agendas', the one dealing with immediate measures to increase women's access (e.g. family-friendly employment policies) and the other revamping institutional life so that it no longer reflects male-defined occupational cultures and working patterns. Rather than deny or assert sexual difference in general, she argues, we should struggle to ensure that it is up to women to say if and when sexual difference is relevant to particular situations.

There is some disagreement as to whether the 'business case' for equal opportunities (justified by ideas about organizational performance rather than fairness or women's interests) works in women's long-term interest, since its relevance is always highly contingent on the type of organization, labour supply and other factors (Dickens 1994).

See also EQUAL RIGHTS.

Equal rights   The language of equal rights and EQUAL OPPORTUNITIES is associated with the feminism of the late eighteenth and nineteenth centuries which exploited the logic of liberal political philosophy to argue for the extension to women of rights claimed on behalf of all INDIVIDUALS, but which de facto and even explicitly excluded women and other categories of persons in terms of RACE, NATIONALITY, and CLASS. This language remained central to second wave feminism in the US particularly, with the growth of organizations such as NOW (New Opportunities for Women) and the strategy of working for legislative reform – in Britain, in measures such as the equal pay and sex discrimination legislation of the 1970s (Cornell 1992; Phillips [ed.] 1987).

Equal rights have been advanced through these means in the areas of employment opportunities and rewards, civil and political liberties and REPRESENTATION, and rights to bodily integrity, including sexual rights. In spite of many formal and even substantive gains, EQUALITY with men in respect of these matters is a long way from being fully realized. In many parts of the world, these goals are simply not accepted. In the countries of the former communist societies of the USSR and Eastern Europe, long-standing rights have been eroded with astonishing rapidity (Peggy Watson 1993). In many cases the first to come under attack have been reproductive rights, especially the right to abortion, and it is interesting that this has coincided with a widespread BACKLASH in the US on these issues. The Equal Rights Amendment (ERA), the flagship of equal rights, has been thwarted.

There has always been considerable reserve amongst feminists about the value of legislative reform in securing change for women, given the central part played by the discourse and institutions of the LAW in PATRIARCHY (Smart 1984; 1989). Some feminist philosophers have developed these reservations to argue, drawing on POSTSTRUCTURALISM, that the discourses of equality, rights, individualism, and the SOCIAL CONTRACT are built upon a false UNIVERSAL human SUBJECT, who is not just contingently a man. The plea to extend his rights to her, it is argued, has to be accompanied by a close DECONSTRUCTION of the manner in which these rights may have built into them the maleness of the 'human' subject, so that winning them on the same terms for women may have unexpected and unwelcome consequences. All selves are embodied, and therefore it is argued, HUMAN RIGHTS must be identified in sex-specific terms (Grosz 1994; Irigaray, in Schor and Weed [eds] 1994; Pateman 1988; Pateman and Gross [eds] 1986).

Others have been anxious that we do not underestimate the dangers of a premature abandonment of the ENLIGHTENMENT project in feminism (Benhabib and Cornell [eds] 1987; Felski 1989b; Lovibond 1989; Soper 1989; 1990). The virulence of racism across the globe shows no sign of abating, and while the language of equal rights and equal opportunities does not necessarily imply any substantive or even formal commitment to egalitarianism – quite the contrary – it does nevertheless provide a platform on which to fight some of the worst abuses of human rights .

See also SEXUATE RIGHTS.

Equality

> The dilemma for a feminist political strategy may be summed up in the tension between the plea for equality and the assertion of sexual difference. If the sexes are different, then how may that difference... be represented throughout culture, without the sex that is different becoming subordinate (Alexander 1987: 162).

The shift in the history of FEMINISMS between equality and DIFFERENCE and various new syntheses of the two is sometimes related as an unfolding over time. 'First-wave' feminism, in the late eighteenth and nineteenth centuries in Europe and the US, founded on the liberal philosophies of Locke and Rousseau and later, John Stuart Mill and Harriet Taylor (Nye 1988; Phillips [ed.] 1987) is said to be a feminism of equality focused on winning legal, civil and political rights for women; second-wave feminism is then presented as a feminism of difference, pointing towards RADICAL FEMINIST celebrations of the specificity of female/feminine CULTURE, practice, desire; and POST-STRUCTURALIST and POSTMODERNIST feminisms, in one or another of their many and various forms, provide the synthesis. Thus Julia Kristeva tells the story in 'Women's Time' (Kristeva 1989), mapping this trajectory within feminism onto her opposition between the 'linear time' of history and political projects, and the 'cyclical time' of reproductive cycles, cycles of birth and death.

Real history is less elegant, more messy and confused, and the tension between demands for equality and the insistence that real differences are acknowledged remains. In Kristeva's third phase, feminism is perhaps more alive to this tension, but the attempts to resolve it in 1990s poststructuralist and postmodernist syntheses are widely variable, ranging from Irigaray's corporeal feminism with its strong emphasis still on the difference and specificity of the female BODY, to cyberfeminisms in which that body is presented as infinitely malleable, losing any clear identity in terms of SEX or GENDER. The tension identified by Alexander is reproduced and reprocessed rather than resolved.

Some poststructuralist critiques of equality have accused EQUAL RIGHTS feminism of 'saming': of denying to women their difference from men, or aspiring to make women identical to men (Irigaray 1993; Schor and Weed [eds] 1994). But this equation of 'equality' with 'the same' has been challenged both inside and outside poststructuralist feminism. The poststructuralist historian Joan Scott argues that 'the antithesis itself hides the interdependence of the two terms, for equality is not the elimination of difference, and difference does not preclude equality' (1990: 138).

The political theorist Diane Coole, on the other hand, deconstructs the discourses of difference/othering, to argue that they cannot encompass certain kinds of material differences of CLASS (1996). Poverty and social deprivation produce differences which provide little cause for celebration. Nancy Fraser discusses the problem in terms of the opposition between political strategies founded on redistribution and on recognition (1995).

Concurrent with the growing interest first in poststructuralism and then in postmodernism as sources for feminist theory was the impact of BLACK FEMINIST criticism of the dominant discourses of feminist theory and practice as white, Western, and middle class in their standpoint, marginalizing women who are positioned elsewhere in social and cultural life. The LESBIAN FEMINIST critique in turn has put the spotlight on the heterosexism of those discourses. The debate over difference shifted attention away from the differences between the sexes, and onto intra-sexual differences. Again, the tension between equality and difference remains strong, but is displaced. For within these critiques feminisms of difference and of the specificity of women's bodies are challenged in new ways in the face of the recognition that the meaning of 'being a woman' is not independent of other social positionings such as those of class, RACE and SEXUALITY (Spelman 1990).

See also EQUAL OPPORTUNITIES; NEEDS; SEXUATE RIGHTS; SOCIAL CONTRACT.

Essentialism Teresa de Laurentis (1989) identifies that sense of 'essentialism' as a conceptual entity which is germane to this debate:

> The totality of the properties, constituent elements, etc. without which it would cease to be the same thing; the indispensable and necessary attributes of a thing as opposed to those which it may have or not... (*Shorter OED*).

Feminists have had good reason for their mistrust of essentialism, for the essential qualities attributed to WOMAN/WOMEN usually turn out to be biological. It is biological reductionism, that old, old weapon in the armory of anti-feminism, that threatens. Early 'second-wave' feminisms, including RADICAL FEMINISM, shared a preference for the view immortalized in Simone de Beauvoir's adage, 'One is not born, but becomes a woman' (de Beauvoir 1953: 249): SOCIAL CONSTRUCTIONISM.

While the accusations and counter-accusations continue, hard-line anti-essentialism has been questioned from within the very POSTSTRUCTURALISM which had been most insistently anti-essentialist (Spivak 1993b). Teresa de Lauretis offers a very positive account of those ITALIAN FEMINISTS indebted to Luce Irigaray, who have 'taken the risk of essentialism', drawing on such concepts as 'female genealogy'; 'symbolic community'; 'entrustment'; 'female authorization'; 'symbolic mediation'; 'the symbolic mother' (de Lauretis 1989).

Diana Fuss's (1989) defence of essentialism is more equivocal and double-edged. Even the most rigorous social constructionism, she argues, cannot avoid it. It may be detected even in the work of Lacan and Derrida. She argues that 'the very staking out of a pure anti-essentialist position simply reinscribes an inescapable essentialist logic (1989: 9). Sarah Franklin and Jackie Stacey's article 'Dyketactics for difficult times' (1988) might serve as an instance of an acceptable 'strategic essentialism'. Strategic essentialism, following the classic displacement strategy of poststructuralist enquiry, shifts the question: not whether, but how and where, does essentialism circulate within any given theory, and in what form? However, 'strategic essentialism' may succeed only in displacing the confrontation between essentialism and anti-essentialism: 'my essentialism is strategic and therefore virtuous; yours however is fundamentalist and vicious'.

See also EPISTEMOLOGY; REAL/REALITY.

Ethics See MORAL REASONING.

Ethnic model Refers to the idea that the formation of collective political IDENTITIES based on ETHNICITY has become a model shaping the articulation of other group identities and politics, such as what is termed the 'ethnic model' of gay identity and gay politics.

Ethnicity   Originally a sociological concept referring to the formation of group identities based on a shared cultural, religious or linguistic heritage, rather than so-called racial distinctions based on skin colour or physical features. As Mary Maynard notes, some commentators prefer the term 'ethnicity' to 'race' because it seems to have fewer ESSENTIALIST connotations (1994a: 11). However, in as much as ethnicity can provide the basis for inferiorization, OPPRESSION, subordination and EXPLOITATION, it too may constitute the basis for racism: 'the markers and signifiers that racism uses need not be those of biology and physiognomy but can be those of language, territorial right or culture' (Anthias 1990: 24, cited by Maynard 1994a: 11). Prompted by the theorization of DIFFERENCE and IDENTITY by BLACK FEMINISTS, the ETHNOCENTRISM of second wave feminism has gradually given way to a greater recognition of diversity and inequality among women.

However, the term 'ethnicity' has begun to be used outside the realm of 'race relations discourse', in which it signals minority status. Feminist analyses of DIFFERENCE seek to articulate how (always already) gendered ethnicities construct sexual difference in specific ways. Moreover, in a globalized world the term connotes the particularity and belongingness which many people value. Since identity is not stabilized by nature or some other essential guarantee, then it follows that it is constructed historically, culturally and politically: the concept which refers to this is ethnicity. Stuart Hall states, therefore:

> The term ethnicity acknowledges the place of history, language and culture in the construction of SUBJECTIVITY and IDENTITY, as well as the fact that all discourse is placed, positioned, situated, and all knowledge is contextual (1992: 25).

See also IDENTITY; RACE; SUBJECTIVITY.

Ethnocentrism   Looking at things from the point of view of one social group or as they apply to one social group. In the 1980s BLACK FEMINISTS and others accused white feminists of assuming the universality of white women's experience of the family and ignoring the importance for women of issues like immigration law and racial discrimination. The WHITENESS of feminist theory and feminist identities had remained invisible. Ethnocentrism sometimes implies a degree of inadvertentence as compared to the more intentional desire to discriminate characteristic of prejudice or racism.

Eurocentrism is a parallel term used by anti-imperialist and POST-COLONIAL critics to draw attention to the ways in which Western, and specifically European, discourses construct themselves as SUBJECT, in the process MARGINALIZING or 'othering' non-western discourse. Edward Said's *Orientalism* (1978) demonstrates how in effect the West discursively constructed the Orient over a 4000-year history through a range of practices including academic DISCIPLINES, historiography, literature and art. Gayatri Spivak focuses on the elisions of Western feminism, showing how it shores up 'the sovereign Subject of the West' (1993: 87).

See also ETHNICITY; ORIENTALISM; OTHER; RACE.

Eurocentrism See ETHNOCENTRISM.

Excess The term is used in POSTSTRUCTURALIST theories of SIGNIFICATION to denote that which cannot be signified. For Derrida there is a continual deferral of the signified; rather than being secured in language, meaning is always in excess of it. In Lacanian PSYCHOANALYSIS desire and the UNCONSCIOUS are excessive: 'IDENTITY' can never fully capture, sum up or adequately REPRESENT myself to myself. Lacan locates excess in the REAL, which is opposed to both the SYMBOLIC and the IMAGINARY realms.

In both theories, 'WOMAN' operates as a sign of excess. As Irigaray, quoting Lacan, states, 'there is no woman but excluded from the value of words' (1985a: 87). And for Kristeva: 'In "woman" I see something that cannot be represented, something that is not said, something that is above and beyond nomenclatures and ideologies' (1989: 137). According to Kristeva, woman's negativity carries with it a revolutionary potential to disrupt PHALLOCENTRIC systems. Similarly, from a Derridean perspective, the sign 'woman' as supplement can be used to undo the phallocentric privileging of MASCULINITY. This, in effect, is what Luce Irigaray's critique of Western philosophy *Speculum of the Other Woman* (1974) achieves. In theories of the CARNIVALESQUE and ABJECTION woman as excess is represented in the figure of the female GROTESQUE whose excessive bodily contours trangress and invert social and sexual norms.

Existentialist feminism

> A woman has no essence, no more than any human being has. In her free choice, she makes herself what she is (Nye 1988: 84).

In the existentialist philosophy of Jean-Paul Sartre's *Being and Nothingness* (1966) the human condition is one of an isolated and vertiginous freedom. Men make themselves through their projects.

Sartrean man is first of all a sovereign INDIVIDUAL consciousness, and the very existence of OTHERS is a threat, although also a necessity, to the transcendent SELF and its projects. Sartrean sociality, at this stage in the development of his ideas, is confrontational and antagonistic, engaged in a fight for dominance and the forced submission of the other.

Simone de Beauvoir mounted her massive study of women as 'the second sex' within these terms (de Beauvoir 1953). Women are press-ganged into immanence by men's strong will to become transcendent SUBJECTS, but also by the treachery of female corporeality. For ABJECTION and immanence have their basis in the physical BODY, and transcendence depends on subduing that body. De Beauvoir's horror of the body, especially of female flesh, matches that of Sartre. Here we have Sartre's nauseated hero in his novel *The Age of Reason:*

> he thought: "She's pregnant. It's fantastic. I can't feel it to be true." It seemed to him shocking and grotesque like the sight of an old man kissing an old woman on the lips... "She's pregnant" – there was a little vitreous tide within her, slowly swelling into the semblance of an eye. "It's opening out among all the muck inside her belly, it's alive." (1961: 20).

And now here is de Beauvoir:

> ...the feminine sex organ... concealed, mucous and humid, as it is; it bleeds each month, it is often sullied with bodily fluids, it has a secret and perilous life of its own... Feminine sex desire is the soft throbbing of a mollusc... man dives upon his prey like the eagle and the hawk; woman lies in wait like the carnivorous plant, the bog, in which insects and children are swallowed. She is absorption, suction, humus, pitch and glue, a passive influx, insinuating and viscous (de Beauvoir 1953: 406–7).

Individual women may escape immanence, to achieve transcendence like men, defining and seeing through their own human projects and creating themselves as full human SUBJECTS; but only by avoiding REPRODUCTION, if not (hetero)sex itself.

It is not difficult, 30 years into second-wave feminism to see the limits of Beauvoir's approach to women's OPPRESSION. But de Beauvoir not only founded a distinctive form of feminism forged in and through existentialist philosophy; she also provided a major work of scholarship from which every subsequent feminism has taken off. Andrea Nye (1988) traces out the influence upon RADICAL FEMINISM, and de Beauvoir's critical engagement (and dissatisfaction with) MARXISM is one of the benchmarks of both MARXIST and SOCIALIST FEMINISM. FRENCH FEMINISM, from MATERIALIST FEMINISM (Delphy 1984; Leonard and Adkins [eds] 1996) to the work of the post-Lacanians (Kristeva 1986; Irigaray 1991), was in part forged in the encounter with de Beauvoir (Moi 1994).

Certain POSTSTRUCTURALIST feminists have identified a way out of de Beauvoir's difficulties in the rejection of her deeply embedded mind/body dualism. The have insisted that all selves are embodied (Battersby forthcoming 1997; Bordo 1993; Braidotti 1994b; Gatens 1991; Grosz 1994; Irigaray 1991; Pateman 1988) and have attempted to develop a 'corporeal feminism' which founds a more adequate approach to subjectivity.

See also GROTESQUE.

Experience   CONSCIOUSNESS-RAISING highlighted women's experience as the source of feminist KNOWLEDGE, as against expert, official or male-defined accounts, and made it the foundation of feminist strategy. Although experience is still privileged in feminism, it has become a much more contested category, first and foremost in relation to DIFFERENCE. As Sandra Harding says 'feminist knowledge has started off from women's lives, but it has started off from many different women's lives' (1993: 63). Secondly, it is argued that experience as the basis of feminist theory is unreliable on EPISTEMOLOGICAL grounds – all human experience being 'mediated by cultural suppositions embedded in language and culture' (Vicki Bell 1993). Some feminist theorists prefer the term 'subjugated knowledges', thereby recognizing women as active producers of (often disqualified) knowledges rather than assuming that their experience speaks for itself.

Experience has played an equally contested role in ACADEMIC FEMINISM. For Donna Haraway (1991) and Diana Fuss (1989) one of the key sites in which experience is produced is 'in the classroom'. Since women's experience does not pre-exist as a kind of prior resource, we can have access to another's life and consciousness only through multiple readings of texts which add and shape each other 'in both cacophonous and consonant waves' (Haraway 1991: 113), building 'just-barely-possible' affinities and connections while, ideally, avoiding appropriating each others' experiences.

See also KNOWLEDGE; POWER.

Exploitation   In Marx's economic theory 'exploitation' refers to the process by which the property-owning classes appropriate the surplus produced by workers, i.e. the value of what they produce over and above what they receive in wages. Since labour is the source of all profit (either 'fresh' labour or the past labour which is congealed in capital) the process of production in class societies is also always simultaneously a process of exploitation.

Partly because economic exploitation was already 'owned' by Marxism, it has been a less popular concept in feminism than the more loosely defined notion of OPPRESSION. However, some feminist theorists have applied the concept of economic exploitation in the family context, treating 'the family as an economic system ... [as] hierarchically structured labour relations in which men benefit from, and exploit, the work of women ... ' (Delphy and Leonard 1992). The work done by women for men within family relations includes housework, work for men's occupations, emotional servicing of family members, childcare, the care of sick and frail family members, sexual servicing of husbands and the bearing of children. FAMILIAL EXPLOITATION is demonstrated when women's contribution to the accumulation of family wealth is inherited by sons from their fathers, bypassing women (Delphy and Leonard 1986). Many feminists also use the term 'exploitation' in sexual contexts, to refer to men's use of women's bodies for their own pleasure. For instance, MacKinnon's famous dictum that 'Sexuality is to feminism what work is to Marxism: that which is most one's own, yet most taken away'

(1982: 516) transposed the concept of exploitation from the economic domain to the personal, seeing the exploitation or appropriation of women's SEXUALITY as the basis of women's oppression.

F

False memory syndrome   False memory syndrome tries to explain (away) the apparently considerable number of adult women who have recovered memories of child sexual abuse while undergoing psychotherapy. Many feminists see the very idea of false memory syndrome as a BACKLASH attempt to limit the impact of women's challenge to male VIOLENCE AGAINST WOMEN.

Clearly the debate over false memory syndrome echoes the debate over Freud's retraction of his first, trauma theory of HYSTERIA (symptoms caused by repression of the trauma of seduction) in favour of OEDIPAL theory (repression of the child's UNCONSCIOUS oedipal DESIRE for the parent) (Masson 1984; Rush 1984). Janet Haaken (1994; 1996) traces the call to validate women's voices – the insistence that all recovered instances of sexual abuse must have occurred – partly to the denial of the existence of hysteria which characterizes the treatment of post-traumatic stress disorder more generally. More importantly, she argues that the insistence on the reality of abuse in every case of recovered memory amounts to a denial of the existence of female sexual FANTASY, indeed of women as sexual actors; it colludes with rather than challenges the prohibition of female desire (all 'bad' thoughts must have come from outside the female psyche). In this sense the debate about false memory syndrome echoes also the attitudes of the feminist campaigners in the moral purity movements of late nineteenth-century Britain, for whom the protection of women seemed to rest on perpetuating the image of women as 'pure' victims of male lust, with no desires of their own.

There is a danger, though, that this kind of argument simply reproduces the polarity between the acknowledgement of women's sexual desire and the recognition of the reality of sexual abuse. What we need is to demonstrate that the one does not rule out the other. Women have faced the same paradox in contesting rape, for it is often difficult for a sexually active woman to prove she did not consent. Ultimately the concept of innocence fails to protect either women or children; we want to be able to punish not those who assault 'innocence' but those who fail to respect sexual autonomy.

Familial exploitation   See EXPLOITATION.

Family In ordinary British usage 'the family' usually refers to the so-called biological or nuclear family – father, mother and dependent children – but sometimes also to the wider KINSHIP network. Use of the term also often naturalizes relationships; as Anne McClintock points out, in nineteenth-century Britain the family was used as a trope 'sanctioning social *hierarchy* within a putative organic *unity* of interests' (1993: 64).

Initially, second-wave FEMINIST theory conceptualized the family as the main site of women's OPPRESSION. Barrett and McIntosh (1982) defined what they termed the 'family-household system' as one in which households are assumed to be based on a male breadwinner, an economically dependent female and their dependent children. It combines two elements, the IDEOLOGICAL and the material. Firstly, what Barrett calls the ideology of familialism (1988: 206) plays a key role in defining ideal family structures, GENDER roles and sexual partnerships, marginalizing people who live outside conventional families from socially acknowledged of adulthood (Barrett and McIntosh 1982). Secondly, the family-household system is the site in which women undertake unpaid labour for those defined as family members, thereby limiting their participation in paid labour. There is a strong implication that the system, if not precisely functional for CAPITAL, is supported by capitalism (through, for instance the welfare policies of the 'capitalist STATE') because it lowers the cost of REPRODUCING the labour force.

The ETHNOCENTRISM of this approach was highlighted by BLACK FEMINISTS, who argued that feminist hostility to the family ignored the solidarity and mutual aid families offer minority women in a hostile society (*Feminist Review* 1984); moreover, motherhood in Black families is a source of female solidarity and POWER, not oppression (James 1993; Phoenix 1987). In retrospect, it also appears that SOCIALIST FEMINIST theory wrongly assumed the willingness of either 'capital' or 'patriarchy' to support women's reproductive labour. As Ehrenreich comments, no one now thinks that 'the decline of American productivity is due to unironed shirts and cold breakfasts' (1992: 143) and men show 'an unexpected ability to survive on fast food and the emotional solace of short-term relationships' (1992: 144). In contemporary capitalist society the control of women's labour has shifted from the family (private PATRIARCHY) to the STATE and paid employment (PUBLIC patriarchy) so that changes in the family-household system partly reduce but partly only reshape women's subordination to patriarchal power (Walby 1990).

Many feminists have tried to deal with the revival of 'family values' political rhetoric by trying to redefine 'the family'. For instance, the gay and LESBIAN movements have tried to widen the meaning of 'family' to include same-sex partnerships and campaigned to have these relationships given the same legal status as heterosexual marriages (for example Weston 1991; see also Herman 1993 for a different point of view).

See also BACKLASH; DEPENDENCY; KINSHIP; KINWORK; MATERIALIST FEMINISM.

Family romance　Freud used the term 'the family romance' to describe children's fantasies regarding parental origin and SEXUALITY, in particular the popular fantasy that one is not really the child of one's parents, but rather the offspring of parents of a higher social class.
　　See PSYCHOANALYSIS.

Fantastic　See FANTASY.

Fantasy　Fantasy constitutes 'the fundamental object of psychoanalysis' (Laplanche and Pontalis 1986: 14). According to Freud, the origins of fantasy lie in autoerotic sexuality, in the separation in the child's psyche of need (to take nourishment) from DESIRE (for sexual satisfaction in sucking the breast). For Lacan desire is for a fantasized rather than an actual object, and for psychoanalysts generally a fantasy is not simply a mental image but a total context in which desire is staged. Burgin (in Wright [ed.] 1992) identifies the importance of the concept to cultural theory:

> Psychoanalysis deconstructs the positivist dichotomy in which fantasy is seen as an inconsequential addendum to 'reality'. It reveals the supposedly marginal operations of fantasy to be constitutive of our identity, and to be at the centre of all our perceptions, beliefs and actions...Fantasy is a complex articulation of both the subject and its unconscious desire in a shifting field of wishes and defences (Wright 1992, 87).

Feminists have not always acknowledged this insight, and fantasy occupies an ambiguous place in feminist discourse. RADICAL FEMINISTS have tended to be suspicious of fantasy, encouraging women to repudiate sexual, especially heterosexual, fantasies modelled on dominance and submission (Jeffreys 1990; MacKinnon 1987 – cf. PORNOGRAPHY). Others (e.g. Segal and McIntosh [eds] 1992; Linda Williams 1990) have criticized this perspective as too simplistic, arguing that fantasy operates in a complex manner and cannot be simply mapped on to a model of gendered social relations. Moreover, fantasy strongly informs feminist UTOPIAN writing, much of which is lesbian and separatist in character. Some of this writing implicitly sets up an opposition between politically correct and incorrect forms of fantasy. Julia Kristeva (1989) is critical of such moves and repudiates the valorization of the 'ARCHAIC MOTHER' in feminist discourse, which she argues is itself a regressive fantasy.

　　PSYCHOANALYTIC feminists evince an interest in relating women's fantasy to forms of (resistance to) OPPRESSION. Jacqueline Rose (1986) identifies resistance to feminine identity in women's UNCONSCIOUS. Fantasy is also a central concept for feminist CULTURAL STUDIES. Feminists have produced valuable studies of fantasies structuring women's romance fiction (Kaplan 1986; Modleski 1982; Radway 1984). They have argued that romantic fantasies are not necessarily as self-punitive as radical feminists have sometimes claimed and can be read against the grain as subversive of PATRIARCHAL norms. Within literary criticism, Rosemary Jackson (1981) has examined the subversive potential of fantasy as a literary GENRE.

Throughout the 1980s, during what became known as the 'Sex Wars' (Ardill and O'Sullivan 1989), feminists hotly debated the role of fantasy in the construction of sexual IDENTITY. Many lesbian and QUEER subjects rejected the critique of fantasy by feminists such as Andrea Dworkin (1981) and Catharine MacKinnon (1987), and began to articulate and act out fantasies which they saw as transgressive of sexual norms. This practice received fresh impetus from the burgeoning of POSTMODERN theories of identity which presented fantasy – in the sense of play – as an element in the discursive construction of identities. Judith Butler's (1991) influential conception views gender as a PERFORMANCE in which desire is always in excess of identity. It is true to say that in postmodern accounts fantasy appears as infinitely more mobile, more subject to choice, and more benign than in the Freudian and (radical) feminist literature and its critics argue that it fails to acknowledge either the embeddedness of certain psychosexual fantasies or the radically destabilizing operation of the UNCONSCIOUS.

See also GROTESQUE; UNCANNY.

Feminine   Moi (1989) makes a distinction between female, feminine and feminist whereby the feminine designates the set of cultural attributes assigned to the female SEX which the political discourses of FEMINISM seek to critique. For example, the feminist writer Virginia Woolf describes the constraints placed on women by the image of the 'angel in the house' produced by nineteenth-century DOMESTIC IDEOLOGY (1977). Theories of the feminine tend to present it in one of two ways: as something basically imposed on women from the outside either through direct or indirect means (sociological), or as a psychosexual process involving the female UNCONSCIOUS (cf. PSYCHOANALYSIS).

Historically, the relationship between feminists and FEMININITY is an ambivalent one. Mary Wollstonecraft set the tone for the RADICAL FEMINIST impugning of femininity, viewing it as a form of romantic illusionism which prevented women exercising their reason. Thereafter femininity has been viewed as a form of false consciousness to be thrown off (Greer 1971). Many feminists, recognizing the theoretical and practical shortcomings of such a position, have turned to psychoanalysis in an attempt to relate theories of IDEOLOGY to the formation of gendered SUBJECTIVITIES.

In many ways the turn to Freud compounds the problem: for Freud every woman was first a little man, and her eventual entry into 'normal' femininity represents her acceptance of her lack in relation to phallic sexuality. However, while challenging aspects of this model, psychoanalytic feminists highlight its valuable features. Jacqueline Rose, for example, argues that

If psychoanalysis can give us an account of how women experience the path to femininity, it also insists, through the concept of the unconscious, that femininity is neither simply achieved nor is it ever complete... (1986: 7).

Rose insists that the concept of the UNCONSCIOUS is crucial to feminist accounts of femininity because 'it represents a resistance to identity...at the very heart of psychic life' (1990: 232). In contrast, Elizabeth Wilson (1990) argues against psychic determinism, emphasizing the sexual division of labour and the importance of social and material pressures in securing IDENTITY.

The strategy of some FRENCH FEMINISTS has been to invert the denigration of femininity and celebrate its DIFFERENCE. Cixous is the major exponent of the practice of *ÉCRITURE FEMININE* which seeks to inscribe femininity in positive terms. Many feminists critique this strategy as ESSENTIALIST and counter-productive, arguing that it ultimately shores up rather than challenges the masculine/feminine polarity. In foregrounding sexual difference, it potentially elides other differences – such as CLASS and 'RACE' – between and within the sexes. Moreover, to return to Moi's point, a theory based on a politicized category of 'femininity' fails to register the critical difference in view between being a WOMAN and being a feminist. Clearly, the challenge for feminists remains one of critiquing the production of femininity within PATRIARCHY without either simply denigrating or celebrating feminine cultures and the investments made by members of the social group 'women'.

See also CULTURAL FEMINISM; WOMEN'S CULTURE.

Feminine language See NEW FEMINIST LANGUAGE.

Feminism Defined in the OED as 'advocacy of the rights of women', dating from the mid-nineteenth century in Europe. Historically there have been many feminisms, variously grounded. Minimally, the term implies the identification of women as systematically oppressed; the belief that GENDER relations are neither inscribed in natural DIFFERENCES between the sexes, nor immutable, and a political commitment to their transformation.

In 1980, Michèle Barrett wrote that 'any feminism must insist upon the specific character of gender relations' (Barrett 1988: 3), but this is no simple matter because the character of gender is bound up with and therefore relative to other markers of social difference including those of CLASS and so-called RACE. What it means to be a WOMAN is variable and context dependent.

Historically, the term emerged as part of the discourse of the European ENLIGHTENMENT, and nineteenth-century feminism was deeply marked by its Western and bourgeois roots. It is this history which has lead some WOMEN'S MOVEMENTS to refuse the term. Alexandra Kollontai, who headed the women's section of the Soviet Communist Party in the early 1920s and was responsible for introducing wide-ranging reforms aimed at women's

EMANCIPATION, rejected the term because of what she considered to be its contamination by bourgeois liberal women's movements in Europe and the United States (Kollontai 1977). Some members of the Indian women's movement that emerged as part of Indian NATIONALISM disputed the label on the grounds of ANTI-IMPERIALISM (Forbes 1990) and this argument still caries weight among some THIRD WORLD and Black women (Kishwar 1990). The Black North American writer Alice Walker prefers to call herself a 'WOMANIST' (Walker 1984a). FRENCH FEMINISM entered yet other reservations. The '*PSYCH ET PO*' group in the mid-1970s defined feminism as 'a reformist movement of women wanting power within the patriarchal system' and marched on International Women's Day in Paris under a banner which read 'Down with feminism!' (Moi [ed.] 1987: 3).

In spite of these reservations, the term has been one under which many women have mobilized in movements aimed at social transformation of SEX and gender. Feminism has created a rich seam of social and cultural critical theory, and political practice which has had a major impact on the everyday, commonsense assumptions that circulate in social practice and in the media. It is at least possible, 30 years into contemporary feminism, for women and girls in many contexts to enter claims for more equitable treatment and the effects, for example in the greatly improved educational attainments of girls in schools, may perhaps be taken as indicators of that change. The strength of the BACKLASH against feminism may also be read as a back-handed compliment.

Feminism has also won a degree of recognition in a number of discourses in the social sciences and humanities, but unevenly. It has presented a challenge, and many more political, cultural and social theorists at least gesture towards feminism in their work. However, a full engagement with feminist theory is still exceptional across many DISCIPLINES.

See also BLACK FEMINISM; CULTURAL FEMINISM; LESBIAN FEMINISM; LIBERAL FEMINISM; MARXIST FEMINISM; MATERIALIST FEMINISM; RADICAL FEMINISM; SOCIALIST FEMINISM.

Feminist counter-public sphere 'An oppositional discursive arena within the society of late capitalism, structured around an ideal of a communal gendered identity' (Felski 1989a: 9).

This concept is an APPROPRIATION of Jürgen Habermas's 'bourgeois public sphere', whose emergence he located in the early modern period in Europe (Habermas 1989). This sphere was constituted through a variety of public forums where opinions were exchanged – in London coffee-houses and other meeting places, and in journals such as the *Tatler* and the *Spectator* which undertook to instruct the morals, manners and taste of the broader PUBLIC and to monitor the conduct of the STATE and public affairs.

Habermas's reworking of CRITICAL THEORY has encouraged the detection of similar forums for the working class – 'the proletarian counter-public sphere' (Negt and Kluge 1993) – centred around the public house, and for women in Felski's concept of a 'feminist counter-public sphere', constituted by the forums of the WOMEN'S MOVEMENT.

Felski's concept is a normative one for feminism, delineating how feminists might ideally negotiate DIFFERENCES in open forums in which all women may participate, undistorted by hierarchies of POWER and privilege:

> The feminist public sphere can be understood as both an ideal and real, as both a utopian ideology and a determinate set of cultural practices governed by given political and socio-economic conditions, as such it provides a model capable of addressing the reasons for contradictions and tensions within the women's movement. The feminist counter-public sphere cannot be understood as a unified interpretive community governed by a single set of norms and values (Felski 1989a: 10).

See also COMMUNICATION; NEW SOCIAL MOVEMENTS.

Feminist stylistics   See *ÉCRITURE FEMININE*; FEMININE.

Feminist therapy   The term refers to the range of therapeutic theories and practices developed by feminists influenced to a greater or lesser extent by PSYCHOANALYSIS. These include Kleinian OBJECT RELATIONS, Lacanianism, existential psychotherapy, anti-psychiatry and the growth movement. In Britain, feminist therapy is closely associated with the Women's Therapy Centre started in 1976 by Louise Eichenbaum and Susie Orbach. Their starting point was classical Freudianism's failure to recognize the theoretical and practical salience of GENDER. They aimed to formulate a feminist psychoanalytic theory and develop a range of psychotherapy services by and for women. The centre's interest in women's interrelationships – especially mother–daughter relations – has led to the privileging of object relations approaches. The Centre has made valuable contributions to both feminist knowledge and women's psychological well-being, including work on the issues of sexual abuse, eating disorders and abortion.

Fetishism   In anthropology, 'fetishism' refers to the practice of using charms for magical purposes. In contemporary theory, the term occurs in two main paradigms: MARXISM and PSYCHOANALYSIS. Marx views fetishism as an inseparable aspect of the process of capitalist commodification whereby the COMMODITY appears not to be the product of human labour, but to exist autonomously.

Recent feminist accounts of postmodern culture make use of the concept; Danae Clark (1993), for example, discusses the appropriation of lesbian iconography by mainstream consumer culture in terms of fetishism.

In PSYCHOANALYTIC theory the term designates a perversion, in which male sexual satisfaction is obtained through the association of a female sexual object with a fetish such as feet, hair, or a shoe. The presence of the fetish is the condition of the male pervert's sexual DESIRE and pleasure. Until recently, commentators including feminists saw fetishism as an exclusively male condition, often reading it as an aspect of HETEROSEXUAL masculinity.

However, some recent feminist work points to the existence of a female fetishism (Coward 1985) and seeks to appropriate it for feminism (Adams 1989; Gamman and Makinen 1994; Grosz 1995). Gamman and Makinen (1994) identify a range of female fetishistic practices including pop fandom, women's engagement with fetish magazines, fetish fashions and sexual subcultures. In particular, they identify widespread food fetishism among women, arguing that some eating disorders such as bulimia are best understood in terms of fetishism. Such projects remain controversial in that it is unclear what relationship fetishistic practices have to feminist politics, and whether they have any subversive, not to say progressive, value.

Field 'A field', in Pierre Bourdieu's terms, 'is a space in which a game takes place, a field of objective relations between individuals or institutions who are competing for the same stake' (Bourdieu 1984: 197, quoted in Moi 1991).

See also DISCIPLINES; DISTINCTION; SYMBOLIC POWER; SYMBOLIC VIOLENCE.

Film theory The history of the emergence of film studies as a recognized field of scholarship articulates in important ways with the rethinking of feminist theory from the late 1960s. A significant amount of contemporary feminist theory has actually been forged in film studies (de Lauretis 1984 and 1987; Rose 1986).

Film studies was closely associated with CULTURAL STUDIES, whose institutional debut occurred in the early 1960s with the founding of the Centre for Contemporary Cultural Studies (CCCS) in Birmingham. But film theory at this time in Britain particularly and in the US, was greatly influenced by the French journal *Cahiers du Cinema* which, under the impact of André Bazin (1958–62), took a purist line on the specificity of film. Film studies in Britain has aspired to become a distinct DISCIPLINE, cultural studies remained more committed to crossing disciplinary boundaries.

The key intervention at this juncture was the transformation of the journal of the Society for Education in Film and Television (SEFT), *Screen*, as it began to orient itself more fully from 1971 towards the new French theories and the application of structural linguistics to film – the work of Roland Barthes (Barthes 1972), Christian Metz (1983) and others. In what became known as '*Screen* theory' the centrality of Lacanian PSYCHOANALYSIS ensured that SEXUALITY and sexual DIFFERENCE would be difficult to sideline and therefore also ensured the interest and engagement of feminist film theorists. It has been argued that 'the narrative and symbolic problem of establishing the difference between the sexes is the primary motivating force of the classical Hollywood film' (Penley 1988: 3). The most influential feminist intervention was made by Laura Mulvey in her widely discussed and reprinted essay 'Visual pleasure and narrative cinema' (Mulvey 1989a). Her thesis was that the relationship between spectator, screen image, and NARRATIVE structure and scopic organization of 'classic Hollywood cinema' positioned the spectator as masculine SUBJECT, the on-screen woman as passive object of the predatory male GAZE.

Women, then, were identified as 'the trouble in the text' in classic Hollywood cinema (Kuhn 1982). Constance Penley, commenting on an essay by Jacqueline Rose (in de Lauretis and Heath [eds] 1980), argues that the on-screen woman '...*comes to represent* (through the textual work of the film) both the difficulty of sexual difference and the problems of cinema as a representational form' (Penley 1988: 13. Emphasis in the original). Addditionally the concept of 'the cinematic apparatus' highlighted the problem of sexual DIFFERENCE. Teresa de Lauretis and Stephen Heath define the term as including both the technology of the cinema and the 'institutions of relations and meanings (a whole machinery of affects and effects)' (1980: ix).

One cannot but be struck by the extent to which the spectator is constructed exclusively through textual analysis in *Screen* theory (Doane 1987). It is the text's positioning of the spectator that is in question and there has been remarkably little curiosity about the way actual spectators might take up, refuse, or re-position themselves in relation to that text. Jackie Stacey's important study of SPECTATORSHIP which included the use of a questionnaire (Stacey 1994b), and some of the articles included in E. Deidre Pribram's collection (Pribram 1988), have begun this work, and in the case of television, Ien Ang's study of *Dallas* viewers and Dorothy Hobson's work on *Crossroads* (Ang 1985; Hobson 1982). As yet there has been no work comparable to Janice Radway's ethnographic study of women ROMANCE readers (Radway 1984). Some interesting feminist studies of 'the monstrous feminine' (Creed 1993; Russo 1994) may be read in terms of Irigaray's project of constructing a less monophallic culture which might feed and support a richer 'female IMAGINARY'. But there is a dearth of studies which seek to find out what may be happening to girls and women as they absorb visual images by listening to what female spectators actually say about their viewing experiences.

See also ENUNCIATION; NARRATIVE; SPECTACLE.

Fixity The term relates to the process of STEREOTYPING by which the identities of social groups are seen as fixed, natural or ESSENTIAL. The term is utilized in the work of the POST-COLONIAL critic Homi Bhabha (1994) to describe the method by which the Western subject attempts to secure the OTHERNESS of the colonized or SUBALTERN subject.

Flaneur The *flaneur*, or urban stroller, is a figure who emerged in mid-nineteenth-century Paris, and came to represent a new way of relating to modern industrial city life.

The fact that the pursuit of sexual experience outside the family, coupled with the seeking out of seedy, decadent locales, was a major preoccupation of the *flaneur* suggests that the figure represents an essentially male IDENTITY. Wolff (1985) and Pollock (1985) argue that (middle-class) women were denied access to PUBLIC spaces and the public GAZE, both of which were coded as masculine. Elizabeth Wilson (1991) remarks that women's relation to the city, mediated by gender IDEOLOGIES, is inevitably different from men's. Apart from individual women artists such as the writer Georges Sand and the painter Berthe Morisot who walked the streets dressed as men, the *flaneuse* did not appear until the early decades of the twentieth century. As job opportunities for women increased and Victorian social mores broke down, the city offered some women a place of anonymity, independence and relative freedom, although some feminist cultural historians (Castle 1986) have argued that the city provided such freedom from a much earlier period.

Much MODERNIST fiction registers the experiences of the *flaneuse*; for example, Miriam Henderson in the middle volumes of Dorothy Richardson's novel sequence *Pilgrimage* (1915–38) lives as an independent woman, working and delighting in the city. Richardson herself lived the life of a *flaneuse*, living in a bedsit and producing pieces of journalism, observing and recording in minute detail her own experiences as the basis of *Pilgrimage*. However, Richardson's work lacks the *flaneur*'s sympathy for the urban underworld; in this respect, Djuna Barnes's *Nightwood* (1950) is more characteristic of the *flaneur* style, with its depiction of a European *demi-monde* made up of prostitutes, lesbians, Jews, travellers and circus entertainers. The themes of *Nightwood* also anticipate contemporary feminist interest in NOMADIC subjectivity.

Foundationalism   A concept central to the deconstructive theories of POSTSTRUCTURALISM and POSTMODERNISM which challenge the foundations of traditional philosophy. 'Foundationalism' refers to the idea that KNOWLEDGE is the reflection of TRUTH and that a stable foundation for it exists in God, reason or history. Postmodernists reject this, arguing that there is no 'view from nowhere', no extra-systemic point from which knowledge can be grounded. Rather, knowledge is conceived of as a network of local games with language (Lyotard 1979) or metaphoric contingencies (Rorty 1989). In fact, there is often an alternative foundationalism operating in many postmodern discourses, based not in subject-centred reason but in, for example, LANGUAGE, or DESIRE, or the BODY.

The Derridean-influenced critic Gayatri Spivak describes her work as anti-foundationalist and links it to Derrida's critique of the METAPHYSICS OF PRESENCE which challenges the centralizing, synthesizing and homogenizing tendencies of (Western) MASTER NARRATIVES. Although Spivak's own work utilizes concepts from feminism, DECONSTRUCTION, MARXISM and psychoanalysis, it resists the attempt to synthesize these discourses, arguing that it is their very differences and discontinuities which are of theoretical value.

See also EPISTEMOLOGY; REALISM; STANDPOINT.

French feminism   French feminism has come to signify those francophone feminisms which are associated with the exploration of the systems of LANGUAGE and SEXUALITY through the work of Lacan and Derrida. The actual range and diversity of French feminisms have not always been recognized in the anglophone context, where three figures – Cixous, Irigaray and Kristeva – have come to represent 'French feminism' *tout court*. In fact French feminism includes not only the RADICAL FEMINISM of Cixous and Irigaray, and Kristeva's psychoanalytic theory, but the LESBIAN FEMINISM of Monique Wittig (1992) and the Quebecoise writer Nicole Brossard, and the materialism of Simone de Beauvoir (1953), Christine Delphy (1984) and Monique Plaza (1978). As Landry and MacLean (1993) note, the overdeterminations of the marketplace are partly responsible for the packaging of French feminism. While anthologies and explications have been invaluable in bringing French feminist ideas to an anglophone audience, they have also shaped the way in which French feminism has been perceived. Important interpreters include Elisabeth Grosz (1989), Toril Moi (1985) and Alice Jardine (1985).

Perhaps the key text in introducing French ideas to an anglophone audience was Elaine Marks and Isabel de Courtivron's *New French Feminisms* (1981). Many of its contributors take as their object the status of WOMAN in Western theoretical discourse and it is this emphasis on FEMININITY as a SUBJECT POSITION in language which has come to characterize the French feminist project. A major obstacle to its anglophone reception is the tradition of linguistic philosophy and PSYCHOANALYSIS in which French feminists work. To more empirically and materially minded anglophone feminists this work has seemed unnecessarily abstract, difficult, and sweeping in its theories of FEMININITY. Anglo-American reactions to French feminism have as a result tended to fall into two categories: either the theory is seen as elitist and irrelevant (radical and LIBERAL FEMINIST response) or it is viewed as ESSENTIALIST (cf. SOCIALIST FEMINISM). Moi's Marxist critique of Cixous and Irigaray as essentialist had a lasting impact on their reception in the anglophone world. Margaret Whitford's (1991) work on Irigaray has done much to redeem her from Moi's dismissal. In addition, Irigaray's interest in feminine specificity and lesbian poetics has made her work valuable to lesbian theorists. Moreover, as anglophone feminists such as de Lauretis (1989), Fuss (1989) and Spivak (1987) have since recognized essentialism can be strategic and political, an insight that permeates Cixous' much discussed, and maligned, still extraordinary, 'The laugh of the Medusa' (1976a).

See also MATERIALIST FEMINISM.

Fundamentalism   Edward Said argues that as a category 'fundamentalism', like terrorism, derives 'entirely from the concerns and intellectual factories in metropolitan centres like Washington and London'. Both are 'fearful images that lack discriminate contents or definition...' (1993: 375). However, many feminists, while recognizing the wider RACIAL and IMPERIALIST politics in which the term fundamentalism is embroiled, would argue that it acquires coherence partly through its negative implications for women. They argue that the phase of 'politico-religious self-definition... invariably happens at the expense of women's and children's autonomy – they are regarded as communal property in need of protection, especially in the sexual sphere, from unholy outsiders' (Connolly 1991: 69).

The British feminist organization Women against Fundamentalism (WAF) defines fundamentalism as 'the mobilization of religious affiliation for political ends' (Connolly 1991), and sees its role as defending women's rights and autonomy against surges of Christian, Islamic, Jewish, and Hindu fundamentalism as and when they arise. WAF was started by an Asian women's organization in London, Southall Black Sisters (SBS), and came to public prominence through its defence of Salman Rushdie in 1989, at a time when, in the name of multiculturalism, many on the left refused to challenge Muslim COMMUNITY leaders' support for the Iranian *fatwah*. WAF's membership now includes women from many communities and organizations; it still focuses mainly on issues arising in Britain, e.g. the expansion of girls-only schooling, but maintains contact with women in other countries where fundamentalism threatens women's autonomy. WAF's success in articulating support for women across DIFFERENCE – while respecting personal religious faith – provides an important counterweight to IDENTITY POLITICS.

G

Gaze   In Freudian theory the gaze is theorized in terms of voyeurism and exhibitionism, the active and passive forms of scopophilia, or the drive to look. For Freud scopophilic drives play an important part in the quest for mastery of the world. In the 1970s FILM THEORISTS adopted the term for their theorization of SPECTATORSHIP. Laura Mulvey's classic essay 'Visual pleasure and narrative cinema' (1989a) utilizes the concept to explore the power relations of looking and represents the cinematic gaze as inherently masculine. Mulvey argued that cinematic pleasure was constructed in such a way as to reassure male subjects of their integrity in the face of sexual DIFFERENCE. Specifically, the sight of the woman on the screen precipitates an OEDIPAL crisis which is resolved through FETISHIZATION of the woman's body thus concealing her 'LACK'. This view was highly influential and became the model for feminist analyses. However, it has been criticized for presenting an overly monolithic conception of the gaze which denies that women have pleasure of their own, and for prioritizing the visual over the tactile (Grosz 1989; Irigaray 1985a). Indeed, Mulvey (1989b) herself has since modified her argument to allow for the possibility of a more active female gaze. Lesbian critics in particular have taken issue with the HETEROSEXISM implicit in the formulation, arguing that lesbian looking represents a different economy of the gaze (de Lauretis 1991a; Roof 1991; Jackie Stacey 1988). Theories of SPECTATORSHIP in the 1990s are moving away from abstract psychoanalytic-based models towards ethnographic research on real audiences.

Gender   Early second-wave feminists adopted the distinction formulated by the psychologist Robert Stoller (1968) between SEX and gender to differentiate the socio-cultural meanings ('masculinity' and 'femininity') from the base of biological sex DIFFERENCES ('male' and 'female') on which they were erected (Oakley 1972).

Within feminist thought in the early period of the second wave the dominant tendency was (and largely remains) one which minimizes the differences between the sexes and privileges gender over sex. Gender began to encroach even upon biology itself. Argument and evidence was accumulated to demonstrate that the BODY and its functionings are formed in interaction with society and CULTURE (Birke 1986; Fausto-Sterling 1985; Oakley 1972). This move to encompass sex within gender, carried to its conclusion, undermines the distinction itself. This 'withering away' of sex was further strengthened by the 'linguistic turn' in social and cultural theory which has sought to dismantle the distinction between words and things (cf. POSTSTRUCTURALISM; POSTMODERNISM; DECONSTRUCTION).

The deconstructionist argument sometimes has the effect of promoting one of a pair of opposed terms to become the overarching category. Yet, typically, the two terms continue to be used in their opposed binary meanings in particular contexts. Thus 'sex' sometimes denotes that which remains *outside* cultural constructions of gender, and sometimes the sex/gender couplet is used to point to distinctions *within* culture:

> Within lesbian contexts, the 'identification' with masculinity [gender] that appears as butch identity [gender] is not a simple assimilation of lesbianism [sex, sexuality] back into the terms of heterosexuality [sexuality]. As one lesbian femme [sex and gender] explained, she likes her boys [gender] to be girls [sex], meaning that 'being a girl' [sex] contextualizes and resignifies 'masculinity' [gender, or here, 'being a boy'] in a butch identity. As a result, that masculinity [gender], if that it can be called, is always brought into relief against a culturally intelligible [gender] 'female body' [sex] (Butler 1990: 123).

The deconstruction/destabilization of both terms that is assayed here depends on a covert but simultaneous maintenance of both terms in opposition to each other. It is only possible to make sense of this complex paragraph if the distinction between sex and gender is borne clearly in mind. The proliferation of quotation marks is telling.

The concept of gender has been criticized on the grounds that the gendering of people, actions and things within cultures is always implicated in differences other than those of sex. There is a powerful case that masculinity and femininity are constructed not alongside 'RACE' and CLASS, ETHNICITY and NATIONALITY, but in and through these and other distinctions, and that it is misleading to privilege sex in accounts of the social construction of masculinity and femininity. 'Are we to assume,' asks Elizabeth Spelman, 'that his [the Black male child's] maleness will be recognized by his mother, his father, his sister, himself, and everyone else, as something separable from his Blackness?' (Spelman 1990: 99).

For all these reasons the need for the sex/gender distinction is increasingly questioned, and feminist theorists are divided in their answers. Some (Plumwood 1993; Keller 1989) argue the necessity for the distinction; others (Gatens 1991; Butler 1990) for its dismantling. Luce Irigaray has made a highly influential attempt to displace the distinction using the concept of MORPHOLOGY (1974) and this suggestion has been pursued by the exponents of a corporeal feminism (Gatens 1992; Grosz 1994). But if the distinction is maintained, overtly or covertly, even in the course of its deconstruction, perhaps it might be more profitable to ask: 'how is this distinction in play? What is it doing in given instances of feminist discourse?' Might it be an example of one of Judith Butler's 'necessary constructions' ('what are we to make of constructions without which we would not be able to think, to live, to make sense at all, those which have acquired for us a kind of necessity?' 1993: xi)? Or of Diana Fuss's (1989) 'strategic ESSENTIALISM'?

Granted that the distinction itself is one that is made *within* culture, although it references the distinction *between* the cultural and extracultural, and given that the body and its functions are formed within society and culture and are by no means simply given and unalterable, there may yet be compelling reasons to maintain the distinction. Keller argues that however the differences between the sexes are produced and maintained, and however difficult it is to disentangle that which belongs to biological sex from that which belongs to the domain of the social, every society must and does distinguish at least two kinds of body, under the presently unavoidable constraints of human REPRODUCTIVE exigencies. All peoples erect a vast superstructure of cultural meanings around this *socially* necessary distinction between the sexes. In a similar spirit Anne Phillips remarks:

> Notwithstanding the conceptual difficulties feminists have raised around the distinction between sex and gender, we will continue to need some way of

dissentangling the differences that are inevitable from those that are chosen, and from those that are simply imposed (Phillips 1992: 23).

See also HETEROSEXUAL MATRIX; COMPULSORY HETEROSEXUALITY; SEXUALITY.

Genderlect A form of discourse, comparable to a dialect, within a larger language system which is identified with or peculiar to a particular gender. Japanese is one example of a language containing recognized genderlects.

Regarding ostensibly non-gender-specific languages such as English, feminists and non-feminists alike have tried to show that women speak differently from men and that there is such a thing as a 'women's language' (Deborah Cameron 1985; Lakoff 1975; Spender 1980). Criticizing the shortcomings of linguistic research on sex-specific discourse Sara Mills states that 'it is clear that male and female sentences do not exist except in stereotypical forms or as ideal representations of gender difference' (1995: 65).

See LANGUAGE; LINGUISTICS.

Gender identity See IDENTITY.

Gender identity disorder See TRANSSEXUALITY.

Gender segregation 'Gender segregation' refers to the concentration of men and women in different sectors, occupations, and workplaces. The idea of occupational segregation was originally developed by DUAL LABOUR MARKET theories (later called segmented labour market theories) to explain why the wage rates of Black American men consistently lagged behind white men's, but it was made more relevant to women's employment by Catherine Hakim's (1979) distinction between horizontal segregation, which refers to segregation between different occupations and sectors, and vertical segregation, which refers to the concentration of men and women at different levels in grade or job ladders. The concept was immensely influential, shifting explanations of patterns of women's employment from a focus on individual role conflicts to the identification of structural barriers in the labour market which prevent women moving into higher paid, higher status occupations.

In contrast to the first, 'sex-blind' explanations of segregation in terms of employers' economic interests, Heidi Hartmann (1979) identified the interests of men as men as a central part of the analysis. She reformulated segmented labour market theory in terms of the conflicting demands of PATRIARCHY (defined as alliances between men, in this case in male-dominated trades unions) and CAPITALISM, a DUAL SYSTEMS theoretical approach. Later feminist accounts of what has become known as gender-specific job typing have given even more emphasis to the IDEOLOGICAL gendering of job characteristics. A further development of segmentation theory is Barbara Reskin and Patricia

Roos's (1990) queuing model, which shows that when women make successful inroads on a male occupation, a process of *re*segregation usually takes place, for instance through the formation of male and female ghettos within the occupation. Other accounts, more influenced by POSTSTRUCTURALISM, focus on 'the cultural [re]production of gendered identities through practices enacted in the workplace' (Smith and Gottfried 1996: 13), thereby highlighting the role of women's own practices in the sex-typing of occupations (Pringle 1989; Cockburn 1991). As Vicki Smith and Heidi Gottfried's typology of gender segregation theories notes, another development is the 'discourse of gender neutrality' model (see especially Acker 1990 and Hearn *et al.* [eds] 1989). It focuses on jobs in large bureaucratic organizations (e.g. corporate management, the civil service, academia) where 'the discourses, structures and routines may appear to be gender neutral, but are in fact predicated on unwritten, implicit gendered assumptions' (Smith and Gottfried 1996: 12). These more recent developments have gone some way towards integrating economic and social factors, structure and agency, into explanations of gender inequality in employment.

See also CULTURE; RESERVE ARMY OF LABOUR.

Genealogy   Refers to the DECONSTRUCTION of concepts by tracing their lines of descent. Foucauldian methodology looks for discontinuities between PRACTICES and IDEOLOGIES and between practices across cultures in order to defamiliarize them and challenge their apparently monolithic or pre-given character. Feminist genealogies often deconstruct totalizing concepts, including those deployed in feminist theory. For instance, rather than looking for a functional relationship between PATRIARCHY and definitions of 'mothering', the Foucauldian asks 'When did the idea of the mother as emotional nurturer emerge? When did women's status as reproducer prevail?' (Sawicki 1991) and concludes that Chodorow's mothering theory obscures differences and heterogeneity in the construction of mothering. Similarly, Fraser and Gordon's (1994) genealogy of the concept of DEPENDENCY challenges unreflective uses of this keyword by feminists: how did dependency come to be stigmatized, they ask, and why is it considered shameful for some and natural or proper for others?

See ARCHAEOLOGY.

Generation   Julia Kristeva uses the concept in her essay on WOMEN'S TIME, to characterize nineteenth-century feminism in terms of the 'linear time' of 'project and history' and the second wave in terms of 'cyclical and monumental time' which measures 'the universal traits of [women's] structural place in reproduction and its representation' (Kristeva 1989: 187–213).

Kristeva's broad sketch leaves out the complexities of the two phases, both of which contain strong elements which might be characterized in terms of both 'linear projects' and reproductive cycles.

Raymond Williams's identification of 'dominant', 'residual' and 'emergent' STRUCTURES OF FEELING offers some means of tracing out these complexities (Jenny Bourne Taylor 1990) but we are still left with a certain lack of attachment of these periodic eruptions of women's activism to the circumstances, material and intellectual, in which they have occurred. Kristeva's time-scale is discontinuous, leaping from about 1920 to 1968. POSTSTRUCTURALIST feminists, part of Kristeva's synthesizing 'third phase', have produced sketches of second-wave FEMINISM in terms of the movement from feminisms of EQUALITY to feminisms of DIFFERENCE which are similar in many respects to Kristeva's categories (Barrett and Phillips [eds] 1992; Gross 1987; Joan Scott 1990) but there has been remarkably little interest in mapping these shifts within feminism and WOMEN'S MOVEMENTS onto contemporaray political and intellectual history: in asking 'why the intellectual cadre in a particular time and place articulated and promoted a particular theory' (Alexander 1995a: 71). What is most interesting in the 'third phase', as delineated in the sketches of poststructuralist feminists, is that it effectively rolls the SOCIALIST and MARXIST FEMINISMS which were dominant in parts of Europe in the 1970s and into the 1980s up into LIBERAL or EQUAL RIGHTS feminism, which then stands forward to represent feminisms of equality, while RADICAL FEMINISM and CULTURAL FEMINISM represent the second phase of feminisms of difference. This has the effect of greatly diminishing the place of socialist traditions in the synthesis of the third phase. As Jeffrey Alexander observes, 'Successor intellectuals tend to invert the binary codes of the previously hegemonic theory' (1995a: 83). He traces the succession in social theory from the postwar HEGEMONY of MODERNIZATION theory to 'the romance of the heroic revival' of the 1960s, the POSTMODERNIST succession, and finally, for those who may have thought that feminist postmodernist syntheses were the end of the story, to 'neo-modernism'. Alexander unwittingly reveals the secret of the disappearance of socialist feminism. Postmodernist critiques simply rolled up post-war modernization theory with its successor, the radical critique of that theory in the 1960s, placing both, indifferently, under the head of MODERNISM. Postmodernist feminism has likewise rolled up socialist and Marxist feminism with liberal and 'equal rights' feminism under the dismissive head of MODERNISM.

Succession from one dominant intellectual formation to another, according to Alexander, is won, as in Thomas Kuhn's account of the clashes between PARADIGMS (Kuhn 1970), not on intellectual merits alone, but in terms of 'plausibility as social myth': as maps of an alternative world. While Alexander's account is utterly innocent of any engagement with feminism, it might perhaps lend itself to APPROPRIATION for the development of a more socially anchored and less homogenizing history of generations within feminism.

Genre   Traditionally referring to a class or type of literature, the term now refers to a formal type in any medium. Theories of genre range from those which ascribe intrinsic and formal properties to genre to those which emphasize the conventional and relatively fluid character of genre BOUNDARIES. Feminist theories of genre tend to belong to the latter type. From her study of feminist reworkings of generic literary forms, Anne Cranny-Francis (1990) argues that genre is a social practice as well as a literary or linguistic practice. While her definition of genre identifies textual attributes such as conventions, codes and formulae, her account moves into discussion of IDEOLOGICAL issues and the relationship between genre, gender and social change. Feminist reworkings of traditionally male-dominated genres suggest that there is nothing intrinsically masculinist about such forms, rather they have typically encoded masculine values and priorities. By inflecting the conventions in new ways, or in some cases recoding them, the PHALLOCENTRISM of generic NARRATIVE may be subverted and the genre appropriated for women.

Feminists have produced an impressive range of work on traditionally 'feminine' genres such as ROMANCE (Modleski 1982; Radway 1984; Helen Taylor 1989) and soap opera (Ang 1985; Geraghty 1991), on genres in which women have always been strongly represented such as crime writing (Munt 1994; Tasker 1991), and on historically male-dominated genres such as science fiction (Bammer 1991; Barr 1987a; 1987b; Lefanu 1988).

Gift   The centrality of the 'gift' emerges first in anthropology, in which 'gift' economies are contrasted to those based on other types of economic exchange, such as the accumulation of profit in CAPITALISM. Claude Lévi-Strauss (1969) identified the exchange of women by men as intrinsic to certain KINSHIP systems. Gayle Rubin (1975) builds on this theory in a famous essay identifying a 'political economy of sex' in which women constitute the 'traffic'. Hélène Cixous and Luce Irigaray employ the concept of 'gift' to contrast 'masculine' and 'feminine' economies – in which the term 'economy' indicates not merely the production and distribution of goods and services, but the psychic organization of individuals. They describe as 'masculine' those economies such as capitalism which involve profitable exchange. In contrast, according to Cixous, feminine economies operate a gift-exchange system which allows for a gift-giving that does not involve a supplementary return. This model clearly draws on the symbolic character of women's unpaid DOMESTIC LABOUR and mothering which, as Cixous and CULTURAL FEMINISTS argue, make possible the most valuable human relations between people. Irigaray's concept of the heterosexual economy (similar in some ways to Rubin's) describes a phallocentric culture based on men's exchange of women and a metaphysical 'logic of the Same' which denies women's difference. Her 'When the goods get together' (1981), a suggestive essay for lesbian theory, describes the possibilities for women of mobilizing their political and sexual desire in terms of another kind of commerce between themselves.

Globalization   Use of the term has followed the economic crisis of the 1970s, the collapse of the Soviet regime, the rise of political Islam and a new perception of ecological interdependence: One World supersedes the postwar division between First, Second and THIRD WORLD. Globalization – the intensification of linkages and interconnections which *transcend* the nation state – is usually seen as having economic dimensions (especially the increasing mobility of capital), political dimensions (nations' declining capacity for control, even within their own territory), and ecological and cultural dimensions (the mobility of cultural signs, including especially the delinking from locality and IDENTITY) (Sklair 1995; Waters 1995).

   Globalization is sometimes seen to instigate a 'race to the bottom', with nations competing for inward investment by eroding legally enforceable labour standards and limiting trades union activity. However, feminist writing on world-wide markets and production regimes preceded the adoption of terms like 'global' and 'globalization' by a good ten years; by the mid 1970s feminists were drawing attention to the ways in which women's work roles were affected by the emergence of a NEW INTERNATIONAL DIVISION OF LABOUR. Particular attention has been paid to the effects of changes in agricultural production, where peasant farms have been replaced by cash crop production for the world market, to the implications of the 'integrated circuit of industrial production', especially in the electronics, textile and garment industries, and to organizing on these issues across national and regional divisions. The increasingly global integration of production, distribution and retailing and their relation to changing patterns of CONSUMPTION has led some feminist analysts to adopt the concept of 'global commodity chains' in place of the (no longer very) new international division of labour (Barrientos and Perrons 1996; see also Sklair 1995).

   The term 'global' in feminist work often connotes links between women's resistance movements. Initially its use tended to highlight UNIVERSALITY rather than differences in the experience of WOMEN in different parts of world. It was first popularized by the title of Robyn Morgan's *Sisterhood is Global: The International Women's Movement Anthology* (1984) which assumed women's universal subjection to PATRIARCHY. However, as Chandra Mohanty and others have argued Morgan fails to see that 'a place on the map is also a place in history' and sees this text as an example of analyses in which universal sisterhood is produced through assumptions about women as a 'cross-culturally singular, homogeneous group' facing a homogeneous 'patriarchal mentality' (1992: 78). The idea that women's nature transcends women's DIFFERENCE is also typical of ECOFEMINISM, which sees itself as a global movement based on women's shared relationship to nature (indeed women as nature) and natural resources, an aspect of their innate relation to REPRODUCTION and/or the sexual division of labour. However, although ecofeminist concepts of women's natural unity clearly rest on ESSENTIALIST notions, they have often fostered or legitimated alliances between women, and their DECONSTRUCTION has to be undertaken cautiously.

Global links have also been fostered through the networks formed at international conferences associated with the United Nations. Although here too the rhetoric may naturalize alliances, in practice these conferences have provided venues in which it has been possible to articulate different positions as well as to identify common interests.

Goddess The grassroots women's movements in second wave feminism has manifested widespread interest in a range of rituals, beliefs, practices, mythical religious and symbol systems that might be claimed for women and for feminism, under the broad head of feminist SPIRITUALITY. Feminist goddess worship flourished within some forms of RADICAL FEMINISM.

See RELIGION.

Grotesque The category of the grotesque – literally, grotto-esque – derives from the image of the cave whose connotations of cavernous, earthy spaces in turn inevitably evoke the female body as represented in MISOGYNIST scatology. For Mikhail Bakhtin, the Marxist theorist, from whose writings contemporary cultural theories of the grotesque derive, the definitive image of the grotesque is that of the 'senile, pregnant hag...decaying, deformed, laughing' (1984: 25–6). As Mary Russo puts it: 'The grotesque body is the open, protruding, extended, secreting body, the body of becoming, process, and change' (1994: 8). In other words, it is FEMININE and EXCESSIVE, and is thus the opposite of the classical, implicitly male, body which is static, discrete and closed.

Russo distinguishes between two types of grotesque: the comic grotesque, associated with Bakhtin's writing on CARNIVAL; and the grotesque as strange and uncanny, associated with Freud's essay on the uncanny and the literary genre of horror. Bakhtin failed to theorize relations of gender within the grotesque and this task has been left to feminist theorists, most notably Julia Kristeva, whose *Powers of Horror* (1982) explores the feminine as a figure of ABJECTION. In contrast to Kristeva's careful tracing of the ambivalence of the category, CULTURAL FEMINISTS and POSTMODERN FEMINISTS alike have valorized and celebrated the female grotesque for its 'natural' earthiness and its playful potential respectively. Feminist artists and writers who utilize grotesque themes and motifs in their work include the photographers Cindy Sherman and Jacqueline Hayden, and the writers Angela Carter and Jeanette Winterson.

Gynesis The term is Alice Jardine's (1985), from her book of the same name, for the textualization of 'WOMAN' within POSTSTRUCTURALIST and POSTMODERN discourses. Jardine counterposes GYNOCRITICISM, the study of the woman writer, to gynesis which focuses rather on woman as a 'writing-effect'. She associates the gynetic putting into discourse of the OTHER/Woman with the collapse of Western MASTER NARRATIVES and the DECONSTRUCTION of Western philosophy.

Gynocritism The term was coined by Elaine Showalter to describe a type of feminist criticism which is concerned with

> woman as the producer of textual meaning, with the history, themes, genres and structures of literature by women. Its subjects include the psychodynamics of female creativity, linguistics and the problem of a female language; the trajectory of the individual or collective female literary career; literary history; and, of course, studies of particular writers and works (1979: 25).

Almost as soon as Showalter elaborated gynocriticism, MARXIST and POSTSTRUCTURALIST feminist critics challenged the ESSENTIALIST premise of her project, in particular its treatment of the categories of FEMININITY, EXPERIENCE, LANGUAGE, and literature, all of which are called into question by theories of IDEOLOGY and TEXTUALITY. Nevertheless, it represents one of two dominant strands – the other being the 'female critique' of male images of women – in feminist literary criticism of the second wave. Exponents include Gilbert and Gubar (1979; 1988), Abel (ed.) (1982) and Homans (1980).

H

Habitus The habitus (Bourdieu 1990a) of an individual is a function of early childhood experience within specific social settings: 'the habitus is a family, group and especially class phenomenon, a logic derived from a common set of material conditions of existence to regulate the practice of a set of individuals in common response to those conditions' (Garnham and Williams 1980: 213).

Bourdieu has always recognized the gendering of habitus, insofar as the male/female opposition is included amongst the fundamental structuring dichotomies of the logic of practice, so that within the shared habitus of family, CLASS, ETHNIC group, experience may be sharply differentiated by gender. However, it is only relatively recently that Bourdieu has explicitly addressed questions of gender (Bourdieu 1990b).

See also CULTURAL CAPITAL; DISTINCTION; SYMBOLIC POWER; SYMBOLIC VIOLENCE.

Hegemony   A key term in the Italian Marxist Antonio Gramsci's theory of the STATE and CIVIL SOCIETY; his work provided a rich seam which was mined by the infant discipline of CULTURAL STUDIES in Britain. In this context, hegemony was taken to refer to the mobilization of the consent of the dominated to the social order in which they are dominated, as opposed to more brutal and direct forms of coercion (McLennan, Held and Hall [eds] 1984). The theory of hegemony offered a fruitful tool for rethinking all that has fallen under the head of IDEOLOGY and CULTURE in left analysis, and it was drawn upon to analyse various popular oppositional subcultures (Bennett, Mercer, and Woollacott 1986; Chambers 1985; Clarke, Critcher and Johnson [eds] 1979; Hall *et al.* 1980; Hall *et al.* 1978; Hall and Jefferson [eds] 1976; Hebdige 1979; Hebdige 1988; Nelson and Grossberg [eds] 1988; Waites *et al.* [eds] 1982; Willis 1977; Willis 1978). This work flourished between two limit positions: a POPULISM which reads such materials for their subversive potential, and more pessimistic readings in terms of the pervasive power of 'the DOMINANT IDEOLOGY' (McGuigan 1992). In between these limit positions a complex model was created of cultural practice as an arena of struggle in which a contest for hegemony and counter-hegemony was fought out. This model is contingent and historically specific. The outcome of the struggle cannot be DETERMINED in advance.

Extending his military metaphor, Gramsci distinguished between the 'war of position', in which the object of struggle is 'the hearts and minds of the people' (Barrett 1991: 55), and the 'war of manoevre' in which, building from the basis of strategic success in the war of position, a decisive bid may be made for the seizure of POWER by the major counter-hegemonic group. For Gramsci INTELLECTUALS, in the broad sense in which he uses this term, play a central role in the cultural and political struggles which characterize the war of position.

While feminists, particularly those working within cultural studies, but also in and with theories of the state (Cooper 1995), have used the term 'hegemony', there has been little systematic exploration/APPROPRIATION of Gramsci's work. As with all Marxisms, Gramsci's chief protagonists are social classes, and the analysis does not transpose unproblematically onto GENDER relations. Gramsci's work has influenced FEMINISM largely via Althusser (cf. STRUCTURALISM).

Debates within feminist cultural studies reproduce the same limit positions which approach populism and paranoia respectively: the popular is almost assumed to be per se subversive (as in the numerous analyses of Madonna, for example Fiske [1987]), or it is viewed as inevitably and inescapably caught within the organizing frame of the dominant 'patriarchal ideology'. Jim McGuigan (1992) provides a useful exploration of these problems of populism in cultural studies.

For those who identify the very language in which we come to acquire a sexed social IDENTITY as structured in terms of the feminine as the negative OTHER on which the positive masculine subject is grounded, populist strategies are of no interest, for all speech and writing is necessarily contaminated, and the only viable 'counter-hegemonic strategy' is one based on MIMICRY, refusal and parody, which has the effect of 'jamming the system' (Irigaray 1985a; Whitford 1991). This replaces the 'dominant ideology' thesis, but makes the task of feminism even more monumental, though some would say, less political: a 'revolution of the word' (Moi 1985).

The intermediate terrain between an overly optimistic populism and profound pessimism in feminist cultural theory is occupied by historically specific analyses in which women's voices are detected and recognized in spite of patriarchal accents and terminology (Stanley [ed.] 1984; Swindells 1985), pulling more or less strongly against the grain. Gramsci's distinction, in the context of class struggle, between working-class 'good sense' and 'common sense' have obvious applications for feminism in this context.

Hermeneutics   A philosophical term referring to the process of interpretation, orginally of biblical texts, now used of texts in general. The hermeneutical PHENOMENOLOGY of Heidegger and Gadamer concerns itself with questions of historical understanding and intepretation. Given this focus hermeneutics has offered a useful paradigm to literary critics interested in whether the meaning of texts is transhistorical – fixed, for example, by authorial intention – or contingent on the understanding of historically specific readers. For Gadamer (1975) interpretation of a past work consists in a dialogue between past and present, between the writer and future readers, in a hermeneutic 'circle' of interpretation which seeks to fit each element of a text into a complete whole. Recently, hermeneutics has developed into reception theory which examines the READER'S role in literature (Iser 1978; Jauss 1982). Feminist engagement with reader-oriented theory has tended to develop in the direction of reader response models (e.g. Fetterley 1978; Tompkins 1980). Two feminist psycho-literary analyses of Virginia Woolf draw on Husserl's phenomenology in arguing for a continuity of consciousness in Woolf's life and work which it is the role of the reader to reconstruct: Roger Poole's *The Unknown Virginia Woolf* (1978) and Stephen Trombley's *'All That Summer She Was Mad': Virginia Woolf and her Doctors* (1981).

Heroinism   Western, particularly but not exclusively LIBERAL, FEMINISM has constructed a narrative comprising individual heroines, usually beginning with Mary Wollstonecraft and including among others – Josephine Butler, Emily Dickinson, the Pankhursts and, of course, Virginia Woolf (Dodd 1990). Much important, if ultimately partial, work has been done on the reclamation of key figures in feminist history. Dale Spender's polemical and remedial *Women of Ideas (and What Men Have Done to Them)* (1983) is a good example. For Hélène Cixous and Catherine Clément (1986) the female hysteric of psychoanalytic discourse is a 'threshold' figure for feminism, symbolizing resistance to patriarchal MASTER NARRATIVES. However, while Cixous celebrates the hysteric's heroism, Clément highlights her victimization by and women's collective struggle against a PHALLOCENTRIC system.

In an important study, Ellen Moers develops the concept of 'literary heroinism', distinct from feminism, to delineate the creation of 'a heroic structure for the female voice in literature' (1977: 123). Dating it back to the late eighteenth century, she cites Richardson's *Pamela*, with her 'knack for writing', as the first heroine of letters. Subsequently, she traces a line from Mary Wollstonecraft of women who 'seized the pen, and [through] female self-consciousness brought heroinism to literature' (1977: 121). Moers identifies different kinds of heroine: intellectual (Wollstonecraft); passionate (Brontë); leader/reformer (George Eliot). A brilliant but partial study, it constructs heroinism as a white anglophone phenomenon and excludes considerations of 'RACE', CLASS and SEXUALITY. As Spivak's (1989) critique of the 'culting' of *Jane Eyre* by Anglo-American feminism points out, the Western feminist subject in the age of IMPERIALISM secures her identity at the expense of the colonial OTHER. Given the elevation of the one over the many, such epistemic or SYMBOLIC VIOLENCE almost inevitably accompanies heroinizing discourses.

Contemporary heroinization within ACADEMIC FEMINISM takes the form of identifying cult or star figures who have accrued CULTURAL CAPITAL. The feminist penchant for heroines would appear at least as insistent as the commitment to egalitarian and democratic organization.

Heteroglossia A Bakhtinian term designating the multiplicity of social voices interrelated dialogically in a text, which include various inserted GENRES and authorial, character and NARRATIVE speech (1981: 263). According to Bakhtin, heteroglossia are determined contextually and extra-linguistically because LANGAUGE is always embedded in social relations. Lynne Pearce (1994) suggests that this makes the concept valuable to feminist writers wishing to explore the multiple accents of women's voices. The novel is an exemplary heteroglossic text owing to the diversity of 'voices' it contains.

Heterosexism The term, central to LESBIAN FEMINIST theory, refers to a system of social relations in which heterosexuality is institutionally and IDEOLOGICALLY privileged at the expense of homosexuality. On a mundane level, heterosexism often manifests itself as the unconscious or explicit assumption that heterosexuality is the only 'normal' form of sexual relations.
See also COMPULSORY HETEROSEXUALITY; HETEROSEXUAL MATRIX.

Heterosexual matrix A term used by Judith Butler (1990), drawing on Monique Wittig's concept of 'the straight mind' (1992) and Adrienne Rich's COMPULSORY HETEROSEXUALITY (1980a), 'to designate that grid of cultural intelligibility through which bodies, genders, and desires are naturalized' (Butler 1990: 151). Butler ceases to use the term in her later work (1993) but continues to argue for the subversion of sexual IDENTITIES and the

disaggregation of SEX, SEXUALITY, and GENDER in the social enactments or PERFORMANCES that are constitutive of all three.
  See also HETEROSEXUALITY; LESBIAN FEMINISM; QUEER POLITICS.

Hexis   'Bodily hexis is political mythology realized, embodied, turned into a permanent disposition, a durable way of standing, speaking, walking and thereby of feeling. The opposition between male and female is realized in posture, in the gestures and movements of the body...' (Bourdieu 1990a: 70).
  See also BODY; HABITUS; SYMBOLIC POWER.

Homeworking   Although the term often refers to all paid work undertaken in the home, some argue that it should be defined more narrowly, covering only waged outworkers who ought to be covered by employment legislation giving them the rights of employees. In Britain the emphasis seems to have followed the wider political situation: research conducted in times when there appears to be a chance of obtaining legislative change has generated narrow definitions, such as that adopted in the unsuccessful Homeworkers' (Protection) Bill of 1979, which excludes not only the self-employed and freelance workers but also childminders and those doing work of an artistic or musical nature (Allen and Wolkowitz 1987; Felstead and Jewson 1996). More recently campaigners have been successful in pushing the International Labour Organization (ILO) to pass an international convention on homework to promote equality of treatment between homeworkers and other wage earners, but it still has to be ratified by member nations (HomeNet 1996). However, where the focus has been on exploring the relation between gender, working at home and the changing structure of the labour market, including the rise in self-employment and in women's professional and managerial employment, some researchers have used a broader definition of homeworking (Phizacklea and Wolkowitz 1995).
  In theoretical terms homeworking is seen by feminists as a striking example of women's employment situation more generally, rather than as a contrast to it (Allen and Wolkowitz 1987; Phizacklea and Wolkowitz 1995). Paid work in the home challenges definitions of work based on men's working lives, which more usually involve a separate workplace and a distinct, bounded working day, and as in women's work outside the home, ethnic inequalities between homeworking women are pronounced.
  Homeworking is the tip of a much wider phenomenon, the casualization of male and female labour and the increasing flexibility of the organization of PRODUCTION (Allen and Wolkowitz 1987; Phizacklea 1990). Although some 'core' workers benefit from 'enabling' forms of flexibility designed to maintain worker commitment (Smith and Gottfried 1996), most feminists have concentrated on its negative impact. Donna Haraway has taken up Richard Gordon's notion of the 'homework economy' (Gordon 1983, cited by Haraway 1991) in her 'CYBORG manifesto'; she argues that the GLOBALIZATION of capital is erasing the boundaries between home, market,

paid work place, state, school and so forth, which are now integrated on a new scale. Similarly, reports Connolly (1993: 60), Gayatri Chakravorty Spivak portrays the position of women homeworkers as 'the central issue in contemporary colonialism' (Connolly 1993: 106). She sees them as caught between the international space of capitalism and the private space of gendering, in which 'internalized constraint work(s) as choice'.

See also POST-FORDISM.

Homophobia The term refers to the conscious or unconscious fear or hatred of sexual love between same-sex partners or of lesbians and gay men themselves. Much used in radical or 'gay-affirmative' psychology, the term has been challenged by some critics as perpetuating liberal and depoliticized accounts of sexual inequality and discrimination. Kitzinger (1987) argues that the concept locates the causes of such discrimination in individual pathology rather than in institutional and structural relations. She offers a political analysis of lesbian and gay oppression as rooted in a HETEROSEXIST system of social relations. The term has been central to the IDENTITY POLITICS of the 1980s and, as Kitzinger suggests, its use has had mixed consequences for political organization. Arguably, however, it has been useful in raising awareness of lesbian and gay issues more generally.

Housework See DOMESTIC LABOUR.

Human rights The DISCOURSE and politics of human rights belongs within the broad liberal HUMANIST frame which encompasses EQUALITY, EQUAL RIGHTS, respect for bodily integrity, and the language of responsibility for OTHERS: therefore to a discourse which has been the target of DECONSTRUCTION by POSTSTRUCTURALISTS and in feminist debates over the BODY.

'Human rights' had already come under criticism from feminists within the human rights movement. Violations of human rights are gendered. To ensure that women's issues within human rights do not remain 'an afterthought' (Peters and Wolper [eds] 1995: 2) it has been strategically necessary to focus on and force acknowledgement of the specificity of violations of women and girls: war rapes; violence against women; genital mutilation; female infanticide; child-marriage, etc.

Secondly, human rights perspectives have been criticized as Western impositions: a residue of IMPERIALIST domination and of traditions in which that domination was defended as 'the white man's burden' with regard to the protection of the more vulnerable members of subjugated COMMUNITIES (Liddle and Joshi 1986; Lorde 1984; Sinha 1987; 1995). Others have attempted a defence of some of the practices in question in the name of cultural pluralism or multiculturalism and have accused feminists of racism (see *Feminist Review* 17, 1984). Picking a path between the dangers of racism on the one hand, and of the silencing of women concerning their OPPRESSION within racialized COMMUNITIES on the other, has not proved easy, and the discussion in Southall Black Sisters ([eds] 1989) brings out this problem with great clarity.

The response to the multicultural argument is often to question the extent to which 'the social groups primarily affected participate in the formation of the cultural practices being protected' (Peters and Wolper [eds] 1995: 6). 'The community' and its CULTURE are structured in domination and are not the property, equally, of all members. Whether we can so identify the origins of cultural practices may be doubted, but what is beyond doubt is that it is very often women who are charged with responsibility for the day-to-day maintenance and enforcement of cultural practices affecting younger women and girls, and a key issue in the politics of human rights concerns implementation. 'Mainstreaming' at international, governmental, and institutional levels often exacerbates the dangers of racist interpretation, and is ineffectual unless accompanied by grass-roots work in the community which involves local women directly (Pietilä and Vickers 1994; Tomasevski 1993).

'Corporeal feminism' is the source of a further critique. It has advanced the necessity for a new model of the human BODY, and has been highly critical of the whole discourse of 'rights' and 'justice' (Diprose 1994; Grosz 1994; Irigaray 1991). Most of those working within this poststructuralist perspective would take exception to the concept of 'bodily integrity' (but see Pateman 1988) which has been so central to the human rights movement, because it is grounded on a model which takes the male body as normative. The preferred alternative model is of bodies not as 'containers' whose task is to resist invasion, but of bodies with fluid BOUNDARIES, engaged in a continuous process of exchange with other bodies and with the surrounding environment, even with machines (Haraway 1991).

However, if we defend our models, as poststructuralists often do, not at the bar of TRUTH or RATIONALITY, but in strategic terms (Braidotti 1991; Fuss 1989), then we must ask whether the model of 'fluidity' offers any strategic advantage over the more traditional 'container' model which allows us to argue so forcibly for bodily integrity. For the violations involved here are gross and brutal, and as long as these abuses continue it would be premature to jettison the politics and discourse of human rights without a powerful and effective alternative.

Humanism Nineteenth-century secular humanism displaces God to position 'Man' at the centre of the universe and history. Humanism has been challenged on a number of counts. Firstly, because it makes a sharp divide between the human species and all other natural forms, claiming dominion over them by virtue of distinctive human characteristics: principally the ability to communicate through LANGUAGE, and to develop SYMBOLIC CULTURES (Outhwaite and Bottomore [eds] 1993: 268).

Mid-twentieth-century STRUCTURALISMS founded on linguistics took this very feature which men had used to affirm their species-privilege to decentre the SUBJECT of humanist DISCOURSE, and to DECONSTRUCT claims to freedom and AGENCY. Language itself was posited as the source of a subjectivity which is based on MISRECOGNITION and social and cultural determinations were held to occur behind the backs of human subjects and without respect for intentionality (Althusser 1969; Derrida 1976; Lacan 1975). MARXIST and EXISTENTIALIST as well as more traditional forms of humanism were rejected in a strident anti-humanism that continued into the successor-theories of POSTSTRUCTURALISM.

Secondly, feminist critiques of science have protested the domination of nature which has historically been part of the humanist project (Harding 1986; Jordanova 1989). Donna Haraway in particular has argued forcibly for the breaching of conceptual BOUNDARIES between animals and humans (Haraway 1991). Linked with this second critique has been the argument first broached within RADICAL FEMINISM, that 'he/man language' (Spender 1980), rationalized as UNIVERSAL, actually related to males. In the nature/culture BINARY, women, notoriously, are aligned with nature (Ortner 1974), and feminists therefore have a special stake in rejecting the project of human dominion over nature, since it includes, implicitly, dominion over women.

The question for feminists remains whether to stake our fortunes upon a reconstructed humanism which is 'post-poststructuralist' and which takes account of these objections (Soper 1986; Taylor 1991) or to reject all languages of the SELF, of freedom and AGENCY as irremediable and opt instead for the radical decentring strategies of cyberfeminism and POSTMODERNISM (Marsden 1996).

See also CYBORGS.

Hybridity Bakhtin refers to a hybrid utterance as one in which two different linguistic registers co-exist (1981). The term is also used in literary criticism to refer to the anti-purist character of POSTMODERN texts which combine a variety of different discursive styles and forms, usually in an ironic or playful way, and often as a means of undermining BOUNDARIES between 'high' and 'low' forms.

Hybridity, according to Homi Bhabha, is a key feature of (post-)colonial subjectivity. Bhabha's work on the ambivalence of colonialism represents a POSTSTRUCTURALIST rethinking of colonial authority and IDENTITY. He argues that the character of colonial identity is not monolithic, but ambivalent or hybrid, and results in the SPLITTING of the SUBJECT of CULTURE (1994).

For Bhabha, hybridity opens up a space of TRANSLATION, useful to POST-COLONIAL THEORISTS of the in-between, allowing them to conceptualize an international culture, 'based not on the exoticism of multiculturalism or the diversity of cultures, but on the inscription of culture's hybridity. We should remember that it is the "inter" – the cutting edge of translation and negotiation, the in-between space – that carries the burden of the meaning of culture' (Bhabha 1994: 38). An older term, 'creole', refers to the hybrid character of certain peoples, cultures or languages

Many feminists, especially post-colonial critics, have adopted the concept of hybridity – or a variant of it – to suggest the shifting and multiple character of cultural identities. However, some critics have pointed out that like related concepts of subjectivity in postmodern discourse, the hybrid subject is invoked by Bhabha with insufficient regard to crucial distinctions of gender, class and caste (Loomba 1993; Parry 1987). Comparable interactive models of subjectivity developed in a feminist context (Anzaldúa 1987; Lorde 1984) suggest that SUBALTERN identity cannot be homogenized in this way even by virtue of its common subjection to colonialism.

Hysteria Hysteria (from the Greek *hysteros* for 'womb') has a long history as an illness in which the uterus is thought to be 'wandering'. In the nineteenth century it was frequently diagnosed in women suffering from 'nervous disorders', and is the disease upon which PSYCHOANALYSIS is based. Freud redefined it as a 'psychic' rather than a neurological disease with sexual disturbance in its aetiology. Hysterical behaviour is therefore a symptom of a disturbance in the psyche. By paying careful attention to the nature of the symptom it is possible to trace its root cause in the UNCONSCIOUS. As Jacqueline Rose (1986) argues, this represented a significant advance in the treatment of women patients in that curing them involved listening to their histories rather than making public SPECTACLES of them.

However, feminist critics have also argued, in a less admiring vein, that psychoanalysis itself effectively hysterizes the (BODY of) woman. Conceived of as a mysterious 'dark continent', the female body is invested with hysterical signifiers by the (male) analyst attempting to discover 'what women want'. During the 1970s and 1980s feminist debates on the significance of women's hysterical discourse focused on the figure of Dora, one of Freud's most famous female case studies (Bernheimer and Kahane 1985). For Hélène Cixous and Catherine Clément (1986) she is a 'threshold' figure for women's liberation. While Cixous sees the female hysteric as the 'hero' of twentieth-century women's writing, Clément sees her as a victim, and Julia Kristeva (1989) rejects Cixous' HEROINIZATION of the hysteric, arguing that there is no benefit for women in immersion in an IMAGINARY realm beyond LANGUAGE.

Women writers have written powerfully about the experience of hysterical diagnosis: the most famous text of this kind is Charlotte Perkins Gilman's *The Yellow Wallpaper* (1981; first published 1892) in which a woman who undergoes an oppressive 'rest cure' literally goes mad as a result of enforced inaction. Gilman wrote the story as a fictionalized account of her own treatment by Weir Mitchell, a famous exponent of rest cures and a follower of Freud. Gilman claims that he was so disturbed by the story that he discontinued the cure.

Lacan sees hysteria as an oscillation of sexual IDENTIFICATION, arguing that it is the condition of the division of all speaking, desiring subjects. Recently, feminist critics have evinced a theoretical interest in the texts of male hysteria. Rereadings of Hoffman's 'The Sandman' (Cixous 1976b) and

David Cronenberg's *Dead Ringers* (Creed 1993) demonstrate the resonance of hysteria within masculine psychic structures.

I

Identification   Social IDENTITY depends strategically upon the recognition by others, formally or informally, that one has indeed a certain identity, and not just on self-recognition.

Identification is a more active process. In film and literary theory, the process of identification on the part of the READER or SPECTATOR may be vital to the effectiveness of the text, and much critical attention has been devoted to the analysis of the manner in which film, literary and other texts position their implied readers and viewers, in attempts to secure particular responses.

We also speak of 'identification' when human actors are able to 'place' themselves in the position of another, to imagine 'what it must be like...': to empathize with another.

Identification is typically seen to follow along the lines of shared identities. But the ability to identify across DIFFERENCES is crucial in social life and in extracting the pleasures offered by certain texts. Laura Mulvey's pathbreaking work on visual pleasure in NARRATIVE cinema assumes identification along lines of identity, but, in characterizing the GAZE as male, makes it difficult to theorize female spectatorial pleasure in other than negative terms as masochistic (Mulvey 1989a). The dominant feminist FILM THEORY when her article was first published in 1975 was hostile to identification:

> identification can only be made through recognition, and all recognition is itself an implicit confirmation of an existing form... Identification enforces a collapse of the subject onto the normative demands for sameness, which under patriarchy is always male (Friedberg 1993: 53).

Elizabeth Cowie, drawing like Mulvey on Lacanian psychoanalytical theory, makes the model more flexible by recognizing the multiple SUBJECT POSITIONINGS offered by many texts, and the ability of viewers to identify across difference, against the grain of social identity (Cowie 1984). Constance Penley summarizes:

> While there are 'masculine' and 'feminine' positions in fantasy, men and women, respectively, do not have to assume these positions according to their assigned gender (Penley [ed.] 1988: 256).

Jackie Stacey makes the objection that there is a danger, in the uncoupling of identification from the actual sex of the viewer, that 'the gender of characters and spectators might cease to be of significance' (Stacey 1994b: 135). The difficulty may be eased if it is recognized that identity and difference are always relational. 'Difference' is not 'absolute otherness', nor does 'identity' always mean 'exactly the same'. Identification perhaps always involves a degree of recognition of sameness but such recognition may, precisely, *not* be 'a confirmation of existing form' but a new recognition of relationship and connectedness across differences in social identity.

Identity 'Identity' as in 'IDENTITY POLITICS', and in the critique of that politics, focuses either upon on the affirmation of common identities by groups of mobilizing individuals, or on the other hand, on the DECONSTRUCTION of these identities as SOCIALLY CONSTRUCTED and therefore open to refusal. However, *social* identity is principally the identity which is recognized and confirmed by others, however strenuously individuals may disavow them. Feminist discussions of identity might be criticized for paying too much attention to self- and group-identity, and not enough to identity as *social* process.

Identity is perhaps best considered alongside its binary partner, DIFFERENCE. As deconstruction has taught us, no term ever stands alone, but is always shadowed by its discursive partners. Contra those who take the view that differences are absolute and incommensurable (Grosz 1994; Irigaray 1974), it may be argued that to be meaningful, differences must differentiate within the same. 'As different as chalk from cheese' differentiates things that may share certain similarities of texture and appearance. 'As different as Norman Mailer from quilting' can only be a joke, as it once was in a *New Statesman* competition which set the task of linking the most unlikely pairs (the prototype was 'Jane Austen and the French Revolution').

If difference is considered not as absolute, but as always contained within some broader frame of comparison, then it is no longer necessary to choose between difference and identity (Joan Scott 1990), and indeed the differences between HUMANIST and postmodernist feminisms may also recede. The difference in question is usually a difference between people, and any two people, differentiated as they may be along every major axis of social and personal identification, are probably more like each other in more respects than either of them is like the member of another species or another category of things. However, Donna Haraway's model of the CYBORG allows for shifts in frames of comparison that may permit the recognition of connection and likeness, therefore possible identification, across species BOUNDARIES and the boundaries between human beings and machines (1991). Haraway's discussion is complex and ironic, and although it would seem to take her decisively outside the humanist frame, she has been criticized for pulling back from the implications of a model of cybernetic rather than cultural

COMMUNICATION, and for implicitly reinstating the mind/BODY and other dualisms which she began by deconstructing (Marsden 1996).

While in principle the differences around which people might construct identities are unlimited, some few recur across all cultures, including differentiation by SEX. And while no axis of difference, including sex, may be taken as given and fixed, mediated as 'natural' differences are by cultural meaning, equally identities do not evaporate once they have been exposed to the deconstructionist pen. Identity and social relation implies at least some degree of continuity, and individual identities, however open-ended, provisional and 'in process', cannot readily be expunged. They may be etched into the very fabric of the body, into gestures, lineaments and markers of who we are, as writers as diverse as Foucault and Bourdieu, and most memorably perhaps Elaine Scarry (1985), have argued. These lineaments disclose what we have been. While they may not determine, they surely have some consequences for, what we may become. Subjectivity may be an ongoing process of becoming, but no-one is ever fully 'born again'. The postmodern politics of temporary alliances, partial identities, is attractive as against the dyed-in-the-wool prejudices and exclusions of xenophobia, racism, sexism; but alliances and affinities mark some degree of ongoing identity and commitment, however provisional.

See also NATIONALISM; OTHER.

Identity politics   The term refers to the practice of basing one's POLITICS on a sense of personal IDENTITY – as female, gay, Black etc. It has been used by ethnic and sexual minorities, in particular, as an organizing tool to build cohesive and vocal political COMMUNITIES. For example, the Combahee River Collective, a US Black lesbian group, mobilized around the issues of sexual, racial and heterosexual OPPRESSIONS:

> This focusing upon our own oppression is embodied in the concept of identity politics. We believe that the most profound and potentially the most radical politics come directly out of our own identity, as opposed to working to end somebody else's oppression (1982: 16).

As the Black lesbian critic Barbara Smith puts it: 'we have an identity and therefore a politics' (cited in Moraga 1983: 131). This suggests the need to claim an identity before articulating a personal politics and that the character of the latter will be determined by the former.

The appeal to a pre-existing identity as a 'natural' basis for political organization has been challenged by a number of critics. For example, POSTSTRUCTURALIST, and specifically Foucauldian, theory has sought to de-essentialize and historicize (homo)sexuality as a discursive construction. Until recently, this project has gained more credence in gay men's studies than in lesbian studies. Fuss (1989) suggests that adherence to ESSENTIALISM may be viewed as a matter of survival for relatively less powerful groups such as

Black and lesbian women. De Lauretis (1989) argues that (strategic) essentialism is in fact constitutive of and necessary to all feminist politics. As a result of the poststructuralist critique all assertions of identity have become problematic and open to charges of essentialism; arguably, to the detriment of political efficacy. A more traditional challenge to identity politics has come from a MARXIST or MATERIALIST perspective from which the elevation of 'the personal' has been at the expense of specifically political analysis. The question 'what is to be done?' is deleteriously replaced by 'who am I?'

During the 1980s identity politics became the dominant form of radical political organization in Britain and the US with mixed results: while encouraging a positive proliferation of new political groupings – such as people with DISABILITIES, sexual minorities etc. – the development also made political mobilization across groups more difficult. The invocation of an identity frequently substituted for analysis and served to silence critical voices. As many critics have pointed out, an unreflective identity politics represents a form of essentialism in which experience can be transparently transposed into discourse to 'speak for itself' and a SUBJECTIVISM in which 'only I can speak for me'.

See NEW SOCIAL MOVEMENTS; STANDPOINT THEORY; QUEER THEORY.

Ideology   This concept as it circulates in Marxist theory is perhaps the most problematic and least well developed, but has been the one with which feminists have leant on most heavily in theorizing PATRIARCHY. Patriarchal institutions, underpinned by patriarchal ideology, it was argued quite widely inside and outside of MARXIST FEMINISM in the 1970s and 1980s, had the effect of reproducing the domination of women by men, and the task of winning the consent (cf. HEGEMONY) of women to that domination (Kuhn and Wolpe 1978; Barrett 1988).

As with many concepts, ideology's 'handiness' is directly proportionate to its multiple CONNOTATIONS and lack of clear definition. Until an array of substitutes was found, however, it was unlikely to be abandoned.

Michèle Barrett (1991), in her critique of 'ideology' and substitution of the twin concepts of CULTURE and subjectivity, identifies no fewer than six distinct uses of the term licensed by various textual references within Marx, Marxists, or their commentators. She follows Jorge Larrain (1979) in distinguishing two basic positions. The first is a negative definition in which ideology connotes ideas and beliefs which are in some sense distorted; they fall short on EPISTEMOLOGICAL grounds, and are motivated by CLASS interests. The second is a more neutral, even positive, conception. For George Lukács (1971) for example and for his follower Lucien Goldmann (1964), all historical forms of class CONSCIOUSNESS are at one and the same time enabling – they give some partial knowledge – *and* tied to class interests.

For Barrett the position developed by Gramsci articulates the limit position of the positive or neutral concept of ideology. She argues that Ernesto Laclau and Chantel Mouffe's (1985) interpretation of Gramsci highlights the turning point beyond which 'ideology' must give way to theories of the production of the human SUBJECT and CULTURE.

'Ideology' has been used fairly loosely within feminism, usually in its critical rather than positive sense. Patriarchal, or GENDER ideology is understood as a cultural ordering in which gender differences present themselves as utterly natural, founded upon biologically given differences of SEX. Girls and boys are socialized to enact and thereby to reproduce this hierarchical gender order. The activity of CONSCIOUSNESS-RAISING in women's groups was used in the women's movement to delve below the carapace of ideology to uncover women's EXPERIENCE, to expose the SOCIAL CONSTRUCTION of gender difference, and in order to generate a 'feminist consciousness' which might serve the interests of women in overthrowing gender OPPRESSION. In this schema, women's experience stands to patriarchy as knowledge to ideology

Marxist feminists linked patriarchal or gender ideology to the DOMINANT IDEOLOGY which served not only the interests of men but also those of CAPITALISM. They were drawn in the early 1970s to Louis Althusser's STRUCTURALIST Marxism, which seemed to have the potential to bring gender ideology into the same frame as that of class. The work of ideology for Althusser was to secure the REPRODUCTION of the forces and relations of production. Feminist theory had returned more than once to Engels's (1972) concept of reproduction, and the Althusserian concept seemed to offer a more satisfactory alternative which continued to focus attention upon institutions which feminists had earmarked in relation to the oppression of women: the FAMILY and the school.

In the second part of Althusser's (1977) essay, he drew upon Lacan to sketch a theory of 'ideology in general'. Althusser's theses are that ideology represents 'the imaginary relationship of individuals to their real conditions of existence' (Althusser 1977: 123); that ideology has a material existence in specific social practices such as the enactment of rituals (125–6); and that ideology produces individual subjectivities through the INTERPELLATION of individuals, who, in recognizing that it is they who are being addressed or 'hailed', (MIS)RECOGNIZE themselves (128–32). Thus the individual human SUBJECT is produced in a subjection that appears to be freely chosen, but which matches the individual to the place which she or he is destined to occupy in society within the parameters of class, gender and 'race'.

It was Althusser's emphasis on 'the lived' rather than upon 'ideas', above all, which proved attractive to feminists (and others): the perception that ideology was inscribed in our day-to-day practices, and therefore taken for granted as unremarkable, natural (Pierre Bourdieu uses the term DOXA for preference, with similar meaning). And secondly, his concept of the 'relative autonomy' of ideology: no mere reflexion of an underlying 'economic base', so that intervention at this level might have real political effects. The feminist emphasis on everyday practice, the 'lived', as the locus of oppression, and the slogan 'the personal is political', could be worked into the Althusserian concept of ideology.

It is but a small step however from the proposition that ideology, where it is effective, is 'lived', inscribed in practice, to the more radical proposition that whatever is 'lived' is ideological. It is this double proposition which Althusser wishes us to accept, and which makes ideology ubiquitous, inevitable, part of the very air we breathe.

Such a very broad conception of ideology begins to lose its analytical power, however. Once Althusser's distinction between knowledge and ideology was DECONSTRUCTED by POSTSTRUCTURALISM, the benefits of continuing to use this broad label diminished. For if ideology equals, without remainder, all lived subjectivity and all that passes for knowledge, then the specific force of the term is lost, a force which the critical concept of ideology retains, and which links it to systematic forms of domination and to systematic, motivated distortions at the level of epistemology. Moreover Gramsci's distinction between 'good sense' and 'common sense', which had identified some positive aspects of dominated cultures was lost in Althusser's formulation.

Poststructuralism sweeps away (or at least under the carpet) all epistemological claims to TRUTH and validity. There remain only competing discourses/discursive practices which constitute competing and multiple subjectivities. If all are equally 'ideological' then the term becomes redundant. This contemporary 'withering away of ideology' has opened up feminism onto contemporary theories of subjectivity, but at a cost, and many feminists prefer to retain the critical concept of ideology, for all its difficulties.

See also REPRESENTATION.

Imaginary In the PSYCHOANALYSIS of Jacques Lacan, the imaginary refers to that state of illusory unity and plenitude, prior to CASTRATION and entry into the SYMBOLIC order of LANGUAGE and DIFFERENCE. Within the Imaginary there is no clear distinction between SELF and OTHER, and initially the child experiences itself as fluid and fragmented. However, during the MIRROR STAGE the child projects an image of itself as unified, producing an imaginary or fictional ego ideal which will later enable it to identify with objects in the Symbolic world as 'others'. While the Symbolic represents a structural break with the Imaginary, the latter persists in the Symbolic in the form of UNCONSCIOUS phantasy, notably the myth of unified selfhood.

FRENCH FEMINIST theorists have widely critiqued Lacan's model, arguing that both the Imaginary and Symbolic realms are theorized in masculine terms with the effect that women are conceived of as defective males. Luce Irigaray, for example, argues that the present PHALLOCENTRIC Symbolic order is completely imaginary:

The Symbolic that you [men] impose as a universal, free of all empirical or historical contingency, is your imaginary transformed into an order, a social order (1985b: 269).

Irigaray and Hélène Cixous have revised Lacanian theory in their attempts to construct a specifically feminine Imaginary. Cixous posits the Imaginary as women's spiritual and linguistic home, a place which exists prior to masculine law and where female creativity is spontaneously expressed. Irigaray, in contrast, has attempted to rethink women's relation to the Imaginary as other than a place of refuge from the Symbolic order, and to formulate it in socio-political terms, thus enabling change to take place. These efforts have been seen as ESSENTIALIST by more materially minded feminists (Felski 1989a; Moi 1985) and as celebrating a regressive pre-Symbolic myth (Kristeva 1989). However, Margaret Whitford (1991) argues that the female Imaginary posited by Irigaray can be seen in two ways: as the unconscious of western thought, and as something which does not yet exist and still has to be created.

Imagined communities   The term used by Benedict Anderson in his influential study of NATIONALISM (Anderson 1983).
   See also POST-COLONIAL THEORY.

Immanence   See EXISTENTIALIST FEMINISM; OTHER.

Imperialism   Edward Said's *Culture and Imperialism* defines it as 'the practice, the theory, and the attitudes of a dominating metropolitan centre ruling a distant territory'; although colonialism, which usually involves settlement, has largely ended, imperialism 'lingers where it always has been, in a kind of general cultural sphere as well as in specific political, ideological, economic and social practices' (1993: 8).
   There is evidence in MARXIST writing for at least two points of view. One sees imperialism instituting harsh new forms of EXPLOITATION in place of pre-colonial systems of material security; the other characterizes imperialism as the highest stage of capitalism, a progressive force sweeping away traditional social relations which stifle development (Warren 1980). Feminist opinion is similarly divided. Many feminist anthropologists (for example Etienne and Leacock [eds] 1980; Draper 1975) have highlighted the negative effects of imperialism, arguing that communal non-class societies in which women exercised considerable POWER and had access to resources in their own right were destroyed by colonial conquest and the penetration of capitalist forms of organization. However, lurking behind some 'Women in Development' approaches to DEVELOPMENT is the idea that Western influence fosters the MODERNIZATION of traditional law and FAMILY structures which OPPRESS women, a view has been much criticized by the anti-imperialist

critique developed by feminist scholars like Chandra Talpade Mohanty (1993), Gloria Anzaldúa (1987) and Trinh Minh-Ha (1990).

Some see the anti-imperialist critique as having been partly displaced in recent years by COLONIAL DISCOURSE analysis and POST-COLONIAL theory, which developed out of radical POSTSTRUCTURALISM and represents a critique of Marxist thinking on the subject. However, many analyses which take a textual turn straddle both perspectives. One development has been the analysis of the complicity and resistance of white European women as members of the colonial elite, sometimes with a view towards showing that their location within the imperialist nexus indicates the racist underpinnings of Western FEMINISM (Burton 1990; Chaudhuri and Strobel 1992; Ramusack 1990; Ware 1992). This research has been accompanied by an interest in uncovering the close connection between imperialist ideals and Western constructions of white manliness (Sinha 1995; 1987).

See also UNDERDEVELOPMENT.

Imperialist subject See HYBRIDITY; POST-COLONIAL THEORY; SUBJECT.

Individualism The doctrine that the individual human being is the basic unit of human society and action. It is contrasted with collectivism and minimizes social obligation to the negative one of not harming others and to the positive ones to those implicit in the SOCIAL CONTRACT. Possession of property in the person is fundamental to the doctrine of individualism: 'Every Man has a Property in his own Person. This no body has any Right to but himself' (Locke 1952).

Locke, in 1689, provided the classic formulation of what has been termed 'possessive individualism' (McPherson 1962) which was to become one of the founding principles of liberal theory, and some half a century later Samuel Richardson's action in allowing his 16-year-old servant/heroine, Pamela, to articulate it in defiance of her master and sexual tormentor, Mr B, was still considered audacious: 'How came I to be his property? What right has he in me, but such as a thief may plead to stolen goods?' (Richardson 1962: 13).

The circumstances under which rights over one's BODY may be forfeited, limited or curtailed are subject to extensive debate which are of critical importance to feminism (Diprose 1994; Pateman 1988). Yet rights over others' bodies are claimed and exercised from infancy to old age – sexual rights, rights to labour, rights to control and fashion that body in illness and health, rights claimed by the STATE to imprison, or place at risk of death or injury in the armed services. Women's rights over their bodies are often breached with impunity even where they are formally recognized.

In the philosophy of the seventeenth- and eighteenth-century contractarians, the contract assumed to have been freely entered into allows only the contractor to abrogate these rights, although some, such as Locke, deny the legitimacy of certain types of contract such as that of slavery. The marriage contract, the only 'free' contract a woman might enter in early modern Europe, was one in which these rights were, in large measure, transferred to her husband, as Pamela learns to her cost. On marriage to Mr B she 'surrenders rights to her only property, her person. Reminded that she now runs the risk of committing "Laese Majestatis", a sort of "Treason against my Leige Lord and Husband" (334) she realises the confirmation of his power over her. Bound by her vow of obedience, Pamela may no longer resist' (Harris 1987: 33).

Feminism and WOMEN'S MOVEMENTS, wherever they have arisen, have frequently made the claim to rights over the person a central article in the struggle for EMANCIPATION, as the title of the book published by the Boston Women's Health Collective in 1972, and in print ever since, testifies: *Our Bodies Ourselves*. Sexual rights, REPRODUCTIVE rights, and the struggle against male VIOLENCE AGAINST WOMEN have rested on this claim.

It has been argued however that the liberal theory of possessive individualism offers treacherous terrain on which to base women's rights. The autonomous, atomized individual is modelled on an idealization to which only men can aspire; an abstraction, but fully embodied only in men. 'Corporeal feminisms' (Diprose 1994; Grosz 1994; Irigaray 1991; Pateman 1988) have argued that all individuals are embodied, and any attempt to define rights over bodies has to take cognizance of their sexual specificity. Otherwise the attempt to extend the rights of possessive individualism to women may, paradoxically, place women in greater jeopardy. The argument has been applied by Diprose and by Pateman, to surrogacy, prostitution, and NEW REPRODUCTIVE TECHNOLOGIES and the so-called 'free' social and SEXUAL CONTRACT is placed under close scrutiny.

Industrialism Feminists have long been concerned about the consequences of industrialization for women, but the emphasis has changed. In the early decades of the twentieth century and again with the revival of academic research on women in the 1970s, feminist researchers have argued that while pre-industrial European societies acknowledged and rewarded women's economic contribution as their husbands' partners in family farming and other family enterprises, industrialism's separation of home and work whittled away women's productive roles (Clark 1992; Oakley 1976; Tilly and Scott 1989). A not dissimilar debate has taken place about the effects of industrialism in the THIRD WORLD, where the role of women as industrial workers is very pronounced. Here an early fear for the consequences of industrialization for women workers has been replaced by a more complex and uneven picture (Elson and Pearson 1981; Lim 1990; Pearson 1992).

Another perspective on the consequences of industrialism is even more pessimistic. ECOFEMINIST and other radical ecology writing sees industrialism as inevitably leading to ecological catastrophe, with particularly acute consequences for women (Merchant 1992). For some feminists Western science and technology are tools for the domination of people and nature and their application – one of the defining characteristics of industrialism –

threatens life on earth. Other commentators try to retain some of the benefits of industrialism through making a distinction between the ecological consequences of unhindered economic growth and 'sustainable development' (Braidotti *et al.* 1994) .

Inscription   In literary criticism 'inscription' describes the process by which textual codes are deployed and activated in a text. It is closely associated with POSTSTRUCTURALIST models of TEXTUALITY which eschew the concept of an 'AUTHOR' communicating his or her thoughts to a READER. For Barthes, it is not the author who speaks in a text, but writing itself which produces a scriptor in the act of writing. Similarly, the text inscribes the reader, inviting him or her to take up SUBJECT POSITIONS within the text.

Inside/Outside   An important BINARY opposition in discursive systems, DECONSTRUCTED by Derrida to demonstrate the mutual dependence of the two terms. It is utilized by lesbian, gay, and QUEER theorists such as Fuss (ed.) (1991) and Eve Kosofsky Sedgwick (1991). Sedgwick demonstrates how the concept structures the 'epistemology of the closet' which works to legitimate the subordination of homosexuality to heterosexuality.

Intellectuals   In its narrowest sense this term refers to the 'stars' of the dominant high CULTURE: creators of ideas who compete for DISTINCTION, and who form the gate-keepers who validate the distinction of others (Bourdieu 1984a).

In the writings of the Italian Marxist Antonio Gramsci, the term is used more broadly to cover all intellectual functionaries, including SUBALTERN strata who staff the various institutions of cultural production, transmission and dissemination. Gramsci distinguishes the 'traditional intellectuals' of social formations. These are the priests and prophets of the old regime, ensconsed in the cathedral, the bishop's palace, the university, the state administration. They appear to be, and indeed are to a degree, independent of the dominant class whose interests they serve. Each newly emergent social group with the means and the ambition to develop a strong counter-HEGEMONIC challenge must generate from within the group a cadre of 'organic intellectuals', Gramsci's second category (Gramsci 1971).

Raymond Williams identifies the intellectual in terms of GENERATION and STRUCTURE OF FEELING. The latter informs the CONSCIOUSNESS of different intellectual generations, and these are classified in terms of dominant, residual and emergent groupings (Williams 1961; 1979; 1983a).

The French sociologist Pierre Bourdieu focuses like Gramsci on the CLASS coordinates of the intellectual and cultural field and ignores those of gender. He delineates intellectual and more broadly cultural PRODUCTION and CONSUMPTION, especially the latter, in his massive study of the sociology of taste in France (Bourdieu 1984a) and in his successive studies of the sociology of intellectual life, especially its institutionalization in the academy (Bourdieu

1988; Bourdieu and Wacquant 1992). For Bourdieu, those who specialize in the acquisition of cultural capital are intellectuals, again used broadly, who constitute 'the dominated fraction of the dominant class' (Bourdieu 1984a). Bourdieu's deconstruction of taste takes him away from Gramsci in more pessimistic directions. For not only are intellectuals engaged in a rather ruthless game which inflicts SYMBOLIC VIOLENCE on those excluded from the field, they are also stripped of their pretensions to superior knowledge. Bourdieu's sociology is a sociology of practice, and his case is that social PRACTICE has a logic of its own which is misunderstood when it is analysed either in terms of an abstract theory superimposed upon it by the outsider/observer, paradigmatically, the intellectual, or by taking the rationalizations of the players at face value (Bourdieu 1990a). However, he has his more optimistic and generous moments in his later writings, holding out the possibility of more emancipatory role for intellectuals who take the approach of 'reflexive sociology', as well as for literature and art (Bourdieu and Wacquant 1992).

Feminist comment upon intellectual life has concentrated upon the critiques of its masculine parameters (Battersby 1989; Jordanova 1989; Kirkup and Keller [eds] 1992; Tuana [ed.] 1989; see also EPISTEMOLOGY). It has generated little systematic analysis of women as intellectuals, however, although some useful case studies are available and there is plenty of material in biographical and autobiographical studies (Berg 1996; Moi 1994). Nor has feminism as an intellectual movement given rise to major studies as yet, although there are some interesting beginnings (Mary Eagleton 1996; Morley and Walsh [eds] 1995). A systematic working through of theories of intellectuals in relation to gender has yet to be written.

See also ACADEMIC FEMINISM.

Interdisciplinarity   Many substantive works of scholarship draw upon more than one DISCIPLINE. Multidisciplinarity is relatively commonplace. Inter-disciplinarity goes beyond this process in carving out an area of study whose organizing theoretical and methodological frame is constructed from cross-disciplinary sources, so that a new synthetic field of study is created over time. The academic study of women and gender typically transgresses disciplinary boundaries, even where these studies began as course units within disciplinary degees.

This characteristic process of reaching beyond established disciplines is partly a function of the questions asked, which arose initially out of the political concerns of a radical social movement, and not out of the PARADIGM of any discipline. Interdisciplinarity comes about in the attempt to pursue questions which are off the disciplinary agenda by a policy of APPROPRIATION from the disciplines to forge the lineaments of new theoretical and methodological frames for inquiry.

Interdisciplinarity has also been boosted by the phenomenon of TRAVELLING THEORY: the writings of intellectuals whose voices are heard in the public world at large, whose approaches are applied outside their originating contexts, and are not confined to any narrow specialism (Said 1983). Many of the theories on which feminism has drawn over the years have been of this kind: Western MARXISM; Foucauldian POSTSTRUCTURALISM; Derridean DECONSTRUCTION; Said's cultural history. But the influence of travelling theory has not been confined to feminism. Many of the disciplines in the humanities and social sciences have had their boundaries redrawn under its impact. Black studies, of lengthier provenance than women's studies, has made a major contribution to this process in turn.

Interdisciplinarity has been a necessity for feminist studies, and its value is manifest in the work of writers such as Gayatri Spivak (1987; 1993b), but it carries dangers of its own. Disciplines focus and direct inquiry, and delimit a manageable field of study, and interdisciplinary studies have to seek other means of performing these functions. Hence perhaps the recurrent preoccupation with METHODOLOGICAL and EPISTEMOLOGICAL questions, which characterizes not only the study of women and gender, but also such fields as CULTURAL STUDIES. Secondly, there is a danger of intellectual tourism when theory is made to travel too far and too fast.

See also ACADEMIC FEMINISM; THEORY.

Interpellation   Interpellation was a key concept in the shift within contemporary theory from STRUCTURALISM to POSTSTRUCTURALISM, and from IDEOLOGY to subjectivity. Interpellation, or 'hailing', according to Louis Althusser in his concept of 'ideological state apparatuses', calls into existence the SUBJECT who therefore has no existence except in and through ideology. This influential concept has been criticized on a number of grounds. Terry Eagleton enquires 'how does the individual human being recognize and respond to the 'hailing' which makes it a subject if it is not a subject already?' How does a girl-child respond to her hailing in the feminine if 'she' is yet to be 'made', as de Beauvoir asserts. 'Are not response, recognition, understanding, subjective faculties, so that one would need to be a subject already in order to become one?' (Eagleton 1994: 215).

Abercrombie, Hill and Turner, in a critique of Göran Therborn, argue for a greater recognition of contingency and pluralism in the discussion of ideologies:

> as ongoing processes of interpellation, they have no natural boundaries, no natural criteria distinguishing one ideology from another or one element of an ideology from its totality. Particularly in today's open and complex societies different ideologies...not only compete and clash, but also overlap, affect and contaminate one another' (1994: 161-2).

The effect of these considerations would seem to be to reinscribe a necessary element of AGENCY and choice into poststructuralist discussions of 'the subject'.

Intersubjectivity The concept is used in MATERIALIST accounts of the SUBJECT to refer to the idea that IDENTITY is constituted dynamically through social and psychic relationships. In their critique of theories of GENDER differentiation, Cornell and Thurschwell (1987) argue that the concept enables theorists to move beyond polarized 'GYNOCENTRIC' and 'UNIVERSALIST' feminisms because it acknowledges that gender is not a substance or an essence but a relation, involving the interlocking interplay of sameness and DIFFERENCE:

> The moment of constitution of subjects qua subjects [occurs] in and through the multigendered flux of the social field of dynamic intersubjectivity. The gender of the I is not established a priori or in the singular; gender identity only maintains itself by virtue of marking its non-identical other (1987: 158).

Intertextuality Intertextuality describes the variety of ways in which texts interact with other texts, and in particular the interdependence between texts rather then their discreteness or uniqueness. It differs from allusion in that whereas the latter works largely through verbal echoes between texts, texts may also interact through formal and thematic echoes.

POSTSTRUCTURALIST accounts of intertextuality go beyond the traditional notion of authorial allusions to emphasize the necessarily intertextual nature of all READING and writing: LANGUAGE is always already there. For Kristeva, who coined the term, intertextuality represents 'in the space of a given text, several utterances, taken from other texts [which] intersect and neutralise one another' (1980: 36). Barthes offers an even more radical version: for him, any text is an intertext: 'a text is ... a multi-dimensional space in which a variety of writings, none of them original, blend and clash' (1977a: 146). The concept is also utilized in New Historicist criticism to signal the textual nature of the social and historical world (e.g. Greenblatt 1991).

Feminist use of the term has emphasized the intertextual character of women's writing. *Jane Eyre*, for example, can be seen as an intertext of Rhys's *Wide Sargasso Sea*, and indeed of any text incorporating the motif of the mad wife. Contemporary feminist fiction is especially rich in intertextual allusion: Angela Carter's work rewrites traditional fairy tales, and Toni Morrison's writing can be seen as reconstructing the suppressed intertext of Black history.

Irony Irony is a non-literal use of language in which we say one thing but mean another. Its subversive potential as a rhetorical device has been exploited historically in texts of all kinds and it has been effectively utilized by feminist writers. For example, Virginia Woolf employs irony to deflate masculine pomposity and bigotry in *A Room of One's Own*:

I thought of that old gentleman ... who declared that it was impossible for any woman, past, present, or to come, to have the genius of Shakespeare. He wrote to the papers about it. He also told a lady who applied to him for information that cats do not as a matter of fact go to heaven, though they have, he added, souls of a sort. How much thinking those old gentlemen used to save one! How the borders of ignorance shrank back at their approach! Cats do not go heaven. Women cannot write the plays of Shakespeare (1977: 70).

More recently, irony has come to characterize a certain kind of POSTMODERN textuality which because of its awareness of *DIFFÉRANCE* – the way meaning can be turned against itself – employs irony to open up a critical space within discourse. Feminism and postmodern irony come together to stunning effect in Joanna Russ' science fiction satire *The Female Man* (1985), and in the fields of feminist theory, in the work of Donna Haraway (1991) and Luce Irigaray (1974; 1985a).

Italian feminism Italian feminism is little known in anglophone feminism, and is often seen, like FRENCH FEMINISM, as having an ESSENTIALIST bias. This is no doubt owing to the fact that for Italian as for post-Lacanian French feminisms, the concept of an originary sexual DIFFERENCE is central. Italian feminists have drawn on the work of both French and American feminists – two of the key influences being Luce Irigaray and Adrienne Rich – to produce a highly politicized account of sexual difference in terms of a social and SYMBOLIC alliance of WOMEN. The appearance in translation of Adriana Cavarero's (1995) study of Plato will begin to rectify this situation. Commentators on and interpreters of Italian feminism include Bono and Kemp (1991), Braidotti (1994b) and de Lauretis (in Schor and Weed [eds] 1994). According to de Lauretis, Italian feminism has been centrally concerned with formulating:

a freedom for women that is not made possible by adherence to the liberal concept of rights – civil, human, or individual rights – which women do not have *as women*, but is generated, and indeed engendered, by taking up a position in a symbolic community, a 'genealogy of women', that is at once discovered, invented, and constructed through feminist practices of reference and address (de Laurentis, in Schor and Weed [eds] 1994: 13).

De Lauretis identifies a number of concepts central to this account of Italian feminist theory and practice: *genealogy*, the *symbolic mother, autocoscienza* and *affidamento*. The term GENEALOGY, suggesting GENDER, GENERATION and KINSHIP, refers to a symbolic 'coming into being of women legitimated by their female origin' (Libreria delle Donne di Milano 1987: 9). The *symbolic mother*, a figure who mediates and guarantees women's relationship to each other and to the symbolic, represents the 'affirmation of women as subjects in a female-gendered frame of reference' (de Lauretis in Schor and Weed [eds] 1994: 24). *Autocoscienza*, the practice of CONSCIOUSNESS-RAISING adapted from the US model, represents the highly politicized and 'self-directed process of achieving consciousness'. It characterized feminist organization in Italy in the 1970s and its separatism was an integral and highly valued aspect of women's interaction.

During the 1980s another political practice developed through the concept of *affidamento* or entrustment. The term designates a relation between women in which one woman 'gives her trust or entrusts herself symbolically to another woman, who thus becomes her guide, mentor, or point of reference – in short, the figure of symbolic mediation between her and the world' (de Lauretis in Schor and Weed [eds] 1994: 21). Entrustment, in contrast to the Anglo-American concept of mutuality among women, positively acknowledges the disparity and lack of EQUALITY between women in terms of status, age, education, income, etc. Inevitably, the concept has been criticized by feminists inside and outside Italy as shoring up a narrow, hierarchical and elitist model of female relationship which at worst posits the symbolic mother as a extension of paternal if not patriarchal AUTHORITY. Nevertheless, de Lauretis argues that feminists in Britain and North America should take seriously the risk of essentialism run by Italian feminism. Arguably, it theorizes an aspect of women's EXPERIENCE that has received scant attention in Anglo-American thought. The theory is particularly suggestive for LESBIAN FEMINISM and the critique of heterosexuality as a socio-symbolic institution which oppresses all women.

J

Jamming A term coined by Luce Irigaray which wittily puns on the two senses of jamming as 'blocking' and 'improvising' and describes her preferred method of subverting PHALLOGOCENTRIC discourse by effectively 'throwing a spanner in the works'. As Irigaray states: 'The issue is not one of elaborating a new theory of which woman would be the subject or the object, but of jamming the theoretical machinery itself, of suspending its pretension to the production of a truth and of a meaning that are excessively univocal' (1985a: 78).

Jouissance The term has no exact equivalent in English and has acquired many connotations. At its simplest it means 'pleasure', but in *The Pleasure of the Text* (1976) Barthes contrasts *plaisir* which he associates with cultural enjoyment of IDENTITY and the ego, to *jouissance*, which he imagines as a kind of pleasure which dissipates that identity and ego. French feminists have adopted the term to designate a FEMININE sexual pleasure which they see as disruptive of the PHALLOCENTRIC symbolic order. Marks and de Courtivron elaborate on the term's inflection in discourses of FEMININITY:

> This pleasure, when attributed to a woman, is considered to be a different order from the pleasure that is represented within the male libidinal economy often described in terms of the capitalist gain and profit motive. Woman's jouissance carries with it the notion of fluidity, diffusion, duration. It is a kind of potlatch in the world of orgasms, a giving, expending, dispensing of pleasure without concern about ends or closure (1981: 36).

Female *jouissance* is celebrated in *ÉCRITURE FEMININE*, the writing of feminine sexuality and TEXTUALITY. This practice has come under criticism from many feminists, especially those of a Marxist bent. Rita Felski criticizes the feminist recovery of *jouissance* in language, arguing that feminists need to understand the material and contextual determinants of literary SIGNIFICATION, rather than simply valorizing the presence of erotic drives in literature (1989a: 39).

See also DESIRE.

K

Kinship   Kinship systems are ways of reckoning relatedness (e.g. next of kin) through descent and marriage. Determination of membership in descent groups is usually either patrilineal (through the father), matrilineal (though the mother) or bilateral (through both parents). Other technical terms which locate people in terms of kinship include 'uxorilocal' and 'patrilocal' (referring to whether newly formed conjugal partners reside with or near the woman's or the man's kin). Nineteenth-century European social theorists wrongly assumed that matrilineal systems were relics of earlier matriarchal systems of group marriage (in which it was impossible to identify a child's biological father). However, some feminist theorists have used their work to construct a *vision* of matriarchy – of a society in which women have power (Webster 1975).

The work of Claude Lévi-Strauss (1969), which shifted the focus of kinship studies from generational descent to relationships between groups, has been APPROPRIATED by feminist theorists like Gayle Rubin (1975), who see the exchange of women by men as the epitome of the objectification of women – the denial of women as SUBJECTS. However, Marilyn Strathern (1988), a feminist anthropologist, argues that equating the exchange of women with the objectification of women assumes that GIFT exchanges are conceptualized in the same way as Westerners conceptualize the exchange of commodities. In Melanesian societies based on a gift economy, she argues, what are exchanged (including exchanged things) are conceptualized as persons (1988: 124).

In feminist sociology dealing with contemporary Western societies, the term 'kin' usually refers mainly to extra-household relatives, as in the term KIN WORK. However, there are important references to the 'politicization of kinship' in the new debates about challenges to the biological basis of descent which have arisen in connection with the NEW REPRODUCTIVE TECHNOLOGIES, so-called surrogate motherhood, and 'blended families' (Edwards *et al.* 1993; Weston 1991).

Kin work   The term kin work was adopted by Michaela di Leonardo (1987) to conceptualize the inter-household work which connects people across households. Kin work involves:

> the conception, maintenance, and ritual celebration of cross-household kin ties, for example visits, letters, telephone calls, presents, and cards to kin; the organisation of holiday gatherings; the creation and maintenance of quasi-kin relations; ... and the mental work of reflection about all these activities (1987: 442-3).

Athough women can 'cede' their kin work to other women kin, it cannot usually be replaced by paid workers.

Knowledge   Both feminist and Foucauldian EPISTEMOLOGIES have foregrounded the links between knowledge and POWER. Second wave feminism saw challenging the expert medical, social scientific and other ruling DISCOURSES which discount women's EXPERIENCES as central to its political PRACTICE. For Foucault too the 'will to knowledge' is primarily malicious, the passion of the inquisitor: 'power produces knowledge (and not simply by encouraging it... or applying it because it seems useful... power and knowledge directly imply each other' (Foucault 1977: 27, quoted by V. Bell 1993: 44).

However, while many feminists have argued that the production of new knowledge from a feminist STANDPOINT is a practical and necessary goal, POSTSTRUCTURALIST feminist EPISTEMOLOGY follows Foucault in preferring the DECONSTRUCTION of knowledge claims to the creation of positive knowledge. Carol Smart argues that feminists who assume that the best knowledge can predict the best political strategies are relying on notions of progressive enlightenment and an outdated view of the coherence of social structures on which knowledge works. This 'orderly universe' in which one agent dominates, she argues, is no longer 'an adequate theorization of our conditions of existence (Smart 1995: 211).

Although according to Foucault knowledge cannot tell us 'the truth', 'subjugated knowledges' have an important place as discourses of resistance. For Foucault subjugated knowledges are:

knowledges that have been disqualified as inadequate to their task...; naive knowledges...beneath the required level of cognition or scientificity;...low-ranking...such as that of the psychiatrist's patient, the ill person,...of the delinquent...and which is...a particular, local, regional knowledge, which owes its force only to the harshness with which it is opposed by everything surrounding it. It is through the reappearance of this knowledge...that criticism forms its work (Bell 1993: 89 quoting Foucault 1980b).

Donna Haraway (1991) stresses that to see from the standpoint of the subjugated is not unproblematic. Her concept of 'situated knowledge', knowledge which is partial and locatable rather than transcendent, follows from her sense that feminism demands some concept of objective knowledge. Her stress on 'how to see' rather than where we stand at least preempts (if it doesn't resolve) the problem of competing feminist standpoints. Hence her stress on vision and positioning – not 'the view from above but the joining of partial views and halting voices' (197). Building accounts of the 'real' world, she says, does not 'depend on the logic of "discovery" but on a power-charged social relation of "conversation"'. (197) Such metaphors are typical of her work, and, she says, characteristic of all conceptions of OBJECTIVITY.

See also DISCOURSE; EPISTEMOLOGY; IDEOLOGY; STANDPOINT.

L

Labour-power Marx defined labour-power as the 'aggregate of the mental and physical capabilities in a human being which he exercises whenever he produces a use-value of any description' (Marx 1970 Vol. I: 35, cited by Kay 1975: 42). In capitalist societies labour is conceptualized as a COMMODITY which the worker sells to the capitalist for a definite time – an hour, a week, a month. The EXPLOITATION of the worker is hidden by the appearance of a 'free contract' between the owners of property and the owners of labour-power. Because labour-power is the average capacity to labour, in measuring labour-power any one hour of one person's labour-power is interchangeable with anybody else's.

Some feminists fear that a gender-neutral abstraction like the concept of labour-power obscures systematic differences in the terms on which men and women sell their labour and therefore systematic differences in the rewards they receive. For instance, Delphy and Leonard (1992) argue that the employment contract depends upon a prior SEXUAL CONTRACT which 'frees' men to sell their labour. The marriage contract gives husbands' rights to their wives' work: 'wives (and daughters and occasionally male kin too) are not free to sell their labour to a third party without their household head authorizing it' (1992: 118), nor do they have the same control over the money they earn.

Several feminist theorists have gone even further, seeing the concept of labour-power as a 'political fiction'. Pateman (1988), Adkins (1995) and Brewis and Kerfoot (1994) argue that in some occupations – prostitution, leisure industries, even secretarial work – it is obvious that it is not abstract labour-power which is purchased but the embodied sexuality of the woman worker. To assume that women treat this as an impersonal, alienable commodity simply rationalizes sexual exploitation. Others have pointed to the increase in 'selved labour', jobs in which workers are required to make use of 'their own' personality traits and empathy, rather than capacities which can be properly conceptualized as detachable from the person (Hochschild 1983). These are usually women's jobs, but there are also men's jobs which involve 'deep acting' and the deployment of particular MASCULINITIES, for instance the intimidating behaviour of the debt collector.

The theoretical implications of focusing on 'selved labour' depends partly on one's starting point. In labour studies, for instance, where gender-blind concepts predominate, almost any attempt to make visible the gender-specific character of both male and female work experience is welcome. Other feminist theorists, however, faced with the increasingly ESSENTIALIZING character of 'corporeal feminism', would prefer to hold onto the existing concept of labour-power precisely because as an abstract way of measuring labour it renders the capacities of men and women comparable and interchangeable.

Labour process The labour process is a Marxist concept which refers to the 'ways in which human labour, working with tools or instruments of production, transforms raw materials into useful products' (Outhwaite and Bottomore [eds] 1993: 318). Rather than focusing on the market relation between capital and labour in determining wage levels, use of the concept draws attention to capital's struggle to shape work tasks so that workers' individual and collective skills and autonomy in their work is reduced (Braverman 1974). Feminists have been particularly concerned to show how labour processes reflect the social relations of gender as well as those of CAPITALISM, for instance by pointing to the design of machinery which assumes male workers or the ways the identification and ranking of skills is 'saturated with sex' (Cockburn 1991; Phillips and Taylor 1986). Although the first studies of labour processes focused on the fragmentation of manufacturing and clerical labour processes, recent studies are beginning to give more attention to jobs like nursing, teaching and leisure industry jobs involving EMOTIONAL WORK.

Lack In Lacanian PSYCHOANALYSIS 'lack' refers to the condition of lacking the phallus, the transcendental signifier within the SYMBOLIC order. It is a product of the SUBJECT'S exclusion from the IMAGINARY realm, and its entry into the Symbolic order of LANGUAGE and sexual DIFFERENCE. Within the Symbolic the subject can never be the origin of meaning, but only its unstable effect as the splitting of the subject mobilizes DESIRE along a chain of signifiers. Although lack is a general human condition, it has a special resonance for women in that according to Lacan it characterizes women's relation to the Symbolic order. FRENCH FEMINISTS have challenged this designation arguing in contrast for a feminine plenitude and an alternative feminine economy (Cixous 1976a; Irigaray 1985a).

See CASTRATION COMPLEX.

Language/linguistics Language constitutes a central field of feminist critical enquiry. This takes a variety of forms: firstly, there is an (Anglo-American) tradition of criticizing 'man-made' or SEXIST language. This involves identifying, tracing the etymology of, and challenging examples of sexist language. Examples include Dale Spender's *Man Made Language* (1980) and Jane Mills's *Womanwords* (1989). Secondly, there is the generation of NEW FEMINIST LANGUAGE (Mary Daly's work [1987; 1991] being the prime example). Thirdly, there is a FRENCH FEMINIST critique of PHALLOCENTRISM in language and the elaboration of *ÉCRITURE FEMININE* or feminine writing with the aim of writing the BODY of WOMAN (Cixous 1981; Irigaray 1985a). In this formulation woman is conceived of as a sign in DISCOURSE, in contrast to the greater Anglo-American emphasis on the socio-political realm independent of language.

One of the consequences of the dissemination of FRENCH FEMINIST ideas is the greater awareness amongst English-speaking feminists of the imbrication of language and the social: REPRESENTATION mediates and constructs our access to social 'reality'. The work of feminist linguists and stylisticians (Deborah Cameron 1985; Sara Mills 1995) draws on and critiques all three strands to demonstrate the central importance of language and representation in the construction and maintenance of gendered inequality. However, as Cameron (1985) argues, linguistic oppression cannot be total or else women would have no means of articulating a critique of those structures and processes encoded in language and society more generally. In addition, POSTSTRUCTURALISTS have pointed out that language itself has a 'DECONSTRUCTIVE' quality working to undermine the fixing of meaning. Women can and do exploit this tendency in order to construct alternative, if provisional, meanings in feminist discourses. As Cameron (1985) argues, language both encodes and constructs social reality. It neither passively reflects, nor wholly determines our gendered social world.

Law Law has played such an important role in institutionalizing heterosexuality and regulating REPRODUCTION and motherhood that looking to the law to further women's interests is bound to be a contradictory project.

Most attention has focused on the theoretical background to different strategies: do we want the law to recognize men's and women's EQUALITY, acknowledge their DIFFERENCES or refuse this polarity (Bacchi 1990; Scott 1988)? Treating women and men as equally autonomous legal SUBJECTS can disadvantage women in many respects. In the past women have often benefited when the specificity of their position was acknowledged, yet this often confirms ESSENTIALIST notions or naturalizes disadvantage. For instance, awarding child custody to the mother often rests on – and reproduces – the assumption of women's natural mothering role and alimony upon divorce confirms women's economic dependence.

Carol Smart (1989; 1995) has stressed two further conceptual minefields. Firstly, although the concept of EQUAL RIGHTS has been a touchstone for feminists, it does not necessarily always work to women's advantage. Not only is there the problem indicated above, in that in the existing set-up women often need special consideration, the DISCOURSE of equal rights is readily APPROPRIATED by men seeking to counter women's advances, for example by the fathers' movement for equal child custody rights or by 'pro-life' anti-abortion campaigns articulating the rights of the foetus.

Secondly, the SEXISM of law is often traced to the overwhelming predominance of men as judges, and, until very recently, as solicitors and barristers. However, Smart argues that the problem is legal regulation itself, not male bias: we have misunderstood 'the power of law' (1996: 213). Using law to further feminist objectives (freedom from rape, reproductive rights) contributes to the further legalization of life which subjugates women's KNOWLEDGES. An example is the way in which the criminal justice system disqualifies women's accounts of their experiences of rape (Edwards 1996; Lees and Gregory 1994; Smart 1989).

Law is therefore a mixed blessing for women, especially when women confront the law as members of racialized groups. Law frequently discriminates among women as well as between women and men, for example in the idea that Black women cannot be raped. As Abena Busia (1993) says, the nineteenth-century legal reality of slavery is still with us as social reality: 'Black women were held to lack the necessary prerequisites of moral womanhood that would make the crime of rape against them conceivable in any social sense' (1993: 288). Indeed, all women's civil rights are dependent on ideas about women's sexual virtue; in Britain women labelled 'common prostitutes' are denied many ordinary civil rights and discrimination against lesbian women is accepted as legitimate, for instance with respect to fostering, adoption and reproductive rights.

Law of the Father In Lacanian thought, the Law of the Father refers to that set of psychosocial injunctions – typically the incest taboo – which constitute the SYMBOLIC order. The term is closely related to Lacan's phrase *le nom du père* in which *nom* – 'name' – is punned with *non*: the 'no' or prohibition of the father. Feminists have used the term to point to the encoding of patriarchal values in phallocentric discourse.

See also CASTRATION COMPLEX; PSYCHOANALYSIS.

Lesbian feminism   Lesbian feminism emerged in North America in the late 1960s and early 1970s and describes a political and ideological grouping within the WOMEN'S MOVEMENT comprising women whose allegiance was divided between FEMINISM of the time, with its prioritizing of heterosexuality, and gay liberation with its predominately male agenda. Although the beliefs and practices the term designates are historically heterogeneous, lesbian feminists have been concerned both to establish lesbians as a distinct group and, in Jill Johnstone's (1973) phrase, to 'liberate the lesbian' in every woman. Like RADICAL FEMINISM lesbian feminism focuses its analysis on the dominant SEX/GENDER system, but has developed unique critiques of COMPULSORY HETEROSEXUALITY (Rich 1980a; Rubin 1975) and the HETEROSEXUAL MATRIX (Butler 1990) as dominant institutional and IDEOLOGICAL practices which are oppressive to all women. As the title of an article by Charlotte Bunch puts it, analysis of heterosexuality is 'not for lesbians only' (1987).

In the last 25 years lesbian feminists have campaigned on a variety of political issues including women's sexual self-determination and PORNOGRAPHY. The issue of male VIOLENCE AGAINST WOMEN has been a priority, and lesbian feminists have been at the forefront in creating feminist institutions and women's spaces such as rape crisis centres and women's refuges.

Some commentators erroneously attribute a monolithic character to lesbian feminism. Its heterogeneity may be partially discerned in the following claims: 'A lesbian is the rage of all women condensed to the point of explosion' (Radicalesbians 1970); 'I mean the term lesbian continuum to include a range – through each woman's life and throughout history – of woman-identified experience' (Rich 1980a); 'Lesbian is the only concept I know of which is beyond the categories of sex (woman and man), because the designated subject (lesbian) is not a woman, either economically, or politically, or ideologically (Wittig 1992).

There is, however, a strategic divergence within lesbian feminism between an emphasis on intervening in order to transform the dominant culture and the goal of a separate, autonomous WOMEN'S CULTURE. While it could be argued that initially the former strategy took precedence, by the late 1970s the movement to develop lesbian institutions and culture, known as Lesbian Nation, had ceased to emphasize the fluidity of sexual identity and increasingly prescribed an exclusionary form of IDENTITY POLITICS. Perhaps as a response to such 'culturalism', political lesbianism emerged in the early 1980s to reanimate the political confrontation with dominant heterosexuality. Like earlier forms of lesbian feminism, it tends to adopt a voluntaristic conception of SEXUALITY but, unlike its predecessors, it is inclined to confuse OPPRESSIVE institutions with sexual practices, as exemplified in a notorious essay by Leeds Revolutionary Feminist Group (1981) in which they apparently equate heterosexual sex and rape.

During the 1980s challenges from a number of sources have resulted in the decentring of lesbian feminism: firstly, 'pro-sex' or sex-radical lesbians rejected feminist prescription of sexual behaviour, appropriated pornography, and introduced a positive concept of lesbian 'perversity'. Secondly, QUEER politics challenged the separatist emphasis of lesbian activism and its location in feminism. In response, lesbian feminists have convincingly argued that 'queer' fails adequately to address the sex/gender system and so elides lesbian specificity. More indirectly, BLACK FEMINISM challenged all white feminists to examine their racism and theorize 'WHITENESS'. As a result of these and other interventions lesbian feminism in the 1990s is a self-conscious, intellectually and politically diverse field which abuts on a wide variety of other discourses including queer theory, CHICANA THEORY and POSTMODERNISM.

The 1980s and 1990s has also seen the development of lesbian and gay studies in the academy which sets out to analyse the 'centrality of sex and sexuality within many different fields of inquiry, to express and advance the interests of lesbians, bisexuals and gay men, and to contribute culturally and intellectually to the contemporary lesbian/gay movement' (Abelove *et al.* 1993: xvi). Lesbian and gay studies gives fresh impetus to INTERDISCIPLINARY work. So far it has had most impact on literary and historical studies. The methodological problems it raises have led to productive debates about who counts as a lesbian or a gay man in history. The so-called SOCIAL CONSTRUCTIONISM VS ESSENTIALISM debate also has radical implications for the status of heterosexuality as an IDEOLOGICAL construct. The work of lesbian and gay theorists radically alters the lens through which we view the past and produces new ways of seeing.

Lesbian and gay studies See LESBIAN FEMINISM.

Liberal feminism Liberal feminism is grounded in the claims of the classical liberal philosophy developed by Locke, Rousseau, Bentham and Mill for EQUAL RIGHTS, INDIVIDUALISM, liberty and justice. Feminists such as Olympe de Gouges in revolutionary France, her contemporary in Britain, Mary Wollstonecraft, and later in the nineteenth century Harriet Taylor, campaigned to extend those rights to women (Nye 1988; Phillips [ed.] 1987; Randall 1982; Rendall 1985). Liberal feminism in the US has been associated with movements such NOW (New Opportunities for Women), and the ill-fated Equal Rights Amendment (ERA) campaign. In Britain it promoted the legislation of the 1970s for equal pay and an end to sex discrimination, and campaigns for changes in the LAW have provided the central plank of liberal feminist politics.

In the late 1960s and early 1970s liberal feminism was usually differentiated from the more radical politics of SOCIALIST and MARXIST FEMINISMS on the one hand, and of RADICAL FEMINISM on the other. POSTSTRUCTURALIST critiques of feminisms of EQUALITY have tended to conflate or SAME liberal, socialist and Marxist feminisms under this head, discounting the significance of any differences between them (Gross 1987; Irigaray 1986), while radical feminism, in these poststructuralist accounts, is opposed to both as a feminism of DIFFERENCE, though one to be transcended in a third, synthesizing form, poststructuralist or POSTMODERNIST (Kristeva 1986; Joan Scott 1990).

Life histories See PERSONAL NARRATIVES.

Liminality The term refers to a threshold or 'in-between' space. The anthropologist Sherry Ortner (1974) draws attention to the way in which women have been culturally constructed as occupying a liminal position between nature and CULTURE (cf. BOUNDARIES). Belonging wholly to neither category, women mediate men's relation to the 'natural' and SYMBOLIC worlds. Feminists might once have lamented this state of affairs, seeking to 'bring women in from the margins'. The term has, however, taken on a positive meaning in POSTMODERN discourses to describe what Bhabha calls 'the in-between space...the connective tissue that constructs the difference' (1994: 4). As a sign of non-IDENTITY or DIFFERENCE, liminality is valued for its unsettling, DECONSTRUCTIVE potential. However, it could be argued in a less postmodern vein that immigration legislation in the West constructs its own liminal space – the detention centre – which shores up rather than calls into question notions of national identity and otherness.
　　See BODY.

Logocentrism Coined by Jacques Derrida, the term refers to systems of thought which are dependent upon what Derrida calls the METAPHYSICS OF PRESENCE, defined as 'a belief in an extra-systemic validating presence or CENTRE which underwrites and fixes linguistic meaning but is itself beyond scrutiny or challenge' (Hawthorn 1992: 136).
　　See also PHALLOCENTRISM.

M

Marginalization An interdisciplinary term, 'marginalization' refers to the process whereby a subject or a sign is rendered marginal to the centre through the exercise of power. Within patriarchal cultures women, despite their numerical majority, are marginalized by a range of practices and discourses including employment law and academic disciplines. EQUAL RIGHTS forms of feminism tend to see EQUALITY in terms of 'bringing women in from the margins to the centre'. Feminisms emphasizing sexual difference, on the other hand, see the marginal status of woman-as-sign as subversive of the phallocentric Symbolic order and exploit the negative, deconstructive potential of femininity.

Marxism The body of social theory and political doctrine derived from the work of Karl Marx and his close collaborator, Friedrich Engels, but much beset by internal division and disagreement. Outhwaite and Bottomore (eds) (1993) summarize the various versions of Marxist and Soviet political doctrine, including some of the differences between the rationalizations of the politics and economic organization of the former socialist states and the diverse 'revisionist', more exploratory analyses which have come to be characterized as Western Marxism. These include elaborations of Marx's conceptual schema analysing capitalist society, as well as the HUMANIST, emancipatory writings of 'the young Marx' focusing on social consciousness.

Second-wave FEMINISM emerged at a time of lively revival in Marxist thought in European intellectual life, in the arts, literature and philosophy as well as in the social sciences. Influenced by the French STRUCTURALIST Louis Althusser and, to a lesser extent, the Italian Marxist Antonio Gramsci, feminist theory borrowed from Marxist theory to articulate its own emerging concerns, with mixed results. Particularly central was the focus on how to understand women's OPPRESSION within different MODES OF PRODUCTION; another example was the attempt to develop a feminist EPISTEMOLOGY, initially based on parallels between the STANDPOINT of WOMEN and the standpoint of the working class. However, feminist theory had ceased to assume 'socialism' as a goal before the demise of the socialist regimes in Eastern Europe, and other aspects of Marxism have tended to be superseded by concepts drawn from PSYCHOANALYSIS and POSTSTRUCTURALISM. But a political economy approach is still very evident in feminist approaches to, for example, work and employment, globalization and migration.

See also MARXIST FEMINISM; MATERIALIST FEMINISM.

Marxist feminism Marxism has a long history of commitment to the emancipation of women, but it brings women into the frame principally in the discussion of the FAMILY in its relationship to capitalist production (Coward 1983). Because Marx uses an abstract concept of labour, his labourers and the labours that they perform are not distinguished by sex. Marxism has no adequate conceptual tools for the understanding of specifically sexual OPPRESSION, of gender differentiation, or SEXUALITY. Marxist feminism therefore has necessarily been revisionist, attempting to achieve some kind of synthesis between Marxist theory and feminist accounts of sex/gender systems and sexuality.

The revisionist imperative may be seen in the writings of the generation of Marxist feminists who emerged in the early years of the twentieth century, particularly those of Alexandra Kollontai in Russia (1977), Clara Zetkin in Germany, and Emma Goldmann (1970), more properly described as an anarchist feminist, in the United States. They attempted to place issues which went beyond the PARADIGM of production, to place oppressive interpersonal behaviour in sexual relations and the family, and issues of domestic life generally, on the agendas of political manifestos of Marxist parties, theoretical analyses, and the policies of the Communist state in the new Soviet Union. Male colleagues, including Lenin, often looked askance at this work, and the Women's Section of the Party was dissolved later in the 1920s by Stalin.

It was principally Engels's *Origins of the Family, Private Property and the State* (Engels 1972) which provided both legitimation and a starting point for consideration of 'the woman question', as it was known. Feminists of the second wave over 40 years on, whose emerging intellectuals, especially in Europe, were deeply influenced by the revival of Marxism in the 1960s, likewise turned to Engels in the first instance (Sayers, Evans and Redclift [eds] 1987). Marxist feminism made major contributions to feminist theories of work and employment, the labour market, and DOMESTIC LABOUR. It exposed in the process some of the weaknesses of a theory of PRODUCTION which had not included the labour of REPRODUCTION and pressed for revisions which would permit Marxism to offer a more fully gendered theory of modern capitalist society (Barrett 1988; Lovell [ed.] 1990).

But the limits of the 'paradigm of production' (Nicholson 1987) were to become increasingly clear. While some struggled to construct a single unified but revised Marxism, drawing heavily on the concept of IDEOLOGY (Barrett 1988), others opted for a DUAL SYSTEMS approach, which left Marxism in place as the theory of MODES OF PRODUCTION, but looked towards other sources for a complementary theory of SEXUALITY.

Veronica Beechey (1979; 1988), among others, expressed reservations over this resolution, not least because sexuality and GENDER cannot be confined to a separate sphere, but pervade the whole social formation, including the world of production. Cynthia Cockburn's work on the print industry demonstrates with great clarity the need for a theory of sexuality and not just of production in the workplace as well as in the home (Cockburn 1983). The feminist critique of Marx's theory of production and the accounts of work which it fosters has been extended by Benhabib and Cornell (eds) (1987), Pateman (1988) and Adkins (1995). Like the lettering in Brighton rock, sexuality and its social structuring goes all the way through and is not confined to personal life inside and outside of families.

In the first instance dual systems theory turned to PSYCHOANALYSIS, especially in its Lacanian revisions, for its complementary theory of sexuality. (Mitchell 1974; Jacqueline Rose 1986; the journal *m/f* 1978–1986). The proposed synthesis faced complex problems of compatibility (Lovell 1980) and once Althusserian STRUCTURALISM had been superseded by POSTSTRUCTURALISM the fragile synthesis around the concept of ideology was openly or tacitly abandoned (Barrett 1991). Dual systems thinking, which had left the Marxist theory of production in place as one of the major players, was abandoned in favour of poststructuralist theories of SUBJECTIVITY. The collapse of communism in Europe from 1989 swept away a form of thought and politics which had already been deeply eroded by this shift from structuralism to poststructuralism.

Successor theories in which there are still 'traces left' include the work of feminists who have turned to Habermas and CRITICAL THEORY in preference to poststructuralism (Benhabib and Cornell [eds] 1987; Felski 1989a); those who have attempted to rework and rethink and reconstruct their socialist commitments from within the context of postmodernity and the collapse of 'actually existing socialisms' (Haraway 1991), and those using highly politicized forms of DECONSTRUCTION (Spivak 1987). Many who retain left commitments have chosen to work under the head of MATERIALIST FEMINISM (Hennessy 1993; Landry and MacLean 1993). The widespread triumphalist declaration of the death of Marxism and socialism is premature, and there is little doubt that we are likely to see a systematic reworking and reassessment of this heritage inside and outside of feminism, in the coming decades.

Masculinity   In Western culture 'man' is conflated with the UNIVERSAL ('mankind') and positioned as the producer of knowledge who is himself unexamined as a GENDER category. The explicit instruction in male culture typical of the new men's magazines may be evidence of a current crisis in masculinity, paralleling the growth of male GENRE fiction at the end of the nineteenth century (Showalter 1992).

The academic focus on men and masculinity has arisen partly as a response to feminism, but also reflects material changes in family composition and the long-term decline in the proportion of men in employment. Sectoral shift in male managerial and working-class employment, from factory, mines and engineering to the service sector, may also contribute to a sense of crisis in definitions of manliness (Roper 1994).

The first theoretical developments in the 1970s, in *Achilles Heel* and other men's movement/men's studies writing (for example Seidler [ed.] 1992; 1989), provided 'insider' subjective accounts of SELF, feeling and vulnerability, often expressing alienation from institutionalized heterosexuality but not heterosexuality as such and ignoring race and class differences (Robinson 1996). However, this focus on individual psychology has been succeeded by a welcome attention to the historical construction of male embodiment as part of the imperialist project, including especially analyses of the military BODY (McClintock 1995; Dawson 1994); torture (Scarry 1985; Theweleit 1993); hunting, games, and sports (Mangan and Walvin [eds] 1987) and the 'built body' (Dyer 1983), all images based on self-control and the denial of vulnerability. Often these explicitly link the construction of white male heterosexuality with the construction of subordinate OTHERS, especially colonized/enslaved men onto whom denied aspects of the self were projected (Chapman and Rutherford [eds] 1988; McClintock 1995; Sinha 1995). However, while within men's studies there is a growing body of analysis of men's involvement in aggressive relationships with each other, men's writing on issues like rape or domestic violence tend to be found outside men's studies, often produced by 'experts' who avoid looking at these issues in gendered terms. Studies of masculinity at work, which deploy the notion of a plurality of masculinities now typical of men's studies as a whole (Collinson and Hearn 1994; David Morgan 1992), focus on the privileges of hegemonic masculinities, as well as exploring the relationships between other class and racially specific forms.

For feminists the key question about theories of masculinity is whether they merely *explore* men's relationship to constructs of masculinity, or even presume that men are equally oppressed by gender STEREOTYPES, or whether they challenge male power and privilege: are these theories 'part of the problem or part of the solution?', asked Canaan and Griffin (1990). However, with the turn from women's studies to gender studies many feminists are contributing to the study of masculinity, in many cases overlapping in focus with men's studies. While the exploration of the contradictory and complex meanings of manhood typical of men's studies refuses the binary opposition between or homogeneity of either gender category, feminists are perhaps more likely to note the ways all men benefit from the valorizing of male CULTURE and privilege, even when they are not themselves participants (Cockburn 1991; Wajcman 1991). But both perspectives are increasingly making apparent the 'vulnerabilities' of the male body, rather than assuming its 'phallic majesty' (Bordo 1993: 697).

Masculinity complex Freud outlines three paths for female sexual development through the oedipal complex: normal FEMININITY, hysterical/neurotic femininity and the MASCULINITY complex where the girl refuses to give up her (phallic) IDENTIFICATION with the father and her desire for the mother (1931; 1933). For Freud, of course, every woman was first 'a little man' and, interestingly, he sees the 'normal' outcome as precarious at best. The term is frequently utilized in PSYCHOANALYTIC theories of female homosexuality. Freud's own 'The psychogenesis of a case of homosexuality in a woman' (1920) views masculine identification as the only trajectory for lesbian desire. Feminist revision of the concept has challenged its (hetero)sexism and normalizing effects, and interprets subjects affected by the complex as resisting oppressive ideologies of femininity which seek to deny their agency. Diane Hamer (1990), for example, argues that the concept can be helpful in theorizing lesbian, particularly 'butch', subject positions as a psychic repudiation of the cultural category 'WOMAN'.

Masochism It was the Austrian novelist Leopold von Sacher-Masoch (1835–95) who gave his name to this term. The masochistic protagonist of his best-known novel, *Venus in Furs*, was a man. Freud, however, contrasting the passive character of masochism to the active one of sadism, calls masochism the 'expression of the feminine essence', effectively aligning the former with FEMININITY and the latter with MASCULINITY. Feminist analyses of the relationship between femininity and masochism have criticized their identification and frequent conflation in patriarchal discursive systems. Kaja Silverman (1988) sees masochism as a central aspect of women's OPPRESSION within the SYMBOLIC ORDER; while Mary Ann Doane (1987) highlights woman's masochistic pleasure within the genre of the woman's film. Angela Carter's *The Sadeian Woman* (1979) represents a bold attempt to challenge the identification of woman with the passive masochism of victimhood. In Carter's reverse-discourse, the masochistic woman of the Sadeian imaginary exerts a sexual and psychic power denied her in the pallid constructions of bourgeois feminine IDEOLOGY.

Masquerade   In an article entitled 'Womanliness as a Masquerade' (1929), the Kleinian psychoanalyst Joan Riviere argues that in a patriarchal society 'womanliness' or femininity is a mask worn by women in order to satisfy the desires of men. The masquerade represents the woman's PERFORMANCE of herself as the man would have her. For Riviere, the masquerade is often a psychological defence against unconscious 'MASCULINITY' (phantasized as the possession of the penis for which the woman fears she will be punished). In psychoanalytic terms, the masquerade is a means of reducing the anxiety engendered by the phantasized paternal retribution. Lacan describes a masculine equivalent in the male 'parade' or display, through which male phallic IDENTITY is displayed in a variety of symbolic fashions.

   In her POSTMODERNIST critique of PSYCHOANALYSIS, Judith Butler (1991) advocates a 'parodic politics of the masquerade' which, through its deployment of MIMICRY, stages gender as a performance and reveals the constructedness of all identity.

Mass culture   See CULTURE; MASS MEDIA; CULTURAL STUDIES; WOMEN'S CULTURE.

Mass media   The term refers to large-scale commodity production of CULTURE, using modern technologies, from the printing press in fifteenth-century Europe to twentieth-century film and television.

   The concept of 'the masses', so salient in twentieth century social theory, has not been prominent in feminist theory, perhaps because it is a de-differentiating concept which does not lend itself very readily to gender analysis. It has its roots in Tocqueville's critique of democracy. In the wake of the rise of fascism it was drawn upon by the Marxists of the Frankfurt School (cf. CRITICAL THEORY) to explain totalitarianism (Adorno *et al.* 1950; Arendt 1958). In the 1950s and 1960s, mass society theory circulated widely in US social and political theory. Modern mass society was theorized as one in which traditional forms of sociality in CLASS, religious and local COMMUNITIES had given way to a structure of bureaucratized élites and atomized masses whose lateral ties to one another had been critically weakened.

The mass media, however, has attracted feminist research (Baehr and Dyer 1987; Lont 1995; Modleski 1986; Van Zoonen 1993). In Britain mass media/culture theory was challenged in the 1960s by approaches which substituted the concept of class-based IDEOLOGIES for the homogenizing concept of 'the masses' (Swingewood 1977). This work included the study of YOUTH CULTURE and of the 'political economy' of the media (Golding 1974; Glasgow Media Group 1977 and 1980). It was the former that inspired feminist work on the media. Feminism has generated a rich body of close textual analysis of gender in REPRESENTATION, rather less on READERS, audiences and SPECTATORSHIP (Ang 1985; Pribram 1988; Radway 1984; Jackie Stacey 1994b).

Frankfurt Marxism (cf. CRITICAL THEORY) from the 1930s generated a distinctive theory of the mass media which has been criticized for its cultural pessimism concerning 'the culture industry'. At the opposite end of the spectrum we find at the turn of the 1950s the rise to prominence of Marshall McLuhan's theory of modern COMMUNICATIONS (1964), famous for his concept of a revolution in electronic communications which was turning the world into a 'global village'. This development finds an echo in certain forms of POSTMODERNIST feminism, for example the work of Donna Haraway (1991).

See also CYBORGS.

Mass society See MASS MEDIA.

Master discourse/narrative In *The Postmodern Condition* (1979), Jean-François Lyotard argues that the *grands récits* or master narratives of the Western philosophical tradition have lost their moral grounds or legitimation. According to Lyotard, the ENLIGHTENMENT project of reason, progress and human liberation has ended in social and political disaster, as evidenced by the Holocaust, nuclear warfare and ecological crisis.

An important aspect of the POSTMODERN critique of MODERNITY is the decentring of the traditional Enlightenment SUBJECT who is of course white, bourgeois and male. His claims to universality and neutrality have been exposed as the particular and partial perspectives of a ruling group. For feminists the possibilities for discrediting the master narratives of gender in the space opened up by postmodernism are welcome, but postmodern discourses do not automatically align with feminism and they, like the discredited master narratives, have had to be gendered by feminists. Moreover, postmodernity has by no means heralded the actual collapse of patriarchal grand narratives. In the BACKLASH against feminisms that took place in the political and cultural realms in the 1980s, master discourses are showing no signs of loosening their hold over the collective IMAGINARY.

Materialist feminism   'Philosophical materialism is the view that all that exists is material or is wholly dependent upon matter for its existence' (Urmson and Rée 1989: 194).

Materialism in feminist theory has taken several forms, including MARXIST FEMINISM and French materialist feminism which was a synthesis of Marxist with RADICAL FEMINISM. A third, emergent, form, which owes much to POSTSTRUCTURALISM with its systematic refusal of mind/BODY dualism, locates the material not in the social forces and relations of PRODUCTION, but in the sexed human body and its exigencies.

Marx's social theory takes as its starting point the material needs of human beings for subsistence, and the labour required to transform historically given forces of production into the means of subsistence, an active, practical, and sensuous social activity which takes place within specific social relations of production.

Marxist materialism is not a materialism of the body, but of the labour of human production. The labour in question is abstract, and this has invited sharp criticism (Adkins 1995; Pateman 1988). It is specified in terms of the primacy of economic production. There are occasional exceptions, most notably the work of Sebastian Timpararo which addresses physical aspects of human existence such as mortality and ill-health (1975). But in general child birth and the exigencies of physical REPRODUCTION are rarely given much attention within the Marxist tradition of thought:

> The maintenance and reproduction of the working class is, and must ever be, a necessary condition of the reproduction of capital. But the capitalist may safely leave its fulfilment to the labourer's instincts of self-preservation and of propagation (Marx 1970: 572).

Many Marxist feminists attempted to make good these limitations by conjoining Marx's theory of capitalist production with Freudian, especially Lacanian, PSYCHOANALYSIS, in what was termed a DUAL SYSTEMS approach (Mitchell 1974).

French materialist feminism prefers to expand the Marxian concept of the material to include the physical world of sexed human bodies, in a synthesis not with Freud but with radical feminist theories of SEXUALITY (Leonard and Adkins [eds] 1996). The paradigm of production is retained, but extended, so that all human activity, including for example, breast-feeding, is understood as labour (Tabet 1987). The concept of CLASS is likewise extended to include sexual classes: men and women figure as distinct social groupings bound together in antagonistic social relationships of gender which have a material basis. Gender is defined as a specific economic relation in which men and women are located in relations of production which are not, however, capitalist processes (Delphy 1984).

Materialist feminist reasoning of this kind informed the wages for housework collective (Dalla Costa and James 1975; see DOMESTIC LABOUR). Those who identified as Marxist feminists mostly distanced themselves from this form of feminist materialism, arguing that men and women did not constitute distinct social classes in Marxist terms. But the two materialisms are occasionally bridged to powerful effect, for example in Cynthia Cockburn's analysis of 'the material of male power' in the print industry (Cockburn 1983), and the current resurgence of interest in the physical body often reprises (without referencing) French feminist materialism.

French materialist feminism has made sexuality central rather than simply adding it on, but with recourse to radical feminist theories of COMPULSORY HETEROSEXUALITY rather than to psychoanalysis. Monique Wittig (1992) developed a highly influential materialist critique of heterosexuality.

The third use of the term is associated with yet another synthesis, this time between SOCIALIST FEMINISMS (including Marxist variants) and POSTSTRUCTURALISM. This approach shares its concern with the material body with French materialist feminism, but rejects both the dualism of mind/body, and also that of material/cultural. It is associated with the CULTURAL MATERIALISM developed principally by Raymond Williams (Williams 1977a; 1980b) which draws on Marxist cultural theory and on the theories of language of Vygotsky and Volosinov rather than French theories of languge which inform poststructuralism (Hennessy 1993; Landry and MacLean 1993).

Maternal body   Redeeming the maternal body from its degraded or invisible status in PATRIARCHAL culture has been an important aspect of many feminisms of the second wave. CULTURAL FEMINISM, in particular, celebrates motherhood, promulgating positive images of the maternal BODY. As generations of feminists have pointed out, Freudian PSYCHOANALYSIS largely ignores the figure of the mother. Freud sees her as 'castrated' and focuses almost exclusively on the father's role in the oedipus complex. It has been left to women analysts and feminists to theorize the place of the mother. Melanie Klein focuses on the early parent–child relation, particularly the child's fantasies about the mother's body. According to Klein, the child feels both love and hate for the mother, fantasizing her alternately as a good and bad mother; and she sees the symbolic loss of the mother as a primary event in the child's life. Nancy Chodorow's (1978) OBJECT RELATIONS theory focuses on the cultural aspects of mother/child relations, highlighting girls' difficulty in separating from their mothers. The work of Julia Kristeva is centrally concerned with the symbolic meanings of the maternal body: her theory of ABJECTION explores its degraded status in the SYMBOLIC order; her theory of the SEMIOTIC locates its repressed traces in language; and her essay 'Stabat Mater' (1986) analyses representations of maternity in the cult of the Virgin

Mary. Kristeva's concept of the 'archaic mother' refers to the myth of a pre-symbolic, all powerful mother figure. The maternal body is a powerful metaphor in both women's writing and literary criticism. Marianne Hirsch (1989) explores the centrality of the mother/daughter plot in women's narrative and Elizabeth Abel (1989) interrogates the text for its repression of the pre-oedipal moment. The work of many FRENCH and ITALIAN FEMINISTS also explores the poetics of the maternal body.

Men's studies See MASCULINITY.

Mestiza See CHICANA THEORY.

Metanarrative In literary criticism a metanarrative, according to Hawthorn, can be 'either a narrative which talks about other, embedded narratives, or a narrative which refers to itself and to its own narrative procedures' (1992: 148). Related to the concepts of metalanguage – 'a language about a language' – and metafiction – literally, fiction about fiction – metanarratives have played an important role in feminist critiques of patriarchal discursive systems. For example, the rewriting of fairy tales by feminist writers such as Angela Carter, Suniti Namjoshi and Emma Tennant using metanarrative strategies challenges the traditional IDEOLOGIES and power relations embedded in such narratives.

Metaphor/metonymy Literary criticism distinguishes between two basic kinds of figurative LANGUAGE. In metaphor one thing is referred to by a word which usually denotes something else but to which it is similar. For example, in the phrase 'her cherry lips', the woman's lips are being likened to cherries on the basis of a shared colour and sweetness. In metonymy terms are linked by association or contiguity rather than by similarity. For example, the sexist phrase 'a bit of skirt' invokes a metonymic connection between a piece of women's clothing and a (sexually desirable) woman. Roman Jakobson sees metaphor and metonymy as two distinct modes which correspond respectively to Saussure's distinction between the selection and combination axes of language. He also relates them to literary movements: Romanticism ostensibly foregrounds the metaphoric mode, whereas REALISM privileges the metonymic. The distinction also has a PSYCHOANALYTIC resonance. It can be related to Freud's concepts of condensation and DISPLACEMENT, the two fundamental operations of the dream-work. For Lacan the phallus metaphorically signifies the LACK or absence which circulates in the SYMBOLIC order and mobilizes desire along a metonymic chain. Metaphor is therefore associated with being and metonymy with non-being. Such terms are not without important and complex gender connotations. Dorothy Dinnerstein (1977) identifies the cultural associations of sexual reproduction whereby women's maternal relation to the child is seen as a metonymic one of association and contiguity, while the father's can only be metaphorically inferred. She views both the cultural privileging of metaphor and the denigration of maternity as men's response to women's more palpable relation to REPRODUCTION. And, returning to the context of linguistics, women's and men's speech has been distinguished in terms of its privileging of metonymic or metaphoric modes. Somewhat contradictorily, women's speech has been accused of being predominantly metonymic and paratactic (emphasizing connections through the use of 'and') and of being elaborate and 'flowery', i.e. abounding in metaphor!

Metaphysics of presence   A term used by Derrida to refer to the character of Western philosophy in which the metaphysical concepts of 'presence' and 'centre' are used to guarantee the grounds of epistemology. Derridean DECONSTRUCTION demonstrated how, in language-based systems, meaning is rather a product of absence and *DIFFÉRANCE* (both difference and deferral). FRENCH FEMINISM is centrally concerned with the critique of metaphysics in the discourses of phallogocentrism.

See also LOGOCENTRISM; OTHER.

Methodology   A useful starting point is Harding's identification of three distinct definitions or aspects of methodology (Harding 1987). *Method* is the narrowest and most concrete level, referring to ways of acquiring information: listening to or interrogating informants, observing behaviour, examining historical traces and records. Here the tendency for feminist sociologists to privilege qualitative methods, especially participant observation, is beginning to give way to a more strategic approach to method. Not only has the ethnographer's status itself been problematized, feminists recognize that quantitative research using large datasets is useful for demonstrating causal relationships and also sometimes makes for a stronger political impact (Phizacklea and Wolkowitz 1995; Maynard 1994b).

Harding's second level is *methodology*, the theory and analysis of how research should proceed. Here reflexivity has emerged as the central concept, referring to researchers' explicit recognition of their involvement as women in the social world they study, and, less frequently noted, their relationships with others in their DISCIPLINE and with their potential AUDIENCE.

For the third aspect of methodology identified by Harding, see EPISTEMOLOGY.

Debate about what is now seen as the prescriptiveness of the first formulations of feminist research methodology focuses on three areas: relationships between women; the relationship between the methodologies of different disciplines; and the relationship between feminist and non-feminist research practice.

In their focus on relationships between women, feminist researchers have seen (or hoped for) the transformative power of research, but at the same time are deeply troubled by issues of DIFFERENCE, POWER, and privilege as between the researcher and the researched, especially but not only when differences of

'RACE' or CLASS are involved. In particular feminists worry that a clash between research objectives and feminist ethics is inevitable; for instance, the friendly woman-to-woman rapport participant observers want to establish may simply deceive women informants into revealing more about themselves than do more conventional, bounded interviews (Finch 1984; Stacey 1991). Recently added to this debate are questions about how these issues are experienced by feminist research students, for whom the usual assumption that the researcher is more powerful than her informants is much less often the case. Moreover, students are often eager to implement what they see as feminist research practices, but are frustrated because as students they lack the time, resources and/or authority to explore them.

Secondly, methodology seems not to travel across disciplines as easily as theory, perhaps because in the humanities methodology is equated with social scientific methods – i.e. the first of the meanings discussed above. Nonetheless, there are strong similarities between developments in different fields, particularly at the level of epistemology, where the assumptions in both STANDPOINT and GYNOCRITICISM about the existence of a distinct women's perspective are readily apparent. In other cases however similarities of approach owe as much to debates over POSTSTRUCTURALIST challenges to knowledge claims as to feminist scholarship.

Ideas about differences between feminist and non-feminist methodologies are still much debated. In sociology feminist critiques of OBJECTIVE, uninvolved mainstream research methodology are sometimes exaggerated, for British sociology has been deeply influenced by the critique of positivism launched by interpretative sociology (of which feminist sociology was part). However, the resemblance between feminist and non-feminist methodologies may be only superficial; as Mascia-Lees states in relation to critics of ethnographic authority, whereas many critics speak for the 'other', 'feminists speak from the position of the "other"' (1989: 11, cited by Diane Bell 1993: 1).

Micropolitics See POWER.

Middle range theory See THEORY.

Migration Migration is usually defined as the movement of people across recognized political or administrative frontiers for the purpose of or in the process of settlement. In recent years both mainstream and feminist social theory have focused on the political economy of migration, relating the causes of migration to economic and political structures in both 'sending' and 'receiving' nations (Cohen 1987). The resistance to now dated notions of assimilation, integration and segregation which dominated the field in the 1960s, however, has meant that questions about migrants' SUBJECTIVITY have been neglected; in this lacuna the concepts related to MIGRATORY SUBJECTIVITY – the exile, the NOMAD – are now more often adopted as a metaphors for the condition of women generally than used to conceptualize women's experience of actual migration (Braidotti 1992).

Women's involvement in migration has a long history. Within Europe and elsewhere industrialization has characteristically involved widespread migration from rural areas to urbanizing centres of economic growth. Women comprised at least a third of the 'forced migrants' slave traders shipped from Africa to the New World; they were incorporated in the 'coolie' labour force in the East Indies (Potts 1990); and they formed a large part of late nineteenth- and early twentieth-century resettlement in America. Even the migration of women to work as prostitutes has a history in the emigration of English, Eastern European and Jewish women to brothels servicing British soldiers in India in the late nineteenth century (Ballhatchet 1980). However, post-1945 migrants face a distinctive situation because the range and intensity of political restrictions migrants face have increased.

Migration clearly involves what are called 'push/pull' factors: not simply voluntaristic decisions made by individuals but structural features of the sending and receiving economies. Push/pull factors have been given a new inflection by feminist analysts focusing on the ways in which structural change affects women. The UNDERDEVELOPMENT of large portions of the Third World which distorted economies often undermined women's traditional employment in family-based agriculture, crafts and marketing more than men's (Phizacklea 1996), while a newly noticed category of 'ecological migrants' (Ekins 1992: 21) have been produced by 'successful' development projects which have destroyed the natural environments on which women's livelihood depended. Whereas some women have migrated as independent workers (for instance Afro-Caribbean women migrating to Britain in the 1950s and early 1960s), others are defined as family dependants whose limited rights of settlement constrain their employment to hidden sectors of employment like HOMEWORKING (Phizacklea 1983; 1990; Phizacklea and Wolkowitz 1995). The proportion of women among those migrating as professional workers within the European Union is minute.

More recently attention has focused on the laws of both sending and receiving countries which specify, for instance, the differential rights of entry and settlement to men and women or which have criminalized work like prostitution (Aoyama 1995) or which are restricting the settlement and employment rights of refugees. Finally, the important structural features affecting women's migration include the SEXUAL POLITICS of sending and receiving countries, including flight from sexual violence, forced marriage and clitoridectomy and demand in the affluent societies for 'mail order brides', prostitutes and domestic workers (Bridget Anderson 1993; Heyzer *et al.* 1994; Phizacklea 1996).

Migratory subjectivities A concept which has little in common with theories of MIGRATION. POSTSTRUCTURALIST and POST-COLONIAL theories purport to examine the effects of migration on the construction of subjectivity, but in reality have little to do with the actual movements of people. Bhabha (1994) argues that the migrant SUBJECT is constituted by a cultural indeterminacy and HYBRIDITY which unsettles fixed notions of IDENTITY and reveals in an exemplary fashion the DIFFERENCE that lies at the heart of identity. Theories of NOMADISM posit subjects who are not necessarily migrants but whose identities are constituted around the notions of mobility and unsettledness; their travels involve the traversing of social spaces and structures of practice (see Braidotti 1994b).

A number of related feminist theories challenge unitary concepts of identity, representing subjectivity as mobile, multiple and migratory; examples include Trinh Minh-Ha's (1990) notion of consciousness as a movement, involving departure and 're-departure'; Lata Mani's (1992) concept of 'multiple articulations' of identity; and Gloria Anzaldúa's (1987) notion of 'borderlands'. Boyce Davies (1994) emphasizes the importance of multiply-articulated approaches to theorizing subjectivity and identity, arguing that the experience of Black women, in particular, lends itself to the notion of fluid, multiple identities. She adopts Zora Neale Hurston's concept of 'going a piece of the way' as a suitable journey metaphor for Black women's critical relations to diverse modes of knowing, suggesting both ARTICULATION and mobility.

Mimicry   In the work of Luce Irigaray, mimicry represents a counter-HEGEMONIC strategy for dealing with the masculinist SYMBOLIC realm of DISCOURSE, whereby the woman parodies the feminine style assigned to her in order to uncover the mechanisms by which it exploits her.

See also MASQUERADE; POST-COLONIAL THEORY.

Mirror phase   A central concept in Lacanian PSYCHOANALYSIS which refers to a formative stage in child development from within the IMAGINARY phase when the child is symbiotically connected to the mother's body and does not perceive itself as an entity as such. During the mirror stage the child begins to experience its body as discrete and projects an image of itself as unified. Crucial to Lacan's account, however, is the idea that the mirror stage represents a MISRECOGNITION of SELF; in other words the sense of wholeness and plenitude it bestows is a fantasy defining the lack inherent in our actual identities which are decentred upon entry into the SYMBOLIC order of LANGUAGE and DIFFERENCE.

For feminists the mirror episode represents the acquisition of FEMININITY whereby the image of the feminine woman is mirrored back to the emerging female subject. Feminist literary critics have shown that women's writing is rich in mirror imagery which they interpret as an allegory of mother–daughter relations, or relations between women generally, and as an expression of pre-oedipal SEXUALITY (Gilbert and Gubar 1979). Gill Frith (1991) identifies the mirror ritual as a common motif in British women's fiction, but argues that it does not coincide with the Lacanian model so much as it represents a form of exchange between women in which what takes place is a kind of DOUBLING with a difference that recalls Irigaray's concept of the 'two lips' of the female IMAGINARY.

Misogyny   The fear or hatred of women. Despite Greer's bald claim in *The Female Eunuch* (1971) that 'women have very little idea of how much men hate them', the term is unfashionable in contemporary feminist theory and has given way in second-wave feminism to the concepts of SEXISM and PHALLOCENTRISM. However, some feminists continue to locate women's subordination in male misogyny (e.g. Dworkin 1981) and the term continues to have a popular resonance, as indicated by the success of Joan Smith's book *Misogynies* (1989). Smith argues that woman-hating is extraordinarily pervasive in contemporary Western culture, locating it in biological determinist IDEOLOGIES.

Psychoanalytic theories suggest that misogyny structures certain popular cultural narratives, and even seemingly positive representations of women can be seen to contain a misogynist subtext. One recent example is the film *Aliens* which pits Sigourney Weaver against a monstrous maternal figure.

See also MONSTROUS FEMININE.

Misrecognition   In Lacanian theory misrecognition refers to the process of IDENTITY formation which takes place during the MIRROR PHASE when the child fantasizes its integrity as an entity or 'SELF', 'misrecognizing' itself as a unified being. Louis Althusser employs a similar concept. Human beings become (IMAGINARY) SUBJECTS in the process of being hailed or INTERPELLATED by an ideology. In this misrecognition we actively produce our own subjection.

For Althusser, following Lacan, all consciousness or lived EXPERIENCE belongs to the realm of ideology and produces KNOWLEDGE neither of the self nor of the social world. Knowledge is the product of specialized, theory-dependent practices which are scientific and which owe nothing to the knowing subject or his or her experience.

Bourdieu's use of the concept, like Althussser's, is located on the terrain which had been occupied by the Marxist concepts of false consciousnes and IDEOLOGY. But he rejects the concept of ideology because of its emphasis on consciousness, albeit false. Misrecognition and recognition for Bourdieu belong neither to consciousness nor to the UNCONSCIOUS, but to PRACTICE: to the realm of what he terms symbolic domination in which the hierarchies validated by a 'sacralized' CULTURE are embedded in the very bodily HEXIS and HABITUS or dispositions of the dominated (Bourdieu 1984a; 1990a). It is a recognition/misrecognition not so much of the self as of the place of the self in a hierarchical world whose values are acknowledged even where they are judged to be 'not for the likes of us'. An example in feminist cultural analysis would be the common finding (Hobson 1982) of a disparity between what women defer to as 'more important' and what they themselves participate in and enjoy.

See also DISTINCTION; SYMBOLIC VIOLENCE.

Mode of production   Althusserian readings of Marx in the 1960s and 1970s challenged orthodox MARXIST theories of IDEOLOGY and CULTURE as mere superstructure of material production. Althusser conceptualized the underlying structure of contemporary Western social formations in terms of Marx's concept of the capitalist MODE OF PRODUCTION, but one in which three levels played a crucial role in the REPRODUCTION of the whole. Each of the three levels – the economic, the political and the ideological – was to be seen as RELATIVELY AUTONOMOUS; the economic was determinate only 'in the last instance' and did not and could not directly shape the myriad developments in state policy or cultural artefacts. Althusser's formulation was extremely influential in shaping new departures in political theory, CULTURAL STUDIES, and anthropological studies of kinship systems. Feminist attempts to theorize women's position took the capitalist mode of production as their starting point, seeing the FAMILY and women's subordination as an aspect of the ideological level or, in DUAL SYSTEMS theory, as a separate intersecting PATRIARCHAL system. However, the rarified level of ahistorical abstraction, absence of subjects and the mechanical nature of the 'system' in the Althusserian development of the concept came to be much criticized; E. P. Thompson (1978) famously compared Althusser's mode of production to an orrery, an early eighteenth-century clockwork mechanism representing the planets revolving around the sun.

See also MARXIST FEMINISM; INTERPELLATION.

Modernism   A contested category which has dominated the writing of twentieth-century literary history. With the emergence of second-wave feminism critics began to point out the exclusion of women from accounts of modernism, to rediscover 'lost' women modernists and to revise interpretation of the work of others. Central to the revisionist project is Jane Marcus's pioneering work on Virginia Woolf (1981; 1983). The rehabilitation of other women modernists, such as H.D., Katherine Mansfield and Gertrude Stein, whose work is increasingly seen as constitutive of modernism – has taken longer. For some – such as Dorothy Richardson – the process of reappraisal and due acknowledgement has barely begun. Key feminist revisions of modernism include Benstock (1987); Gilbert and Gubar (1988); Hanscombe and Smyers (1987) and Bonnie Kime Scott (ed.) (1990). Such accounts demonstrate how important women were to the modernist enterprise not only as writers, but also as publishers, patrons, editors, translators etc. They point to the existence of significant networks and COMMUNITIES OF WOMEN modernists which are now in the process of being uncovered and documented.

A key question concerns whether or not women practised a modernism qualitatively different to that practised by men. The affirmative answer given by many women modernists themselves has greatly influenced the debate: Virginia Woolf and Dorothy Richardson, for example, argue strongly for the specificity of female modernism. Both view features such as NARRATIVE fluidity and elasticity, achronology and lack of plotting as quintessentially 'feminine'. However, these features can also be observed in the work of male modernists such as Joyce and Mallarmé. Indeed, FRENCH FEMINISTS have argued that it is not the gender of the writer but rather the 'writing effect' of such aesthetic practices that determines the ostensible 'femininity' of the modernist text. Their work overlaps in significant ways with the POSTMODERNIST construction of modernism. Peter Brooker argues that modernism and postmodernism stand in a relation of reciprocal definition, and that while 'postmodernism has functioned to further undefine [modernism's] supposed unitary identity [it has often collaborated] in the construction of that very identity as fit only for DECONSTRUCTION' ([ed.] 1992: 3).

Postmodernism causes confusion not only by the appropriation of literary modernism to itself, but also by its use of the term in an EPISTEMOLOGICAL sense. All pre-postmodern epistemologies tend to be enveloped together under the label of 'modernism', from realism to scientific positivism to Marxism. Given the fact that in literary usage 'modernism' is *contrasted* with nineteenth-century realism and naturalism, this redefinition of the terms allows important distinctions to be elided.

Modernity The widespread perception of living in a new, modern form of society dates from seventeenth-century early modern Europe. 'Modernity' carries connotations of scientific rationality, progress, freedom of the INDIVIDUAL, and the political institutions of emergent nation states. Above all, modernity designates a state of mind, a commitment to the new: 'Its pull is constantly towards the future' (Outhwaite and Bottomore [eds] 1993: 392).

Modernity is therefore necessarily unfixed in time, or rather, fixed in the present, constantly superseded.

Modernity is deeply implicated in ENLIGHTENMENT RATIONALITY, which has come under intense critical and philosophical scrutiny in POSTSTRUCTURALIST and POSTMODERNIST theory. Feminism, in its EQUAL RIGHTS form, is a child of the Enlightenment, as is MARXISM. However, in feminist critiques of Enlightenment rationality, the projects of liberal 'equal rights' feminism and Marxist and socialist feminisms are not always very carefully differentiated (Cocks 1989).

Feminist critiques of Enlightenment rationality are to be found in feminist STANDPOINT EPISTEMOLOGY in both neo-Marxist (Harding 1990; Hartsock 1983) and RADICAL FEMINIST forms. British (Stanley and Wise 1983) and French (Cixous 1976a; Irigaray 1974) and many feminist poststructuralist exegeses now begin with the DECONSTRUCTION of Enlightenment rationality and its binary habits of thought.

Modernity has its feminist defenders (Felski 1989a; Lovibond 1989; Soper 1989). Felski argues for an understanding of modernity as ambivalent, 'simultaneously dialogic and contestatory' (1989a: 47). While the wholehearted embrace of the modernist promise of progress is cautioned against, she argues that 'feminism is itself profoundly implicated in and indebted to rapid transformations of intellectual and social life endemic to modernity' (1989a: 49). A cautious reappraisal of the Enlightenment project is under way, and a carefully qualified UNIVERSALISM is defended:

> Those who argue...that the core of present conceptions of justice and equality needs to be retained as the condition of future emancipation...have the interests of the vast majority of women more closely at heart than those holding out the promise of a utopia of multiplying difference (Soper 1989: 111).

See also MODERNIZATION.

Modernization   The term 'modernization' was originally associated with Weberian as against Marxist approaches to social transformation. It was associated with breathtaking Western ethnocentrism and neo-evolutionary assumptions. Until recently it was considered almost completely discredited. As Jeffrey Alexander comments,

> Sometime in the mid 1960s, between the assassination of President Kennedy and the San Francisco 'summer of love' of 1967, modernization theory died... because the younger generation of intellectuals could not believe it was true (1975a: 75-6).

However, Alexander argues, in reaction to dramatic changes and heroic visions in Eastern Europe and South Africa post-postmodernist theorizing is now sometimes taking the form of what he calls neo-modernity theory. Its key foci are the emancipatory possibilities of CIVIL SOCIETY, democracy, UNIVERSALISM and market rationality and, in place of tradition, it demonizes NATIONALISM as its OTHER. Examples of neo-modernity theory are the various versions of the concept of reflexive modernization, which see late modernity typified by an increasing awareness of and orientation of action around perceptions of risk (Beck 1992); the projection of self through elaborate bodily regimes and non-traditional forms of personal relationships (Giddens 1990); or the redirection of economic life around the production and consumption of aesthetic signs (Lash and Urry 1994).

In so far as Western feminism centres on examining women's own PRACTICES and POLITICS, recreating them anew, it is undoubtedly itself part of the heightened reflexivity spotlighted by some neo-modernity theorists. But this is not the whole story. Although in its earlier guise modernization theory was influential among those feminists seeking to integrate women *into* DEVELOPMENT, its main postulates were rejected in favour of theories of

UNDERDEVELOPMENT. Indeed the relatively adverse impact of global integration for women constitutes an important critique of neo-modernity theories, as does the development of what are in effect the '*male* democracies' (Molyneux 1995) of Eastern Europe and the ambiguous relationship between gender and civil society more generally. 'Neo-modernity' theorists also fail to notice that market rationality does not usually permeate institutions like the FAMILY (when it does enter family decision-making it often perpetuates women's disadvantages) or that universalist values often implicitly apply only or mainly to men. This general failure to integrate either women's experiences or feminist insight is evident in Alexander's own account of reactions to what he sees as the failure of the NEW SOCIAL MOVEMENTS of the 1960s and 1970s, which takes no notice of later feminist activity or of feminists' less than whole-hearted acceptance of the POSTMODERNISM he sees as totally dominating 1980s social thought.

See also MODERNITY; UNDERDEVELOPMENT.

Monstrous feminine   In Bakhtin's (1984) work the term refers to the image of the repulsively fecund mother-figure whose generative powers inspire horror.

See also ABJECT; GROTESQUE; MATERNAL BODY.

Moral reasoning   Freud notoriously 'explained' women's alleged lesser sense of justice in terms of their weaker super-egos. For girls, the internalized Law of the Father is less imperiously demanding.

In the history of cultural constructions of gender, women have often had their moral integrity thus traduced. In the legal system of Pakistan at present, it takes the evidence of two women to counter that of a man. In Britain and elsewhere, women's evidence may be doubted in certain cases on the grounds of their sex, as in the notorious comment made by Judge Sutcliffe in a rape case, that 'It is well known that women in particular and small boys are liable to be untruthful and invent stories' (cited in Smart 1989: 35).

A second rather contradictory theme runs in tandem, that of women's essential moral superiority, and feminists have sometimes attempted to capitalize on this, for example in the campaign for the repeal of the Contagious Diseases Acts in the second half of the nineteenth century (Walkowitz 1980) and in the moral purity movements of the close of the century (Bristow 1977). Something of the same logic is invoked in the special claims made for women in relationship to environmentalism (care for the earth), the peace movement (life-enhancing, nurturant), and animal rights (care for all living creatures).

Claims that women's moral sense differs from that of men are found in feminisms of DIFFERENCE. Carol Gilligan identifies two types of moral reasoning, only one of which gains widespread recognition, that based on an ethic of justice and rights. The other, an ethic of care or responsibility for others is, she argues, usually more highly developed in women, whose moral judgements tend to be more contextual and particularistic, concerned less with abstract judgements of right than with the assessment of the consequences of any given action for the fabric of relationships and responsibilities in which the actor is enmeshed.

The 'justice' perspective focuses upon abstract or 'generalized' OTHERS, the 'care' perspective on 'concrete' or 'particular others' (Benhabib 1987). While critical of aspects of OBJECT RELATIONS theory, Gilligan draws upon this approach, particularly the work of Nancy Chodorow and the account it offers of the differential relationship which mothers have with same-sex and different-sex babies.

Gilligan's work has been immensely influential in the resurgence of feminist moral theory, and has occasioned extensive debate (Kittay and Meyers [eds] 1987; Porter 1991). She has been criticized for over-generalizing, and for paying insufficient attention to the manner in which RACE and CLASS intersect with GENDER differences (Spelman 1990). Sandra Harding (in Kittay and Meyers [eds] 1987) has drawn attention to the striking similarities between Gilligan's characterization of women's moral reasoning and claims which have been advanced concerning African morality and law, which suggests that if indeed there are two types of moral reasoning, they are not aligned in any simple way with gender differences.

From a very different theoretical perspective Luce Irigaray has called for 'a revolution in thought and ethics' (Irigaray 1991: 166; 1993) which would be thought through in terms of sexual difference, or MORPHOLOGY, rather than equality. This strand of feminist moral theory informs feminist contributions to bioethics, or the ethics of intervention on and transformations of the human BODY.

See also ECOFEMINISM; NEW SOCIAL MOVEMENTS.

Morphology Luce Irigaray uses the term, in preference to 'anatomy' or 'biology', to describe the connection of the BODY of woman to her DISCOURSE and her IMAGINARY. As the sign *morphe* – 'form/figure' – suggests, the term functions on literal and metaphorical levels simultaneously. Unlike the other terms, it implies a 'shape' or 'form' rather than an ESSENCE, and therefore better captures the non-reductive sense of her deployment of feminine DIFFERENCE. For 'corporeal feminists' morphology displaces the problematic feminist distinction between SEX and GENDER by deconstructing the binary opposition between the material and the non-material (see Grosz 1994).

Myth Myth may be understood as history – the imagined past of a CULTURE, as in myths of origin; and as charter (the setting up of binding values of the COMMUNITY/culture) (Larrington [ed.] 1992). In one sense the project of FEMINISM throughout its history has been to dispel what have come to be known as PATRIARCHAL myths about woman. Ever since Wollstonecraft's critique of Rousseau's Sophie, feminists have been concerned to reveal the IDEOLOGICAL and political motivations for symbolic REPRESENTATIONS of FEMININITY. Feminist writing of all kinds has a strongly demythologizing emphasis: feminist linguistics challenges assumptions about women's speech; feminist anthropology examines the myths about sexual difference which structure not only human CULTURES but also (men's) accounts of them; much contemporary feminist fiction deconstructs patriarchal myths and/or reworks them in woman-friendly ways; and feminist literary critics challenge the myths which inform male-stream theories of reading and writing. Maggie Humm (1994) discusses myth criticism as a significant strand within feminist literary theory. Her delineation of the category strongly resembles what Hawthorn (1992) calls archetypal criticism. She identifies Mary Daly (1991), Adrienne Rich (1977) and Annis Pratt (1982) as key myth critics. In addition to the DECONSTRUCTION of patriarchal myth, feminists such as Rich and Daly have also been concerned with the construction of alternative feminist myths or 'stories of origin'. GYNOCRITICISM seeks to identify those myths and motifs which are specific to women's writing. Gilbert and Gubar (1979), for example, identify the 'madwoman in the attic' as a central motif in nineteenth-century women's writing. Marina Warner has analysed fairy-tales from a myth-critical feminist perspective (1995).

N

Narcissism   In the Greek myth Narcissus fell in love with his own image. Freud adopts the myth to refer to self-obsessive psychosis and the 'pathology' of homosexual object-choice. He distinguishes between primary narcissism, in which the child's libido is focused entirely on itself, and secondary narcissism, where libido is disinvested in others and returned to its own ego. Freud also argues that narcissistic women cannot, unlike nurturing women, love others, and that men who love such women transfer their own primary narcissism onto their love-object. (That Freud reportedly gave Virginia Woolf a narcissus on meeting her in the 1930s is a fascinating piece of feminist trivia.) Sarah Kofman (1985) critiques Freud's view, arguing that his discourse mirrors his own narcissism.

Lacan differs from Freud in assigning narcissism a normative role in the constitution and maintenance of the ego-function. He sees it as a necessary IDEOLOGY which masks the gaps between the SYMBOLIC, the IMAGINARY and the REAL.

Some gay, QUEER and MASCULINITY theorists are beginning to explore male subcultural practices such as bodybuilding in terms of narcissism (see Goldstein [ed.] 1993); although gay men are understandably cautious about employing the term (Fletcher 1989). This work overlaps in significant ways with feminist work on women and MASOCHISM in film studies (Doane 1987).

See also PSYCHOANALYSIS.

Narrative Gerald Prince defines 'narrative' as 'the recounting of one or more fictitious events' (1988: 58). But as Hawthorn (1992) points out, the term is elastic and has been used in a variety of other ways. Gerard Genette distinguishes between three uses of the term: firstly, to refer to oral or written statements that tell of events; secondly, to indicate the succession of real or fictitious events that are the subject of DISCOURSE; and thirdly, to describe the act of narrating (1980: 25–6). Genette advocates using the term to refer to the first of these, while the second he calls 'story' or 'diegesis', and the third 'narrating'. Theorists agree, however, that the recounting of an event or events is a precondition of narrative.

During the 1970s SEMIOTICS and PSYCHOANALYTICALLY-oriented critics rejected the narrative basis of what they called 'the classic realist' text. Whether in the form of the nineteenth-century REALIST novel or the classic Hollywood film, it was attacked as inherently reactionary and in thrall to bourgeois IDEOLOGY (MacCabe 1974). Mulvey (1989a), for example, argued that the very structure of narrative cinema privileged masculine subjectivity and she advocated the development of a feminist anti-narrative cinema. However, it is important to acknowledge, as many feminists have since done (e.g. Felski 1989a), that realism has historically been a valuable mode for feminist writing. Indeed, many classics of the second wave are realist narratives.

Of course, this debate has a long history within feminist literary criticism, which poses the question of whether there is something specific to women's use of narrative. The female modernists such as Virginia Woolf and Dorothy Richardson certainly thought so, setting out to create 'the psychological sentence of the feminine gender' (Woolf 1979) and 'a feminine equivalent of the...masculine realism' (Richardson 1938). Their feminine prose was characterized by a lack of punctuation, breaks in syntax, the use of elisions and ellipsis, a lack of explicit plotting and a narrative unsupported by the conventional devices of character, chronology and exposition of events. While Richardson was one of the first to utilize such a narrative style, the features are as much a part of a modernist aesthetic as they are of a specifically feminine or feminist one. Felski (1989a) and Sara Mills (1995) argue that sexual difference cannot be exclusively identified with the use of particular narrative elements, but that stylistic features have historically been associated with particular gender ideologies. Nevertheless the association of an anti-narrative style with femininity persists in the work of French feminists such as Hélène Cixous and Luce Irigrary, who view the fluidity and multiplicity of *ÉCRITURE FEMININE* as disrupting the logic of PHALLOCENTRIC discourse.

Nation See IDENTITY; NATIONALISM ; POST-COLONIAL THEORY.

National identity See IDENTITY; NATIONALISM; POST-COLONIAL THEORY.

Nationalism Ernest Gellner stresses the contested nature of the term 'nation': 'neither cultural nor political boundaries are generally neat; cultural traits such as language, religious adherence or folk custom frequently cut across each other. Political jurisdiction may be multilayered' (cited in Outhwaite and Bottomore [eds] 1993: 402).

The term 'nationalism' designates movements of peoples to establish nationhood, or to reestablish it contra IMPERIALISM. Nationalist movements aim to foster markers of national IDENTITY and the building of solidarities around membership of nations and would-be nations. A number of attempts have been made to distinguish different types of nationalism (Benedict Anderson 1983; Anthony Smith 1986).

Virginia Woolf famously wrote: 'As a woman I have no country. As a woman I want no country. As a woman my country is the whole world' (1943: 197). This is a common stance among feminists, but it has been challenged because it downplays women's part in imperialism and racism. Floya Anthias and Nira Yuval-Davis (1991) identify three component elements of nationalist IDEOLOGIES: CITIZENSHIP, or membership of the national community; the sharing of a common CULTURE, especially a common language; and religious affiliation. All three may be gendered. Membership may depend on the maternal line; women play an immensely important role in most such COMMUNITIES in the transmission of culture, including religious practice and belief, and the 'mother-tongue'. Despite the inclination in the literature concerning nationalism to figure it as masculine, and the willingness of many feminists also to distance women from its excesses (Woolf 1943), women have been actively involved in the reproduction of national identities and ideologies, and in policing the boundaries of national identity.

National liberation movements, especially those which are anti-imperialist, have often provided fruitful soil for the emergence of women's movements and for the questioning of traditional gender hierarchies and divisions, and of their subsequent reassertion (Jayawardena 1986; Rowbotham 1972; Visweswaran 1994; Margaret Ward 1983).

Needs Essential human requirements. Within Western ethical theory, the language of need stands alongside ideas of reciprocity, mutuality, and an ethic of responsibility or care for others, and is in some tension with the language of the rights and autonomy of the atomized INDIVIDUAL. All of these terms have been challenged within POSTMODERNISM and POSTSTRUCTURALISM.

But the concept of need had already become contentious in twentieth-century Marxist social theory. Marx's concept of 'necessary labour' was defined in terms of the subsistence needs of the labouring class, but he recognized that there was a social or moral element to 'subsistence', related to customary patterns of working-class life in a given place and time, rather than to bare human survival. The second generation of Frankfurt School Marxists, Eric Fromm, Herbert Marcuse, and Wilhelm Reich, distinguished between basic human needs, and 'false needs' created by CAPITALISM to stimulate demand and habits of mind that would be functional for capitalism. Marx himself equivocated between 'needs' and 'wants'. But Marxism had been predicated on the capacity of the capitalist, and then the socialist MODES OF PRODUCTION, to release the forces of production and create an abundance which would take us beyond the 'realm of necessity' to the 'realm of freedom'.

An era become more conscious of ecological questions is less sanguine about the possibility of a world whose resources may be exploited indefinitely so that all wants may be satisfied. In a context of scarcity, the issue of basic human needs and the right to their satisfaction is once again a pressing one.

Attention has been drawn by feminists to the differential distribution of need-satisfaction along lines of gender. Poverty, across the globe, affects more women and children than men. But it is possible to argue, further, that 'human needs' themselves cannot be identified in sex-indifferent ways (Sen and Heyzer [eds] 1995; Nussbaum and Glover [eds] 1995). The critique of ENLIGHTENMENT RATIONALITY, and the insistence that the human subject of liberal theory is actually male (Nye 1988; Pateman 1988), and that all subjects are embodied, raises the question whether differences of sex and gender may not be relevant to the specification of needs, rights, subjectivity, and the other furniture of such discourses. However, these questions have been explored more fully thus far in feminist theory on possible gendered differences in MORAL REASONING (Gilligan 1982; Kittay and Meyers [eds] 1987; Porter 1991) than on basic needs.

See also BODY; ECOFEMINISM.

New communitarianism See COMMUNITY.

New feminist languages New feminist languages are attempts to supersede the constraints of patriarchal discourse by inventing wholly new terms and concepts based on women's experience, or by giving old terms new meanings. Many feminists have titled journals and books with puns and other verbal plays which reclaim disparaging epithets as a source of strength (for instance the British feminist journals *Trouble and Strife* [Cockney rhyming slang for wife], the defunct journals *Spare Rib* and *Red Rag*, and the publishing house Virago). Best known is the work of Mary Daly, especially *Gyn/Ecology: The Metaethics of Radical Feminism* (1991), first published in 1978, and her later glossary of new feminist concepts, *Webster's First Intergalactic Wickedary of the English Language* (1987). Daly suggests that

> spinsters can find our way back to reality by destroying the false perceptions of it inflicted upon us by the language and myths of Babel. We must learn to dis-spell the language of phallocracy, which keeps us under the spell of brokenness (Daly 1991: 4).

The term gyn/ecology, Daly says, combines the then newly coined French term *eco-féminisme* with an attempt to 'wrench back some wordpower' (1991: 9) by reclaiming the term gynaecology from the control of male doctors. However, she implicitly refuses to recognize any links between the feminist critique of language and other challenges to the transparency of phallocentric discourse.

A more ambitious attempt to go beyond the invention of individual words is the science fiction of Suzette Elgin, herself a specialist in linguistics. The world she creates in *Native Tongue* (1985) and *The Judas Rose* (1988) is dominated by linguistic households which control communication with other planets. As Lucie Armitt (1991) suggests, the plot involves the entrance of girls into the Symbolic Order in Lacanian terms, while the creation of a new language by discarded women living in Barren House allows Elgin to critique – but despite her attempts, not really replace – the linearity and binary logic of male discourse.

See also LANGUAGE; *PARLER FEMME*.

New international division of labour In the 'old' international division of labour established by the colonial powers, the European nations and the United States were to monopolize industrial production while the colonies specialized in producing 'primary' products, especially agricultural commodities required by European markets. Since the oil crisis of the 1970s, however, rising costs of production in the OECD countries have led many manufacturers to export part of their manufacturing industry to take advantage of much lower labour costs in THIRD WORLD countries. This new international division of labour was supported by many Third World governments through tax concessions and the specification of Free Trade Zones (FTZs) where trade union law, health and safety and other worker protection regulations were relaxed. Much of this overseas production was concentrated in labour-intensive, export-oriented manufacturing industries employing mainly female labour. Feminist economists were among the first to highlight the mixed effects of the new international division of labour, especially the incorporation of Third World women in INDUSTRIALIZATION on a subordinate basis (for example Elson and Pearson 1981; Fuentes and Ehrenreich 1982), and they have contined to document the varied and contradictory implications of women's employment in manufacturing (Lim 1990; Pearson 1992).

In more recent years the emergence of the new international division of labour has been reconceptualized as part of the broader process of GLOBALIZATION. However, some of the analytical issues remain the same. For instance, Elson and Pearson (1981) noted some years ago that rather than trying to weigh up the balance between the costs and benefits of the NIDL for women, we do better to identify in the changed terrain new opportunities for women to struggle for empowerment and self-determination, a point just as pertinent for students of globalization.

See also INDUSTRIALIZATION; POST-INDUSTRIAL SOCIETY; POST-FORDISM.

New Left   The broad label for a range of radical NEW SOCIAL MOVEMENTS and ideas which emerged in the late 1950s in Europe and the US, and which was usually non-aligned politically. It stimulated the search for new, non-aligned and less formal modes of political mobilization and organization, which would later to characterize the WOMEN'S MOVEMENT (Rowbotham, Segal and Wainwright 1979). In the US, it is associated with the Civil Rights movement, the opposition to the Vietnam war, and a flourishing counter-culture (Roszak 1969). In France the events of May 1968 provided the focal point and climax, and everywhere, it stimulated student radicalism (Caute 1988). In Eastern Europe, the 'Prague Spring' of 1968 was brutally crushed but presaged the dramatic events of 1989. Another lasting strand was the ecological movement which was central to this alternative CULTURE (see ECOFEMINISM).

Intellectually, the New Left was associated with the revival of interest in twentieth-century MARXISM, especially that of the Frankfurt School. Herbert Marcuse was particularly influential in the US and elsewhere (Marcuse 1964). Other major influences included Antonio Gramsci, Jürgen Habermas, George Lukács, and Louis Althusser, whose STRUCTURALIST Marxism can be seen in retrospect as marking the watershed between 1960s left radicalism, and its successors, POSTSTRUCTURALISM and then POSTMODERNISM (Jeffrey Alexander 1995a).

This complex of radical social movements and thought provided the crucible for the resurgence of FEMINISM and the women's movements of the second wave.

In the 1980s and 1990s there has been a certain retrenchment of both the women's movement and the New Left. Yet new social movements continue to flourish, including movements in which women figure very prominently, such as the ecology, animal rights, and SPIRITUALITY movements. The sharp social divisions exacerbated by the widespread dismantling of welfare states have generated a so-called underclass (Coole 1996), and an alternative economy which is a rich breeding ground for alternative cultural movements. But these no longer necessarily place themselves under a single banner, or identify themselves in terms of left and right. The New Left still provides a significant focal point, however, through journals such as *New Left Review*, and associated publishing ventures, around which a re-focusing of the non-aligned left may yet occur.

New reproductive technologies (NRTs)   Shulamith Firestone (1971) called for a revolution in the technology of REPRODUCTION that would liberate women by bypassing our BODIES, enabling us to avoid a process which makes us vulnerable to male domination. She has been widely misread as a technological determinist. But she was clear that such technologies only had liberatory potential in the context of a parallel revolution in the social relations of reproduction, so that they came under the control of women.

NRTs such as in vitro fertilization, as well as less high-tech practices such as surrogacy, have continued to attract controversy inside and outside feminism. The argument within those legal and institutional forums concerned to regulate such practices (for example, the Warnock Committee in Britain in 1984) is usually framed within the terms of 'rights' and 'responsibilities', as is the case in the principles articulated by the Australian National Bioethics Consultative Committee in 1990 concerning surrogacy: the principle of personal autonomy and freedom of choice, bounded only by the injunction against harming others; the principle of justice; the principle of the common good (Diprose 1994: 2).

Feminist disputes over NRTs often invoke anxiety over the privileging of normative heterosexuality which informs access to these technologies, and the policing of 'fitness' for mothering which they permit. Legitimizing high-tech/high-cost interventions to 'remedy' infertility also naturalizes the 'maternal instinct' once more (Stanworth 1987). FINRRAGE (the Feminist International Network of Resistance to Reproductive and Genetic Engineering), formed in Sweden in 1985, objects to NRTs for their violation of women's bodies and of our unique capacity to create human life. Other feminists have disputed FINRRAGE's outright rejection of all technological interventions in favour of a strategy of selection combined with seeking greater control for women over their use, on the grounds that technology per se is not hostile to women, and that some NRTs may be liberating and empowering (Birke, Himmelweit and Vines 1990; Smart 1989)

POSTSTRUCTURALIST and POSTMODERNIST feminisms have relocated the debate over NRTs in terms of the concept of embodiment and the recognition of the interdependence of human bodies. Feminist ethics has experienced a resurgence in this context, focusing on issues of NRTs, alongside surrogacy, abortion, and pregnancy (Diprose 1994; Gilligan 1982; Pateman 1988).

See also CYBORGS; NORMALIZATION.

New social movements   The women's, Black, peace, anti-nuclear, gay and lesbian, DISABILITY and green/environment/ecology and animal rights movements inherited the mantle of 1960s radicalism. Not dissimilar to related notions of emancipatory politics or radical democratic movements, new social movements are movements in which subject positions previously considered apolitical have become the foci of political mobilization (Mouffe 1992: 372). The implicit or explicit contrast is with liberal interest group politics, on the one hand, and, on the other, class politics centring on what Marxists see as objective positions defined by the 'implacable logic' of the system of capitalist production (Plotke 1995). New social movements are often concerned with changes in ways in life, posing objectives which go beyond conventional political reform. Large-scale representative organizations are less typical than more informal, less hierarchical modes of organization among groups which are conceptualized more like the American notion of a 'minority' than the European tradition of a class formation (Touraine 1995). Foucault's writing (in Dreyfus and Rabinow 1983: 211-212, cited in Plotke 1995: 116) highlights the ways in which the new social movement asserts and validates individual DIFFERENCE but also 'ties the individual to his identity in a constraining way'.

For feminists the crucial question is whether the formation of alliances between new social movements works in women's interests. In Britain Rowbotham, Segal and Wainright's *Beyond the Fragments* (1979) tried to establish a common ground for new social movements working as pressure groups alongside the Labour Party. The theoretical issue is whether an alliance of radical democratic movements allows for or denies sexual difference in political practice. For example, Iris Young (1990a) has argued that alliance allows for sexual difference because new social movements share an image of a 'differentiated public that directly confronts the allegedly impartial and universalistic state'; they share the desire to celebrate 'private' differences in PUBLIC. However, Mouffe (1992) argues that the idea of a differentiated public, along with sexually differentiated CITIZENSHIP as defined by Pateman (1988), or a Gilligan-type feminist politics based around gender-specific identities derived from the private sphere do not go far enough. She argues that an alliance of radical democratic movements should encourage the individual parts to redefine the multiplicity of their overlapping identities rather than try to put together a rainbow coalition around already constituted interests.

See also ECOFEMINISM.

Nomadic subject/theory   In his essay 'Nomad thought' (1985), Gilles Deleuze argues that philosophical discourse with its origins in imperial state apparatuses is part of a cultural drive towards immobility and fixity. In contrast, he sees nomadic counter-discourse as working to 'DETERRITORIALIZE', that is to unfix and mobilize cultural dynamism. Typically, nomadic subjectivity blurs boundaries, making transitions between categories, states and levels of experience. It represents a form of critical consciousness that resists settled, HEGEMONIC patterns of thought and behaviour. Nomadism as a transgressive subjectivity is central to contemporary POSTSTRUCTURALIST and POST-COLONIAL THEORIES, but the concept also has a history in feminist criticism. Rosi Braidotti (1994b) points to the association of female identity with statelessness and worldly exile within feminist theory, citing Woolf's *Three Guineas* (1943; originally published 1938) as a seminal text of feminist nomadism. In it Woolf states, 'As a woman I have no country, as a woman I want no country, as a woman my country is the whole world' (1943: 197).

Braidotti, adopting Deleuze's nomadic EPISTEMOLOGY, employs the term to describe the nomadic character of feminist theory in the POSTMODERN era, arguing that the concept of nomadism affords opportunities to go beyond PHALLOCENTRIC and monologic modes of thought and create a 'new female feminist subjectivity'. Recent figurations of alternative feminist subjectivity which could be termed nomadic include Donna Haraway's (1991) political fiction of the CYBORG, Luce Irigaray's (1985a) image of the 'two lips', de Lauretis's (1990a) notion of the 'eccentric' subject, and Trinh Minh-Ha's (1990) concept of 'inappropriated others'.

As Braidotti makes clear, post-colonial nomadism is not simply a geo-political category, but an IMAGINARY and SYMBOLIC one: 'It is the subversion of set conventions that defines the nomadic state, not the literal act of travelling' (1994b: 5). However, contra Woolf, she warns against the blanket ascription of nomadism to women regardless of their different locations. Homelessness means different things in different contexts; moreover, all women are not homeless, either literally or metaphorically, and neither are they equally 'at home'. Feminist critics of poststructuralist theories of nomadism and MIGRATION have highlighted inter- as well as intra-sexual difference, pointing to the fact that the experience of movement described in theories of migration and nomadism cuts across the axis of gender. Janet Wolff (1993) argues that the metaphors of travel in various 'TRAVELLING THEORIES' are male-gendered, and Boyce Davies (1994) asserts that it is mainly 'men who are asserting the right to theory and travel', pointing to 'the masculinised set of formulations with woman as object' which are common to men's nomadic discourse (1994: 45). Nevertheless, like Braidotti, she argues that the emphasis on modes of interruption, disrupting linearity, fixity and sedentariness characteristic of nomad discourse is useful to feminist projects.

Normalization   In her *Speculum of the Other Woman*, Luce Irigaray argues that Western thought, from Freud back to Plato, offered no place in its construction of the (masculine) self for 'the other, woman': 'the silent allegiance of the one guarantees the auto-sufficiency, the auto-nomy of the other' (1974: 135). Within this 'economy of the same' where only men may be full subjects, woman, the OTHER, is fundamentally lacking, pathological, outside the norm. Hence Irigaray's dismissal of feminisms of EQUALITY which seek only to lay claim to this masculine 'sameness' (in Schor and Weed [eds] 1994).

Foucault, in his work on the disciplining of bodies and populations, argued that the various DISCIPLINES of hospital, school, army, prison, along with disciplinary knowledges of clinical medicine, psychiatry, child and educational psychology, etc., served, in nineteenth-century Europe, to produce socially adapted 'docile bodies' (1977).

In feminist theory, the concept of 'normalization' has focused on the bodies of women. Irigaray's work has inspired a 'corporeal feminism' which looks for another model of bodies which is not founded on integrity, independence and separation, measured against which all women's bodies will inevitably be found wanting. The proffered alternative emphasizes fluidity, interaction with the environment, exchange across BOUNDARIES, and mutability of form (Braidotti 1994b; Diprose 1994; Gatens 1995; Grosz 1994).

Foucault emphasized the malleability of the BODY, so that social norms may be inscribed on its surface and in its very form. But if conformity may be written on the body, so too may subversion, and this thought lies behind feminist valorizations of body-modifications which challenge the boundaries between masculine and feminism – such as female body-building and a variety of subversive bodily PERFORMANCES (Butler 1992; 1993). Conversely, body-management techniques such as diet, exercise and cosmetic surgery, aiming to produce the normatively desirable feminine body, are usually excoriated (Bordo 1993).

This late-twentieth-century resurgence of interest in the body as the site of both normalization and resistance converges with debates over DISABILITY as the voices of those whose bodies are non-standard have begun to command more attention. Michael Oliver (1991) draws on Foucault to argue that the standardization of bodies, and the marking out and segregation of those bodies which fall outside the 'normal' range, was related to the demand for a standardized worker for mechanized factory production. The consensus within the discussions of disablement increasingly shifts attention from the bodies that are 'different' and onto the socio-physical environment which disables certain bodies, because our environment is designed to accommodate only those within the 'normal' range (Swain *et al.* 1993). Political demands focus on changing the environment rather than adapting the body. There has been fierce opposition to normalizing techniques and therapies, such as conductive education for brain-damaged children, hearing implants, prostheses, etc.

Disability is only beginning to be discussed in terms of the differential experiences of men and women. An affinity has been claimed between able-bodied women and people with disabilities on the grounds that women's bodies are already discounted as 'not up to standard' in the dominant discourses of PATRIARCHY. This approach encourages the acceptance of 'DIFFERENCE', but may ring hollow to the person suffering for example from a progressive disabling disease.

Further uncomfortable paradoxes emerge in the application of theories of the corporeal subject in this context. The feminist celebration of bodily diversity has drawn on the concept of the GROTESQUE, and generated interest in a whole range of non-standard bodies – conjoined twins, the unusually large and the unusually small, multiple identical births, obesity – and in the representation of these bodies (Russo 1994). There is a very fine line between the celebration of diversity and an all-too-familiar horrified fascination, and this development has not been welcomed unequivocally by many of those working for the self-REPRESENTATION of people with disabilities (Hervey 1992).

The double emphasis on the malleability of bodies and the prohibition on modification in normalizing directions has the paradoxical effect of unfixing 'normal' bodies, whilst putting those whose bodies are 'non-standard' under pressure to accept them as they are, not to seek modifications in the direction of normalization. And the Foucauldian prohibition on surveillance – the measuring and comparison of individuals and populations – and on the acceptance of difference obscures the detection of certain kinds of difference which are not revealed at the level of the individual body. A long series of empirical studies have amply demonstrated the manner in which poverty affects the development, including physical attributes such as height, of children and their subsequent life-chances (for a recent example which surveys this history, see Wadsworth 1991). These differences are increasing in 'postmodern' society at the present time, with increasing inequality and widespread poverty. Class is a difference that makes a difference, as Diana Coole puts it (1996). In the 1940s, the average height differential of boys from working-class and upper-class backgrounds was about two inches. Such differences offer little cause for the celebration of diversity.

O

Object relations theory A branch of PSYCHOANALYSIS derived from the work of Melanie Klein which takes as its study the relationship between mother and infant in the first year of life. Object relations theory views the child's development as occurring through its relations with 'objects' separate from itself which include whole persons or parts of the body, both real and fantasized. In contrast to Freudian theory which largely ignores the mother figure, object relations theory privileges the MATERNAL BODY. Klein (1928) proposes a primary femininity stage in which both sexes identify strongly with the mother. She posits womb envy as a male complex analogous to Freud's concept of penis envy in the girl. For Klein the child fears maternal rather than paternal retribution for its fantasies of aggression against the mother's body, which it sees in terms of the good/bad breast.

The centrality of the mother has made object relations theory attractive to feminists. Whereas Kleinian theory emphasizes biological drives and fantasy, the feminist object relations theory which emerged in the 1970s is distinguished by the emphasis it gives to the cultural construction of mothering and to the nature of maternal care as the primary influence on infant development. Dorothy Dinnerstein's *The Mermaid and the Minotaur* (1977) and Nancy Chodorow's *The Reproduction of Mothering* (1978) locate female subordination in women's exclusive mothering and call for joint parenting by men and women. Chodorow argues that the dissolution of the boundaries between SELF and OTHER characteristic of mothering makes it difficult for women to achieve autonomy and active desire. Chodorow's work has influenced feminist cultural studies (see, for example, Radway's [1984] study of women's romance fiction) and feminist psychology and moral philosophy (see, for example, Gilligan's [1982] account of women's MORAL REASONING and 'different voice').

While object relations theory has undoubtedly been valuable to feminists wishing to shift the psychoanalytic lens from fathers to mothers, feminists have also been critical of its tendencies to ESSENTIALIZE female experience. Lacanian feminists criticize it for eliding the concepts of LANGUAGE and the UNCONSCIOUS (Jacqueline Rose 1986); and lesbian feminists (Ryan 1990) highlight the HETEROSEXISM informing much object relations work which ignores the implications of desire between women.

Objectivity There are now several important attempts to define objectivity in ways which are compatible with feminist recognition of the socially located nature of the production of knowledge. However, this 'invitation to have it both ways' (Harding 1993: 50) is rejected by those who assimilate situated knowledge to the debate between RELATIVISM and objectivism.

Objectivism sees the only alternative to relativism as value-free, dispassionate impartial research, which is a very narrow reading of the concept. Harding (1993) suggests that the application of conventional scientific methods does not usually make visible or eliminate sexist and androcentric assumptions – the beliefs of an age. 'Strong objectivity' is achieved only through 'strong REFLEXIVITY' (Bourdieu and Wacquant 1992) which applies objectivity-maximizing procedures to the scientific communities themselves (to the subjects and not only the objects of knowledge) from the perspective of the marginalized. The need to develop forms of strong objectivity applies not only to those scientific communities where the relative absence of disadvantaged ethnic minorities and women of all groups means that unspoken, unnoticed assumptions are not challenged from within, but also to ethnically homogeneous feminist communities. Like Cain (1990), Harding insists that the social locations feminist knowers should take as their starting points are not ethnocentric, individual, idiosyncratic or biologically founded; they are constituted politically, theoretically and reflexively.

See also EPISTEMOLOGY; STANDPOINT.

Occupational segregation/segmentation See GENDER SEGREGATION.

Oppression The language of oppressor/oppressed, exploiter/exploited, entered FEMINISM as part of the MARXIST legacy. While MARXIST and SOCIALIST FEMINISMS retained the original reference to CLASS, RADICAL FEMINISTS transposed these concepts to the relationship between the sexes, developing analyses of PATRIARCHY, SEXISM, and male VIOLENCE AGAINST WOMEN. The terms had earlier been applied in the context of RACISM and IMPERIALISM, and the concept of women as an oppressed group drew upon these sources too. But radical feminism insisted that the oppression of women was a fundamental and primary form of oppression in its own right, and was not to be reduced to that of class (Burris in Koedt, Levine and Rappone [eds] 1974).

The DISCOURSE of oppression and exploitation attracted some criticism on political grounds, for it is one which is in danger of positioning women as victims, and feminism has an equally important need to stress women's AGENCY and POWER of resistance. This reluctance to be positioned exclusively in the role of victim was reinforced by the shift in feminist theory from Marxism to the POSTSTRUCTURALISM of Michel Foucault (Barrett 1991; Bartky 1990; McNay 1992; Ramazanoglu 1989; 1993; Sawicki 1991).

Foucault argued, famously, that power is not a zero-sum win-or-lose game but is structured through KNOWLEDGE in discursive social practices within various fields. No players are totally bereft of power, which is productive rather than distributive. This view resonated with feminists' use of the concept of empowerment which is as central to feminist analysis as is the concept of oppression.

Where there is power, argued Foucault, there is also resistance, and some feminists influenced by Foucault have used this idea to give an optimistic gloss which his own writings scarcely sanction. Susan Bordo, placing emphasis rather on Foucault's concepts of DISCIPLINE and NORMALIZATION, contests such optimistic POSTMODERNIST readings in which power figures as 'a terrain without hills and valleys, where all forces have become "resources"' (1993: 261):

> This conception of power does *not* entail that there are no dominant positions, social structures, or ideologies emerging from the play of forces; the fact that power is not held by any *one* does not mean that it is equally held by *all* (262).

Perhaps after all the languages of empowerment and of oppression are not necessarily opposed and indeed may be mutually implicated with each other?

Oral history   See PERSONAL NARRATIVES.

Orientalism   Edward Said (1978) coined the term in his book of the same name to describe the overlapping fields of cultural and historical relations, the scholarly disciplines and ideological and imaginative representations by which the West has constructed and come to know the non-Western world as 'OTHER'. Influenced by Foucault's concept of the discursive dissemination of KNOWLEDGE/POWER, Said inaugurated a new field of study called colonial discourse analysis. Feminist theorists who take COLONIAL DISCOURSE as the object of ideological critique include Lata Mani (1992), Chandra Mohanty (1993), Benita Parry (1987), and Gayatri Chakravorty Spivak (1989, 1993a).

While *Orientalism* demonstrated the involvement of culture in processes of imperial domination, its approach is not without problems. Dennis Porter (1993) criticizes Said for giving an overly monolithic account, of 'overworlding' the Orient, and of silencing counter-hegemonic voices. From a feminist perspective, Jane Miller (1990), while admitting to the 'seductions' of his theory, enters reservations over Said's failure to analyse the sexually differentiated sexual meanings of the metaphors of Orientalist discourse: 'It is possible to feel that within his analysis it is with the distortions of male sexuality produced by the language of Orientalism that he is chiefly concerned' (1990: 118). Liddle and Rai (in Rai and Lievesey 1996) likewise draw on Said's concept in their work on Indian nationalism, but are also concerned to extend the analysis to the gendering of sexual metaphors in that context.

See also POST-COLONIAL THEORY.

Other   The concept of 'the other' cannot be disentangled from that of 'the SELF'. The Canadian moral philosopher Charles Taylor, in a major study of 'sources of the self' in European thought, locates its emergence in the early modern period (Charles Taylor 1989). But the other which the self is invited to contemplate, within this tradition of thought, whether 'generalized' or 'concrete' (Mead 1955), is another 'self': another therefore of 'the same': another whose subjectivity is acknowledged.

Both feminist and post-colonial theory (Bhabha 1990; 1994; Said 1978) have used this concept to identify a more radical form of 'othering', in which the various 'others' to the white Western heterosexual male are denied selfhood, ABJECTED (Kristeva 1982). The other of Simone de Beauvoir's EXISTENTIALIST FEMINISM and of Said's ORIENTALISM is not another self, but one whose selfhood is denied in the interest of securing the centred subject's own soaring ego. Full selfhood, for de Beauvoir, was transcendent, achieved through active human projects.

Woman-as-other is one of the major themes of contemporary feminist theory in its critique of the male Western philosophical tradition (Irigaray 1974). But while de Beauvoir's feminist project was to remove the obstacles to women's freedom and AGENCY, enabling them to become in turn transcendent selves, Irigaray's, like that of Derrida and Lacan, is the DECONSTRUCTION of the transcendent subject, to reveal its foundations in the operations of language and in the radical MISRECOGNITION through which the human infant begins to acquire an (illusionary) coherent self (see PSYCHOANALYSIS).

Naomi Schor (Schor and Weed [eds] 1994) clarifies this distinction in terms of 'saming' and 'othering':

If othering involves attributing to the objectified other a difference that serves to legitimate her oppression, saming denies the objectified other the right to her difference (1994: 48).

Saming and othering are diametrically opposed strategies of the self, in this account, but it is not always easy to distinguish them, since both seem able to happen simultaneously to the same 'others'. Ethnic and 'racial' groups have been 'othered' and 'samed': attributed a difference that is fundamental, yet also fantasized as the unknowable 'dark heart' of the (white, Western) self. This presents a dilemma which Schor uncovers: if difference is denied by those who are thus othered, then the risk is of saming ('women are exactly like men; Black people are just like white'), the trap into which Schor claims de Beauvoir falls; on the other hand, if IDENTITY is affirmed in terms of a significant DIFFERENCE then the risk is of being 'othered' once more: defined by an essential difference. Schor argues that it is this risk which Irigaray takes. The charge laid against her of ESSENTIALISM (Moi 1985), against which she is defended by Schor and by Whitford (1991), recurs with a frequency which suggests that she has not been entirely successful in negotiating that risk.

What is at stake in contemporary feminist theory, and indeed in POST-COLONIAL THEORIES also, is the possibility of escaping this dilemma by rejecting 'othering' while yet insisting upon the recognition of important but non-essential differences. Judith Butler attempts to achieve this goal through the concept of the subject as PERFORMANCE: a subjectivity which knows itself to be a MASQUERADE; the copy of a copy, in no way AUTHENTIC (Butler 1992; 1993). These are the terms on which we might all be (provisional, unfixed, ironic) subjects without either saming or othering any others.

The awkwardness of this last sentence suggests that we need to ask who or what may be 'samed' or 'othered'? It is clear that the 'others' in question are (mostly) other people. The ironic subject of anti-humanist POSTMODERNIST discourse sometimes comes, ironically, to bear a close resemblance to the reworked INDIVIDUAL of modern (post-poststructuralist) HUMANISM (Charles Taylor 1991).

P

Paradigm   Developed especially through the work of Thomas Kuhn, a paradigm is the set of shared beliefs of a scientific community which defines researchable, resolvable problems. Kuhn's *The Structure of Scientific Revolutions* (1970, first published 1962) was not the first challenge to science's view of its own practice but has proved to be among the most influential. Karl Popper (1959) had dissected the positivist view of science which corresponds so well to how research looks from the laboratory bench (Bhaskar 1989, cited by Harding 1993: 76), but while Kuhn, like Popper, challenged the distinctions between fact and THEORY (or in Popper's terms, conjectures and refutations) he scandalized not only the positivist scientists but also the Popperian philosophers of science. For he refused the distinction between discovery and invention, and rejected any possibility of unequivocal falsifiability as well as of verifiability of theories by 'facts'. There was, he argued, no unmediated KNOWLEDGE of the REAL.

Parler femme The term was coined by Luce Irigaray to describe 'speaking (as) woman' (1985a). It refers to an experimental mode rather than a definitive practice, and emphasizes the relationship between female sexuality and writing. According to Irigaray, *parler femme* seeks to disrupt the syntax of conventional discourse, which operates according to a PHALLOCENTRIC logic of the same, in order to express the multiplicity of feminine DIFFERENCE. Irigaray's model of feminine speech/writing has been widely criticized by feminists for its ESSENTIALISM (Moi 1985; Felski 1989a); however, others have defended it, arguing that Irigaray's references to the female body represent poetic METAPHORS and analogies, symbolic challenges to phallocentrism rather than an example of biological essentialism (Burke 1981; Grosz 1989; Schor and Weed [eds] 1994; Whitford 1991).

Patriarchy The 'patriarch' was 'the father and ruler of a family or tribe' (*OED*) and metaphorically, of the church or religious order. FEMINISM has made 'patriarchy' its own, attributing its source to the realm of IDEOLOGY. Kate Millett (1971) broadened its scope, to reference an over-arching system of male dominance. Other feminists such as Juliet Mitchell (1974) have argued that the term should be reserved for the rule of the father over his wife, immature children, and any other household dependants. Michèle Barrett has also objected to the extension of the term to include all forms of male dominance over women, in an attempt to avoid the danger of a UNIVERSALISM which can only fuel ESSENTIALISMS rooted in the biological differences between the sexes (Barrett 1988). Veronica Beechey (1979) offers a useful overview of feminist and sociological usage and debate current at that time.

The feminist sociologist Sylvia Walby defends the broader definition. Patriarchy, for Walby, is 'a system of social structures, and practices in which men dominate, oppress and exploit women' (1990: 214). However, she hopes to avoid the charges of universalism and essentialism by breaking 'patriarchy' down into six component structures: husbands' exploitation of their wives' labour; relations within waged labour; the state; male violence; SEXUALITY; CULTURE. She makes each of these components relatively autonomous, and argues that the variable combinations of these structures give the concept of patriarchy the flexibility it requires.

The feminist philosopher Carole Pateman focuses upon changes occuring during the early modern period to argue that patriarchy per se was not overthrown at this time, but only its traditional form. It was succeeded by fraternal patriarchy, in which the brotherhood of men qua men, and not as qua fathers, entered the notorious SOCIAL CONTRACT in which they gained rights as CITIZENS which women (and others) were denied. For women were deemed, implicitly at least, to have placed themselves under the authority of their husbands on entering the prior SEXUAL CONTRACT, which, for Pateman is founded on rape or its threat. Her theory is closely linked to the concept of 'COMPULSORY HETEROSEXUALITY' (Pateman 1988).

Gayle Rubin was influential in the development of this latter theory. But she argued against 'patriarchy', favouring the more neutral term 'sex-gender system'. Sex-gender systems are universal, but need not necessarily be hierarchical systems of male–female domination. Or so we must hope (Rubin 1975).

Peace and war The Greenham Common women's peace camp catapulted issues of war and peace into feminism and was a remarkable achievement (Roseneil 1995). The camp was maintained continuously from September 1981 until 1994, when most of the women left soon after celebrating the departure of the missiles whose presence had set off the occupation; a small number of women still remain at the camp. It attracted large numbers of women who lived there on a temporary or semi-permanent basis in conditions of great discomfort, and even larger numbers of visitors for mass demonstrations. It attracted a great deal of media attention and may rightly claim to be part of a lengthy tradition of feminist REPRESENTATION through visual display in political demonstrations (Parker and Pollock 1987; Tickner 1988).

Militarism glorifies the supposed virility of war, especially of wartime combat, while concealing and camouflaging war's dependence on women. The polarization of men as fighters and women as the protected may be reproduced by those feminists who naturalize men's association with war and women's with peace, equating 'maternal thinking' with the politics of peace (Ruddick 1990). As Wajcman (1991), Enloe (1983) and Elshtain (1987) suggest, many women have been involved in war and many men have been pacifists and conscientious objectors. Combat depended on women's production and use of weaponry in both world wars and later regional conflicts, as munitions workers and battle 'support' staff (Braybon and Summerfield 1987; Enloe 1983; Summerfield 1984) as well as in other roles. Yuval-Davis (1985) and Enloe (1983) highlight the ways in which women are both integrated into but marginalized within the armies to which they are recruited.

Increasingly feminist theory sees women fighting for peace not as an example of women's natural pacifism but as a rejection of masculine technocratic CULTURE (Braidotti *et al.* 1994; Haraway 1991; Wajcman 1991). Carol Cohn's (1995) study of the world of nuclear deterrence experts is an important instance of recent emphasis on sign and text; she locates masculinity in the highly sexualized DISCOURSE of nuclear defence, which reduces anxiety about nuclear war and denies knowledge of its effects; it frames the IDENTITY therefore of participants rather than mirroring their maleness.

Performance theories Literary studies traditionally distinguishes between the performing and the non-performing arts. However, as theatre theorists complain, text-based critics such as the New Critics are apt to elide important distinctions between written and staged versions of plays. Theatre criticism employs a threefold distinction between the 'play text' – the material text of the play; the 'performance text' – the script which contains theatrical instructions to actors; and the 'production text' – the individual and unique staging of the play by a company.

Feminist writers have frequently adopted a theatrical concept of performance to explore the cultural construction of GENDER: Joan Riviere (1929) refers to FEMININITY as a performance or MASQUERADE, while Virginia Woolf, in her cross-dressing, bisexual fantasy *Orlando*, argues that 'it is clothes that wear us and not we them; we may make them take the mould of our arm or breast, but they mould our hearts, our brains, our tongues to their liking' (1992: 120).

More recently, the term has achieved prominence in relation to POSTMODERN theories of IDENTITY. The lesbian philosopher Judith Butler (1990) conceptualizes gender, and indeed all, identity in terms of performance, stating that it produces 'through the gesture, the movement, the gait (that array of corporeal theatrics understood as gender presentation) the illusion of inner depth' (1991: 28). Butler's suggestive theory has been enthusiastically taken up many feminist, lesbian and gay, and QUEER THEORISTS. However, it is not without its detractors, and some reject as idealist the theoretical basis of performance theory:

> If gender can no longer be reduced to self-evident identities (man or woman), neither can it be conjured away as the compelling but ultimately illusory product of performance. Gender no more resides in gesture and apparel than it lies buried in bodies and psyches ... Social relations are gendered, not persons or things (1993: 17).

In the context of speech and theory, J.L. Austin (1962) distinguishes between performatives, or verbal actions, and constatives, which state whether something is true or false. However, Austin suggests that constatives are also performative in that they perform the act of assertion. Austin's view of LANGUAGE as performance shares two features with POSTSTRUCTURALIST theories of language: a repudiation of the correspondence theory of language – where words simply describe things – and an emphasis on language as a performative set of conventions rather than as a description of the world. Recent inflections of performativity overlap with postmodern reconceptions of identity as performance, as the title of *Performance and Performativity* (1995) edited by Eve Sedgwick and Andrew Parker testifies.

See HETEROSEXUAL MATRIX; SEX AND GENDER.

Performativity See PERFORMANCE THEORIES.

Personal narratives Personal narratives include several kinds of 'life history writing' (Stanley and Morgan 1993) which, seen to be couched in terms of women's own categories and values, are much privileged in feminist social theory and research. They include autobiography and biography, conventionally the province of literary studies, diaries (whether or not written for publication), the life histories collected by oral historians, and those ethnographies in which an anthropologist presents an informant's account in the first person singular 'in her own words'. Personal narratives also include testimonial writing, i.e. accounts based on having been present which testify or bear witness to important political events and tragedies which might otherwise be forgotten or disbelieved. There are obvious tensions between the use of personal narratives as data for sociology, where their popularity is part of a move toward the acceptance of situated KNOWLEDGE, and the kinds of analysis offered by literary theory.

Personal narratives are, like all forms of writing, necessarily constructions of experience, and feminist literary theorists have given particular attention to the literary techniques through which they are constructed. Rita Felski (1989a) explains that rather than prescribing rules for defining a text as autobiography, the distinction between autobiography and fiction has come to focus on the cultural conventions through which the AUTHOR establishes an 'autobiographical contract' with the reader signalling the identity of author and protagonist and her effort to tell the TRUTH. However, some autobiographical writing itself undermines any unproblematized notion that experience speaks for itself. For instance, in Sara Suleri's *Meatless Days* (1991) language is not a transparent window on the author's life but itself one of the book's subjects, an unreliable and constantly shifting indicator of meaning.

When life history writing is crafted by an editor based on another person's oral narrative, serious ethical questions arise concerning the production and control of the text, the distribution of the rewards of publication and the claiming of authorship (for two examples see Shostak 1989 and Mbilinyi 1989). Power relations are also involved in TRANSLATION. In order to make a text accessible to prospective readers its production may involve translation from one (usually subordinate) culture to another (usually metropolitan) one. An example is when oral narratives are edited so as to conform to the cultural conventions of European/American autobiography, whether or not these are a feature of local discourse; for example the testimonial *I, Rigoberta Menchú* (1994).

Although this kind of textual DECONSTRUCTION of a personal narrative inevitably brings the truth claims of the narrative into question, it is arguably progressive if it illuminates the cultural politics involved in the narrative's construction.

Phallocentrism   A term derived from Lacanian PSYCHOANALYSIS, it designates the PATRIARCHAL SYMBOLIC order in which the phallus is positioned as the primary SIGNIFIER, privileging MASCULINITY at the expense of FEMININITY. According to Lacan, the phallus is distinct from the penis; however, while no one possesses the phallus as such, men and women occupy a different relation to it owing to their asymmetrical positions in the symbolic order. The feminist critique DECONSTRUCTS the phallocentrism of male DISCOURSES, not least psychoanalysis itself which in its Freudian form sees the girl infant as a 'little man', and women as the 'castrated' victims of penis envy. The term is now widely used in feminist discourse generally. Smart (1996) employs it to refer to the assumption that all sexual pleasure derives from penile penetration.

The related term phallogocentrism combines the meanings of phallocentrism (from Lacanian thought) and refers to any DISCOURSE which attempts the phallic mastery of the world through the sign. FRENCH FEMINIST theorists are centrally concerned with the critique and subversion of phallogocentrism. They advocate a range of strategies including *PARLER FEMME* and MIMICRY (Irigaray 1985a); *ÉCRITURE FEMININE* and the deconstruction of binary oppositions (Cixous 1976a; 1981).

Phallogocentrism   See PHALLOCENTRISM.

Phallus   See PHALLOCENTRISM.

Phenomenology   Drawing on Outhwaite and Bottomore's summary (1993) and at risk of over-generalizing, it can be said that phenomenological approaches focus on the lived EXPERIENCE of individuals and their perception and consciousness of objects and relationships, rather than the structural organization of institutions or macro-systems. Although this focus on experience inevitably makes phenomenology ego-centred, in some forms of phenomenology the ego is envisioned as a highly abstract 'wide-awake adult' (Outhwaite and Bottomore [eds] 1993: 462) rather than a situated or gendered subject.

Among feminist interpretative sociologists phenomenology has been integrated into feminist EPISTEMOLOGY rather than challenged. Their research tends to prioritize women's lived experience as against – indeed as a challenge to – the categories of scientific, official or expert discourses (e.g. Dorothy Smith 1988). In terms of concrete METHODS, feminist researchers have preferred the situated knowledge produced through interview or participant observation to attempts to grasp structural configurations or causal relationships through, for instance, statistical regularities. However, the failure to acknowledge the problems in phenomenology's ego-centredness reared its head in disputes, typical of IDENTITY POLITICS, over how to resolve differences between competing accounts of women's experiences.

French POSTSTRUCTURALIST feminists, as well as Judith Butler (1990) and others, have also undertaken a (rather different) critical engagement with

phenomenology. Elizabeth Grosz has drawn heavily on Maurice Merleau-
Ponty in formulating a gender-specific theory of bodily based SUBJECTIVITY.
She commends his focus on the BODY as the very condition of lived
experience (not, as Sartre or de Beauvoir would have it, as something to be
transcended) and his view of the 'constructed, synthetic nature of experience'
(1994: 95).

See also EXISTENTIALIST FEMINISM.

Politics   The *Shorter OED* defines politics as 'the art and science of
government' and as 'that branch of moral philosophy dealing with the state or
social organism as a whole'. In this tradition of thought, 'politics' and 'the
political' are linked to PUBLIC life, the STATE, and political parties. But there
is widespread recognition of broader and more historically and culturally
variable connotations. Vicki Randall identifies the common ground in terms
of the social nature of the political, and its relationship to scarce resources
and conflict over their distribution (Randall 1982). Beyond that broad
agreement she differentiates the concepts of politics as activity and as
relationship.

In relation to the arena of public life, FEMINISM has been concerned to
expose the gendered nature of political activity, and to win full political
participation for women (Hollis [ed.] 1979). The second sense, politics as
relationship, locates it less narrowly in the 'public sphere' and affairs of state,
and feminist interventions have been directed at mapping the differential
distribution of a variety of scarce resources, and even more importantly, of
their control and allocation according to sex and gender.

Feminists who have been active in left political life more generally have
urged the transformation of many of its practices along the lines developed
within the WOMEN'S MOVEMENT, to make such political forums more user-
friendly, democratic, and open (Rowbotham, Segal and Wainwright 1979).

RADICAL FEMINISM in the second wave, using politics in the second,
relational, sense, has founded the project of extending the concept of the
political even further beyond the arenas of public life and economic
distribution, to uncover the gendered politics of personal life. The slogan 'the
personal is political' was one of the most influential rallying calls of the
second wave. Kate Millett coined the term SEXUAL POLITICS, and in her book
of that title, defined politics as 'power-structured relationships, arrangements
whereby one group of persons is controlled by another' (Millett 1971: 23).

This expansion of 'the political' has taken a further turn in
POSTSTRUCTURALIST FEMINISM, particularly that which has drawn upon the
work of Michel Foucault, who has reformulated the concept of POWER so that
it is ubiquitous, diffuse, and multi-directional. Poststructuralist and
POSTMODERNIST feminisms generate radically extended understandings of
'the political' which display little interest in traditional forms of politics
(Butler and Scott [eds] 1992). In turn this move has provoked a certain

anxiety among some feminists: 'When everything is political, the sense and specificity of the political recedes' (Fraser 1989: 76).

See also AUTHORITY; CITIZENSHIP.

Popular culture The short history of CULTURAL STUDIES until it took the 'linguistic turn' associated with SEMIOLOGY and POSTSTRUCTURALISM was coterminous in Britain with the project of separating an authentic and popular working-class CULTURE from a superimposed 'Americanized' commercial culture that was initially presented as undermining this authenticity (Hoggart 1958).

F.R. Leavis, who had dominated the English School at Cambridge from the 1930s, inspired an army of 'cultural missionaries' (Eagleton 1984; Mathieson 1975) to go into schools as teachers of English. As well as teaching children to distinguish 'the best which has been thought and said' (Arnold 1960: 6), 'practical criticism' scrutinized mass culture, especially advertising and the products of the MASS MEDIA, in order to arm children against them (Leavis and Thompson 1933).

Leavis inspired what became known as 'Left Leavisism' in the 1950s (Mathieson 1975; Mulhern 1979), which departed from Leavis in refusing any absolute distinction between 'literature' and 'mass culture', and sought instead to foster discrimination within popular cultural forms. Stuart Hall and Paddy Whannel's *The Popular Arts* (1967) inaugurated this project.

The concept of 'the popular' proved attractive to many feminists working in cultural studies to whom the common dismissal of cultural forms popular with women as what Germaine Greer (1971), writing of ROMANCE fiction, once termed 'dope for dopes', was unacceptable.

Some studies throw caution to the wind, to embrace almost anything, just so long as it is popular. This full-blown populism, exemplified by 'the Madonna industry', may be seen in some studies framed by POSTMODERNISM (Fiske 1989. For a critique, see McGuigan 1992). Judith Williamson comments on the spectacle of 'left-wing academics... busy picking out strands of "subversion" in every piece of pop culture from Street Style to Soap Opera' (Williamson 1986: 14). It is not easy, however, to pick a path between the recognition of women's investments in cultures of FEMININITY and an optimistic 'anything goes' populism. The idea of popular forms such as romance fiction as compensatory carves out some middle ground (Modleski 1982; Radway 1984). Romance neither produces subversion nor reproduces patriarchy *simpliciter*, but rather reproduces an already deeply ambivalent relationship to both (Lovell 1987).

See also FEMININE; WOMEN'S CULTURE.

Pornography Along with debates about prostitution and sado-masochism, pornography was a key issue in the feminist 'sex wars' of the 1980s (Snitow *et al.* [eds] 1984). Feminists continue to disagree over how pornography should be defined, its status as REPRESENTATION, and the role of FANTASY in its construction and use.

Traditionalists fear that pornography lowers public morals, threatens the privacy of sexual relations (ideally confined to marriage), degrades respectable women and introduces innocent children to sexual knowledge, while liberals perceive little harm in pornography, unless people can be shown to have been harmed. In contrast, feminists oppose pornography not because of its explicitness (revealing what should not be seen) but because pornography glamorizes and eroticizes women's submission to men.

Writing in 1989, Carol Smart distinguished two distinct feminist positions. The RADICAL FEMINIST pornography-as-violence position distinguishes pornography, which is defined as material that combines sex or the exposure of genitals with the abuse or degradation of women (and which appears to endorse or encourage such abuse), from erotica, which it defines as arousing material free from sexism, racism and homophobia (Russell 1993). A comparison of the sexualized violence depicted in pornography with non-sexualized racial violence (for example, photographs or films eliciting pleasure by showing a lynching, beating and murder of a black man) shows that we have come to accept horrific images of violence as normal fare when women are the objects of violence in a sexualized scenario (Kappeler 1986; MacKinnon 1994). According to MacKinnon's view, to see pornography as mere representation is to license what goes on there; pornography is no less an act than the rape and torture it represents. Whether or not pornography actually leads men to commit SEXUAL VIOLENCE, legal restriction is required because the woman-hating climate created by pornography censors women's freedom of movement and contravenes EQUAL RIGHTS.

In contrast, the second feminist critique identified by Smart, which she terms pornography-as-representation, argues that the pornographic GAZE which objectifies and fragments women and their BODIES is as much a part of the wider contemporary CULTURE as of sexually explicit pornography, so that the same political critique should apply to both. (Braidotti [1994a] even extends the notion of the pornographic gaze to the objectification and fragmentation of women's bodies in ultrasound imaging.) From this point of view pornographic images require continual interrogation, not legal restriction, which is if anything more likely to curtail images feminists support (lesbian erotica, safe sex education) than mass market sexually explicit material. In any case, some argue, those countries and localities which massively restrict pornography are characterized by a more traditionalist anti-egalitarian climate than where liberal regimes allow it to flourish.

However, partly in response to attempts to censor pornography, especially in North America, a third feminist position has emerged which actively defends pornography as a source of sexual pleasure (Assiter and Carol 1993; McIntosh and Segal [eds] 1992; Strossen 1996). Partly because challenges to the particular theory of the male GAZE on which the pornography-as-representation argument rests have weakened its intellectual credentials (Linda Williams 1994), this third position seems to be becoming the main feminist opposition to RADICAL FEMINISM. Although supported by liberal ideas, it argues that radical feminists are trying to define and limit acceptable female fantasies and images to wholesome, so-called 'vanilla' egalitarian relations, effectively reproducing the DOMINANT IDEOLOGICAL representation of women as sexually pure or innocent. Pornographic images do not put alien ideas in our heads; rather they excite because they echo and elaborate already established fantasy scenarios constructed unconsciously in childhood. Moreover, identification with pornographic images is not FIXED in gender terms, but often transcends the male=active, female=passive scenarios which form the manifest content of much pornography.

Positioning See SUBJECT POSITION.

Post-colonial theory Post-colonial theory represents a major field in cultural and sociological theory in the 1990s, drawing on the more radical implications of POSTSTRUCTURALISM in its analysis of colonial discourse. While its appearance overlaps with debates on POSTMODERNISM, it carries a heightened awareness of power relations between Western and 'Third World' cultures. Linda Hutcheon (1994) makes a useful distinction between their respective aims and agendas by suggesting that whereas postmodernism and poststructuralism both challenge notions of the unified humanist SUBJECT, post-colonialism offers a specific critique of the imperialist subject. Key texts of post-colonial criticism include Franz Fanon's *The Wretched of the Earth* (1967), Jacques Derrida's 'White mythology' (1974) and Edward Said's *Orientalism* (1978).

While diverse in character, post-colonialist theorists share, according to Sally McWilliams, an attempt to

> unweave the complex structures put in place by colonialist rule ... revealing the complex interactions of colonizer and colonized ... to discuss how subjects are constituted now that the colonial powers no longer have overt political control (1991: 102-3).

Gayatri Spivak (1990), associated with both feminist and post-colonial criticism, adopts an ambivalent if not contradictory attitude to post-coloniality, in keeping with the problematizing, DECONSTRUCTIVE emphasis of her work, arguing that post-coloniality represents a new colonialism which is not space-based.

As is the case with critiques of QUEER, and postmodern discourses, some feminists prefer to retain an oppositional IDENTITY signalled by the categories BLACK FEMINISM, or THIRD WORLD feminism. Boyce Davies (1994) sees post-colonial theory in rather negative terms as a Western-initiated and oriented attempt to manage epistemologically a range of disjunctive realities and argues that it is not necessarily helpful for theorizing Black and Third World women's identities. Ama Ata Aidoo remarks succinctly that 'colonialism has not been "post"-ed anywhere' (quoted in Boyce Davies 1994: 95). Clearly, there is a need to acknowledge and theorize the ways in which societies and their subjects are positioned differently and unequally in relation to (post-) colonialism and/or imperialism. The persistence of neo-colonial and imperialist policies and strategies ensures the continued problematizing of the designation 'post-colonial'.

Postfeminism   Postfeminism parallels other 'post-' compound concepts (POSTSTRUCTURALISM, post-Marxism) in focusing on CULTURE and LANGUAGE in the adoption of what are seen as freely chosen IDENTITIES. Whereas the term BACKLASH refers to those opposed to feminism, feminists who use the term postfeminism welcome what they see as feminism's success in having changed women's position, or explore what they see as the altered terrain of cultural politics; not necessarily implying that the battle has been won, they would argue, but leading to the production of new kinds of texts which need to be read differently, especially those of POPULAR CULTURE. An example is Cora Kaplan's (1993) analysis of Kathryn Bigelow's film *Blue Steel* in terms of male reactions to women's increased power (epitomized in the film by the phallic confusion of the policewoman with a gun). However, critics of postfeminism argue that the term inevitably reproduces the assumption that feminist politics are no longer relevant, 'contributing to the backlash against feminism in its very name' (Modleski 1991). Modleski sees the poststructuralist rejection of women as a category ('feminism without women') as an example. Such critics argue that still necessary political struggles are being replaced by the play of images, for example around cultural icons like Madonna. Here it may be useful to bring a CLASS analysis to bear, for differences in women's social positioning, and thus their ability to sustain postfeminist lifestyles based on economic and sexual independence, have undoubtedly increased.

Post-Fordism   A way of conceptualizing transition in capitalist development from the 'Fordist' era of assembly-line mass production and consumption of standardized goods to a new set of organizational principles, especially flexible specialization and the deployment of information technology. As Ash Amin ([ed.] 1994) suggests, the term applies not only to changes in economic organization. The break-down of class homogeneity in lifestyles and outlook is leading to political and cultural shifts, for instance the decline of class-based mass political parties and trades unions and the rise of non-class NEW SOCIAL MOVEMENTS based around conceptions of individual IDENTITY, lifestyle choices and personal CONSUMPTION. Emily Martin (1994) points out that concepts like 'flexibility' have come to shape late twentieth century culture; not just business management but also now used in models developed in immunology and health care advice, as well as feminist theory.

Other ways of conceptualizing contemporary changes are also possible, for example Lash and Urry's notion of reflexive MODERNIZATION, based on the transition from 'organized capitalism' to 'disorganized capitalism' (Lash and Urry 1987, 1994). However, such schematic theorizations are criticized by others who reject the idea of binary contrasts, turning points and distinct phases in favour of analyses which highlight the heterogeneous, open-ended evolutionary nature of social change (Amin [ed.] 1994: 3). Some also argue for the essentially unchanged nature of capitalist organization of production, seeing in examples of 'flexibility' new ways of intensifying work (Pollert [ed.] 1991).

The changes which have been associated with post-Fordism and flexibility are having uneven effects for both women and men. The decline or, in some places, the restructuring of manufacturing has usually meant a decline in the availability of men's employment and a rise in women's, in revamped manufacturing labour processes or in the expanded service sector. The gains made by the growing number of women in management jobs through, for instance, more flexible family-friendly employment policies need to be set against the relaxation of employment protection law, collective trades union wage agreements and so on, which previously governed working conditions; although employment regulations covered more men than women, at least there was a 'gold standard' for women to aim for. Now growing inequality among women in employment has made it harder to generalize about women's condition (Smith and Gottfried 1996).

See also POSTFEMINISM; POST-INDUSTRIAL.

Post-industrial In post-industrial societies the service-based and information-based sectors of the economy have outstripped manufacturing industries as a source of profit and employment (Outhwaite and Bottomore [eds] 1993). This shift affects regions differently, often leading to heightened inequalities, and affects household relations between husbands and wives, parents and their grown children, as well as the balance between men's and women's employment (Smith and Gottfried 1996; Stacey 1987). A greater proportion of manufactured goods are imported or, where the production of consumer goods can compete with lower waged economies elsewhere, as in the clothing industry, manufacturing is hidden in undocumented inner-city small-scale workshops, especially those employing recent migrants, or in the homes of HOMEWORKERS.

See also GENDER SEGREGATION; POSTFEMINISM; POST-FORDISM; HOMEWORKING.

Postmodernism A term coined by Jean-François Lyotard. It labels certain features of contemporary Western society 'after modernity'; it is claimed as the successor to MODERNISM in the arts; and finally, it shares many elements of the philosophy of POSTSTRUCTURALISM (Lyotard 1979).

Central to the 'postmodern condition' as delineated by Lyotard is a revolution in communications led by computer technology and cybernetics, which dispenses with the 'Fordism' of classic nineteenth-century industrial CAPITALISM. POST-FORDIST production is dispersed, flexible and information-based. Frederic Jameson (1991) has exploited this residual technologistic neo-Marxism with its base/superstructure frame, to argue that postmodernism constitutes 'the cultural logic of late capitalism'.

Postmodernist philosophy is anti-FOUNDATIONALIST, echoing Wittgenstein's argument that philosophy does not ground knowledge or social criticism. Postmodernism is pragmatic, contextual and local (there are displaced echoes here of Karl Popper's [1966] impassioned plea for 'piecemeal social engineering' and of Hayek [1962], both staunch postwar defenders of liberal thought). Postmodernism refuses MASTER NARRATIVES which purport to explain the whole movement of history and social life as a single interconnected totality. It offers instead 'little narratives' which do not necessarily add up, but which may be woven together as a succession of short threads into a blanket. The search for the fundamental causes of injustice, OPPRESSION, the movement of history, is ruled out of court, and this places it in tension with many feminisms: 'There is no place in Lyotard's universe for critique of pervasive axes of stratification, for critique of broad-based relations of dominance and subordination along lines like gender, race, and class' (Fraser and Nicholson 1990: 22).

Nevertheless postmodernism provides one influential framework within which feminism is today constructed. Conversely, issues of GENDER (although not necessarily of WOMEN or of POWER: Jardine 1985; Modleski 1991) sometimes gain attention within postmodernist theory, although male postmodernists do not always return the compliments paid them by feminism.

It is not easy to attach the postmodernist label with any degree of confidence to feminist thinkers. Many of the most notable feminist theorists who sometimes attract the label might more accurately be described as poststructuralists, for example Julia Kristeva. But none of these and other associated positions such as DECONSTRUCTION are mutually exclusive, with carefully policed boundaries. Between them they constitute a net which catches up most of the major social theorists of the second half of the twentieth century. It is possible to pick out an almost infinite variety of pathways and combinations, and the refusal of 'grand narrative' combined with theoretical as well as political pragmatism encourages a certain eclecticism.

The relationship to MARXISM is critical. For if postmodernism is the dominant idiom of social and cultural theory in the late twentieth century, Marxism(s) held pride of place in the 1960s and 1970s and, INTELLECTUALS often outlasting the currents of thought in which they were formed, many of today's postmodernists were yesterday's poststructuralists and/or Marxists. The poststructuralist Luce Irigaray, like many of her generation, shows the influence of Marxism in her early work, as well as of Lacanian

PSYCHOANALYSIS and the structural anthropology of Lévi-Strauss – a common combination on the left in the 1960s and 1970s (Irigaray 1985a; Mitchell 1974; Rubin 1975). Donna Haraway, among the most original of postmodernist feminists, in her influential article in 1985 on CYBORGS and feminism (Haraway 1991), was still referring to herself as a SOCIALIST FEMINIST, and is attempting to rethink and rebuild what might be meant by socialism in the present conjuncture. Judith Butler, another major figure in contemporary postmodernist feminism, freewheels with Foucault, Derrida, Freud, Lacan and many more (Butler 1990; 1993). Gayatri Spivak combines deconstruction with continued political and theoretical commitments to feminism and Marxism, in her highly original contribution to POST-COLONIAL THEORY.

Many postmodernist feminists argue that feminism has special affinities with postmodernism (Butler and Scott [eds] 1992; Ferguson and Wicke [eds] 1994; Nicholson [ed.] 1990). But because postmodernism invites eclecticism, and because many of the principal male architects of postmodernism (and poststructuralism) have often neglected feminism, postmodernist feminism is, typically, as much critique as APPROPRIATION. However when Nancy Fraser and Linda Nicholson end their extremely useful essay on postmodernism and feminism by affirming 'contra Lyotard' that 'postmodernist critique need forswear neither large historical narratives nor analyses of societal macrostructures', it leaves one wondering whether there is anything in postmodernism that is 'write-protected' or whether postmodernisms share only loose 'family resemblances'.

Poststructuralism   The term designates not a single approach, but a range of overlapping positions: Jacques Derrida's DECONSTRUCTION; Julia Kristeva and the SEMIOTIC; Michel Foucault's theory of POWER and DISCOURSE; Gilles Deleuze and many others, all of whom are in some sense 'after' the STRUCTURALISM they had in many cases helped forge. Poststructuralism 'represents at the same time both a development and a deconstruction of structuralism' (Hawthorn 1992: 190). It breaks with many of the characteristics which structuralism shared with the structural-functionalism it attacked: firstly, with the distinction, central to the Marxist structuralist Louis Althusser, between KNOWLEDGE and IDEOLOGY, which grants epistemological privilege to scientific discourse over all others; secondly, with the metaphor of depth and surface, and the attribution of causal primacy to the former; thirdly, it eschews in a more thoroughgoing manner than structuralism the search for guarantees of discursive truth, whether in the world itself or in the protocols of science.

But much of the structuralist legacy remains. The two have in common their strident anti-HUMANISM; their displacement of the human SUBJECT; their critique of historicism: Althusser's three *bêtes noires*; and the influence of structural linguistics via Lacanian PSYCHOANALYSIS.

The branch of poststructuralism which has been most influential in literary studies is that referred to by Alex Callinicos (1989) as 'textualism', chiefly associated with Derrida, who, notoriously, holds that there is nothing outside the text, no possibility of referring text to world, nothing therefore to underwrite any definitive interpretation of the text, (although it must be said that distinctions between concept, term, and referent are not always scrupulously maintained, especially in secondary exegeses: Lovell 1980). Not surprisingly, textualism has been deployed most successfully in literary and other textual studies.

The second type of poststructuralism identified by Callinicos is associated above all with Michel Foucault, and hinges on the relationship between power and discourse. However the possibilities of combination and variation are almost infinite, and certainly there are many theorists indebted to both strands. Within feminism, Judith Butler may be cited as a good example (Butler 1990; 1993), and in literary studies, Nancy Armstrong (1987) who takes a Foucauldian approach. 'New historicist' cultural theory draws freely on both. But Foucauldian poststructuralism has taken hold more firmly in social and historical studies (Barrett and Phillips [eds] 1992; McNay 1992; Ramazanoglu 1993; Sawicki 1991; Joan Scott 1988). Among feminists working in the social sciences and social policy (Smart 1989) there has been a marked shift in recent years from Marx to Foucault (Barrett 1991). Marxist feminism has always been more powerfully present in socio-historical studies than in literary and other textual studies, with CULTURAL STUDIES perhaps dividing the honours evenly, perhaps even leaning more towards Foucault than Derrida, at least in the case of those forms whose project is to locate texts in the social world in which they are embedded.

In philosophy it is post-Lacanian psychoanalysis, especially as mediated by FRENCH FEMINISM, which has had the greatest impact (Battersby 1997 forthcoming; Gatens 1995; Grosz 1989; 1994; Irigaray 1991; Kristeva 1986). Gayatri Spivak (1987) has been a key actor in the making of poststructuralism. She translated Derrida's *On Grammatology* and uses the techniques of deconstruction in the service of anti-imperialism and feminism. Kristeva was a member, along with Derrida, of the *Tel Quel* group in Paris in the 1970s. Irigaray turns the weapons of deconstruction quite mercilessly against the whole tradition of Western philosophy. For her pains she was expelled from the Lacanian *École freudienne* on publication of her *Speculum of the Other Woman* (Irigaray 1974). Rosi Braidotti has made innovative use of Gilles Deleuze (Braidotti 1991), and the list of major feminist theorists working within and on poststructuralism is long and growing.

Even in the case of literary studies, feminism's tendency towards a political aesthetic has moderated the attraction of whole-hearted textualism. Of course this is not to deny that Derridean and other textualisms may be political, as indeed the work of Spivak amply demonstrates.

See also POSTMODERNISM.

Power   The power relations between men and women, especially struggles over the control of women's BODIES, have been a key focus of feminist analysis, as indicated by titles like Kate Millett's *Sexual Politics* (1971). Feminist objectives are defined by women's individual and collective empowerment.

The conception of power incorporated in the feminist definition of PATRIARCHY, is one in which 'men possess power which they hold over women (and subordinate men and children)' in a 'relatively stable sex/gender system' (Ramazanoglu and Holland 1993: 239). However, whether or not this way of conceptualizing power best illuminates the character of gender relations has received sustained debate as a result of the increasing influence of Foucault's notion of power, which it is argued, illuminates power's productive, and not merely repressive, aspects. Foucault sees power as exercised rather than held; rather than emanating from a single source, a multiplicity of power relations are being produced at every moment and at every point.

Feminists sympathetic to Foucault argue that his formulation parallels and develops many of the strengths implicit in the way feminists have conceptualized power, which is as concerned with power in everyday life (Foucault's 'micropolitics') as with the power of the STATE, especially the interactions between various sets of experts and laity; the power relations in which women are involved in a range of sites cannot be pinned down to any one institutional base nor reduced to any single factor. Feminists have always refused to limit their notion of power to one which operates within structures, and the relationship between power, KNOWLEDGE and DISCOURSE, as elaborated by Foucault, parallels feminist concern with how power defines situations and SUBJECTS. Moreover, the Foucauldian notion of surveillance as a key regulatory mechanism aptly captures the persistent surveillance of women, especially in relation to their reproductive capacities, family roles and mental health. Foucauldian feminism has been particularly successful in thinking through the way in which power 'has gotten such a grip on us' (Sawicki 1991: 21). Others argue that Foucault's notion of power is a useful corrective to feminist strategies which in trying to overcome women's position as victims replicate and perpetuate discourses which position the female as victim.

Less sympathetic critics argue that Foucault's formulation makes it impossible to analyse – and even rejects the existence of – the systematic power of men as a group over women as a group, the 'massive continuity of male domination' (Balbus cited in Sawicki; 1991: 58) and underestimates the continuing importance of state power and legal regulation in relation to women.

See also DISCIPLINES; ITALIAN FEMINISM.

Practice   In Marxism the cognate term 'praxis' has several meanings. Most relevant to feminist APPROPRIATIONS, it denotes, firstly, human sense activity, 'the practical, object-constituting activity of human subjects as they confront

Nature' and secondly, as in the phrase 'revolutionary praxis', a point of fundamental transition in which objective social conditions and understanding coincide (Outhwaite and Bottomore [eds] 1993: 83).

The French sociologist Pierre Bourdieu prefers to use the term 'practice'. He analyses the myriad empirical social practices in different fields, through which agents reproduce CLASS distinctions: for instance, their practices as INTELLECTUALS or professionals (Bourdieu 1984a; 1990a; Bourdieu and Wacquant 1992; Lash 1993). Bourdieu's 'practice' belongs not to CONSCIOUSNESS nor to the Freudian UNCONSCIOUS, but is embedded in the HABITUS of actors, or their dispositions, and in the rules which govern the field in question. In uncovering these rules, Bourdieu privileges not the actors' accounts of what they are doing, still less those of the outside observer who subjects them to theoretical analysis, but rather what he terms 'the logic of practice' itself. The logic of practice may only be uncovered by a scrupulously reflexive sociology in which observer and observed are located in their differential relationship within the same social field.

In feminism the term is sometimes used to distinguish activity from its SOCIAL CONSTRUCTION or institutionalized forms – for example, in Adrienne Rich's distinction between motherhood as institution and as EXPERIENCE (Rich 1977) or in the argument that sexual practices are open to different constructions (Smart 1996). But 'practice' is more often used to refer to theoretically and/or politically informed activity, as in Liz Stanley's (1990) notion of feminist research praxis.

Praxis   See PRACTICE.

Pre-oedipal   In Freudian thought the pre-oedipal is the phase preceding the oedipal stage of the child's psychosexual development prior to the full acquisition of an ego and super-ego. Freud's work scarcely mentions the little girl's pre-oedipal development until his late essay on 'Female sexuality' (1931) in which he acknowledges that the girl's pre-oedipal attachment to the mother is more protracted and significant than he had previously thought. Melanie Klein's (1928) work privileges the mother–child dyad in the first year of life and identifies an earlier maternally motivated oedipal complex.

Feminist accounts of the pre-oedipal seek to identify the specificity of the woman's pre-oedipal phase. Nancy Chodorow's (1978) OBJECT RELATIONS approach focuses on the pre-oedipal attachment between mother and daughter to explain why women mother. Joanna Ryan (1990) critiques the heterosexual bias in Chodorow's work, extending it to suggest the possibility of a strong pre-oedipal profile in lesbian relationships. Julia Kristeva's (1984) concept of the SEMIOTIC, analogous to Lacan's notion of the IMAGINARY, is counterposed to the SYMBOLIC as a pre-signifying energy. Closely associated with the maternal body, the semiotic is aligned by Kristeva with MARGINALITY, and by association with FEMININITY, and seen as disrupting the (Lacanian) Symbolic order of SIGNIFICATION. However, Kristeva dismisses as a regressive FANTASY any belief in the pre-oedipal realm as a refuge from PATRIARCHY. Nevertheless pre-oedipal motifs feature prominently in women's writing, especially speculative fiction, in the form of (politicized) UTOPIAN fantasy.

See also MATERNAL BODY.

Private   See PUBLIC/PRIVATE.

Production   As Benhabib and Cornell (1987) point out, second-wave feminist theory began by trying to work within a productionist paradigm drawn from MARXISM. Many theorists who identified themselves as SOCIALIST FEMINISTS located their interest in women, the FAMILY and REPRODUCTION in relation to Engels's analysis of the 'twofold character' of social production: 'on the one side, the production of the means of existence, of food, clothing and shelter and the tools necessary for that production; on the other side, the production of actual human beings themselves... ' (1972: 71). They justified the feminist focus on DOMESTIC LABOUR and women's OPPRESSION by showing how these mirrored or were linked to capitalist production rather than stressing their singularity. Empirical studies in sociology also looked to production, although this may have been due as much to masculinist bias in the sociology of work as to Marxist concepts. For instance, Ann Oakley's (1974) pathbreaking research on housework made housework visible as work by comparing it to low-paid, unskilled factory labour, while many of the first feminist ethnographies of women's waged employment focused on women's factory employment (Cavendish 1982; Pollert 1981; Westwood 1984), even though for women the service sector was a more important source of employment.

In fact, as Benhabib and Cornell suggest, women's work is more typically interpersonal and affective than men's concentration in the production of material objects and is often perceived by women themselves to be guided by different assumptions and standards. Of course Marx was concerned primarily with capitalist production, and since in his day, as Benhabib and Cornell point out, it was mainly in the factory-based production of objects that production was organized on a capitalist basis, it is not surprising that he gave this so much attention. But we should therefore be wary of taking Marx's analysis of commodified labour as the basis of a more general sociology of work, especially if unpaid work is to be included.

A second challenge to the production paradigm has come with POSTSTRUCTURALISM. Although second-wave feminism has always given as much attention to other areas of social life – cultural forms, leisure, the environment – as to production, what has been variously termed the 'cultural turn', the 'linguistic turn' and the 'turn to TEXTUALITY' all draw attention to roles of text, LANGUAGE and DISCOURSE in creating meaning, rather than the centrality of material production to social STRUCTURE. These too have led to what Benhabib and Cornell term 'the displacement of the centrality of production' ([eds] 1987: 1) in social theory. However, there is an important dissenting current in the CULTURAL MATERIALISM influenced by Raymond Williams, which refuses the separation of text and materialism.

Projection   A PSYCHOANALYTIC defence mechanism which describes 'the process whereby the SUBJECT'S ego disowns unacceptable impulses by attributing them to someone else; the intolerable feelings are then perceived as coming from the other person who, from then on, appears to the subject as a persecutor' (Wright [ed.] 1992: 352-3). Projection also describes woman's relationship to the image in sexual FANTASY. According to Lacan, woman becomes an object of fantasy, the place where lack is projected. The male subject disowns his own experience, producing an idealized or degraded image of the woman. Irigaray (1974) develops this idea, arguing that the psychoanalytic concept of woman as a castrated man is a product of male IMAGINARY projections.

See also UNCONSCIOUS.

Proper   Cixous (1976a) associates the proper – in the dual sense of property and propriety – with masculine or PHALLOCENTRIC systems and economies. Unlike man's economy, with its titles, its 'pouches of value', its 'cap and crown', woman's economy eschews property and profitable exchange and is symbolized by GIFT-giving. *ÉCRITURE FEMININE* – the privileged site of feminine *JOUISSANCE* – explodes the category of the proper, exceeding what is deemed proper to each gender. 'If there is a 'propriety of woman',' she states, 'it is paradoxically her capacity to depropriate unselfishly, body without end' (1976a: 259). Cixous' delineation of the term has been widely criticized as ESSENTIALIST and reductive, romantically reinscribing women into the (Lacanian) Symbolic order as selfless givers. Feminists insist that women's 'gift' of unpaid domestic labour must not be confused with any notion of essential female/feminine generosity.

Psychic repression   A central concept within PSYCHOANALYTIC theory, 'repression' refers to the operation whereby the SUBJECT attempts to repel or to relegate to the UNCONSCIOUS those REPRESENTATIONS – including thoughts, images and memories – which are too painful or dangerous to admit into CONSCIOUSNESS. Repression plays an important part in the causes of mental illness such as neurosis, hysteria and psychosis. The psychic effort required to keep repressed material confined to the unconscious causes the patient to exhibit compromising symptoms and become ill. However, the act of primary repression, the repression which first opens up the unconscious, is a universal mechanism.

Psychoanalysis   Psychoanalysis occupies a central place in feminism: historically, the relationship between the two has been a close and dynamic one, in which feminist responses to Freudian ideas have ranged from denunciation and rejection to enthusiastic APPROPRIATION; but rarely have they been indifferent. During his lifetime, Freud worked with many women who, as both patients and analysts, made valuable contributions to or criticisms of his work. Notable amongst them are Bertha Pappenheim (the Anna O of the case study), with whom Breuer discovered the 'talking cure', and Emma Eckstein, from whom Freud learnt about the importance of wish-fulfilment in psychotic episodes. In fact, Eckstein went on to become the first trained analyst. Other key women analysts include the feminists Karen Horney, who challenges the male-biased character of Freud's account of femininity; Joan Riviere, who theorized femininity as a MASQUERADE; and Helene Deutsch, whose work focuses on female psychology and sexuality. Melanie Klein, arguably the most famous and influential woman psychoanalyst, revolutionized the psychoanalysis of children with her invention of play analysis.

During the early second wave of feminism, de Beauvoir (1953), Friedan (1963), Greer (1971) and Millett (1971) all attacked Freud's account of the oedipal and castration complexes, particularly his concept of 'penis envy'. They accuse him of biological determinism and of participating in an anti-feminist 'counter-revolution' (Millett 1971). Millett's uncompromising critique stands out as a key text which set the tone of feminist analyses until Juliet Mitchell's (1974) important Lacanian reworking of Freud (see below). While this history has resulted in a variety of feminist responses to and versions of psychoanalysis, two main paradigms can be discerned: Lacanian psychoanalysis, which predominates in French-oriented and POST STRUCTURALIST criticism; and the OBJECT RELATIONS school, which draws on the work of Melaine Klein, Karen Horney and Nancy Chodorow. The latter has been influential in the development by Susie Orbach and others of the feminist therapy movement in Britain. Some of its practices, such as interpretations of child sexual abuse, eating disorders and approaches to false memory syndrome, are controversial.

Following Lacan's reworking of Freud, psychoanalytic theory has provided tools for a number of influential feminist accounts of the acquisition of gendered SUBJECTIVITIES in patriarchal societies. Within psychoanalytic feminist discourse the term 'PATRIARCHY' refers to the internalized Law of the (Symbolic) Father and the oedipal structure of human subjectivity. Feminist discussion of the issue has turned on the paradox that while in Lacanian theory the fact that sexual identities are constructed allows for mutability and change, the pre-given and universal character of the SYMBOLIC order would seem to preclude change. Mitchell (1974), for example, argues that psychoanalysis provides an indispensable description of the mechanisms by which patriarchy perpetuates itself. She takes a 'DUAL SYSTEMS' approach, locating CAPITALISM at the economic level and patriarchy at the IDEOLOGICAL level, and calls for an ideological revolution to overthrow patriarchy. However, her belief in the Law of the Father as the psychic foundation for human society would seem to undermine this demand.

Irigaray (1985a) challenges the necessity of the monolithic Law of the Father, arguing for the possibility of specifically female IMAGINARY and Symbolic realms. Like Mitchell she omits to theorize the relationship between the symbolic and material levels; however, her exclusive focus on the Symbolic order has led to criticism from some feminists that her work is ESSENTIALIST. Whitford argues that the problems of Irigarayan theory lie not in essentialism but in

> the impossibility of finding a position outside patriarchy from which to contest it; the contradiction of challenging patriarchy from within (which seems to promise psychosis rather than a different order); and the unimaginable transition to a new Symbolic order (Whitford, in Wright [ed.] 1992: 303).

Still other critics have questioned the usefulness of psychoanalytical theory for a feminist political programme. Elizabeth Wilson (1990), for example, argues that resistance to external social and ideological constraints are imperative. Jacqueline Rose (1990), responding to Wilson, nevertheless insists that it is the very existence of the unconscious and the resulting psychic discontinuities that enable women to resist the patriarchal law at all. Indeed, it is the notion of the unconscious which is central to psychoanalytic theory and distinguishes it from other perspectives.

Moreover, lesbian critics (Butler 1990; Jackie Stacey 1988) have criticized the privileging of heterosexuality within psychoanalytical theory, arguing that it establishes a heterosexist model in which all identities are subordinated to one of two gendered poles – masculine, feminine – from which sexual IDENTITY is seen to follow.

Notwithstanding its problems, psychoanalytical theory continues to be drawn on by lesbian and feminist theorists concerned both with the ways in which women collude with heterosexual patriarchy and the ways in which they resist it.

Public/private   This distinction is at once fundamental to contemporary feminist theory's conceptualization of the subordination and OPPRESSION of women and deeply problematic as analytic device. B. Honig writes of the distinction's 'permeability, inexactness and ambiguity' (Honig in Butler and Scott [eds] 1992). As such it is characteristic of the IDEOLOGICAL concepts that are effective in ordering social life precisely because of this ambiguity. Where such concepts are taken into social and political theory however, their ambiguity needs to be consciously addressed and not simply imported into the theory.

Elizabeth Spelman, in discussing the relationship between 'RACE' and GENDER, uses the metaphor of a portable bank of labelled doors which, depending on the order in which they are successively erected, and the context in question, sort the population who walk through them into different groupings (Spelman 1990). The public/private pair can most usefully be considered in conjunction with a series of related pairs which, taken together, provide the means to slip the terms from one context to another without registering the change of meaning. These pairs would include:

public	private
STATE	CIVIL SOCIETY
POLITICAL	personal
social	INDIVIDUAL
workplace	household
landed classes	bourgeoisie
politics founded on family/kin	separation of spheres

The distinction between public and private realms is central to liberal political philosophy, and represents a further differentiation of the Hegelian distinction between the state and civil society. The state belongs unequivocally to the public realm, but civil society is in turn divided along this axis, into public and private components. The economy and the world of work is part of civil society, but is not excluded from the public gaze; personal life is outside of civil society and, provided its conduct does not infringe the law or the rights of others, is protected from that gaze; but the family/household, whilst being one of the major loci in which personal life is conducted, is also a primary institution of civil society (Habermas 1989). Slippage between the two pairs of concepts, however, obscures the public or political aspect of civil society (Pateman in Butler and Scott [eds] 1992: 107). Feminist scholarship has uncovered the extent to which this division continues into the topology of the home: private houses have their public rooms which allow entrances from outside, and their more private quarters (Davidoff 1983). Conversely, attention has been drawn to privileged and powerful private spaces within the public sphere, such as men's clubs (Fahey 1995).

The idea of gendered public and private spheres was discussed in feminist anthropological writings as a quasi-UNIVERSAL feature of social life which went some way towards accounting for women's subordination and OPPRESSION (Rosaldo in Rosaldo and Lamphere [eds] 1974, but see her auto-critique, 1980). It has been located by feminist historians as a development associated with the separation of the workplace from the home from about 1780 in Europe and the United States, with the emergence of a distinctly middle-class or bourgeois culture. Historians working within this frame have both drawn upon the distinction to order their findings on nineteenth-century women's history (Cott 1977; Davidoff and Hall 1987) and simultaneously uncovered the myriad ways in which these boundaries might in practice be more honoured in the breach than the observance. Actions and practices could always be presented to the self and to others as being in conformity with such very flexible terms.

Attempts to use the terms analytically have encouraged their DECONSTRUCTION, to expose the interconnections and dependencies between the two (Eisenstein 1981; Elshtain 1974; Pateman 1988). The distinction has been challenged in the wake of the deconstruction of 'the industrial revolution' and the recognition that the transformations of the eighteenth and nineteenth centuries were complex and convoluted, as often creating new work opportunities and ways of surviving for small family units as dispersing their members into factory production outside the home (Berg 1994). The separation of home from work, insofar as it ever occurred, did so unevenly and incompletely, and indeed those boundaries have proved extremely permeable in the twentieth century context of homeworking (Allen and Wolkowitz 1987) and 'working from home'. And the argument that this division represented a specifically bourgeois cultural development has also been challenged (Vickery 1993 in Brewer and Porter [eds] 1993).

Assertions, therefore, that there was an increasingly sharp and gendered separation of public and private spheres from the late eighteenth century, with the effect of removing women from public places or from the world of work, must now be carefully qualified, and we need rather to ask 'how is this distinction circulating and with what effect, to create what social groupings?' in any given historical or social context.

Q

Queer Nation   See QUEER THEORY.

Queer theory   The term entered theoretical discourse in the early 1990s: Teresa de Lauretis apparently coined it in her introduction to the lesbian and gay issue of DIFFERENCES (1991b). De Lauretis distinguishes between Queer Nation and the new queer theory, seeing the project of the latter as having a double emphasis – 'on the conceptual and speculative work involved in discourse production, and on the necessary critical work of deconstructing our own discourses and their constructed silences' (1991b: v). This statement clearly aligns queer theory with POSTSTRUCTURALISM and a commitment to anti-ESSENTIALISM and the strategies of DECONSTRUCTION.

Its relationship to feminism is controversial: clearly, 'queer' represents an assertion on the part of self-styled queer women of a sexual difference among women which cannot be assimilated to FEMINISM. It asserts the relative autonomy of sexuality and seeks to separate questions of SEXUALITY from those of gender. It therefore represents a rejection of forms of LESBIAN FEMINISM in which sexuality follows from gender IDENTITY. Queer theory/politics are partially responsible for the decentring of LESBIAN FEMINISM in the late 1980s and 1990s. (But see McIntosh in Bristow and

Wilson [eds] 1993 for an interesting discussion of points of contact between Queer and feminist politics.)

While 'queer' is meant to mark a critical distance from the term 'lesbian and gay', to overcome its exclusions and elisions, it could be argued that in sexist and racist societies it is subject to the same kinds of exclusions as the terms which it seeks to replace.

R

Race/racism Although the West assumed its superiority from 'the rest' from their first encounters, the idea of 'race' as a particular way through which the West distinguished itself from its 'OTHERS' first appeared in the nineteenth century, along with the new importance given to biological difference to justify men's dominance over women. The claim that there is a scientific basis to biologically distinct, hierarchically ordered races dates only from the 1930s (Miles 1989; Ratcliffe [ed.] 1994). Despite new attempts to discover systematic 'racial' differences in intelligence (Herrnstein and Murray 1994), generally speaking the idea of biologically fixed subdivisions has generally been replaced by new racial discourses which discriminate between 'bounded groups' defined in terms of COMMUNITY and nation. Although the precise role of racism in determining disadvantage is contested among sociologists, in ordinary usage it refers mainly to institutionalized direct and indirect discrimination against racialized minorities: once groups have been differentially located in the social structure (for instance through slavery, colonialism, labour market discrimination) they can be affected differently, indirectly by policies which are not directly racist in intent. In Britain the term 'race' is often put in quotation marks to indicate that the writer recognizes it as a SOCIALLY CONSTRUCTED category with no biological basis.

One of BLACK FEMINISTS' concerns has been to theorize the relationship between 'race' and GENDER. As Rose Brewer states, 'gender as a category of analysis cannot be understood decontextualized from race and class in Black feminist theorizing' (Brewer 1993: 16). Racist constructions persistently and pervasively inflect cultural understandings of gender and SEXUALITY in ways which privilege or empower women treated as members of the dominant group. In now well-known critiques Black feminists and women of colour argued that second-wave feminism failed to recognize the extent to which all women's experiences are shaped by racism and ETHNICITY, resulting in different political priorities and loyalties (for instance Carby 1982; Davis 1982; hooks 1982; 1984; Phoenix 1987 and later Collins 1990; hooks 1989; 1991 and James and Busia 1993). They have pointed out that when struggles against inequality centre on the dynamics of either race or gender this 'translates into discussions of white women or Black men ... eras[ing] African-American women' from the analysis (Brewer 1993: 18). Eaton adds that US anti-discrimination law, couched in terms of race- *or* sex-bias, has made it difficult for black womanhood 'to be recognized as an identity category in its own right' (Eaton in Herman and Stychin [eds] 1995). This invisibility is reproduced by phrases like 'women and ethnic minorities'. An important corrective is the documentation of the history of WHITE women as a racialized category (Jayawardena 1995; Morrison 1992).

Radical feminism   In the public imagination at large, 'women's libbers' and FEMINISM generally are linked most strongly with radical feminist thought and politics, and its impact is widely acknowledged:

> Radical feminism... offered a breathtakingly audacious understanding of relations between the sexes in history. Sexual divisions prefigure those of class was the message that Shulamith Firestone and Kate Millett flung at a male dominated intellectual world, patriarchy the concept which they restored to the centre of debates around social formations and social relations between the sexes (Sally Alexander 1984: 125).

Radical feminism was born in North America out of dissatisfaction with radical left politics, and radical feminism in the late 1960s and early 1970s usually included some commitment to the goals of socialism, while the questions posed by radical feminism about SEXUALITY, personal relations, marriage and the FAMILY and VIOLENCE AGAINST WOMEN identified issues with which all feminisms had to engage. Some of the tenets of radical feminism might be identified as follows:

- that women are oppressed as women and that their oppressors are men. Male POWER had to be recognized and understood, and was not to be reduced to anything else, for example, the power of capital over labour;

- that the whole gender order in which people, things and behaviour are classified in terms of the distinction between masculine and feminine is SOCIALLY CONSTRUCTED and has no basis in natural differences between the sexes. A common goal was 'the annihilation of sex-roles'.

- that male OPPRESSION has primacy over all other oppressions, for which indeed it provided the template.

Radical feminism informed the women's refuge movement, uncovering the extent of violence against women. It motivated the setting up of Rape Crisis centres, and 'reclaim the night' marches. The emergence of a strong women's health movement whose slogan was 'our bodies ourselves' (Boston Women's Health Collective 1978) was powered by radical feminist initiatives, and it was radical feminism that was most closely associated with the emergence of LESBIAN FEMINISM and the critique of COMPULSORY HETEROSEXUALITY (Rich 1980a; Koedt, Levine and Rappone [eds] 1974). The development of CONSCIOUSNESS-RAISING groups, widespread during the late 1960s and early 1970s, and the insistence that 'the personal is political', were both associated with radical feminism (see also Coote and Campbell 1982; Echols 1993; Tong 1989).

Radical feminism has affected almost every emergent feminism since the late 1960s. The SOCIALIST FEMINISM which was dominant in Britain (Rowbotham 1972; 1973a; 1973b; Barbara Taylor 1983) owes as much to radical feminism as to Marx. FRENCH FEMINISM, particularly that of Luce Irigaray and Hélène Cixous, represents an interesting convergence of radical feminism and Lacanian psychoanalytic feminism, which is repeated in the 'corporeal feminism' of Elizabeth Grosz (1994) and Moira Gatens (1995), and Foucauldian POSTSTRUCTURALISM joins hands not infrequently with radical feminism (Cameron and Frazer 1987). But the chief 'successor-feminism' is that which has been labelled cultural feminism, a feminism of difference grounded in the belief that there is a distinctive WOMEN'S CULTURE (Segal 1987).

See also PATRIARCHY; WOMEN'S MOVEMENTS.

Rationality 'Reason' and 'rationality', like many key concepts of Western thought, occur in tandem with contrasting terms, variable from context to context, each serving to fix and positively define the privileged principal term, and many feminists (Gatens in Barrett and Phillips [eds] 1992; Irigaray 1974; Wittig 1992) have aligned these oppositions others, including CULTURE/nature and MASCULINE/FEMININE.

There is a long history in feminism, at least since the publication in 1792 of Mary Wollstonecraft's *Vindication of the Rights of Woman*, of contesting men's exclusive claims to reason. A common strategy was to concede the ways in which women frequently fall short of reason's exacting standards, but to place the blame on men who have denied them the necessary education, and their training instead in an artificial and constricting FEMININITY.

RADICAL FEMINISM first gave voice to the charge that what presents itself as abstract and UNIVERSAL in Western thought de facto excludes women. A particularistic masculine subjectivity is made to stand in for all humanity. (Daly 1991). Within feminist EPISTEMOLOGY, reason's sovereignty was challenged. Feminist research protocols favoured qualitative over quantitative methods, subjectivity over the objectivity (Smith 1988; Stanley and Wise 1983). Some influenced by radical feminism draw on philosophical and sociological PHENOMENOLOGY (Grosz 1994; Smith 1988; Stanley and Wise 1983), but others turn their backs upon philosophy and theory generally as 'malestream' (Daly 1991) to celebrate instead reworked stereotypes of feminine ways of knowing: the subjective; intuition; the emotional, but leaving their gender associations firmly in place (cf. NEW FEMINIST LANGUAGE).

The critique of rationality, OBJECTIVITY, and MODERNITY emanating from POSTSTRUCTURALIST and POSTMODERNIST feminism is sometimes sutured onto this radical feminist critique (Gatens 1995; Irigaray 1974). It is strongly anti-FOUNDATIONALIST.

There is an emergent 'post-poststructuralist' feminist defence of rationality and the Enlightenment project which argues that the balance sheet for women is a fine one in terms of gains and losses, risks taken, costs incurred (Felski 1989a; Jardine 1985; Lovibond 1989; Soper 1989). The argument for the necessity of risking a 'strategic' or 'ironic' ESSENTIALISM (de Lauretis 1989; Fuss 1989) opens up the possibility of recognizing the strategic necessity of certain Enlightenment concepts, including that of rationality, as opposed to their demolition.

Reader   In recent years the reader has become a major focus of literary-critical discussion. A variety of approaches have emerged, notably German reception theory, French POSTSTRUCTURALISM and feminist reader-response criticism, which all work to decentre the role of the sovereign AUTHOR who determines the meanings of a text (Barthes 1977a; Iser 1978; Jauss 1982; Tompkins [ed.] 1980).

Exemplified by Kate Millett's *Sexual Politics* (1971), the 'female critique' of male authored images of women is one of two major strands in feminist literary criticism, the other being the study of the woman writer (cf. GYNOCRITICISM). Millett surveys a range of twentieth-century male authors including Freud, Lawrence, Miller and Mailer, refusing their depiction of women and indicting their work as sexist. Subsequently, a feminist variant of reader response criticism was developed by critics such as Jane P. Tompkins ([ed.] 1980) and Judith Fetterley. Fetterley (1978) argues that much American literature posits an implied male reader which requires that the woman reader either adopt a 'male' reading position or construct an oppositional reading position. She uses the term 'resisting reader' to describe the reader's refusal to take up the position offered by the text. Extremely suggestive for feminist readers, Fetterley's politics of textual opposition has however been criticized as somewhat simplistic, positing a unified concept of the female reader which elides the distinction between 'female' reader and 'feminine' SUBJECT POSITION. Moreover, as Gill Frith points out, historically women themselves have been 'positively encouraged, indeed consistently exhorted, to read' (1991: 72) and reading itself has more often than not been constructed as a feminine activity.

Sara Mills (1995) offers an account of the gendering of the reader which draws on linguistics to offer a critique of models which ignore the literary aspects of texts, and on pragmatics to highlight the complex relations of SUBJECTS to text. In addition to the concept of 'direct address' – based on Althusser's notion of INTERPELLATION whereby subjects are 'hailed' by texts –

Mills advances the concept of 'indirect address', 'where elements of background knowledge are assumed to be shared and where certain information is posed to readers as if it were self-evident' (1995: 26). Mills argues that texts contain linguistic codes and cues about how 'ideally' they should be read, but that they make available a number of possible subject positions which may be adopted or resisted. Some of these ideas are indebted to CULTURAL STUDIES and media analysis which are centrally concerned with how readers of media texts construct meanings in specific cultural contexts according to a complex process of negotiation. They have developed a number of theories to account for it. For example, the encoding/decoding model developed at the CCCS seeks to analyse how a cultural product can evoke different responses in an audience. A related theory of meaning posits three potential responses to a media message: dominant, negotiated, and oppositional. Jacqueline Bobo (in Pribram [ed.] 1988) uses this model in her analysis of Black women as cultural readers.

Poststructuralist theories overlap with feminist debates about the reader. A long-standing debate concerns the issue of reading like or as a woman/man (Culler 1982; Gill Frith 1991; Fuss 1989). Culler (1982) deconstructs the concept of the 'woman reader', viewing it as a position that anyone, male or female, can adopt in relation to a text, thus enabling them to read 'like a woman'. This view has been criticized by feminists (see especially Frith 1991 and Mills 1995) who point out that Culler's model divorces textual subject positions from sexed reading subjects entirely and destabilizes the very concept of 'woman'. Reading, they argue, is not simply a matter of 'MASQUERADING' and while there are multiple subject positions in relation to a text, these are not equally available for everyone to adopt. Mills argues that the category of 'women readers' 'needs to be maintained for the simple reason that women are still discriminated against *as* women' (1995: 33).

Real Another category which has been discredited in the climate of POSTMODERNISM and POSTSTRUCTURALISM. While most exponents of these philosophies do not deny that a real world exists, they insist that since our KNOWLEDGE of it is necessarily mediated by and formed in language, we cannot know whether or not our propositions about the real are 'adequate' to it, because we cannot ever compare the two. There is no 'skyhook – something which might lift us out of our beliefs to a standpoint from which we glimpse the relations of...beliefs to reality' (Rorty 1991: 9).

If this makes 'the real' redundant it persists remarkably, and not only in common-sense discourse – it is covertly in play in the writings of many relativists. Necessary or not, the residual longing for 'the real' resonates most fully where it has been most radically cast out. Ludwig Wittgenstein likened language to a net cast over the world which both organized reality, and permitted us to act within it, as members of linguistic communities. The fantasy of getting 'under the net' (the title of one of Iris Murdoch's early novels) is powerfully present in Wittgenstein and his followers. The unsayable and unknowable haunt his work.

Has 'the real' perhaps become a spectre of postmodernity? The feminist 'postmodernist materialist' Kathryn Bond Stockton (in Ferguson and Wicke [eds] 1994) speculates that the near-obsession with the BODY in poststructuralist and postmodernist thought may represent a clinging to 'the real body' as an escape, or perhaps an anchor. She reads it as an expression of the longing to get 'under the net', to something that is 'outside of language'.

Pragmatism offers another kind of accommodation. Richard Rorty gives an anti-REPRESENTATIONALIST account of the relationship between language and the world: 'one which does not view knowledge as a matter of getting reality right, but rather as a matter of acquiring habits of action for coping with reality' (1991:1): a pragmatic realism?

Diana Fuss's concept of 'strategic essentialism' might also be applied to 'the real'. Instead of assiduously rooting out and exposing the concept of 'the real' as it lurks in theory we might ask 'how and where is this necessary concept circulating in the theory in question? What work is it being made to do?' The term 'real' is used in a special sense by Lacan, who distinguishes between three orders: the SYMBOLIC, the IMAGINARY and the Real. The Lacanian Real contrasts with Freud's reality principle, suggesting rather a principle of irregulation. It derives from pre-Symbolic reality and is, according to Lacan, absolute and unconceptualized. It returns as a need – such as hunger – which cannot be satisfied because the object is really an impossible plenitude. He uses the term '*objet a*' to refer to whatever the subject hopes will compensate for the loss of the Object, plugging the hole that prevents us experiencing ourselves as One. The Real appears in connection with the radical loss at the heart of language and subjectivity. It lies beyond language as 'an impossible core' or place of excess which blocks the smooth flow of communication. Feminist theorists have picked up on Lacan's association of woman-as-mother and the Real where, as Ragland-Sullivan puts it, 'woman dwells beyond language and gender identity in a closer proximity to sexuality and pain than man does' (in Wright [ed.] 1992: 376).

See also STRUCTURALISM; TRUTH.

Realism   Roy Bhaskar distinguishes three historically important types of realism: predicative (asserting the existence of UNIVERSALS); perceptual (asserting the existence of material objects in space and time independently of their perception); and scientific (asserting the existence and operation of objects of scientific enquiry absolutely or relatively independently of the enquiry, or more generally, of human activity) (Bhaskar in Outhwaite and Bottomore [eds] 1993). It is primarily this third sense which has been disputed within feminist EPISTEMOLOGY and these and related debates are also discussed under the heads of DETERMINISM, anti-FOUNDATIONALISM, IDEOLOGY, KNOWLEDGE, and THEORY.

There is a fourth sense of the term, however, with which we shall be concerned here: AESTHETIC realism, or realism in art and literature, which has been as contentious within feminism as the issue of epistemological realism.

Realism, in the Hungarian critic and aesthetician Georg Lukács's terms, refers to art and literature which aims to 'show things as they really are' (1970). It has been comprehensively discredited in the critical climate dominated by Marxist STRUCTURALISM, POSTSTRUCTURALISM and POST-MODERNISM in the second half of the twentieth century.

It is not difficult to establish that what passes for realism is historically and culturally variable, and as convention-bound as any other approach to cultural production. Ian Watt, untouched by any of the 'isms' above, as long ago as 1957 established the thesis that realism is a matter of convention in relation to the history of the novel (Watt 1957).

However, the poststructuralist critique of realism was not limited, like Watts's, to establishing that realisms are governed by clearly discernible conventions, and to disallowing realism's claims to special epistemological privileges, to leave realism as one approach among others in cultural production. In the climate of left film theory, as well as of literary criticism, especially in France and Britain from the late 1960s, realism was effectively demonized as the form par excellence of bourgeois IDEOLOGY: the 'classic realist text' (MacCabe 1974). There were of course dissenting voices. Raymond Williams in particular did not mince his words: 'the diagnosis of "realism" as a bourgeois form is cant' (Williams 1977b).

The critique of the classic realist text, however, carried the day in left critical theory and practice during the 1970s and into the 1980s. Most feminist cultural theory in Britain and Europe followed this line of argument, looking towards non-realist forms, whether within the avant garde favoured by FRENCH FEMINISM (Cixous 1990; Kristeva 1986; Moi 1985) or to popular GENRE fiction (cf. CULTURAL STUDIES) as the sources of interventions which were of interest to feminism from both a political and an aesthetic perspective. US feminist literary criticism, heavily concentrated until the late 1980s on nineteenth-century women's fiction (cf. GYNOCRITICISM) which worked with an unproblematized concept of realism, was criticized in turn for so doing by those influenced by and familiar with the critique of 'classic realism' (Moi 1985).

Moi's critique is mounted from a position which aligns itself with French critical theory and the valorization of the avant garde, but feminist critical theory which aims to redeem popular forms also sometimes buys into this critique of realism, arguing that these forms, for example, melodrama and the 'woman's film', are potentially more 'subversive' (Gledhill [ed.] 1987). But those whose concern is with POPULAR CULTURE have to engage with the fact that many of the fictions most popular with women, including conservative and radical 'middlebrow' novels of the 1930s (Light 1991), as well as contemporary feminist fictions (Palmer 1989), often draw on realist traditions.

The situation has changed with the publication of Felski's major study, *Beyond Feminist Aesthetics* (1989a). Felski registers the pull of realism, and challenges the arguments which had equated realism with bourgeois ideology and the inevitable production of 'ideological effects' inimicable to feminism. She looks at two common and popular forms of women's writing, both of which are heavily implicated in an aesthetic of realism: the confessional form found in autobiography and other PERSONAL NARRATIVES and the feminist *BILDUNGSROMAN*.

Reason   See RATIONALITY.

Reductionism   Reductionism assumes that phenomena are hierarchically ordered and that 'phenomena in the upper levels of the hierarchy can ultimately be explained in terms of "more fundamental" events at a lower level in the hierarchy' (Birke 1986: 56). Characteristic of many biological accounts, it also appears in analyses in which the behaviour of higher-order social phenomena – for instance, of collectivities or groups – is reduced to the psychological or biological characteristics of individuals. It is usually a central component of explanations of differences between men and women in terms of biological DETERMINISM or psychological traits.

Reification   Strictly speaking any second-order abstraction as against the first-order perception of lived EXPERIENCE involves reification. But the term usually refers to 'the process by which the products of the subjective action of human beings come to appear as objective, and so autonomous from humanity' (Outhwaite and Bottomore [eds] 1993: 552). In practice reification often involves treating concepts or social constructs as if they were wilful persons or unitary things.

Relative autonomy   See IDEOLOGY

Relativism   Relativism denies that moral or EPISTEMOLOGICAL TRUTHS, semantic constructions, entities and categories exist independently of point of view; rather these only reflect or are relative to LANGUAGE, locality, CULTURE and situation (Outhwaite and Bottomore [eds] 1993: 554). Relativism comes in strong and weak variants and has developed through debate with various forms of UNIVERSALISM, OBJECTIVISM and FOUNDATIONALISM (Harré and Krausz 1996). Feminist theorists have generally argued that universalism 'consists in conflating the masculine viewpoint with the general, "human" STANDPOINT, thereby confining the feminine to the position of "OTHER"' (Braidotti *et al.* 1994: 37). Gilligan (1982) rejected moral theory's preference for universal moral principles as the basis of MORAL REASONING, arguing that the interpretation of abstract rules by a disinterested observer is in no way superior to women's more concrete, relational style of moral reasoning. However, her position has been rejected by many other feminists as

ESSENTIALIST and, in so far as its generalizations are based on the moral reasoning of middle-class American women, ethnocentric. Similarly there is much disagreement as to whether objectivity should be rejected outright or redefined in ways which recognize the situated character of KNOWLEDGE (Haraway 1991; Harding 1993). Again, some feminist theorists have tried to develop criteria for evaluating knowledge (for instance, Cain's [1990] notion of good quality knowledge) whereas others see the suggestion of hierarchies of knowledge as suspect (Smart 1995).

Religion FEMINISM has a history of opposition to PATRIARCHAL world religions. Elizabeth Cady Stanton mounted an attack on institutionalized Christianity in 1895 (1985), and eighty years later Mary Daly resumed the attack (1974). Feminist critiques of androcentrism, sexism, exclusive language, the exclusion and marginalization of women in religious practices and writings have mushroomed since then in relation to all major world religions (Carmody 1979; Christ and Plaskow 1979; King 1995; Ruether 1974).

Secular forms of Western feminism which dominate feminist theory have by and large neglected religion, but others have preferred the strategy of critique, appropriation and transformation. 'Because religion has such a compelling hold on the deep psyches of so many people feminists cannot afford to leave it in the hands of the fathers' (Christ 1986). The STRUCTURALIST anthropologist Mary Douglas likewise castigates contemporary intellectual neglect of the significance of rituals and symbolic practices in generating and confirming social identity and belonging (Douglas 1970), and Luce Irigaray refers scathingly to feminists who '...hope to be done with these religious traditions without having gauged their impact on the societies in which they live' (Irigaray, in Schor and Weed [eds] 1994: 85). Finally the immense significance of religion in the lives of so many women should alert secular feminists to the need to understand women's religious life without dismissing it as an opiate.

The first impulse of feminist intervention in this field, as with feminist literary-critical theory, was to DECONSTRUCT and critique the male theological canon and the exclusion of women from the institutional practices and hierarchies of religion. Images of women criticism (Brown 1974; O'Faolain and Martines 1979; Warner 1985) was accompanied by demands for the elimination of sexist language and exclusive practices in institutionalized religions and theological beliefs, and by the work of recovery of the history of women's religious lives and writings. This work was common both to those who wished to transform existing religious traditions (Ruether 1974; 1986) and those who, like Mary Daly, felt obliged to forge alternative woman-centred forms.

Feminist religious historiography uncovered the traces of women's religious lives and practices. Women have participated massively in the religious lives of their COMMUNITIES, and women have been allocated religious roles, or have seized, transformed and made them their own, across different religious traditions and at different points in time (Holden 1983; Koltun 1978; Maitland 1983; Mukta 1994; Richardson 1980; Rudd 1981). For, as King points out, women have been simultaneously excluded from religious hierarchies, yet attributed 'great moral and spiritual authority' within their communities (King 1989: 33). This work of recovery has led to an interest in religious COMMUNITIES OF WOMEN (Bernstein 1976), and in the AUTHORITY which women have from time to time been able to exercise as preachers, prophets and mystics, within some religious traditions (Mukta 1994).

A further phase, which also has parallels in feminist criticism, has been to ask whether there is a distinctive 'women's religious experience', and indeed there have been widespread attempts to create women-centred forms of religious life, as in the Womanspirit movement (Christ and Plaskow [eds] 1979; Daly 1974; Neitz 1993). For the EQUALITY/DIFFERENCE opposition structures and divides feminist religious theory and practice as sharply as it does all other areas and it is the point at issue in Irigaray's review of Schüssler Fiorenza's *In Memory of Her: A Feminist Theological Reconstruction of Christian Origins* (Fiorenza 1983; Irigaray in Schor and Weed [eds] 1994).

'Alternative feminisms' which attract little attention within academic women's studies flourished in the grassroots women's movements of the second wave, many of them associated with NEW SOCIAL MOVEMENTS, and various new feminist religiosities/spiritualities have drawn freely on creative interpretations of religious traditions, as well as on frank innovations at the level of ritual, symbol, and belief (Daly 1974; 1984; 1991), often drawing on conjectural histories of MATRIARCHY. Monique Wittig provides the slogan which informs much work in this area: 'make an effort to remember. Or, failing that, invent' (Wittig 1971: 89). The idea of the Goddess is an example of this creativity, drawing as it does upon a variety of sources: ancient Greek; pagan witch or 'wicca' worship; native American traditions; Hinduism; African religions (*Encyclopaedia of Religion* 1987).

Carol Christ interprets the Goddess as 'an acknowledgement of the legitimacy of female power... symbol of the life and death and rebirth energy in nature and culture' (1986: 213–4). Goddess worship is frequently associated with the recovery of a prehistorical or mythical period of matriarchy, allegedly overthrown by patriarchal religions, evidence for which is found in the remains of the Minoan/Mycenean civilizations overlaid by those of ancient Greece.

Powerful symbol systems that structure personal and social identities also powerfully divide, marking off those who do not belong. Feminists who do not wish to turn their backs upon religion often address this problem by searching out commonalities across different religious traditions, and especially by marking out religious forms developed and practised by women, or that may in some sense be identified as 'feminine', as the source of synthesis and integration. King draws on OBJECT RELATIONS feminism, and on Carol Gilligan's claim that women speak in 'a different voice' when it comes to MORAL REASONING (Gilligan 1982). The MATERNAL BODY provides the common ground for much new feminist theology. But Irigaray distinguishes between the maternal and the divine, and insists upon the need for women to lay claim to both, in distinctively feminine form, before there can be any question of synthesis or even full relationship (Irigaray in Schor and Weed [eds] 1994).

In spite of these developments, the dominant feminist voice is perhaps still sceptical and secular. Donna Haraway is wary of the associations of the Goddess and the divine with radical feminist alignments of women with nature, the organic, the holistic, and with an emnity towards the machine: 'Though both are bound in the spiral dance I would rather be a cyborg than a goddess' (1991: 181).

See also CYBORG.

Representation   'An image, likeness, or reproduction... The fact of representing or being represented in a legislative or delibertive assembly...' (*OED*). Feminism has a long standing concern with the manner in which women are represented in both senses. The demand has been for self-representation, but the BLACK FEMINIST critique establishes the problematic nature of this demand. No woman or group of women may represent all women. There is no perfect likeness, no single voice.

Gayatri Spivak's essay 'Can the subaltern speak?' (1993a) analyses both senses of representation, citing Marx's distinction between *darstellen* (to re-present in the aesthetic sense) and *vertreten* (to represent or speak for politically), and shows their mutual imbrication, thus deconstructing the classic literary-critical and social science opposition.

Feminist POSTMODERNISTS such as Judith Butler (1990) take the view that all representation is re-presentation – there are no originals before representation of which representations are more or less imperfect copies: no authentic IDENTITY which may be misrepresented.

Pierre Bourdieu suggests that this eternal regression of representation may be halted not with any appeal to an authentic identity, but at the point of DOXA: the taken-for-granted, naturalized assumptions and beliefs that inform everyday social PRACTICE in a given field. POSTSTRUCTURALISTS after Lacan might demur on the grounds that even the UNCONSCIOUS is representational. It operates 'like a language', using condensation, displacement, and symbolism. But while Bourdieu refuses the term 'IDEOLOGY' because it too strongly suggests consciousness, insisting that the doxic is neither conscious nor representational, he is equally guarded with respect to the concept of the unconscious. The doxic is pre-representational but socially constructed, embedded in practice and in bodily HEXIS. It is only when challenged and deconstructed by heterodoxy that doxa begins to articulate itself as orthodoxy, and to become representational.

The advantage of this approach is that it avoids both a FOUNDATIONALISM based upon LANGUAGE or CULTURE, but also the new foundationalism which, paradoxically, shadows much postmodernist discourse in which the (ironic) individual is somehow able, in spite of all, to free fall out of *socially* constructed identities into self-representation (see Spivak's critique of Deleuze, 1993a). For although Bourdieu might be accused of a certain romanticization of doxic COMMUNITIES such as the one he studied in North Africa (the Kabyle), feminists hardly need to be reminded that it is in our lived doxic practices in that powerful locus of ROMANCE, 'the community', that women's oppression is most deeply entrenched and hardest to see – which was the whole point of the practice of CONSCIOUSNESS-RAISING. Butler's concept of gender as PERFORMANCE suggests a script, and a greater degree of consciousness, than does the concept of gender as PRACTICE.

See also AESTHETICS; FILM THEORY; GAZE; PERFORMATIVITY; SYMBOLIC POWER.

Reproduction   FEMINISM necessarily has to confront the strikingly uneven sexual division of labour in human reproduction, but has often been at pains to deny that PATRIARCHY and the widespread OPPRESSION of women are necessary outcomes of, or explained by, these biological exigencies. One important exception in early second-wave feminism was Shulamith Firestone, who put reproductive technology and its social relations at the forefront of her theory of women's oppression (Firestone 1971).

The concept has featured most often in feminist theory in the sense in which it is used within MARXISM: the reproduction of social forces and relations of production, or social reproduction. This concern places the spotlight firmly upon the economic, class, and production. MARXIST FEMINISTS in the second wave turned for preference to Engels's formulation:

> the determining factor in history is, in the last resort, the production and reproduction of immediate life. But this itself is of a twofold character. On the one hand, the production of the means of subsistence, of food, clothing and shelter and the tools requisite therefore: on the other, the production of human beings themselves, the propagation of the species (Engels 1972: 26).

This formulation made it possible to bring the biological exigencies of reproduction, and domestic life generally, into the frame of Marxist theory. The paradigm of production/reproduction in the economy was applied in the domestic sphere in an attempt to identify the contribution made by women's DOMESTIC LABOUR, childbearing and rearing, to the reproduction of capitalism. Domestic reproductive activities were typically analysed in the same terms as economic production under the heads of the material and technological forces of (re)production, and the social relations of (re)production. Firestone adopted this terminology to argue for a revolution in the forces of reproduction which would enable the womb to be bypassed, using NEW REPRODUCTIVE TECHNOLOGIES.

The feminist politics of human reproduction remains a live issue in contemporary feminist thought. But there is widespread recognition that human reproduction cannot be explored effectively within the Marxist paradigm alone (Coward 1983; Mitchell 1974; Rubin 1975), and a turning towards Freud and the post-Freudians for an understanding of the economies of DESIRE which structure human SEXUALITY and reproduction. The whole issue of mothering has achieved great prominence, both in the work of neo-Freudians such as Mitchell (1974), the work of OBJECT RELATIONS feminists (Chodorow 1978; Rich 1977) and the French post-Lacanians (Irigaray 1991; Kristeva 1982).

Romance   The critique of the GENRE and IDEOLOGY of romance has been central to feminist cultural criticism. In *The Female Eunuch* (1971) Germaine Greer captured a traditional feminist reaction towards romance fiction, famously calling it 'dope for dopes', but a more nuanced account of women's investment in romance has since been produced. Rosalind Coward (1985) sees the ideology of romance as bound up with FANTASIES of heterosexual domination, arguing that it encodes a desire for power through subordination. Ann Barr Snitow (1984) also highlights the way that in romance fiction sexual feeling is contained within a timeless and agonistic heterosexual frame and examines its pornographic appeal for women.

In two influential studies Modleski (1982) and Radway (1984), both adopting PSYCHOANALYTIC modes, argue that the fantasies encoded in the romance genre fulfil important compensatory and escapist functions. In Modleski's view romance enables women to work through the contradictions and conflicts of kinship relations, in particular assuaging their fears of male violence. Radway sees romance reading as a way for women to claim time to themselves, away from domestic responsibilities. Her ethnographic study found that women favoured romances which presented an image of the hero as the 'good mother', inviting the woman reader to see herself in the role of the nurtured rather than the nurturer.

More recently, Bridget Fowler (1991) employs Marxist theory in her analysis of the PRODUCTION and CONSUMPTION of the popular romance in the twentieth century. She argues that romance can be seen as the 'dream-book' of the family, encoding the symbolic erasure of industrial capitalism through the images of the rural retreat, fulfilled love and female entrepreneurship.

Feminist writers have reworked the traditional romance narrative in a number of ways. Fay Weldon's *The Lives and Loves of a She-Devil* (1983) and Margaret Atwood's *Lady Oracle* (1982) reveal the oppressive IDEOLOGICAL implications of the genre through comic subversion and parody. Another strategy, exemplified by lesbian romance fiction, is to offer women an alternative to the heterosexuality of the traditional genre (Uszkurat in

Griffin [ed.] 1993). Examples include Katherine V. Forrest's *An Emergence of Green* (1986) and Jane Rule's *Desert of the Heart* (1986).

S

Saming   See OTHER.

Second wave   See FEMINISM; WOMEN'S MOVEMENT.

Self   One of the fundamental categories of Western MODERNITY, which grounds the ideas of human AGENCY, autonomy, and the INDIVIDUAL. In a major study, the Canadian philosopher Charles Taylor also finds central to it the principle of respect for 'the life, integrity and well-being, even the flourishing, of others' (1991: 4) He adds the rider that

> the scope of the demand notoriously varies: earlier societies and some present ones, restrict the class of beneficiaries to members of the tribe or race, and exclude outsiders... But they all feel these demands laid upon them by some class of persons, and for most contemporaries this class is coterminous with the human race...' (1991: 4).

Feminist POSTSTRUCTURALISTS and POSTMODERNISTS have contested the HUMANIST account of selfhood which Taylor reworks and defends, arguing that the very process of constructing a coherent autonomous self is through the systematic exclusion of the OTHER. It is a process which Julia Kristeva refers to as ABJECTION (Kristeva 1982), while Luce Irigaray argues that Western philosophical discourse is PHALLOCENTRIC, with no place in LANGUAGE from which women may position themselves in other than masculine terms: 'the other of the same'. The modern self may present himself as an abstract 'human person' but the terms of personhood are such that only (white, middle-class) men may hope fully to achieve it. Woman/(m)other is what she terms 'the blind spot in a dream of symmetry' (Irigaray 1974). No real sexual DIFFERENCE is acknowledged.

Poststructuralist (and postmodernist) feminist strategies in the face of this radical othering of women and other Others varies from the 'corporeal feminism' of Irigaray or Grosz (1994), rooted in the affirmation of female bodily difference, to those with strong reservations over corporeal feminism's willingness to identify and idealize 'the feminine' as 'the elsewhere' of modern subjectivity (Butler 1992). However, as postmodernists, feminist and non-feminist, begin to address questions of ethics and politics, they often move back towards quasi-humanist positions (Butler and Scott 1992; Diprose 1994), and indeed, Foucault, in his later work, returns to the concept of the self and 'care of the self' (1986). Points of convergence or overlap become particularly visible in New Age philosophies, and in such activities as AIDS awareness campaigns, which lend themselves to framing both within the terms of certain forms of postmodernist politics of difference and within Taylor's 'ethics of AUTHENTICITY'; Taylor addresses this overlap in his book of that title (Taylor 1991). Both positions insist on the need to respect difference. Where the two discourses diverge is at the point of relativism:

> To come together on a mutual recognition of differences – that is, of the equal value of different identities – requires that we share more than a belief in this principle; we have also to share some standards of value on which the identities concerned check out as equal... Recognizing difference, like self-choosing, requires a horizon of significance... (Taylor 1991: 52).

Animals aside, the others whose differences we are enjoined to respect in both humanist and postmodernist discourse are principally other human beings or persons. Whether we opt in the meantime for a politics based on the radical affirmation of differences between people founded on MORPHOLOGY, or any other axis of differentiation, is a matter of strategy rather than of ontology.

See also MORAL REASONING.

Semiology/semiotics   The term derives from the Greek word *semeion*, meaning 'sign'. The American philosopher C.S. Peirce coined the term *semiotic* to describe a new method for the study of signs. Saussure's semiology of the sign, laid out in his *Course in General Linguistics* (1974), became the foundation for modern semiotics. Saussure distinguishes between *langue*, the LANGUAGE system, and *parole*, the individual utterance. The proper object of linguistic analysis is the set of rules or *grammar* which underlies and generates any one signifying practice. Saussure rejects the correspondence theory of language whereby each word or symbol refers to a thing in the world. He argues that the sign is quite separate from its referent and is made up of two parts which are only arbitrarily and conventionally connected: the signifier, which is the sound-image of the sign, and the signified, which is the concept evoked by the sound-image.

Notwithstanding its formalist origins in linguistics and STRUCTURALISM, semiotics has been adopted by those working within CULTURAL STUDIES to explain the IDEOLOGICAL meaning of signs embedded in particular cultural contexts. Although it is difficult to identify any feminist semiologists as such, semiotics has been used by feminists working within the fields of FILM THEORY, art history and literary criticism. Judith Williamsons' (1978) *Decoding Advertisements*, for example, combines semiotics and Marxist analysis.

See also SIGNIFICATION.

Semiotic   The term, not to be confused with semiotics – the study of signs – occurs in the work of Julia Kristeva to describe a disposition which is contrasted to the SYMBOLIC ORDER identified by Lacan. Roughly corresponding to Freud's notion of the PRE-OEDIPAL and Lacan's concept of the IMAGINARY, the semiotic exists not as a separate realm, but as a pattern or play of forces within language which bears the trace of the earlier stages. It is associated with the pre-linguistic child's connection to the MATERNAL BODY which is experienced as an extension of self. The semiotic is thus associated with FEMININITY whereas the Symbolic is connected with the LAW OF THE FATHER. Kristeva refers to the flow of drives in the pre-oedipal body as the chora, a term borrowed from Plato's *Timaeus*. She describes the chora as: 'an essentially mobile and extremely provisional articulation constituted by movements and their ephemeral stases' (1984: 25–6). Contrasted to symbolic SIGNIFICATION and without identity or unity, the semiotic chora is present in the cry, the sounds, and the gestures of the baby.

Kristeva sees the semiotic as a means of undermining the PHALLOCENTRISM of the Symbolic order. She points to the work of avant-garde writers and poets in which the stable meanings of ordinary language are disrupted by the rhythmic, tonal and physical aspects of the sign. Until recently the bisexual kind of writing associated with the semiotic had, ironically, been identified in the work of mainly male writers, but a number of recent feminist studies trace the semiotic in women's writing (e.g. Minow-Pinkney 1987).

See *ÉCRITURE FEMININE, PARLER FEMME*.

Separate spheres   A high degree of separation between the sexes in social life has the effect of producing largely segregated worlds of men and women. This phenomenon was discussed by feminist historians in relation to the emergence of the new 'middling classes', middle class, or bourgeoisie, in Europe and the United States. The dating of this emergence is contested. Most commonly, the period 1780–1850 is earmarked (Cott 1977; Davidoff and Hall 1987) but increasingly attention has been drawn to the significance of the early modern period, from the end of the seventeenth and into the early eighteenth centuries (Armstrong 1987; Bermingham and Brewer [eds] 1995; Vickery in Brewer and Porter [eds] 1993). The historical thesis has been modified in the light of evidence that the separation of spheres may not have been as clear-cut as has sometimes been supposed, and that there was considerable movement between PUBLIC and PRIVATE realms, which in any case are not always clearly demarcated, by both men and women. A related criticism has been that many of the values of DOMESTIC IDEOLOGY were actually fairly commonplace across other social classes, especially those associated with land and finance capital (Vickery in Brewer and Porter [eds] 1993). It may be that many of these oppositions were sharper in the discourse of IDEOLOGY than in social practice, and that their ambiguity and flexibility permitted many different kinds of unacknowledged accommodations.

Probably the vast majority of societies over space and time have maintained high degrees of separation between the social worlds of men and women. While the aim of much nineteenth- and twentieth-century feminism has been to storm the citadels which have been wholly or mainly reserved for men, breaking down this segregation and exclusion, more positive aspects of the separation of spheres have begun to be appreciated. For the effect was to create COMMUNITIES OF WOMEN and distinctive WOMEN'S CULTURES which have been highly valorized in much RADICAL FEMINISM and CULTURAL FEMINISM, and in some of the writings from anti-IMPERIALIST and BLACK FEMINISMS concerned to challenge common cultural stereotypes about women in non-Western cultures.

See also DOMESTIC IDEOLOGY.

Sex   In Anglophone feminist theory (the distinction is less readily available in certain languages including French), 'sex' was defined in opposition to GENDER in order to differentiate the biological markers of sexual difference from the socio-cultural meanings attached to them. Implicit in feminist social theory at least since Mary Wollstonecraft, the distinction was succinctly formulated in 1968 by the psychologist Robert Stoller, and was taken up in early second-wave feminism by writers such as Kate Millett (1971) and Ann Oakley (1972).

The distinction has come under close scrutiny in recent feminist theory. One potent source of the DECONSTRUCTION of 'sex' has been the feminist critique of biology. For the 'givens' of biological sexual differences are, it is argued, by no means immutable. Much of the work of feminist biologists aims to document the ways in which biological difference is affected – enhanced or reduced – by the social environment (Birke 1986; Bleier 1984; Fausto-Sterling 1985). The dominant model, in which mutable distinctions of gender are grafted onto immutable differences of sex, is replaced by an *interactive* model of the relationship (Birke 1986). Biological sex, it is held, is more indeterminate and more open to modification than had been supposed. This critique has been radically extended to challenge the basis of the distinction between sex and gender from POSTSTRUCTURALIST and POSTMODERNIST perspectives, sometimes substituting for this opposition the concept of MORPHOLOGY (Butler 1990; 1993; Gatens 1992; 1995; Grosz 1994; Irigaray 1991).

The second form of deconstruction, often found in tandem with the first, places under scrutiny not so much bodily processes as the terms of biological theory, and this provides a second path through which the natural/biological and the cultural may be made to converge. Biological science is part of CULTURE rather than of the world of 'nature' it purports to describe, and its concepts and theories have been deconstructed to uncover their recycling of *gender* stereotypes in the terms in which processes such as menstruation, impregnation, and objects such as egg and sperm, have been described (Martin 1987).

Finally, the effects of modern technology in extending biological limits, such as NEW REPRODUCTIVE TECHNOLOGIES, organ transplants, etc., have inspired Donna Haraway to posit a world peopled not by biologically distinct entities, but by CYBORGS, for whom the BOUNDARIES separating humans on the one hand from simians, and on the other from machines, are permeable (Braidotti 1991; Haraway 1991).

See also BODY; SEXUALITY.

Sex class   Developed at a time when many French Marxist feminists followed Althusser in focusing on the IDEOLOGICAL functions of the family, Christine Delphy's (1984) concept of sex class underpins her materialist analysis of women's oppression. Under the domestic mode of production male household heads exploit and profit from women's domestic labour (housework and childcare) and their work as unpaid family labour in family enterprises. Delphy's main example was the dependence of French family farms on the housewife's labour, but her formulation has also been used to analyse the roles of factory workers' wives (Delphy and Leonard 1992), the contribution the wives of diplomats and local vicars make to their husbands' careers (Finch 1983) and large firms' employment of married couples as hotel and pub managers (Adkins 1995).

See also FAMILY; KIN WORK; MATERIALIST FEMINISM.

Sex-gender system   Gayle Rubin argues for this term as a substitute for 'PATRIARCHY' (Rubin 1975) on the grounds that it does not carry the implication that such systems must inevitably be hierarchical and oppressive of women.

Sexual contract   Marriage has been subjected to close critical scrutiny and critique throughout the history of feminism. Late twentieth-century feminist political philosophy has forged a close link between the 'sexual contract' including, although not exclusively, marriage, and the SOCIAL CONTRACT of seventeenth- and eighteenth-century political philosophy which had been held to found modern CIVIL SOCIETY. Submission to the LAW and the STATE, in spite of the consequent curtailment of the sovereign rights of the individual human being in his person (possessive INDIVIDUALISM), was held to be rational by virtue of the gains in protection for which this freedom was rescinded.

Although only men were envisaged as having the characteristics necessary to so contract, yet, paradoxically, women were assumed to have freely entered into a prior sexual contract which placed them in subordination to their husbands. In most versions of the social contract, marriage and the subordination of women are held to have pre-existed the social contract in the state of nature. Carole Pateman argues that 'the construction of sexual difference as political difference, is central to civil society.... Men's patriarchal right over women is presented as reflecting the proper order of nature' (Pateman, 1988: 16) and she rejects feminisms which work for gender-neutral individual rights on the grounds that all individuals are embodied. 'The story of the sexual contract is about (hetero)sexual relations and women as embodied sexual beings' (Pateman, 1988: 17). It is as female persons, she argues, that women's rights must be pursued if the pitfalls of contractarianism are to be avoided.

Pateman raises the question of how women may be deemed unable to contract, yet simultaneously be assumed to have rescinded, in the state of nature, their absolute rights over their persons to their husbands in a marriage contract freely entered into. She argues that conjugal relations and rights have their roots, implicitly, in superior force, and posits a (mythological) original rape, to stand alongside Freud's horror story of parricide (Pateman 1988: 107).

See also BODY; COMPULSORY HETEROSEXUALITY.

Sexual division of labour   See DIVISION OF LABOUR.

Sexual politics   Coined by Kate Millett in her book of that title which became a founding text of second-wave FEMINISM (1971). Millett used the term in the spirit which informed the popular slogan 'the personal is political', but also to draw attention to the manner in which divisions of SEX and GENDER structured every aspect of the social organization of PATRIARCHY, from the economy to FAMILY organization, to MYTH and RELIGION.

The politics of SEXUALITY came to occupy the foreground of feminist theory and politics from the late 1970s, focusing less upon the reform of heterosexual politics than upon the exposure of the institution of COMPULSORY HETEROSEXUALITY and a redirection of attention onto lesbianism.

The keyword in these discussions, the POLITICS of sex, was challenged subsequently by the notion of 'pleasure'. Carole Vance (1984) argues that there had been an overemphasis on the dangers of sexuality in the context of patriarchal control. 'Feminists must speak to sexual pleasure as a fundamental right' (1984: 24).

See also LESBIAN FEMINISM.

Sexuality   In common-sense definitions 'sexuality' usually refers to a biologically based inner drive or impulse, based on Freud's notion of the libido, or indicates an individual's sexual orientation or sexual IDENTITY ('her sexuality'). However, in feminist writing 'sexuality' usually refers not only to 'individual erotic desires, practices and identities' but also to the DISCOURSES and social arrangements which construct erotic possibilities at any one time (Jackson and Scott 1996: 2). Since what is defined as erotic varies, what is encompassed by the term is far from fixed. Most feminists, along with sexologists and sociologists more generally, now reject a 'universalist conception of the sexual' (Gagnon and Parker 1995: 8) for some form of SOCIAL CONSTRUCTIONISM.

In feminist history sexuality has been analysed less in terms of sexual morality or choice than as SEXUAL POLITICS. For example, middle-class Victorian women, who were limited by women's economic and legal dependence and the denial of autonomous female sexual feeling, are seen to have adopted the DOMINANT IDEOLOGY of women's 'passionlessness' (Cott 1979) in their own interests, making it a source of moral power and resistance. Only in the late nineteenth century did the 'New Woman' begin rejecting formulations and practices which stifled the possibility of sexual pleasure for women (Bland 1986). Feminist historians have also been involved in deconstructing the still powerful racialized sexual imagery of the period (Cranny-Francis 1995).

Second-wave feminism began by demanding women's right to define their own sexuality, initially in their relations with men but later by challenging the arrangements of institutionalized heterosexuality. Writers critiqued male-defined assumptions – in sexology, for example – especially the equation of sex and sexual pleasure with heterosexual coitus (Greer 1971; Hite 1988; Jeffreys 1985; Koedt, Levine and Rappone 1974; Millet 1971). As Hilary Allen (1982) comments, some adopted a voluntaristic view of the malleability of female sexual DESIRES; for instance, Adrienne Rich (1980a) and others who developed political lesbianism saw women abandoning COMPULSORY HETEROSEXUALITY for more profoundly female experience in which 'the erotic is not genitally focused' but 'pervades female comradeship' (McIntosh in Bristow and Wilson [eds] 1993: 35), in what Rich termed the lesbian continuum.

However, most feminist theory continued to see sexual desire as inextricably linked to gendered SUBJECT positions. As Diana Fuss (1989) and Mary McIntosh point out, although RADICAL FEMINISTS highlighted the socially constructed character of male-defined sexuality, their yearning for an authentic female sexuality suggests that they did not totally reject ESSENTIALIST thinking. In contrast, recent feminist theory has been much influenced by debate about Foucault's social constructionist project. For Foucault sexuality is not a natural given which is held in check but merely 'the name given to a historical construct' (1980b: 105); rather than being a source of liberation, modern sexuality is a field of KNOWLEDGE constructed by the medical and other public DISCOURSES through which POWER gains access to the BODY.

Catharine MacKinnon (1992) has argued that Foucault's gender-blind history of discourse on sexuality ignores virtually the entire history of women's sexual OPPRESSION by men, the rape and abuse which go far beyond discursive construction; Jackson and Scott argue that in Foucault's social constructionism the material or experiential 'it' which these discourses construct disappears. However, the Foucauldian emphasis on the discursive production of sexuality has strengthened feminist deconstructions of new discourses as they arise, for example televized accounts of abuse (Alcoff and Gray 1993; Vikki Bell 1993) or the role of expert knowledge in disciplinary regimes and legal regulation (Smart 1989; 1995); it forces feminists to confront their own writing as examples of the discursive construction of sex (Vikki Bell 1993).

Feminist debates of the 1980s (the so-called 'sex wars') about the extent of women's real sexual agency and choice still come to the fore in discussions of sado-MASOCHISM, PORNOGRAPHY and prostitution. Further challenges have arisen with the development of QUEER THEORY (McIntosh in Bristow and Wilson [eds] 1993), especially its separation of sexuality from GENDER.

See also SEXUAL POLITICS; VIOLENCE AGAINST WOMEN.

Sexuate subject/rights   Luce Irigaray (1991) uses the term 'sexuate' to refer to a SUBJECT who is sexually embodied through SYMBOLIC, psychic and socio-political processes. It is closely linked to the concept of sexual DIFFERENCE which implies distinct masculine and feminine economies of DESIRE and symbolization. The centrality of the UNCONSCIOUS to Irigaray's conception of sexed subjectivity means that the term carries a different significance from the Anglo-American concept of the GENDERED subject as a product of SOCIALIZATION. The political projects attached to each conception are in consequence distinct. Women's sexuate rights cannot be won through a legal/social struggle in which the inequalities of social gender are erased. They require rather the construction of a female Symbolic to give women the symbolic placement they have historically lacked in the PHALLOCENTRIC order. Such a Symbolic would 'guarantee women's claim to self-affirmative existence as subjects in the social' (de Lauretis in Schor and Weed [eds] 1994: 25). (Anglo-American) critics are suspicious of what they see as

Irigaray's ESSENTIALIZING account of WOMAN'S subjectivity; however, for Irigaray the construction of a female Symbolic is an eminently political and historical task.

Signification   The term's contemporary importance is a product of the STRUCTURALIST revolution. It registers the fundamental shift from PHENOMENOLOGICAL models of LANGUAGE and intentional theories of meaning, where language is seen as a tool of human COMMUNICATION and self-expression, to a SEMIOTIC model where language is seen as a system of signifying elements or signs. As Saussure's model of the linguistic sign demonstrates, signs exist in relations of similarity and difference to each other, are purely arbitrary and conventional, and have no relation to their referents in external reality. As Barthes (1977a) suggests, language recognizes not individuals but SUBJECT POSITIONS which exist prior to and independently of particular speakers. Whereas in structuralist models the sign is a relatively stable entity, in POST-STRUCTURALIST accounts the instability of the signifying process is emphasized. Barthes' concept of writing where meaning is ceaselessly posited and deferred captures the poststructuralist emphasis.

Signifying practice   See SIGNIFICATION.

Sisterhood   The language of sisterhood was commonplace in 1970s FEMINISM, especially in RADICAL FEMINISM, but in the 1990s the term has come to stand for the failings of that feminism with regard to the problem of DIFFERENCES that separate women. However, the term was powerful in mobilizing women, and encouraging solidarities where they were extremely difficult to forge in the face of the widespread cultural disparaging of women. Above all, it pointed towards a political project of alliances which might be forged, rather than a definition of 'WOMAN' in her essence, although ESSENTIALISM was certainly risked in the process (Morgan [ed.] 1970). However, it is worth making the point that '1970s feminism' was not actually so naive as it is made out to be in certain of its 1990s re-presentations.

Situated knowledge   See KNOWLEDGE.

Social capital   In his accounts of the reproduction of domination, Pierre Bourdieu differentiates two types of capital, the cultural and the economic, and argues that the dominant class may be located in terms of the variable composition of the capital of its members (Bourdieu 1984a; 1990a). The dominant fraction of the dominant class is high on economic capital, while those high on CULTURAL CAPITAL alone constitute what he terms 'the dominated fraction of the dominant class', or INTELLECTUALS. Bourdieu refers in addition to social capital, and this concept is potentially of great interest to feminism. For 'social capital' is a function of the density of the net of influential connections possessed by the (classed) individual. FAMILY and kinship networks are one key forum for the accumulation of social capital, and it is marriage alliances, and the KINSHIP WORK which frequently falls to women, which are critical in this process of accumulation.

Paradoxically, those daughters who have high value in terms of social capital and therefore marriageability may be more circumscribed in the competition for DISTINCTION in the cultural field than those who have less. Toril Moi argues that this was the case with Simone de Beauvoir, who was able to accumulate more cultural capital than her schoolfriend Zaza by securing a better education, because of Zaza's importance in her family's strategies for the accumulation of social capital through marriage alliances (Moi 1994: 46–7).

See also HABITUS; SYMBOLIC POWER; SYMBOLIC VIOLENCE.

Social constructionism Contemporary feminist theory has by and large shared with sociology the axiom that social reality is constructed, variable across history and CULTURE, and open to change through POLITICAL intervention. Gender-differences are learned in the course of SOCIALIZATION. The distinction between SEX and GENDER has wide currency, and has been used not only to demarcate the domain of the social from the residue left to biology and 'nature', but also to maximize the responsibility of the socio-cultural domain for differences between the sexes and to minimize the effects of the biological. To this end even many physical differences of sex were attributed so far as possible to social circumstances (Oakley 1972). Feminist theory, like sociology, defended itself vigorously against the incursions of biology, and made frequent counter-raids, particularly against socio-biology (Sayers 1982) and in the growing critique of biological thought (e.g. Bleier 1984; Martin 1987).

The intellectual task therefore which confronted second-wave FEMINISM gave priority to the extension of the sociological principle of social constructionism to gender and the relations between the sexes, about which the sociological tradition had been notably silent, tacitly ceding this area to the domain of 'nature' or, at best, to a social psychology which paid heavy dues to biology (Coward 1983; Haraway 1991). Women occupied a LIMINAL position within sociological and anthropological thought – on the margins between 'nature' and 'CULTURE' (Lévi-Strauss 1969; Ortner 1974).

The intermediate terrain of the psychic was the ground on which feminist PSYCHOANALYSIS was founded. The psyche was understood by feminists such as Mitchell (1974) to be socially constructed in the sense that it was produced through the processes of interaction in the family through which the infant acquired a SELF. But, crucially, the psychoanalytic self was in large part UNCONSCIOUS, while sociological discourses had laid emphasis on CONSCIOUSNESS, or at least on activities and behaviours which might readily be brought into focus through CONSCIOUSNESS-RAISING.

By the late 1980s the dominant influence of sociological theory on feminism had given way to the newer TRAVELLING THEORY emanating from France, which was rooted, like Lacanian psychoanalysis, in STRUCTURALIST and POSTSTRUCTURALIST theories of LANGUAGE, as most of the disciplines of the social sciences and humanities began to feel the effects of 'the linguistic turn' in social and cultural thought.

The HERMENEUTIC properties of social life have long been acknowledged. Social action and interaction are meaningful, and it follows that it may perhaps be 'read' rather in the manner of text, although it might be more accurate to speak, following Wittgenstein, of 'knowing how to go on' – of learning to participate in a culture, rather than of 'reading' it (Bourdieu 1990a; Wittgenstein 1967). The new language-based theories affected most fundamentally and earliest the humanities whose business was the study of texts: feminism, literary-critical theory and above all, FILM THEORY. However, there is a tendency to substitute the study of texts for the study of social action, and to treat social action as though the latter were no more than the points of intersection of textual effects. Thus while it is helpful to understand that words are almost always an immensely significant constituent of social action and interaction, and that verbal interventions constitute actions in their own right, there remains a stubborn 'thingness' about social action. If social action may be read 'like a text', it is not the same kind of text as, for example, a film. And while texts have effects, these are usually less immediate and tangible than the effects of social actions.

Pierre Bourdieu founds his sociology of culture on a similar guardedness against what he regards as over-interpretation, or rather, interpretation of the wrong kind. He privileges what he terms HABITUS, and HEXIS, over both the theorizations of the observer, and the rationalizations of the actor, arguing that what is required in the case of social action is an understanding of what he terms the 'logic of practice', which is inscribed first and foremost in the PRACTICE itself (Bourdieu 1984a; 1990a).

Foucault declared for words rather than things; but he also yields a sociology of practice rather than of texts, because of the rootedness of much of his work in the analysis of social institutions. His form of poststructuralism has been more influential on sociological theory than the more exclusively textual approaches of DECONSTRUCTIONISTS such as Derrida.

The battle whose lines were drawn between social constructionism and ESSENTIALISM has lost much of its force in the 1990s (Fuss 1989; Schor and Weed [eds] 1994). The more pressing problem in social theory remains that of theorizing sociality, including gender, in ways that give full significance to language without reducing the social to the textual, and without privileging text over action.

See also CULTURAL STUDIES; READER; TEXTUALITY.

Social contract Seventeenth- and eighteenth-century European contractarian philosophers (Hobbes, Locke, Rousseau) posited an implicit contract which all free and rational citizens were deemed to have entered into voluntarily, and which guaranteed their civil rights and obligations.

After a lengthy period in which the concept was widely discredited, there has been renewed interest in the second half of the twentieth century in a generalized contractual model as paradigmatic of all free social relations per se (Rawls 1972; cf. discussion of social choice theory in Outhwaite and Bottomore [eds] 1993).

It has been recognized widely that the parties to the ENLIGHTENMENT social contract did not include all adult human beings, but assumed CLASS, GENDER and racial exclusions. It was men who held property rights, in particular, rights over their own persons, who were 'stakeholders' in CIVIL SOCIETY and who might thereby enter into free and binding contracts. Feminists have been divided over the strategy of claiming these rights for all excluded groups, including women. Anti-contractarian feminists, RADICAL FEMINIST (Wittig 1992), POST-STRUCTURALIST, or a combination of both (Gatens 1991; Grosz 1994; Irigaray 1985a; Pateman 1988; Whitford 1991), warn that the abstract INDIVIDUAL of the social contract is not just contingently male, and that attempts to extend his rights to women run grave risks. For the individual is embodied, and sex cannot simply be laid aside as irrelevant in the specification of political and social rights.

Carole Pateman has subjected contract theory to an extended feminist critique, which detects behind the overt stories of the contract an anterior but covert SEXUAL CONTRACT which established men's conjugal rights over women. The social contract is mistakenly read as the defeat of PATRIARCHY. It deposes the paternal patriarch, but ushers in the fraternal brotherhood of men: 'Political right originates in sex-right or conjugal right' (Pateman 1988: 3).

See also BODY.

Social history A great deal of feminist THEORY is embedded in feminist historiography, for the point that was once made about Marxism – that 'Marxist history is a history in the making' (Vilar 1973) – is also true of feminism. Theoretical concepts and propositions reveal their power only when they are used to frame and structure scholarly and carefully documented analyses, and indeed, the analysis often preceded the elaboration of THEORY, as for example in the stunningly original historiography of Natalie Zemon Davis (1965).

Each of the various intellectual contexts within which the second wave of feminism emerged had its own distinctive historiographical landscape, and the feminist project of recovering women's history began by taking its bearings within that landscape. In the USA labour history was transformed by feminist interventions (Tilly and Scott 1989) and the culmination of this work and its convergence with the current focus upon gendered SELF-formation and SUBJECTIVITY is exemplified in Deborah Valenze's *The First Industrial Woman* (1995).

In Britain, feminist historiography found a niche within the school of socialist working-class history. A group of feminist historians emerged as part of the History Workshop movement, and they defined their object as much in terms of CLASS as of GENDER. The institutional base was provided by the adult education movement in its working-class constituency. Ruskin College was founded in Oxford in 1899 as a residential college for working-class adults, and it was Ruskin which hosted the History Workshop Conference from the mid-1960s which in turn led to the founding of the *History Workshop Journal* in 1976. Many of the feminist historians who wrote for the *Journal* had been adult students themselves, and had in turn taught in colleges of adult education. In the *Journal* women's history was produced as the history of working-class women, defined primarily as workers, paid or unpaid, industrial or domestic, and the characteristic stamp of British feminist thought owes much to this originating source (Lovell [ed.] 1990).

The History Workshop hosted the first national Women's Liberation Conference in Britain at Ruskin in 1970. Sheila Rowbotham describes this moment in the history of the British women's movement (Rowbotham 1990) in a collection of essays written by feminists of this generation (Wandor 1990).

Socialist feminism   Socialism – the term and the movement – came into existence in the early decades of the nineteenth century in France and Britain, in the form which was dismissed later in the century by Marx as 'UTOPIAN'. It was a theory which emphasized COMMUNITY over INDIVIDUALISM; EQUALITY; and a commitment to the common, collective good. It found practical expression both in the political parties which sprang up all over Europe in the second half of the century, and in a variety of experiments in creating prefigurative socialist communities.

Marxism is of course a socialism, but the preference among feminists for one self-stylization rather than the other is always significant. Although MARXIST

FEMINISM is always to a degree 'revisionist', to so style oneself is to take out an exacting theoretical and political mortgage that the alternative term does not require.

The attraction of socialist over Marxist feminism for those who made this choice was not least the record of utopian socialist writings and social experiments in placing the issue of women, of relations between the sexes, sexuality, and domestic life, high on the agenda.

Socialist feminism has not distanced itself from RADICAL FEMINISM in the same manner that Marxist feminism tends to, and the willingness of socialist feminists to take the traditions of utopian socialism seriously opened up important lines of interconnection. This may be seen for example in the work of Sheila Rowbotham (1972; 1992). Socialist feminists in Britain also tried to forge links with the male left, urging that there were important lessons to be learned about more open and accessible styles of political organization from the women's movement (Rowbotham, Segal and Wainwright 1979).

The 1990s are hard times for Marxist and socialist feminists alike, caught between the scissor blades of POSTSTRUCTURALIST and POSTMODERNIST repudiation, and the collapse of communism. But it may be hoped that traditions of more democratic, open forms of political life and theoretical engagement have left a permanent heritage for a feminism struggling yet again, within the newer theoretical discourses, with issues of community, commonalities across DIFFERENCE, and ways of developing the skills required to listen, to hear, to engage with and make exchanges across those differences. And it is already becoming apparent that accounts are by no means now settled once and for all between feminism and socialism, utopian or scientific.

Socialization In psychology and sociology, the acquisition of GENDER IDENTITY and gender roles is often conceptualized as taking place through socialization. Originally drawn from Talcott Parsons' functionalist account of individual adaption to social structural prerequisites, socialization was given major analytical weight by feminists concerned with the IDEOLOGICAL construction of feminine subjects who seemed willing to 'accede to their own oppression' (Crowley and Himmelweit 1992: 18). However, it often connotes a form of learning theory or cognitive development which assumes that gender characteristics are inscribed on a blank slate. In much ACADEMIC FEMINISM it has been superseded by PSYCHOANALYTICALLY oriented understandings of UNCONSCIOUS psychosexual development which focus on 'the specificity and psychosexual meaning of the sexed BODY' (Grosz 1990) or by other theories of SUBJECTIVITY and IDENTITY.

See IDEOLOGY.

Spectacle The concept of woman as spectacle is central to feminist FILM THEORY. PSYCHOANALYTIC theory offers an account of the processes of disavowal and fetishism whereby woman stands for and assuages LACK, or as Jacqueline Rose puts it: the 'woman in the image [functions] as safeguard against the trouble of the image' (in de Lauretis and Heath [eds] 1980: 178). According to Rose this works in one of two ways: either woman represents plenitude, the totality of cinema; or she represents disturbance, the figure troubling community and image. In the context of SPECTATORSHIP, feminist film theorists have argued that the screen functions as a mirror, reflecting the specular image of the woman back to the female spectator who masochistically identifies with it (e.g. Doane 1987). Arguably, over-emphasis on woman as spectacle in the 1970s and 1980s obscured the ways in which women were active as spectators. More recent film criticism has used ethnography to discuss women as spectating SUBJECTS (Ang 1985, 1991; Jackie Stacey 1988). This has proved an important corrective to the formalist psychoanalytic model, in which DESIRE was always already marked as masculine. Rose (in de Lauretis and Heath 1980), for example, was led to ask 'what is at stake when Dietrich kisses a woman [in the film *Morocco*]?', without considering the possibility of reading lesbian desire in the relationship between image and spectator.

The mirroring of FEMININITY through the lens of sexual difference is a central theme in Luce Irigaray's *Speculum of the Other Woman* (1974) which explores the ways in which women have been made to reflect masculine desire, creating a specularized image of woman with no desire of her own. Angela Carter's fiction addresses a similar theme and explores women's strategies of resistance.

Apart from psychoanalytic models, the other context for the theorization of spectacle is Bakhtin's concept of the CARNIVALESQUE. It provides a more populist, celebratory model and potentially more scope for AGENCY. However, Russo (1994) warns that the opportunities it affords women to make spectacles of themselves are distinctly double-edged. This can be seen in contemporary gendered examples of the carnivalesque such as streaking and skinny-dipping which, while in some sense UTOPIAN, clearly also involve women in a network of sexual POWER relations.

See also GROTESQUE.

Spectatorship FILM THEORY generally, including feminist film theory, has paid a great deal of attention to the viewing relationship, but this body of analysis has been dominated by PSYCHOANALYTICAL 'scopic' theory and is almost entirely focused upon the text, rather than actual spectators, or upon what has been termed 'the cinematic apparatus' (de Lauretis and Heath 1980): the technology of the cinema (the machines and techniques used to make and screen films) and the 'institution of relations and meanings (a whole machinery of affects and effects)' (1980: ix). This approach is likewise indebted to psychoanalytic theory.

Psychoanalytically informed film theory is concerned to map out spectator positionings offered by the narrative organization and the scopic economy of looks between camera, screen actors, and implied spectators. Its dominance has discouraged the development of theoretically informed work on audiences which attempts to find out how actual viewers watching films in movie theatres or on television, rather than under the special circumstances of film studies courses, actually relate to the textual positionings identified in film theory (Mayne 1993; Studlar 1988).

One exception to this generalization is the work of Jackie Stacey (1994). She explores the interplay between film star and spectator, utilizing sophisticated forms of textual analysis, but alongside and interwoven with the analysis of the responses of women to questions about the significance in their lives of their favourite stars of Hollywood cinema in the 1940s and 1950.

Stacey is reserved about the dominant psychoanalytic paradigm although she does not reject it entirely. It produces, she argues, an overly passive account of female spectatorial pleasure in looking which can only be masochistic within the terms of the theory and is locked within the parameters of a heterosexual economy of desire.

There has been a greater degree of interest in theorizing audience response in television studies (Ang 1985; Hobson 1982; Morley and Brunsdon 1978) but work analagous to Janice Radway's ethnographic study of a group of mid-western ROMANCE readers in the United States, or Bridget Fowler's work on working-class women's reading in Glasgow (1991), remains rare in feminist film and television studies.

Spirituality An amorphous, polysemic concept, broad in its CONNOTATIONS. The term circulates inside and outside formal religious discourses, and secular spirituality retains a certain aura of 'religiosity'. The term provides an umbrella which shelters notions of 'transcendence', 'fundamental values', 'the goals and meaning of life', 'human fulfilment', 'creativity', 'wholeness', 'healing', 'connection (with others/nature/the earth/ the cosmos)' (King 1989: 5–6).

Secular celebrations of spirituality are ubiquitous in the NEW SOCIAL MOVEMENTS which emerged in the West from the 1960s, and which frequently drew for their inspiration upon Eastern religions. The language of spirituality frequently informs many radical political movements, such as ecology; the peace movement and animal rights activism.

Feminism is usually understood to be a secular political movement whose roots lie in the emancipatory projects of the ENLIGHTENMENT. But it also 'points to new religious and spiritual developments which affirm the resacralisation of nature, the earth, the body, sexuality, and the celebration of the bonds of community' (King 1989: 224). The RADICAL FEMINIST invention/re-discovery of rituals and symbols of female POWER and COMMUNITY has mined traditions of religious and secular spirituality. While rejecting PATRIARCHAL world religious traditions, it has returned to, or re-invented, ancient female-centred pre-patriarchal religions including witchcraft or Wicca, paganism, and goddess-worship, which have often been read as evidence of earlier MATRIARCHAL societies.

Feminism and spirituality intersect at the point at which the question is raised as to the existence of specifically female forms of spiritual EXPERIENCE, and an affirmative answer leads almost inevitably to a consideration of the female BODY. The transcendence of spirituality is not that sought in the EXISTENTIALIST FEMINISM of Simone de Beauvoir, in which the female body is presented as that which ties women to immanence, that which must be transcended. Rather is may be aligned with POSTSTRUCTURALIST 'corporeal feminism'. They share not only this concern with the specificity of the female body, but also a greater degree of openness than is displayed by more traditionally political feminisms to the DISCOURSES of religiousity and the divine (Irigaray 1974).

The discourse, symbols, and rituals of feminist spirituality circulate freely in the 'revisionings' of the historical and mythological past (Rich 1979) in feminist fiction, poetry, and myth-making, for example Alice Walker's *The Temple of my Familiar*.

Splitting The term refers to the splitting of the SUBJECT as an effect of its entry into the SYMBOLIC ORDER of LANGUAGE and DESIRE. Subjected to division and loss (of imaginary unity), the subject will forever be non-identical to itself. Within FILM THEORY, Christian Metz (1983) argues that NARRATIVE cinema provides compensation for subject splitting by offering the spectator an experience of imaginary union. Feminist film critics have argued that this process is structured across sexual difference so that the system of pleasure is geared to a masculine viewing subject and the woman functions as image. Female IDENTIFICATION with – or fetishistic desire for – a female object on the screen therefore involves a further splitting.

See also SPECTATORSHIP.

Standpoint epistemologies For both proponents and critics the term 'standpoint' groups together a number of feminist EPISTEMOLOGIES which privilege women's 'ways of knowing' above others (Braidotti 1994b; Harding 1986; Maynard 1994b; Smart 1995). Standpoint theorists look two ways, offering on the one hand a critique of dominant conventional EPISTEMOLOGIES in the social and natural sciences and defending the coherence of feminist KNOWLEDGE against postmodern uncertainty on the other.

Initially seen to be based on women's unique position in the sexual DIVISION OF LABOUR or distinctive styles of MORAL REASONING, standpoint's ESSENTIALIST assumption of a universal woman's perspective and its tendency to conflate women's EXPERIENCE and feminist political insight led by the late 1980s to a more critical approach to women's experience as the foundation of feminist knowledge. Donna Haraway's (1991) notion of situated knowledge (cf. KNOWLEDGE) tried, not altogether successfully, to counter the apparent RELATIVISM of standpoint theory. Most standpoint theory developed in feminist sociology now sees feminist standpoint as a relational standpoint (Cain 1990); rather than arising inevitably from the experience of women, which is recognized to be extremely diverse, feminist standpoints are consciously chosen political and social vantage points available to men as well as women. Moreover, in an explicit rejection of IDENTITY POLITICS Harding (1993) suggests that feminists adopt the 'starting point' of women in circumstances very different from their own, in order to get outside their own experiential limitations, while Cain (1990) outlines the need for a feminist public discourse which is independent of personal experience. Along with the continued importance of feminist empiricist theoretical arguments, such attempts to strengthen feminist standpoint by objectivizing its perspective make it impossible to argue that feminist epistemology rejects OBJECTIVITY; rather it redefines objectivity through specifically feminist justificatory epistemic strategies (McLennan 1995).

However, these attempts to revise standpoint have not been accepted by its POSTSTRUCTURALIST critics. Standpointism is seen as a knowledge project which assumes that correctly produced knowledge will lead to the adoption of the best political strategies, an assumption which is no longer tenable in an unpredictable postmodern world (Smart 1995). However, it is arguable whether standpoint theorists really aspire to the total certainty or absolute TRUTH in research which critics read into their work.

State The state is conventionally defined in terms of the existence of a distinct set of centralized institutions which monopolize the use of legitimate force over a given territory (Walby 1990: 150). State societies can be contrasted with the organization of POWER in non-state societies, in which decisions are taken more informally by (men in) family or kin groups, rather than by a separate apparatus.

Although the women's suffrage campaigns show the centrality of access to state power for first-wave feminists, second-wave feminism initially focused on the micropolitics of gender relations in the private sphere; but feminist theories of the state evolved alongside the development of campaigns around male violence, welfare rights, reproductive rights and family and employment law.

Although for feminists the key question is how male power becomes embedded in the different branches of the state apparatus and in state policies, feminist theory is deeply marked by theories of the state which do not see gender as a dimension of power (or which take for granted its male character). Whereas liberal political theory sees the state as an autonomous 'watchdog' whose role should be restricted to the establishment and protection of INDIVIDUAL liberties (a view which presents many contradictions for liberal feminism [Eisenstein 1981]), deterministic views of the state see its structure and policies determined by the nature of the society of which it is part. For instance, British SOCIALIST FEMINIST attempts in the 1970s to theorize the relation between women's OPPRESSION and the state developed initially in relation to the then current Marxist conception of the capitalist state, focusing on the role of the welfare state in reproducing women's dependence on men (McIntosh 1978; Wilson 1977) or arbitrating between the competing interests of capital and PATRIARCHY (Summerfield 1984).

This view of 'the state', as a single entity determined by class interests, made it difficult to explore questions regarding women's representation in state office (Wolkowitz 1987), while the focus on the exploitation of women's labour provided little space for developing theory of the state's 'prerogatory monopoly' (Brown 1992) of organized VIOLENCE. It was also incompatible with a (different but equally deterministic) view of the state as male in its very inception, founded on a 'fraternal contract' between men (Pateman 1988). Moreover, state theory has to take account of the GLOBAL economic interests which limit NATION states' capacity to determine and enforce public policies within their own borders.

Feminist theory has been affected even more by the recent rejection of grand theoretical schema and the pluralization of what were previously seen as single social phenomena. Theoretical rejections of the 'deterministic paradigm' (Rai and Lievesey [eds] 1996: 12) and the recognition of diversity among states (e.g. post-colonial states, or what Molyneux [1995] calls the 'male democracies' of formerly socialist Eastern Europe) have been accompanied by more feminist interest in access to power through state office. For example, in Australia 'femocrats' have come to have considerable influence in the corridors of power and have argued that although in the past the state has been male, there is now a possibility of altering that fact (Watson [ed.] 1990), as neat a recapitulation of liberal political theory within feminism as one could hope to find. But while some theorists are embracing what is seen as women's 'expanding relationships to state institutions' (Brown 1992: 11), others question whether increasing state interference in the family and sexuality, even if it has the apparent aim of protecting women, really empowers women or whether it rather increases female DEPENDENCE and widens the 'pervasively disciplining' capacity of the state (Brown 1992: 9).

As against POSTSTRUCTURALISTS who see the state as merely 'a plurality of discursive forums' (Yeatman in Watson 1992: 63) Shirin Rai suggests using 'the state' as a 'shorthand term' for 'a network of power relations existing in co-operation and also in tension, . . . situate[d] within a grid composed of economic, political, legal and cultural forms all interacting on, with and against each other' (Rai and Lievesey [eds] 1996: 5). Her relatively open definition provides scope for exploring a variety of different structural configurations and situations without denying a 'significant structuring of power' (Walby 1990: 31).

Stereotypes 'Almost always a term of abuse', according to Dyer (1993), who explores certain functions of stereotypes that might be viewed more positively: as an ordering process, as 'short cuts' etc. The term has also been discussed in PSYCHOANALYTICAL terms (Gilman 1985).

Tessa Perkins's essay on stereotypes reveals the influence of Dyer's discussion, but points to the need to differentiate between types. She analyses the complex negotiations of prevailing social typologies and stereotypes in the self-presentations of individuals and groups to themselves and to others and in the REPRESENTATION of others (Perkins 1979). She reinforces the positions of those feminists who have, against the grain of the dominant psychoanalytically informed traditions of feminist FILM THEORY, argued for more positive valorizations of popular fictions which draw heavily upon stereotypes (Stacey 1994b). Such fictions have the advantage of accessibility and of offering familiar pleasures, which yet may be turned through imaginative play upon stereotypical images to the point of subversion.

See also REALISM.

Strategic essentialism See ESSENTIALISM.

Stratification See CLASS.

Structuralism A structure is 'a set of interconnecting parts of any complex thing' (*Shorter OED*). In sociological and anthropological theory the idea that societies have structures which are reproduced in similar or modified form over time, underpinned the dominant paradigm of these disciplines up to the early 1960s: structural-functionalism.

Structuralism displaced structural-functionalism in the social sciences but it retained a number of the latter's characteristics. Both were OBJECTIVIST, laying claim to rigorous scientific status. Both had depth/surface explanatory models which, with deep underlying structures exercising determining causality over the phenomenal social world. Neither had much place for human AGENCY. Social causality occurred behind the backs of human actors and their intentions in both structuralism and structural-functionalist accounts.

The 'structure' of a building, a sentence, the economy, may all be said to consist of interconnecting parts. Nineteen-sixties structuralist thought, however, departed from structural-functionalism in that it was rebuilt upon a linguistic base. Ferdinand de Saussure had identified the structure of LANGUAGE in complex sets of BINARY oppositions. It was the relationship between the elements that was significant rather than the relationship to the referent. As Michel Foucault was to put it, there occurred a shift within the social sciences and humanities from things to words.

Structural linguistics informed Jacques Lacan's reworking of Freudian PSYCHOANALYSIS, Lévi-Strauss's structural anthropology, Louis Althusser's reinterpretation of Marx, and Roland Barthes' SEMIOLOGY or the study of cultural systems of MYTH and IDEOLOGY. The common premise was that the UNCONSCIOUS, myth, and CULTURE – the very mind itself, 'savage' and 'civilized' – were structured like language (rather than, for example, like buildings or economic systems).

Second-wave FEMINISM emerged at the moment of structuralism's greatest influence, when it was challenged only by that group of theories which placed their emphasis on human agency in action and interaction: PHENOMENOLOGY; ethnomethodology; symbolic interactionism. Feminisms, as they built up their theoretical repertoire, tended to be influenced by one or another of these two groupings of theory, with MARXIST FEMINISM drawing on structuralism, while RADICAL FEMINIST EPISTEMOLOGY turned to the sociological phenomenology of Alfred Schutz (Stanley and Wise 1983). In the case of Dorothy Smith's influential contribution, Schutz's phenomenology was combined with the early work of Marx (Smith 1988).

Anthropology has been used as a reserve which feminists who were not anthropologists often raided for good counter-examples of gender systems which might disrupt the DOXA, in theory and in social life, of naturalized gender divisions (Rosaldo 1980). Margaret Mead's work was frequently cited (Mead 1963). Lévi-Strauss's structural anthropology seemed promising in that he placed at the very centre of all social worlds the exchange of women between men, and identified an opposition, which he claimed was universal in cultures, between nature and culture, leading Sherry Ortner to ask 'Is female to male as nature is to culture?' (1974). Her answer was equivocal. Women occupied the LIMINAL space on the margins between.

Juliet Mitchell, one of the pioneers of feminist psychoanalysis, attempted to explain the subordination of women through a combination of Althusserian Marxism, Lacanian psychoanalysis, and Lévi-Strauss's theory of the exchange of women (1974. See DUAL SYSTEMS THEORY), and great many Marxist feminists followed her in explaining women's subordination through this double focus, using Althusserian Marxism and Lacanian psychoanalysis. Other feminists retained the traditional reserve about psychoanalysis, but the basic structuralist premise was widely accepted.

Structuralism also influenced feminism through lesbian critiques and APPROPRIATIONS. In 1975, Gayle Rubin wrote an important article which in turn was greatly influenced by Mitchell, which engages critically with the concept of the exchange of women. For Lévi-Strauss it was the incest taboo which motivated that exchange and ensured sociality. Rubin draws attention to an implicit and unacknowledged prior taboo on same sex sexuality. Luce Irigaray went on to ask what happens 'when the goods get together'? (1981).

See also POSTMODERNISM; POSTSTRUCTURALISM.

Structure of feeling The work of Raymond Williams has had less impact on feminist theory than it deserves, having been overlooked in many cases in favour of TRAVELLING THEORY from continental Europe – STRUCTURALISM, DECONSTRUCTIONISM, POSTSTRUCTURALISM and SEMIOLOGY. Williams distanced himself from these theories, yet fully recognized the place of LANGUAGE in social and cultural life. He drew for preference upon the work of Vygotsky (1978) and Volosinov (1986). The importance of Williams's early work in the development of British CULTURAL STUDIES is fully registered, but it is almost as though he ceased to write after producing these 'founding texts' (*Culture and Society* and *The Long Revolution*). His later works in which he spelled out his distinctive CULTURAL MATERIALISM (1977a; 1980b) and in which the impact of Volosinov's linguistic theory is most evident, have been virtually ignored in feminist writings.

Williams defines 'structure of feeling' as being

as firm and definite as 'structure' suggests, yet it operates in the most delicate and least tangible parts of our activity. In one sense, this structure of feeling is the culture of a period: it is the particular living result of all the elements in the general organization (1961: 64).

'Structures of feeling' are registered in intellectual GENERATIONS, and Jenny Taylor suggests that these terms might be used to trace out the impact of generation within the history of FEMINISM, both in relation to the second wave, and historically. This concept of might be utilized to add further nuance to contemporary discussions of DIFFERENCE. Across the diversity of 'race', culture and class unexpected commonalities sometimes come into view that may be a function of feminist intellectual generations.

Williams's work has had considerable impact on feminist theory and cultural studies in the United States (Cocks 1989), especially on certain strands of MATERIALIST FEMINISM (Landry and MacLean 1993).

Subalternity Originally a Gramscian term for the subordinated consciousness or SUBJECTIVITY of non-elite social groups, the concept has been developed by Ranajit Guha ([ed.] 1982) and the group associated with the South Asian journal *Subaltern Studies* in the attempt to recover subaltern voices in Indian historiography. Their project is defined as a rethinking of 'Indian colonial historiography from the perspective of the discontinuous chain of peasant insurgencies during the colonial occupation' (Spivak in Williams and Chrisman [eds] 1993).

In response to this initiative the term has recently been appropriated by post-colonial theorists such as Bhabha and Spivak. In her challenging essay, 'Can the subaltern speak?' (1993a), Spivak addresses the way the 'subaltern' woman is already POSITIONED, constructed or spoken for as lacking credibility, absent, silent or erased in a variety of DISCOURSES. Other feminists question the usefulness of the term, arguing that it is deterministic and homogenizes disparate groups of subaltern women (Loomba 1993) and that Black female subjectivity cannot be defined primarily in terms of domination, subordination and 'subalternization' (Boyce Davies 1994). Boyce Davies prefers the term 'MIGRATORY SUBJECTIVITY' to suggest both the fluidity and agency of Black femininity in an international frame.

See also SYMBOLIC VIOLENCE.

Subject A term whose ambiguity as between conscious AGENCY and passive subjection was exploited by Louis Althusser (1977). His essay on 'ideological state apparatuses' was highly influential upon contemporary feminist theoretical understanding of the 'subject', which was placed on the terrain previously occupied on the one hand by the sociological theory of SOCIALIZATION and on the other by the Marxist concept of IDEOLOGY.

Althusser had drawn on Lacan to sketch out a quasi-functionalist account of the 'fit' between 'social formations' and individual subjectivities and IDENTITIES.

He drew on the Lacanian analysis of the production of the subject through '(MIS)-RECOGNITION' in the psychic processes of family life (see PSYCHOANALYSIS). The production of the requisite subjectivities or self-identities was the work, for Althusser, of the 'ideological state apparatuses': in modern capitalism, principally the family and the school. The process of INTERPELLATION, or ideological address to the subject, when answered by the subject's own (mis)-recognition, ensures that the subject accepts his or her own subjection while retaining the illusion of coherence and agency.

How far this Marxist functionalism was actually compatible with the Lacanian theory of the subject is questionable, and FRENCH FEMINIST post-Lacanians such as Irigaray (1974), in developing theories of feminine subjectivity, engaged in more critical APPROPRIATION of Lacan. Irigaray's concern was with the 'sexuate subject' rather than the reproduction of social formations (see SEXUATE RIGHTS).

In Britian, however, the first major work of appropriation of psychoanalysis for feminism by Juliet Mitchell (1974) was cast in terms of Althusser's project of fleshing out the Marxian concept of ideology with Lacanian psychoanalysis. Her focus, too, was on feminine subjectivity, but the ambition was to place this account alongside the Marxist theory of capitalist production, in a DUAL SYSTEMS approach. Mitchell told the story of how the BISEXUAL female infant acquired a feminine psychic identity that served to reproduce the gender identities and relations of CAPITALISM.

Jacqueline Rose critiqued this functionalist logic in a response, ostensibly, to Elizabeth Wilson's critique of Mitchell:

> the unconscious constantly reveals the 'failure' of identity... Feminism's affinity with psychoanalysis rests above all...with this recognition that there is a resistance to identity which lies at the very heart of psychic life (Rose 1986: 91).

Foucault has largely replaced Althusser in those feminist theories of the subject that are more distanced from psychoanalysis, although there is an almost infinite possibility of combination. Foucauldian feminists have retained Rose's insistence that subjective identity in general, and feminine identity in particular, are always contested. Foucault goes beyond the Althusserian (mis)-recognition and consent model of ideological subject-formation/subjection in his concept of 'regimes of KNOWLEDGE/POWER', which he analyses in such institutions as the prison, school, and asylum. These regimes, he argues, have the effect of inscribing identity onto the very BODIES of those subject to them. This work has been highly influential in the development of 'corporeal feminism' (Braidotti 1991;1994b; Butler 1992 and 1993; Gatens 1995; Grosz 1994; McNay 1992; Ramazanoglu [ed.] 1993).

Foucault has been criticized however for the rather passive, overdetermined subject yielded by his concept of DISCIPLINARY regimes, a subject who could have little real agency. He countered with his dictum of resistance:

> There are no relations of power without resistance; the latter are all the more real and effective because they are formed right at the point where relations of power are exercised (Foucault 1980b: 142)

It is this qualification which founds the more optimistic versions of Foucauldian feminism. Susan Bordo, herself a feminist who draws extensively on Foucault, enters a reservation about POSTMODERN appropriations of Foucault, such as that of John Fiske (1987) and Judith Butler (1992), which utilize a conception of power as 'a terrain without hills and valleys – where all forces have become "resources"' (Bordo 1993: 261):

> For Foucault, the metaphorical terrain of resistance is explicitly that of the 'battle'; the 'points of confrontation' may be 'innumerable' and 'instable', but they involve a serious, often deadly, struggle of embodied (that is, historically situated and shaped) forces (Bordo 1993: 263).

Subject-in-process   In POSTSTRUCTURALIST accounts the subject is split into subject and object, conscious and UNCONSCIOUS aspects and is always in the process of being constituted in and through psychic and discursive systems. The fluidity of SUBJECTIVITY is such that it never fully coincides with IDENTITY. Landry and MacLean (1993) argue that, notwithstanding subjective instability, the subject is always in the process of CENTRING itself in order to act at all.

Subject position   According to the linguist Emile Beveniste (1969), 'I', 'you', 'he', 'she' etc. are subject positions offered in LANGUAGE which the speaking subject adopts or enters into. 'I' does not belong to or refer exclusively to 'me' any more than it does to 'you'; the character of language is the very reversibility of persons. For DISCOURSE theorists, discourses and texts offer us, and invite us to take up, a range of IDEOLOGICALLY implicated subject positions. Lacan argues that subjects enter a pre-existing system of signifiers which enables them to take up gendered and familial subject positions within a relational system (father/mother/daughter/son). The system is organized around the phallus or transcendental signifier and the process of subject positioning is governed by the UNCONSCIOUS.

Feminist theories of location refer to the ways in which the subject is positioned in relation to a network of discourses organized around CLASS, 'RACE',

ETHNICITY, SEXUALITY etc. In the light of a number of challenges, particularly from POSTMODERNISM and from BLACK FEMINISM, feminists generally have recognized the need to situate their discourse within multiple and often contradictory fields of POWER. Increasingly, too, feminist theories of KNOWLEDGE emphasize the process of positioning as itself an EPISTEMOLOGICAL act. Donna Haraway (1988) calls for 'accountable positioning', exhorting feminists to recognize the limited and situated character of the knowledge they produce.

Subjectivity See SUBJECT.

Subjugated knowledge See EPISTEMOLOGY; KNOWLEDGE.

Symbolic Traditionally, human LANGUAGE and CULTURE have been seen as realms invested with symbolic meanings. The anthropology of Lévi-Strauss has demonstrated that the human subject is an animal who creates and lives by symbols. And while Marx crucially showed how symbolic systems arise from particular socio-economic contexts, generations of cultural producers and consumers have shown that human culture is not reducible to its economic base. The concept itself is central to Lacanian theory, and it is this PSYCHOANALYTIC resonance that has come to dominate contemporary critical theory. Lacan distinguishes between three orders: the Symbolic, the IMAGINARY and the REAL. Building on Saussure's linguistic theory, Lacan views the Symbolic order as above all a product of language which as a system imposes rules upon the human infant. Central to Lacan's conception of language and the constitution of the subject is the concept of loss: it is only when the infant loses a primary object – the mother as presence – that symbols enter the field of language and the infant becomes a speaking subject. Entry into language requires that the infant takes up a SUBJECT POSITION in a system of sexual difference, thereby acquiring a GENDER IDENTITY. The process is governed by the LAW OF THE FATHER, symbolized by the phallus. Woman, associated with the Imaginary figure of the mother, represents loss and LACK and cannot therefore be a Symbolic signifier. As Lacan infamously claims, woman does not exist within the Symbolic.

While acknowledging some of the implications of Lacanian theory for feminism, notably the fact that women live, speak and struggle under the sign of the phallus, feminists have challenged aspects of Lacan's account. Deborah Cameron (1985), from a linguistic perspective, rejects the linguistic DETERMINISM implied by the claim that language is always already PHALLOCENTRIC, offering women no place within the Symbolic. She argues that language per se cannot be ascribed to masculinity and that as women clearly do use language, it makes more sense to analyse language use in terms of asymmetric POWER relations. Feminists in the French tradition have tended to agree with Lacan that the Symbolic is phallocentric, but have rejected his claim that woman has 'no place' anywhere. Cixous (1981) and Irigaray (1985a) argue that women have a separate Symbolic, characterized for Cixous by plenitude, and for Irigaray by multiplicity, in contrast to the logic of the Same and lack which characterize the phallocentric Symbolic. Kristeva (1980) locates resistance to the Symbolic not in a separate female symbolic which she rejects, but in the SEMIOTIC. Analogous to Lacan's Imaginary, the semiotic represents a trace of pre-oedipal DESIRE which irrupts into the Symbolic and disrupts its phallocentric logic. It refers to the non-symbolic, physical aspects of language, such as sound, rhythm, and tone. Associated with the mother's body and therefore coded as FEMININE, the semiotic is not, however, the prerogative of women, and in her discussion of the semiotic in literature the examples Kristeva cites derive from the work of male writers.

Kristeva (1980) characterizes the history of FEMINISM in terms of those feminists who want a place for women within the Symbolic, and those who want to create an alternative female Symbolic according to WOMEN'S TIME. She problematizes both these goals, insisting that, as there is no human culture outside the Symbolic realm, political programmes which seek to break or transcend the Symbolic order are UTOPIAN, regressive or misguided. This view is shared by (feminist) psychoanalytic theorists generally who hold that the Symbolic, as the condition of being human, necessitates SPLITTING, separation and the production of DESIRE. Indeed, as Jacqueline Rose (1986) argues, this is where desire, including political desire, comes from. However, this leads to something of a paradox for psychoanalytically oriented feminists: if there is no alternative to the Symbolic and the Symbolic is inimical to women, then what is POLITICS for?

Symbolic power One of a battery of related concepts developed by the French sociologist Pierre Bourdieu. He is a POSTSTRUCTURALIST in the strict sense that his work is built upon a critique of STRUCTURALISM (Bourdieu 1990a), but his name is not often included in the poststructuralist roster. Yet he, too, seeks to cut a path through the pervasive BINARIES of social thought: structure/AGENCY; OBJECTIVITY/subjectivity; MATERIAL/ideal; mind/BODY.

For Bourdieu the social world is constituted by a set of 'FIELDS' of social PRACTICES whose participants interact according to the specific logic of the field in question, and who compete with one another for something akin to Max Weber's 'status honour'. Those who are rich in 'symbolic capital' may exercise symbolic power, or domination. Those whose CULTURE lacks recognition, either generally, or within that particular field, are subject to SYMBOLIC VIOLENCE.

'Fields' are rule-governed only in Wittgenstein's sense: the rules are tacit, exhibited by the participants' knowledge of 'how to go on' (Wittgenstein 1967);

by their 'feel for the game'. Neither the rules which may be articulated by participants, nor the formal models of 'underlying generative structures' developed by 'objective' observers taking a theoretical stance, such as Lévi-Strauss's 'savage mind', corresponds to what Bourdeu terms 'the logic of practice' (1990a). Bourdieu refuses to privilege either 'objectivity' or 'subjectivity'.

The skilled practitioner acquires not 'knowledge of the rules' but an appropriate HABITUS: a set of general dispositions which are developed through practical experience of interaction within the field. It is laid down in early childhood, family, class in the contexts of neighbourhood, and revealed in shared habits, posture, everyday likes and dislikes, propensities to act and react in certain ways – above all in the dispositions of the body itself, bodily 'hexis'. Thus, like Erving Goffman whose work has influenced him (Goffman 1976), Bourdieu reads women's subordination in terms not of what is said or even done, but in the bearings of male and female BODIES, especially in traditional or 'doxic' societies (Bourdieu 1990a; 1990b).

Through his deployment of these terms Bourdieu occupies the territory of IDEOLOGY. But he uses a term which avoids the implication of consciousness: DOXA, or those beliefs which are absolutely taken for granted, embedded in practice. Once articulated, doxa becomes orthodoxy, but is more readily challenged.

Feminism has been slow to recognize the potential of Bourdieu's work for the analysis of gender relations. It is no more (and no less) in need of critique from the point of view of gender and feminism than that of the better known poststructuralists who have been APPROPRIATED for feminist theory, such as Derrida and Foucault. Toril Moi draws on Bourdieu in her study of the making of Simone de Beauvoir as an INTELLECTUAL woman (Moi 1994). Ann Phoenix's work on young unmarried Black mothers in a context of high Black male unemployment might be used to support Moi's analysis. She argues that it makes sense for these mothers to adopt the strategy of educating their daughters for the labour market through educational qualification rather than schooling them in FEMININITY with an eye to the marriage market (Phoenix 1987; 1991).

Bridget Fowler's study of Scottish working-class women readers (Fowler 1991) adapts elements of Bourdieu's theory of DISTINCTION, and she has written a more extended overview and critique of Bourdieu's sociology of culture (Fowler 1997).

Symbolic violence Symbolic violence is possible, argues Pierre Bourdieu, because of the cultural and symbolic legitimacy conferred by powerholders within a whole broad range of cultural practices. The violence entailed in this process consists in the fact that other cultures and cultural practices are, by the same token, delegitimated, discounted.

In terms reminiscent of Gramsci's 'common sense', Bourdieu argues that the values and judgements of those who 'sacralize' the dominant culture are endorsed, if only negatively, in the lived experience and practice of the dominated. A recurrent phrase in Bourdieu's work is 'not for the likes of us'. The dominated live out, embody, and in many cases accept as 'natural' or 'doxic' their own domination. The first stage in conscious opposition lies in bringing DOXA into question by showing its constructed nature – rather in the manner of feminist CONSCIOUSNESS-RAISING.

Feminism itself is no stranger to symbolic violence. The critique from DIFFERENCE forces recognition of the exclusions in feminist theory and practice which has been constructed from particular vantage points while presenting itself as valid for all women. But in turn, feminist revisionist critiques de-legitimate, subjugate. earlier feminisms.

See also CULTURAL CAPITAL; DISTINCTION; HABITUS; SYMBOLIC POWER.

T

Teratology   The science of monsters (Schor 1987). .
    See also DISABILITY; GROTESQUE; NORMALIZATION.

Testimony   See PERSONAL NARRATIVES.

Textuality   In POSTSTRUCTURALIST theories the term refers to a conception of the text-as-writing which is radically at odds with traditional concepts of texts as *works*. Roland Barthes distinguishes between 'text' and 'work' in the following way:

> The work is a fragment of substance... the Text is a methodological field... the work can be seen (in bookshops, in catalogues, in exam syllabuses), the text is a process of demonstration...the work can be held in the hand, the text is held in language, only exists in the movement of discourse...*is experienced only in the activity of production* (1977b: 156-7).

In this model, textuality is seen not as a finished product but as a process of inscription, whereby meaning is ceaselessly posited and deferred according to the play of DIFFÉRANCE. A major consequence of this view is the rejection of mimetic theories of REPRESENTATION whereby the text is viewed as an expression of an author. Indeed Barthes displaces altogether the author as the guarantor of a text, arguing that if anything it is the READER who represents the place where the multiplicity of writing is focused.

Feminist criticism has posed the question of whether textuality is gendered. The GYNOCRITICISM of Elaine Showalter and Gilbert and Gubar suggests that there are distinctive stylistic qualities to women's writing. Other feminists reject the identification of particular textual forms with gender-exclusive interests. Landry and Maclean (1993), for example, argue that 'a theory of textual agency that attributes formal, textual features with gender-specific qualities relies on an essentializing tendency' (1993: 93).

See AUTHORSHIP.

Theory

> Systematic conception or statement of the principles of something; abstract knowledge...: often used as implying more or less unsupported hypothesis: distinct from or opposed to *practice* (*Shorter OED*).

In any given DISCIPLINE, theory consists in the systematic framework of interrelated concepts and propositions, and the EPISTEMOLOGICAL, ontological and methodological assumptions which govern a given field of KNOWLEDGE. The term is also used more loosely for any speculative inquiry.

While the need for theory has been widely recognized in the various branches of knowledge production, the status accorded theoretical terms and propositions has been a matter of dispute. For positivists, theoretical terms were convenient fictions: props for the production of positive, verifiable knowledge; for the critic of positivism, Karl Popper, theories were nominal or conventional, but necessary to knowledge production. They were falsifiable rather than verifiable by empirical tests. Unfalsifiable (and therefore unscientific) theories, for Popper, included Marxism and Freudianism.

During the period of dominance of structural-functionalism and then STRUCTURALISM within the social sciences, theory was privileged and was often set out formally in axioms and propositions (Parsons 1951), and seen as an essential guide to practice (and politics).

With the advent of POSTSTRUCTURALISM theory's status has become more enigmatic. On the one hand, abstract philosophical theory has, de facto, immense prestige. On the other, science is stripped of epistemological privilege, which is dispersed equally among theoretical and extra-theoretical discourses including those of literature, personal writing and popular forms. As 'systems' have fallen into disrepute, so 'theory' has become less a matter of developing systematic interrelated concepts and causal propositions, and is become more freewheeling and eclectic, ranging imperiously across the whole field of social and political thought: in Edward Said's term, it has become TRAVELLING THEORY, philosophical, general and abstract, and uncontained by disciplinary boundaries (Said 1983).

Feminist theory has always had an uncomfortable relationship with feminist practice and politics (Evans 1982), especially where it has borrowed from twentieth-century 'travelling theory', as it increasingly does. 'Theory' is still frequently denounced as 'malestream', elitist, mystificatory. The great weight given within RADICAL FEMINISM to experience and CONSCIOUSNESS-RAISING has often placed feminism in greater sympathy with empiricism. On the other hand, the need is widely felt to 'go beyond' appearances, the 'givenness' of experience, the lived 'naturalness' of everyday understandings in which women's subordination is inscribed, and this opens up feminism to the claims of theory.

But what kind of theory? Within the social sciences in the second half of the twentieth century there has been a recurrent tension between OBJECTIVIST theories which place explanatory emphasis on underlying structures and relations that operate 'behind the backs' of human agents, such as structuralism, structural-functionalism, and Marxisms based on Marx's later works, and on the other hand more SUBJECTIVIST theories which take the point of view of the participant: PHENOMENOLOGY, ethnomethodology, symbolic interactionism, and (early) Marxism, which stress AGENCY over against structure. Poststructuralism has dismantled this opposition between structure and agency, problematizing both. It recognizes no determining structures, but neither does it reinstate human agency, being in most of its forms as anti-HUMANIST as had been structuralism and structural-functionalism.

Joanna de Groot and Mary Maynard (1993) suggest adopting the sociological structural-functionalist Robert Merton's (1968) concept of 'middle-range theory' as a strategic choice for feminism. It has the advantage, they claim, of recognizing and attempting to explain structured inequalities while forbearing the kind of determinist account – the part explained in terms of the whole – critiqued by poststructuralism. Middle-range theory may develop 'grounded' theory (Glaser and Strauss 1967) which moves back and forth between the experiential/empirical and general and more abstract levels.

Third World   The connotations of the term 'Third World' are given by the different DISCOURSES in which it is located. Originally a Cold War term for the unaligned countries which supported neither the 'First World' parliamentary democracies nor the 'Second World' Communist Bloc, it rapidly became a term in neo-evolutionary DEVELOPMENT discourse. As Chandra Talpade Mohanty (1992; 1993) and others have pointed out, its uncritical adoption by Western feminist discourses constructs 'the Third World woman' as a singular, monolithic and helpless victim of PATRIARCHY and/or MODERNIZATION (Chowdhry 1995). However, it could be argued that much ACADEMIC FEMINIST writing has not *homogenized* Third World women; even traditional mainstream anthropology was concerned with specifying differences among so-called 'primitive' societies and feminist anthropology and development studies, whatever their other defects, usually present detailed accounts rooted in particular locales.

The Third World is also a term in the political economy of UNDERDEVELOPMENT which explains Third World poverty in terms of economic distortion created by colonialism, imperialism and the practices of international agencies and, although sometimes replaced by the term 'the South', is still used by many in that sense. For instance, Shirin Rai favours its continued use as 'a term of political opposition, as well as indicative of the colonial experience of these states' (1996: 2). However, others argue that even as a term in political economy its use 'reveals the hierarchical, dualistic nature of Western thought' and tends to reify and reinforce the North/South divide (Marchand and Parpart [eds] 1995: 16).

Transcendence   See EXISTENTIALIST FEMINISM; OTHER.

Transgression   The term has achieved currency in critical theory to describe the exceeding of SYMBOLIC, socio-political and/or bodily norms. Kristeva (1982) incorporates Bakhtin's theory of the CARNIVALESQUE and Lacan's theory of SUBJECTIVITY in her account of ABJECTION, seeing the GROTESQUE, archaic mother as the principal site of transgression. In *Revolution in Poetic Language* (1984) she identifies transgression of the codes and structures of language with the transgression of social and political norms. Significantly, Kristeva views rupture of phallocentric discourse as a *feminine* practice. This model encapsulates the key question for feminist theorists and critics: what is the political status of gender transgression? Prior to Kristeva, Natalie Davis, in her study of carnival and gender in early modern Europe (1965), had argued dialectically that the image of the carnivalesque woman simultaneously undermined and reinforced the existing social structure. Russo similarly points up the double-edged character of transgression for women, asking 'In what sense can women really produce or make spectacles of themselves?' (1994: 60). Nevertheless, she argues that the

figure of the female transgressor as public SPECTACLE still possesses powerful possibilities of redeployment as a demystifying or UTOPIAN model of FEMININITY.
See also NORMALIZATION.

Translation   Susan Bassnett-Maguire describes translation as a process which involves

> the rendering of a source language (SL) text into the target language (TL) so as to ensure that (1) the surface meaning of the two will be approximately similar and (2) the structures of the SL will be preserved as closely as possible but not so closely that the TL structures will be seriously distorted (1991: 2).

She notes that translation has historically been seen as a secondary activity; as a mechanical rather than a creative process and, in consequence, as a low status occupation. Commentators have been divided on whether translation constitutes an art, a craft or a science. The dominant nineteenth-century Western models conceived of the translator's role as either 'servant' to the text or its civilizer; either humbly reproducing the (usually classical) text or confidently 'improving' the (usually ORIENTALIST) text. This view, consistent with colonial imperialism, was challenged in the twentieth century by the Russian formalists and by the subsequent development in the 1950s, mainly in Eastern Europe, of translation studies.

Andre Lefevère (1992) identified translation studies as a discipline concerned with the 'problems raised by the production and description of translations' and, more ambitiously, 'to produce a comprehensive theory which can be used as a guideline for the production of translations'. It is a multidisciplinary field encompassing linguistics, stylistics, SEMIOTICS, literary history, and AESTHETICS. Key questions for translation studies include the problems of evaluation, equivalence and cultural untranslatability. A major issue concerns the nature of the relationship between the SL and the TL. Lefevère suggests that it is one of 'refraction' – a change of perception – rather than one of reproduction. Given the complex character of translation, Susan Bassnett-Maguire concludes that:

> it is pointless...to argue for a definitive translation, since translation is intimately tied up with the context in which it is made....There can no more be the ultimate translation than there can be the ultimate poem or the ultimate novel, and any assessment of translation can only be made by taking account both of the process of creating it and its function in any given context (1991: 9-10).

These concerns overlap in significant ways with those of POSTSTRUCTURALISM, whose theorists argue that language yields up no definitive meanings.

In addition Bassnett-Maguire points to the development since the mid 1980s of a feminist translation studies concerned with women's writing in translation. Examples include Myriam Diaz-Diocaretz's (1985) study of Adrienne Rich in translation and the special issue of the journal *Tessera* in 1989.

Transsexuality   Transsexuality has a long history in various guises including theories of hermaphroditism and androgyny. Recently, postmodern, QUEER and lesbian and gay theorists have begun to explore transsexuality as a LIMINAL SEXUALITY which calls conventional concepts of GENDER and sexuality into question. Examples include Marjorie Garber's (1992) study of cross-dressing and Kate Bornstein's (1994) account of her own transsexuality in *Gender Outlaw*. Virginia Woolf's high camp classic *Orlando* (1992, first published 1928) is a key text for feminists. Orlando's gender transgression – male-to-female across three centuries – describes a witty upper-class fantasy in which transsexuality and transvestism are linked and one is the consequence of the other. However, the issue sits uneasily in feminist contexts, where there is a clear tension between the more sympathetic accounts of QUEER theorists, and the hostile and suspicious approach adopted by some feminist and LESBIAN FEMINIST commentators. Feminists as different as Elaine Showalter and Janice Raymond criticize male transsexuality as a male attempt to usurp the prerogatives of feminist criticism and female affection respectively. Such responses indicate a fear of the sexual unknown, suggesting that feminist attitudes to gender difference are more ESSENTIALIST, if not fundamentalist, than we would like to think. However, the issue of social POWER relations and men's greater access to resources – including surgery – cannot be ignored. Moreover, the gap between gender IDENTITY and sexual orientation is frequently being elided in recent mainstream arguments in support of gender realignment procedures. In some cases of female-to-male transsexuality, young women with 'masculine' gender identity are undergoing physical surgery when it may be their sexual orientation (towards other women rather than men) that it is the cause of their 'disorder'. The relationship between sex, gender and sexuality which transsexuality so sharply foregrounds is therefore a highly complex one.

Travelling theory   'Like people and schools of criticism, ideas and theories travel – from person to person, from situation to situation, from one period to another' (Said 1983: 226).

Joan Cocks identifies the major travelling theories of contemporary feminism in the work of Karl Marx, Antonio Gramsci, Raymond Williams, Michel Foucault, and Edward Said himself (Cocks 1989). Jacques Derrida, Jacques Lacan and Roland Barthes must surely be added, along with many more. But travelling theory is transfigured in its journeying, 'to some extent transformed by its new uses, its new position in a new time and place' (Said 1983: 226–7).

Has feminist theory travelled? Sometimes it seems only within feminism itself. Consulting other reference books in the preparation of this volume, it is difficult to avoid the conclusion that feminism's close engagement with, critique and creative APPROPRIATION of the range of contemporary theories in the social sciences and humanities has rarely been fully reciprocated.

Truth Contemporary feminist theory has engaged successively or simultaneously and variously, with STRUCTURALIST MARXISM, sociological PHENOMENOLOGY, Lacanian psychoanalysis and theories of LANGUAGE, DECONSTRUCTIONISM, POSTSTRUCTURALISM, and POSTMODERNISM. In each of these theories, 'truth' and related epistemological concepts have come under close scrutiny.

This critique of EPISTEMOLOGY runs parallel to and at points merges with, the feminist critique which was developed primarily in relation to the DISCIPLINES of biology and sociology. Insofar as it went beyond RADICAL FEMINIST refusals of 'malestream' THEORY, this critique drew either upon sociological phenomenology (Dorothy Smith 1988; Stanley and Wise 1983) or Marxism (Harding 1986; Hartsock 1983; Haraway 1991) in contructing a feminist STANDPOINT EPISTEMOLOGY. The difficulty of finding a firm enough point on which to stand, however, with the increasing recognition of the plurality of 'subjugated knowledges' further emphasized in the Black feminist critique of white middle-class feminisms, led some standpoint theorists to abandon this anchorage. Haraway attempts to provide a remaining vantage point in her concept of 'situated knowledge', and this probably represents in the mid-1990s the position around which feminist consensus converges. Others have chosen the free-fall of full postmodernist epistemological refusal, although many feminists who have identified themselves as poststructuralist or postmodernist have been more hesitant about interpreting the concept of truth in entirely relativist terms (Barrett 1991).

For the post-Lacanian FRENCH FEMINIST Luce Irigaray 'phallogocentric' Western philosophy works within an economy of truth, the METAPHYSICS OF PRESENCE, and dependence on the transcendental signifier (the phallus). It has no place for women except as the OTHER who keeps the PATRIARCHAL psychic and philosophical economy functioning. Whitford offers this reading of Irigaray:

...if you produce an account of truth which includes, or is derivative of, an imaginary scene in which the role of the mother is written out, leaving engenderment entirely to the father, then your whole theory and its consequences will be marked by that forgetting (Whitford 1991: 112).

Post-Marxist feminists who have turned to poststructuralism have often been particularly attracted to Foucault's approach. In his early work, Foucault traced out the relationship between 'regimes of truth' and regimes of POWER (Foucault 1977; 1980b). There are traces left in this early work of the Marxian privileging of the standpoint of the oppressed in his concept of 'subjugated knowledge'. Later he recognized the problem of granting greater authenticity to such 'knowledges' (Foucault 1986; 1988), but while 'truth' remains pinioned by qualifications, parentheses and emphatic inverted commas, several feminists sympathetic to his approach have argued that 'truth' continues to circulate nevertheless in his writings (Barrett 1991; McNay 1992). Other feminist philosophers have urged caution in prematurely and comprehensively rejecting the Enlightenment tradition within feminism (Lovibond 1989; Soper 1986; 1989 and 1990).

Secondary accounts of poststructuralist and postmodernist feminism are full of sweeping generalizations about the assumptions of 'Western philosophical thought' and 'Western science', but it is actually quite difficult to find very many examples of those working 'within the true' of these scientific and philosophical traditions in the last several decades who operate with the absolute concept of Truth. There is a long history of dispute and debate over the meaning and criteria of truth within philosophical discourse (Outhwaite and Bottomore [eds] 1993; Urmson and Rée [eds] 1989). 'Western philosophy' and 'Western science' speak with one voice no more than do these new twentieth-century theories, and it is sometimes possible to wonder whether the ruthless hunting out of Truth does not indicate a paradoxical hankering after an absolute that such scientists and philosophers have long since learnt to live without.

U

Uncanny A key category in AESTHETICS and PSYCHOANALYSIS. In his essay 'The Uncanny' (1919), Freud provides a psychoanalytic interpretation, initially defining the uncanny as that class of the frightening which 'arouses dread and horror' in old and familiar things. Assessing a range of definitions, Freud argues that the term 'uncanny', *unheimlich*, tends to merge into its opposite, *heimlich*, signifying simultaneously the familiar, homely and comfortable and the unfamiliar, alien and unknown. The term's meaning can therefore be seen to develop in the direction of ambivalence: the familiar *becomes* unfamiliar and uncanny. Freud uses Schelling's definition of the uncanny as 'that which ought to have remained hidden but has come to light' to inflect it psychoanalytically, suggesting that the uncanny is what ought to have remained repressed and UNCONSCIOUS but which has frighteningly emerged into consciousness. Analysing E.T.A. Hoffman's short story 'The Sandman', Freud argues that in modern scientific cultures the uncanny takes a literary form, confounding the distinction between FANTASY and reality in a way characteristic of examples of Romantic literature.

The category is of interest to POSTSTRUCTURALISTS and literary critics who interpret it as a demonstration of the literariness of PSYCHOANALYSIS, with literature as the uncanny double of theory. Feminist theorists have explored the gender implications of Freud's account of the uncanny. Cixous's (1976a) critique highlights Freud's repression of certain uncanny motifs in the story, in particular the figure of the doll. Jane Marie Todd (1986) explores the question of whether it is the castrated female BODY or the (phallic) female *gaze* which evokes horror in the male SUBJECT. Within literary criticism, Shoshana Felman (1982) proposes a model of reading for uncanny effects in literature, thereby problematizing rather than literalizing sexual identities and meanings. Rosemary Jackson (1981) invokes Freud's association of the uncanny with fantasies of taboo-transgression and consequently highlights its potential as a literature of subversion. In her theory of the ABJECT, Kristeva (1982) develops Freud's notion of the uncanny as taboo, identifying the MATERNAL BODY as the expression of women's power of horror. Freudian theories of the uncanny are now dovetailing with the Bakhtinian concept of the GROTESQUE in feminist work on the MONSTROUS FEMININE (Creed 1993; Russo 1994).

Unconscious The central term in PSYCHOANALYSIS, which distinguishes the theory from all other psychological models. Freud conceived of the human psyche as radically split, made up of several 'states', namely the pre-conscious state, conscious awareness and unconscious activity of which the individual is necessarily unaware. The unconscious operates according to an entirely different logic to the conscious mind, which is based on prohibition; in contrast, the unconscious 'knows no negation'. The emergence of the unconscious coincides with the resolution of the oedipal complex and is a product of the repression of illegitimate wishes and desires. Carl Jung (1972) proposed an alternative model in the concept of a transindividual or collective unconscious, containing primordial images or archetypes which recur in dream symbols. This model has had more influence on feminist literary practice and ARCHETYPAL criticism than on feminist theory more generally.

Within feminist theory there are different accounts of the place and status of the unconscious. Jacqueline Rose (1986), whose work has been concerned to elaborate a politics of the unconscious, argues that any politics will founder if it fails to recognize the unconscious and its ability to undermine political programmes. Landry and Maclean (1993), however, warn that feminism is concerned rather with a *social* and *political* programme in which an understanding of the unconscious should have *a*, but not *the*, central place. They ask whether an approach which always privileges the unconscious 'would ever allow any straying into the social, *any movement outside* the unconscious. Or are we always to be, as it were, on the couch, exploring sexual difference?' (1993: 170).

Psychoanalytic ideas about the unconscious have had considerable influence on CULTURAL STUDIES, FILM THEORY and literary criticism. Literary critics have drawn on Freud's ideas in three main approaches, focusing on the author, the reader and the text. The concept of a textual unconscious was developed by Macherey (1978) in his theory of textual absence. Roman Jakobson (1971) applies to literary language Freud's concepts of condensation and DISPLACEMENT which characterize the unconscious dream-work. Feminist literary critics whose work invokes the concept of the unconscious include the Marxist-Feminist Literature Collective (1978), Gilbert and Gubar (1979), Mary Jacobus (1986) and Jacqueline Rose (1991).

Underdevelopment Although writing on underdevelopment was initially gender blind, development studies has had to take cognizance of feminist research on women's economic roles, especially in agricultural and household production. However, much of the feminist writing on gender and development since the 1970s has been produced in the context of particular theories of underdevelopment whose relevance is now frequently challenged.

Whereas American MODERNIZATION theory saw THIRD WORLD economies suffering from the absence of DEVELOPMENT, Left-leaning economists conceptualized the problem as 'the development of underdevelopment' (Frank 1978), a historical process created by colonial and neo-colonial exploitation, one which could be challenged only if Third World states, led by their national bourgeoisie, rejected participation in the world capitalist system. However, by the 1980s underdevelopment theories were seen to have reached an impasse (Schuurman [ed.] 1993); they were vitiated by, among other factors, rapid economic growth in the Newly Industrialized Countries (NICs) and, to a lesser extent, India and parts of Latin America, combined with worsening conditions in other Third World countries, the continued GLOBALIZATION of capital, and the failure of the socialist model of state planning in Eastern Europe, which has made alternatives to the market appear unrealistic. Although a neo-liberal PARADIGM now holds sway in mainstream circles, a new left-oriented, macro-economic development paradigm which can counter it has yet to emerge (Leys 1996), partly because environmental devastation and growing inequality between and within Third World countries suggests to many that development poses as many problems as underdevelopment.

Feminist writing in Britain was initially influenced by the Marxist conceptions of underdevelopment, especially those which pointed to the persistence of non-capitalist modes of production subordinated to capital. What various authors call the 'political economy' approach or the 'gender and development' approach was linked with SOCIALIST FEMINIST theoretical perspectives. Some argue (see especially the essays in Marchand and Parpart 1995) that this has now been superseded by POSTSTRUCTURALIST critiques of 'development discourse' which challenge the modernist assumptions in all gender and development thinking. The impasse in wider underdevelopment theory is also reflected in feminist writing by the focus on women's empowerment and the validation of subjected KNOWLEDGES.

Universalism   The problem of universals in philosophical thought has entered feminist discourse as the problem of over-generalizing about 'women'. The *Concise Encyclopaedia of Western Philosophy and Philosophers* suggests that the term 'particulars' be reserved for 'that element of a concrete object which...distinguishes it from everything else, however similar in character' and that 'individuals' is used to denote 'concrete objects in space and time' (Urmson and Rée [eds] 1989). Thus each woman is a particular individual. The question about what, if anything, women share in common remains, and it is this which has so troubled contemporary feminism.

Much effort has gone into the task of deconstructing WOMAN and 'women' in feminist theory, so great is the fear of ESSENTIALISM, reinforced by the charges laid against white middle-class feminists of ETHNOCENTRISM and the tendency to overgeneralize on the basis of historically and culturally specific experiences and characteristics. Elizabeth Spelman states baldly that 'the more universal the claim one might hope to make about women... the more likely it is to be false' (1990: 8–9).

However, general terms are unavoidable, and it is tacitly acknowledged in such critiques that we may, indeed must, continue to refer to 'women' without any serious difficulties concerning the reference of the term. But it does not follow that there is some single, or several, property or properties which all women possess, the essence of 'womanness', although the relationship to the sexed division of REPRODUCTIVE labour is scarcely accidental. Not all generalizations are universal statements about whole classes, although it is certainly true that great caution is required in qualifying general statements. But the climate of anti-essentialism has been limiting in some respects, and a more relaxed attitude towards 'the risk of essentialism' (de Lauretis 1989; Grimshaw 1996) allows the recognition of commonalities shared by some if not all women, without undoing the respect for DIFFERENCE upon which both BLACK FEMINISM and POSTSTRUCTURALISM have rightly insisted.

Utopia   'No place': 'a place, state or condition ideally perfect in terms of politics, laws, customs, and conditions' (*Shorter OED*). Utopian hopes, wishes, and imaginings are common in Western social thought and literature (Bloch 1988; Dyer 1981; Jameson 1979; Kumar 1987), and oppositional groups and movements are frequently associated with the production of utopian blueprints, imaginings, and experiments in the creation of new forms of COMMUNITY. It is not surprising that utopianism is seldom far from the surface in feminist thought, practice, and imaginings.

Utopian elements circulate in FEMINISM in a number of ways. Firstly, feminist social historians have been interested in the utopian socialist communities that were constructed in France, Britain, and the US from the early period of the nineteenth century, because of the fact that questions of sexual difference, SEXUALITY, marriage and domestic organization were all key issues for the utopian socialists (Barbara Taylor 1983). For this reason, many have chosen to call themselves SOCIALIST FEMINISTS rather than MARXIST FEMINISTS, even some who have been deeply influenced by Marxism. Marx distinguished between scientific and utopian socialism, and was dismissive of the latter. The view of many of the socialist feminists of the second wave of feminism was that in certain respects the utopian socialist tradition had more to offer to feminism than the 'scientific' variety which succeeded it.

Secondly, the WOMEN'S MOVEMENT in Europe and the US succeeded the radicalism, sexual and political, of the 1960s, and continued many of its concerns. This period had been associated with an oppositional counter-culture, and the spread of large numbers of small-scale experimental communes. Feminisms, socialist, RADICAL, and LESBIAN, have experimented in the setting up of pre-figurative feminist communities, including radical and lesbian feminists in the case of COMMUNITIES OF WOMEN (Auerbach 1978; Bammer 1991; Rowbotham, Segal and Wainwright 1979).

Thirdly, feminist thought has been produced in the form of fictional feminist utopias, usually in the GENRE of science fiction, from Charlotte Perkins Gilman

(1979, first published 1915) to Marge Piercy (1979), Joanna Russ (1985) and Monique Wittig (1971).

And finally, feminist theory itself often incorporates important utopian elements. For example, in addition to this tendency in socialist and radical feminisms, it is of significance in much FRENCH FEMINIST thought, especially that of Irigaray, Cixous, Le Doeuff, and Kristeva (Grosz 1989; Moi 1985; Whitford 1991):

> Utopian thought has always been a source of political inspiration for feminists and socialists alike. Confidently assuming that change is both possible and desirable, the utopian vision takes off from a negative analysis of its own society in order to create images and ideas that have the power to inspire to revolt against oppression and exploitation (Moi 1985: 121).

V

Violence against women   Rather than seeing violence as the idiosyncratic behaviour of a few deranged men, feminist theory views male violence as a universal aspect of male POWER over and control of women; 'violence from men to women is likely to be sexual...' (Radford *et al.* [eds] 1996: 3). Although the prevalence of intra-family violence is now usually recognized by social work agencies these often favour models of family dysfunction which ignore the vast predominance of men as perpetrators (Bell 1993; Driver and Droisen [eds] 1988).

In targeting violence against women, feminists at first developed a political account of abuses which had previously been defined as personal problems, such as domestic violence ('wife-beating'), rape, especially marital rape, and child sexual abuse. They also identified other kinds of abuse, such as genital mutilation, witch-burning and foot binding (Daly 1991; Rich 1980a) which seemed to demonstrate the trans-historical aspect of male violence, although sometimes with little attention to the colonial politics which influenced their sources (Liddle and Rai in Rai and Lievesey [eds] 1996). Western feminists usually saw the STATE as protecting women against male violence, except in so far as it defined the home as a private domain in which it was reluctant to interfere (Barrett 1988). Increasingly, however, feminists focus on the violence of those acting as agents of the state. Partly as a result of the mass rape of women in the former Yugoslavia, feminists and PEACE movement activists have become more concerned about the connections between militarism, NATIONALISM and male violence, including rape, forced prostitution and torture during invasions and civil war (Enloe 1989; Hughes and Foster 1996; Seifert 1996). For many women male violence is inextricably enmeshed in state violence, including rape, murder and beatings in police custody (Rai and Lievesey [eds] 1996).

Feminists have created a number of institutions to combat or provide refuge from male violence; these include rape crisis centres, women's refuges and self-help groups. While abuse of women does not appear to be decreasing, there is evidence for Britain and perhaps elsewhere that feminist CONSCIOUSNESS-RAISING around the issue has reaped benefits: women are more willing to report incidents of abuse and 'battered woman syndrome' entered public discourse in the 1990s, providing abused women who kill with a stronger defence in court (although medicalizing them in the process).

Two issues at least have divided feminist theorists. Firstly, BLACK FEMINISTS have argued that white feminist analyses of and campaigns against rape and other forms of male sexual violence have been completely insensitive to the racism which constructs Black men as likely rapists, while ignoring the ways Black women's experience of violence is disqualified (Carby 1982; Davis 1982; hooks 1989). Secondly, the centrality of discursive constructions of male violence has been much debated. Some POSTSTRUCTURALIST feminists have seen rape as a language, script or narrative in which women are 'always either already raped or already rapable', i.e. one which defines women by their violability (Marcus 1992: 386; see also Smart 1995). They argue that focusing solely on improvements to the criminal justice system's treatment of rape risks reinforcing these DISCOURSES and intensifying women's involvement in speaking them. However, analysing rape as merely the effect of discourse could be yet another way of 'disqualifying' women's own accounts of their experience (Smart 1989). That being said, there is a problem when violence against women becomes the *main* feminist issue. Besides diverting attention from other issues, it can construct HETEROSEX primarily as danger, replicate dominant discursive constructions of women as passive objects of male DESIRE and violence and leave little scope for the emergence of a feminist discourse fostering active female SEXUALITY and pleasure (Smart 1996).

In recent years the term abuse has been associated particularly with child abuse, especially child sexual abuse, focusing fears around both child and adult sexuality. In 1990s Britain the cases of Rosemary West and Beverley Allitt disturbingly drew attention to the capacity of women themselves to abuse.

See HUMAN RIGHTS.

Voyeurism In Freudian PSYCHOANALYSIS voyeurism designates the active form of SCOPOPHILIA, the drive to look. It is commonly associated with a form of *unseen* looking. The concept is often connected with but is not identical to the GAZE which refers to a perceptual mode which feminists have identified with MASCULINITY (Mulvey 1989a) because it operates in a PATRIARCHAL POWER relation in which the male subject looks at a female object. Theories of voyeurism and the gaze are central to feminist FILM THEORY which explores cinematic relations of looking. Mulvey's correlation between masculinity and voyeurism and femininity and exhibitionism long set the standard for feminist cinema studies despite being widely criticized as overly monolithic (Rose 1986). More recently, new theories of female SPECTATORSHIP, produced from psychoanalytic and ethnographic perspectives, emphasize an active female gaze, and lesbian and QUEER theorists (Roof 1991) have posited the concept of a specifically lesbian gaze.

W

Whiteness A term which makes white people visible to themselves as a racialized category. As Toni Morrison says of her essay exploring whiteness and the literary imagination, *Playing in the Dark*:

> My project is an effort to avert the critical gaze from the racial object to the racial subject; from the described and imagined to the describers and imaginers, from the serving to the served (1992: 90).

Asking 'What does the inclusion of Africans or African-Americans do to and for the work?' (1992: 16) Morrison brilliantly illuminates the 'sycophancy of white culture' on the constructed, imagined character of blackness, which she terms American Africanism:

> For the settlers and for American writers generally this Africanist other became the means of thinking about body, mind, chaos, kindness, and love, provided the occasion for exercises in the absence of restraint, the presence of restraint... for bearing the cross of religion and following out the ramifications of power (1992: 47-8).

Ruth Frankenberg's sociological analysis also identities the context as one in which 'white people have too often viewed themselves as nonracial or racially neutral (1993: 1). She identifies three aspects of whiteness: (1) as a location of structural privilege; (2) as a STANDPOINT from which whites look at themselves, others and society; and (3) as previously unmarked cultural practices.

Because one of his themes is the anxiety present in Hollywood film depictions of whiteness, Richard Dyer (forthcoming) is particularly well placed to proffer a warning about focusing on whiteness, the possibility that it represents a 'guilt trip' or a form of the 'Me too-ism' one sometimes sees in men's studies: 'look at us for a change', the white man cries. For many Black people or those placed at the fringes of what Dyer calls the hierarchical 'aspirational structure of whiteness' the idea of whiteness being a SOCIAL CONSTRUCTION is scarcely novel.

See also ORIENTALISM

Woman/women   At once central to the feminist enterprise and deeply problematic, these terms circulate in everyday DISCOURSE with multiple, context-dependent and imprecise CONNOTATIONS. The terms continue to trail these associations in the more analytic discourses of feminist theory.

'Woman' in the singular was commonplace in nineteenth-century discourse inside and outside FEMINISM. Marxists and socialists spoke of 'the woman question', and Mary Wollstonecraft's vindication was of the rights of 'woman' (Wollstonecraft 1982). In twentieth-century feminism this usage has attracted the charge of ESSENTIALISM and an unwarranted UNIVERSALISM. 'Women' has fared little better. The LESBIAN FEMINIST Monique Wittig argues that it is the context of COMPULSORY HETEROSEXUALITY which defines these terms: 'what makes a woman is a specific social relation to a man, a relation...which implies personal and physical obligation...which lesbians escape by refusing to become or stay heterosexual' (Wittig, 1992: 20).

'One is not born, but becomes a woman' wrote Simone de Beauvoir (1953: 249), and there is widespread agreement across feminisms that women are socially contructed rather than biologically given. Females become women in very different ways in different social and historical contexts (Spelman 1990).

Another tendency within contemporary feminism, however, sometimes referred to as CULTURAL FEMINISM, moves some distance from SOCIAL CONSTRUCTIONISM in insisting on the radical DIFFERENCE between women and men, and on the existence of a specifically female CULTURE and way of being in the world (Gilligan 1982; Chodorow 1978; Rich 1977). In this approach, the specificity of female (and male) BODIES is often highlighted. But locating women in the body by no means settles the matter, as is evidenced by TRANSSEXUALITY and hermaphroditism.

A similar insistence upon embodiment is generated within some POSTSTRUCTURALIST feminisms (Braidotti 1994b; Gatens 1995; Grosz 1994; Irigaray 1974; Pateman 1988). Other feminisms of embodiment, for example, that of Judith Butler, Mary Russo and others, allow a greater degree of freedom to acknowledge that there is no single 'woman's body' (Butler 1993; Russo 1994). Yet in common-sense thinking, and indeed in much feminist theory, the 'specificity' of femaleness is not merely contingently linked with the sexual division of labour in REPRODUCTION (Battersby forthcoming; Diprose 1994; Grosz 1994; Fox Keller 1989).

In an influential book-length DECONSTRUCTION of 'women', Denise Riley struggles with the problem of referring to what she is deconstructing. Her strategies include placing 'women' in inverted commas, and substituting 'female persons'. The latter, however, merely becomes a synonym for the term thus avoided, and paradoxically emphasizes the fact that what 'woman' denotes is never entirely detachable from biological femaleness even in remoter metaphorical connotations. Riley closes on an oblique acknowledgement of this necessity: 'The temporalities of 'women' are like the missing middle term of Aristotelian logic; while it's impossible to thoroughly be a woman, it's also impossible never to be a woman' (Riley 1988: 114) – impossible, that is to say, for a 'female person' (or a woman?).

Womanism   A term coined by Alice Walker (1984a) to describe the specificity of BLACK FEMINISM and contrast it to what she sees as an ethnocentric and separatist white feminism. Womanism designates a political continuum of Black women whose struggles and alliances occupy several fronts in a non-exclusive manner.

Women's culture   Within Western feminism since Wollstonecraft, women have protested their systematic denial of full participation in cultural life. Granted only an inferior education, their aspirations at best patronized, more usually ridiculed, women have been schooled within a demeaning CULTURE of FEMININITY.

Yet alongside the demand for equal access to the dominant culture lies both a critique of that culture as PATRIARCHAL, and the shadow of a poorly articulated, largely unacknowledged, but more 'authentic' culture circulating among women. This concept has come into sharper focus with the development of what has been termed CULTURAL FEMINISM from the late 1970s. This label is not self-chosen, and is usually applied critically (Segal 1987). Included under this head are a variety of approaches: RADICAL FEMINISM (Daly 1991; Dworkin 1981; Rich 1977); OBJECT RELATIONS THEORY (Chorodow 1978; Gilligan 1982), and post-Lacanian FRENCH FEMINISM (Cixous 1976a; Irigaray 1974). Yet insofar as something called 'women's culture' circulates in these approaches, it is articulated in very different ways, and the value of a common label is doubtful.

The main charge laid against those who posit such a culture is that of ESSENTIALISM, and there is a further difficulty in general in deciding what aspects of women's cultural lives carry the stamp of AUTHENTICITY free from the insignia of the subjugating patriarchal, commoditized cultures of femininity. Can we ever distinguish 'woman's own voice' (Gilligan 1982) from patriarchal ventriloquisms (Irigaray 1974)? Probably not. Gramsci's concept of IDEOLOGY recognizes very clearly the manner in which positive elements of working-class culture are 'gathered up' and re-worked within the DOMINANT IDEOLOGY, and the task of distinguishing the 'authentic' from the 'inauthentic' would be a thankless one.

But 'women's culture' may be interpreted not as the description of an authentic culture shared by all women, but as a political project. Across a wide range of cultural forms, there has been self-conscious intervention to *create* a culture by and for women, by creating feminist forums for women's cultural production, or new and creative forms of political action, such as the Greenham Common women's peace movement. Margaret Whitford interprets Irigaray's feminism in this light, as a project for creating a richer IMAGINARY *for* women rather than an essentializing description *of* it (Whitford 1991).

Women's language   See GENDERLECT; NEW FEMINIST LANGUAGE.

Women's movements   While FEMINISM has usually developed out of activist women's movements aimed at changing women's situation, not all such movements have styled themselves 'feminist'. The term has sometimes been refused on the grounds that it is too closely linked with the sectional interests of women who are privileged in terms of CLASS, 'RACE' or IMPERIALISM. But the debt owed by feminism to women's movements, feminist or no, across the globe and over time, is immeasurable: 'How was it possible for small bands of women to have such enormous impact, to change our thinking so radically in such a short period of time?' (Jessie Barnard, quoted in Dahlerup [ed.] 1986: 1).

Women's movements include single-issue campaigns such as those for abortion rights; more broad-based campaigns such as the Working Women's Charter movement in Britain in the 1970s; and the mobilization of particular categories of women. There is some degree of tension, apparent in many contexts, between mobilization around women's rights to equal treatment with men on the one hand, and mobilization based on the belief in women's particular needs or qualities (cf. EQUAL RIGHTS). The former, broad-based and inclusive, immediately runs up against the problems of global overgeneralizations based upon the experiences and situation of particular and more local constituencies. This problem highlights the related issue of the POWER to give voice; to speak *for* women, which is unequally distributed and which masks important differences, political and cultural, *among* women. This concern with cultural DOMINATION within feminism has greatly exercized feminist theoretical debates in the 1980s and 1990s.

The issues around which independent women's movements have emerged include civil rights, especially suffrage; equal political, economic and sexual rights; social purity and temperance; anti-slavery; lesbianism; DISABILITY; environmentalism; PEACE; and in 'Third World' contexts, popular women's consumer movements concerning prices and inflation. They range from left radicalism to the conservatism which has often been attached to campaigns premised upon the superior moral qualities of women.

The emergence of autonomous women's movements has been closely associated with social revolutionary movements, movements for national liberation and anti-IMPERIALIST struggles (Jayawardena [ed.] 1986; Jelin 1990; Liddle and Joshi 1986; Rowbotham 1972; Ward 1983). Nationalist and anti-imperialist feminist struggles have often suffered from a tension between MODERNIZATION and the influence of the West, and TRADITIONALISM:

> Nationalist movements had a profound ambiguity about the proper place of women. The exceptional circumstances of struggle required a break with custom. The enlightenment heritage sometimes envisaged women educated and in production. Yet the creation of a nation involved also the legitimation of continuity (Rowbotham 1992: 108).

This tension is particularly evident in reconstructions of the LAW (Stewart 1996).

The greater the stress on EQUALITY in women's movements, the greater the emphasis on comparison with men. One effect of movements of DIFFERENCE has been to draw closer attention to COMMUNITIES OF WOMEN; actual attempts at single-sex communitarianism motivated by feminist goals, and subcultural formations within a variety of broader social communities, where women are placed in close relationships with other women. Experiments in creating feminist communities of women have been particularly valued by RADICAL FEMINISTS and by LESBIAN FEMINISTS. Attention to women–women relationships has sometimes involved an over-idealization and homogenization. But it has also had the effect in the longer term of drawing attention, paradoxically, to the differences among women which women's movements and feminism have to negotiate.

Women's time   The concept of women's time possesses a number of resonances in feminist theory and politics. The idea of a temporality specific to women has been advanced by some second-wave feminists interested in the existence of ancient matriarchies prior to the emergence of *his*tory. Interestingly, Engels also speaks of the 'world historic defeat of the female sex' and the replacement of matriarchy by PATRIARCHY as a key moment in human CULTURE. CULTURAL FEMINISTS have emphasized the historical importance of the rhythms and cycles of the female body in women's experience. Feminist historians such as Carroll Smith Rosenberg (1985) have identified female-specific cultural practices by which women define their own spaces and temporalities in certain highly sex-segregated cultures. Other feminists, however, guard against essentializing women's experience at any one historical moment, rejecting accounts which perpetuate what Julia Kristeva (1982) has called the myth of the 'archaic mother'.

Kristeva's important essay 'Women's time' (1989, first published 1981) suggests that women have occupied a temporal economy distinct from men's: whereas men monopolize and define linear or historical time, women have been relegated to an 'ahistorical' or monumental time which is seen as immanent, unchanging and eternal.

Kristeva identifies three generations of feminist enquiry: the first GENERATION which characterizes liberal feminism up to the second wave seeks equal access for women to the SYMBOLIC order. The second generation, emerging after 1968 and associated with RADICAL FEMINISM, rejects the patriarchal symbolic order and emphasizes women's difference from men. The third generation, with which Kristeva aligns herself and the present moment, moves beyond EQUALITY and DIFFERENCE and rejects the dichotomy man/woman as belonging to metaphysics. Recognizing the contemporaneity of all three 'moments', third-generation feminism represents a new theoretical space in which the notion of 'IDENTITY' and 'sexual identity' is challenged.

See also GENERATION

Women of colour An American term of self-identification highlighting alliances between women who experience racial oppression. The British use of 'Black' has been much less enduring. As Mary Maynard (1994a) states, while it was initially used to signify a common experience of racism and marginalization ('political blackness'), it has been criticized by Avtar Brah (1992) and others for, among other problems, its tendency to refer to those of sub-Saharan African descent, for its denial of the existence and needs of other cultural groups, and for 'assigning a label to those who do not necessarily define themselves in this way' (Brah 1992: 11).

See BLACK FEMINISM.

Y

Youth culture   During the 1950s and 1960s, a key, though not uncontested, element of the dominant PARADIGM in US and much European social theory was the concept of 'the masses'. Modern industrial society was understood as an atomized MASS SOCIETY, in which intermediate and localized forms of sociality and COMMUNICATION had atrophied. In the 1960s this dominant paradigm was displaced by neo-Marxism and by theories and approaches rooted in PHENOMENOLOGY (Jeffrey Alexander 1995a). The homogenizing concept of 'the masses' was deconstructed through attention to counter-cultural movements and subjugated cultures – in particular in studies of working-class CULTURE and 'subcultures' structured around RACE and youth. Working-class youth culture became the subject of scholarly scrutiny in sociology, but above all in the developing field of CULTURAL STUDIES (Hall and Jefferson [eds] 1976).

With the advent of the WOMEN'S MOVEMENT from the late 1960s, feminists interested in this area of study subjected subcultural studies in turn to DECONSTRUCTION and critique. For the 'youth' in question, and its 'culture' was overwhelmingly that of 'the lads': football (Clarke *et al.* [eds] 1979); reworkings of working-class styles of masculinity among 'mods' and 'rockers' (Hebdige 1979); rock music (Simon Frith 1981); playground and street-corner activity (Corrigan 1979); work (Willis 1977). The running theme throughout this literature echoed the title of Hall and Jefferson's 1976 collection: resistance through rituals. The work drew heavily on Gramsci's theory of HEGEMONY and Althusser's reworking of the concept of IDEOLOGY.

Feminists began to analyse youth culture in terms of gender, and to turn attention to 'girls' culture': the 'bedroom culture' of femininity of young girls at home – fashion, make-up, teenage romance magazines, etc. (McRobbie 1987; McRobbie and Nava [eds] 1984); schooling (Steedman 1982); SEXUALITY and sexual harassment (Cowie and Lees 1981).

See also POPULAR CULTURE; WOMEN'S CULTURE.

Z

Zami Audre Lorde's 'biomythography', *Zami: A New Spelling of my Name* (1983) blends sexual and racial politics, Caribbean island history and matriarchal MYTH in mapping the complex layerings of Lorde's outsider identities as a Black LESBIAN FEMINIST.

See also BLACK FEMINIST; WOMEN OF COLOUR .

Bibliography

Abel, Elizabeth (ed.) (1982). *Writing and Sexual Difference*. Brighton: Harvester.

Abel, Elizabeth (1989). *Virginia Woolf and the Fictions of Psychoanalysis*. Chicago: Chicago University Press.

Abelove, Henry, Barale, Michele Aina, and Halperin, David M. (eds) (1993). *The Lesbian and Gay Studies Reader*. London: Routledge.

Abercrombie, Nicholas, Hill, Stephen, and Turner, Bryan (1980). *The Dominant Ideology Thesis*. Hemel Hempstead: Allen & Unwin.

Abercrombie, Nicholas, Hill, Stephen, and Turner, Bryan S. (1994). 'Determinacy and indeterminacy in the theory of ideology'. In Zizek, Slavoj (ed.) (1994).

Acker, Joan (1990). 'Hierarchies, jobs, bodies: a theory of gendered organisations'. *Gender and Society*, 4, 2, 139–58.

Adams, Parveen (1982). 'Family Affairs'. *m/f*, 7.

Adams, Parveen (1989). 'Of female bondage'. In Brennan, Teresa (ed.), *Between Feminism and Psychoanalysis*. London: Routledge.

Adkins, Lisa (1995). *Gendered Work: Sexuality, Family and the Labour Market*. Buckingham and Philadelphia: Open University Press.

Adorno, Theodor W. *et al.* (1950). *The Authoritarian Personality*. New York: Harper & Row.

Aitkenhead, Marilyn and Liff, Sonia (1991). 'The effectiveness of equal opportunities policies'. In Firth Cozens, Jenny and West, Michael (eds), *Women at Work: Psychological and Organisational Perspectives*. Milton Keynes: Open University Press.

Alcoff, Linda and Gray, Linda (1993). 'Survivor discourse: transgressional recuperation'. *Signs*, 18, 2, 260–90.

Alcoff, Linda and Potter, Elizabeth (eds) (1993). *Feminist Epistemologies*. New York and London: Routledge.

Alexander, Jeffrey C. (1995). 'Modern, anti, post and neo'. *New Left Review*, 210, 63–101.

Alexander, Sally (1984). 'Women, class and sexual differences in the 1830s and 1840s: some reflections on the writing of a feminist history'. *History Workshop Journal*, 17, 125–49.

Alexander, Sally (1987). 'Women, class and sexual difference'. In Phillips, Anne (ed.) (1987).

Allen, Hilary (1982). 'Political lesbianism and feminism – a space for sexual politics'. *m/f*, 7, 15–34.

Allen, Sheila, and Macey, Marie (1990). 'At the cutting edge of citizenship: race and ethnicity in Europe 1992'. Unpublished paper presented at the Conference on New Issues in Black Politics, University of Warwick, May.

Allen, Sheila, and Wolkowitz, Carol (1987). *Homeworking: Myths and Realities*. Basingstoke: Macmillan.

Althusser, Louis (1969). *For Marx*. Trans. Ben Brewster. London: Allen Lane.

Althusser, Louis (1977). *Lenin and Philosophy and other Essays*. London: New Left Books.

Althusser, Louis (1994) (first published 1970). 'Ideology and ideological state apparatuses (notes towards and investigation)'. In Zizek, Slavoj (ed.) (1994).

Althusser, Louis, and Balibar, Etienne (1970). *Reading Capital*. Trans. Ben Brewster. London: New Left Books.

Amin, Ash (ed.) (1994). *Postfordism: A Reader*. Oxford: Blackwell.

Anderson, Benedict (1983). *Imagined Communities*. London: Verso.

Anderson, Brigit (1993). *Britain's Secret Slaves*. London: Anti-Slavery International.

Ang, Ien (1985). *Watching Dallas*. London: Methuen.

Ang, Ien (1991). *Desperately Seeking the Audience*. London: Routledge.

Anthias, Floya (1990). 'Race and Class revisited – conceptualising race and racism'. *Sociological Review* 31, 1, 19–42.

Anthias, Floya, and Yuval-Davis, Nira (1991). *Racialized Boundaries: Race, Nation, Gender, Colour and Class and the Anti-Racist Struggle*. London and New York: Routledge.

Anzaldúa, Gloria (1987). *Borderlands/La Frontera: The New Mestiza*. San Francisco: Spinsters/Aunt Lute Book Co.

Aoyama, Kaoru (1995). '"Force" and "choice": sexual slavery, prostitution and women's agency through a case study of international trafficking in women from Thailand to Japan'. University of Warwick , Centre for the Study of Women and Gender, unpublished MA dissertation.

Arcana, Judith (1983). *Every Mother's Son*. London: The Women's Press.

Ardill, Susan, and O'Sullivan, Sue (1989). 'Sex in the summer of '88'. *Feminist Review*, 31, 126–34.

Arendt, Hannah (1958). *The Human Condition*. New York: Doubleday Anchor.

Armitt, Lucie (ed.) (1991). *Where No Man Has Gone Before: Women and Science Fiction*. London: Routledge.

Armstrong, Nancy (1987). *Desire and Domestic Fiction: A Political History of the Novel*. New York and Oxford: Oxford University Press.

Armstrong, Nancy and Tennenhouse, Leonard (eds) (1987). *The Ideology of Conduct: Essays in Literature and the History of Sexuality*. New York and London: Methuen.

Arnold, Matthew (1960) (first published 1869). *Culture and Anarchy*. Cambridge: Cambridge University Press.

Assiter, Alison and Carol, Avedon (1991). *Bad Girls and Dirty Pictures: The Challenge to Reclaim Feminism.* London: Pluto.

Atwood, Margaret (1982). *Lady Oracle.* London: Virago.

Auerbach, Nina (1978). *Communities of Women: Ideas in Fiction.* Cambridge, MA: Harvard University Press.

Austin, J.L. (1962). *How To Do Things with Words.* Oxford: Oxford University Press.

Aziz, Razia (1992). 'Feminism and the challenge of acism'. In Crowley, Helen and Himmelweit, Susan (eds), *Feminism and Knowledge.* Cambridge: Polity Press/The Open University.

Bacchi, Carol (1990). *Same Difference.* London: Unwin Hyman.

Badinter, Elisabeth (1989) (first published 1986). *Man/Woman: The One is the Other.* Trans. Barbara Wright. London: Collins Harvill.

Baehr, Helen, and Dyer, Gillian (eds) (1987). *Boxed In: Women and TV.* London: Pandora.

Bakan, Abigail, and Stasiulis, Daiva (1995). 'Making the match: domestic placement agencies and the racialization of women's household work'. *Signs,* 20, 2, 305–35.

Bakhtin, Mikhail (1981). *The Dialogic Imagination.* Ed. Michael Holquist. Trans. Caryl Emerson and Michael Holquist. Austin, TX.

Bakhtin, Mikhail (1984). *Rabelais and His World.* Trans. Helen Iswolsky, Bloomington: Indiana University Press.

Ballhatchet, Kenneth (1980). *Race, Sex and Class under the Raj.* London: Weidenfeld and Nicolson.

Bammer, Angelika (1991). *Partial Visions: Feminism and Utopia in the 1970s.* London and New York: Routledge.

Banks, Olive (1981). *Faces of Feminism.* Oxford: Martin Robertson.

Barnes, Djuna (1950). *Nightwood.* London: Faber and Faber.

Barr, Marleen (1987a). *Alien to Femininity: Speculative Fiction and Feminist Theory.* Westport, CT: Greenwood Press.

Barr, Marleen (ed.) (1987b). *Feminism Faces the Fantastic.* New York: Gordon & Bread; London: Eurospan.

Barrett, Michèle (1988) (first published 1980). *Women's Oppression Today: The Marxist Feminist Encounter.* Second edition. London: Verso.

Barrett, Michèle (1991). *The Politics of Truth: From Marx to Foucault.* Cambridge: Polity.

Barrett, Michèle, and McIntosh, Mary (1982). *The Anti-Social Family.* London: New Left.

Barrett, Michèle, and Phillips, Anne (eds) (1992) *Destabilizing Theory: Contemporary Feminist Debates.* Cambridge: Polity.

Barrientos, Stephanie and Perrons, Diane (1996). 'Fruit of the vine: flexible women workers in the production and retailing of winter fruit'. Paper presented at the Conference on Globalisation of Production and Regulation of Labour, University of Warwick, September.

Barron, R.D. and Norris, E.M. (1976). 'Sexual divisions and the dual labour market'. In Barker, Diana, and Allen, Sheila (eds), *Dependence and Exploitation in Work and Marriage.* London: Longman.

Barthes, Roland (1972). *Mythologies.* London: Paladin.

Barthes, Roland (1976). *The Pleasure of the Text.* Trans. Richard Miller. London: Cape.

Barthes, Roland (1977a). 'The death of the author'. In Barthes, Roland (1977b).

Barthes, Roland (1977b). *Image, Music, Text.* London: Fontana.

Bartky, Sandra (1990). *Femininity and Domination.* London: Routledge.

Bassnett-McGuire, Susan (ed.) (1991). *Translation Studies.* London: Routledge. quote (translation).

Battersby, Christine (1989). *Gender and Genius: Towards a Feminist Aesthetics.* London: Women's Press.

Battersby, Christine (1997 forthcoming). *The Phenomenal Woman: Feminist Transitions and Metaphysical Traditions.* Oxford: Polity Press.

Beck, Ulrich (1992). *Risk and Society: Towards a New Modernity.* Trans. M. Ritter. London: Sage.

Beechey, Veronica (1979). 'On patriarchy'. *Feminist Review,* 3, 66–82.

Beechey, Veronica (1988). 'Rethinking the definition of work'. In Jenson, Jane, Hagen, Elizabeth and Reddy, Ceallaigh (eds), *Feminization of the Labour Force: Paradoxes and Promises.* Cambridge: Polity.

Beechey, Veronica, and Perkins, Tessa (1987). *A Matter of Hours: Women, Part-Time Work and the Labour Market.* Cambridge: Polity.

Bell, Diane (1993). Introduction 1: the context. In Bell, Diane, Caplan, Pat and Karim, Wazir Jahan (eds), *Gendered Fields: Women, Men and Ethnography.* London: Routledge.

Bell, Vikki (1993). *Interrogating Incest: Feminism, Foucault and the Law.* London and New York: Routledge.

Belsey, Catherine (1989). 'Towards cultural history'. *Textual Practice,* 3, 2, 159–72.

Belsey, Catherine, and Moore, Jane (eds) (1989). *The Feminist Reader: Essays in Gender and the Politics of Literary Criticism.* London: Macmillan.

Benhabib, Seyla (1987). 'The generalized and the concrete other'. In Kittay, Eva Feeler, and Meyers, Diana T. (eds) (1987).

Benhabib, Seyla, and Cornell, Druscilla (eds) (1987). *Feminism as Critique.* Cambridge: Polity Press.

Bennett, Tony (1994). 'Popular culture and the "turn to Gramsci"'. In Storey, John (ed.), *Cultural Theory and Popular Culture.* Hemel Hempstead: Harvester Wheatsheaf.

Bennett, Tony, Mercer, Colin, and Woollacott, Janet (eds) (1986). *Popular Culture and Social Relations.* Milton Keynes: Open University Press.

Benstock, Shari (1987). *Women of the Left Bank.* London: Virago.

Berg, Maxine (1993). 'Women's property-holding in eighteenth-century England'. *Journal of Interdisciplinary History.*

Berg, Maxine (1994). *The Age of Manufacture, 1700–1820: Industry, Innovation and Work in Britain.* Second edition. London: Routledge.

Berg, Maxine (1996). *Women in History: Eileen Power, 1889–1931.* Cambridge: Cambridge University Press.

Bermingham, Ann, and Brewer, John (eds) (1995). *The Consumption of Culture, 1600–1800: Image, Object, Text.* London and New York: Routledge.

Bernheimer, Charles, and Kahane, Claire (1985). *In Dora's Case: Freud, Hysteria, Feminism.* London: Virago.

Bernstein, Marcelle (1976). *Nuns.* London: Collins.

Beuveniste, Emile (1969). *Indo-European Language and Society.* Trans. Elizabeth Palmer. Coral Gates, RAFL: University of Miami Press.

Bhabha, Homi K. (1990). *Nation and Narration.* London: Routledge.

Bhabha, Homi K. (1994). *The Location of Culture.* London: Routledge.

Bhaskar, Roy (1993). 'Realism'. In Outhwaite, William and Bottomore, Tom (eds) (1993), 547–49.

Birke, Lynda (1986). *Women, Feminism and Biology: The Feminist Challenge.* Brighton: Harvester.

Birke, Lynda, Himmelweit, Susan, and Vines, Gail (1990). *Tomorrow's Child: Reproductive Technologies in the 'Nineties.* London: Virago.

Birmingham Feminist History Group (1979). 'Feminism as femininity in the nineteen-fifties?' *Feminist Review,* 3, 48–65.

Bland, Lucy (1986). 'Marriage laid bare: middle class women and marital sex: 1880–1914'. In Lewis, Jane (ed.), *Labour and Love.* Oxford: Basil Blackwell.

Bleier, Ruth (1984). *Science and Gender: A Critique of Biology and its Themes on Women.* New York: Pergamon.

Bloch, Ernst (1988). *The Utopian Function of Art and Literature.* Cambridge, MA: MIT Press.

Bono, Paula, and Kemp, Sandra (1991). *Italian Feminist Thought: A Reader.* Oxford: Basil Blackwell.

Bordo, Susan (1993). *Unbearable Weight: Feminism, Western Culture, and the Body.* Berkeley, Los Angeles and London: University of California Press.

Bornstein, Kate (1994). *Gender Outlaws: On men, Women, and the Rest of Us.* London: Routledge.

Boston Women's Health Collective (1978) (first published 1972). *Our Bodies Ourselves.* Second edition by Angela Phillips and Jill Rakusen. Harmondsworth: Penguin.

Bourdieu, Pierre (1984). *Distinction: A Social Critique of the Judgement of Taste.* Trans. Richard Nice. London: Routledge & Kegan Paul.

Bourdieu, Pierre (1988). *Homo Academicus.* Cambridge: Polity Press.

Bourdieu, Pierre (1990a). *The Logic of Practice.* Trans. Richard Nice. London: Routledge.

Bourdieu, Pierre (1990b). 'La domination masculine'. *Actes de la Recherche en sciences sociale,* 84, 3–31.

Bourdieu, Pierre, and Wacquant, Loic J.J. (1992). *An Invitation to Reflexive Sociology*. Cambridge: Polity.

Bowlby, Rachel (1985). *Just Looking: Consumer Culture in Dreiser, Gissing and Zola*. New York and London: Methuen.

Boyce Davies, Carole (1994). *Black Women, Writing and Identity*. London: Routledge.

Brah, Avtar (1992). 'Difference, diversity and differentiation'. In Donald, James and Rattansi, Ali (eds) *Race, Culture and Difference*. London: Sage.

Braidotti, Rosi (1991). *Patterns of Dissonance: A Study of Women in Contemporary Philosophy*. Trans. Elizabeth Gould. Cambridge: Polity.

Braidotti, Rosi (1992). 'The exile, the nomad and the migrant'. *Women's Studies International Forum* 15, 1, 7–10.

Braidotti, Rosi (1994a). 'Body-images and the pornography of representation'. In Lennon, Kathleen and Whitford, Margaret (eds), *Knowing the Difference: Feminist Perpsectives in Epistemology*. London: Routledge.

Braidotti, Rosi (1994b). *Nomadic Subjects: Embodiment and Sexual Difference in Contemporary Feminist Theory*. New York: Columbia University Press.

Braidotti, Rosi, et al. (1994). *Women, the Environment and Sustainable Development: Towards a Theoretical Synthesis*. London: Zed Books in association with INSTRAW.

Braverman, Henry (1974). *Labour and Monopoly Capital*. New York: Monthly Review Press.

Braybon, Gail, and Summerfield, Penny (1987). *Out of the Cage: Women's Experience in Two World Wars*. London: Pandora.

Brewer, John and Porter, Roy (eds) (1993). *Consumption and the World of Goods*. New York and London: Routledge.

Brewer, Rose M. (1993). 'Theorizing race, class and gender: the new scholarship of black feminist intellectuals and black women's labour'. In James, Stanlie, and Busia, Abena (eds) (1993).

Brewis, Joanna, and Kerfoot, Deborah (1994). 'Selling our selves: sexual harassment and the intimate violations of the workplace'. Paper presented at the BSA Conference, Sexualities in Context, Preston, March.

Bristow, Edward (1977). *Vice and Vigilance: Purity Movements in Britain Since 1700*. Dublin: Gill and Macmillan.

Bristow, Joseph and Wilson, Angelia (eds) (1993). *Activating Theory*. London: Lawrence & Wishart.

Brooker, Peter (ed.) (1992). *Modernism/Postmodernism*. Harlow: Longman.

Brown, Cheever Mackenzie (1974). *God as Mother: A Feminine Theology in India: An Historical and Theological Study of the Brahmavaivarta*. Hartford/Vermont: Claude Stark.

Brown, Wendy (1992). 'Finding the man in the state'. *Feminist Studies* 18, 1, 7–34.

Bruegel, Irene (1995). 'Economic reasoning and family relations'. *Work, Employment and Society*, 9, 1, 183–86.

Brunsdon, Charlotte (ed.) (1986). *Films for Women*. London: BFI Publishing.

Bunch, Charlotte (1987) (first published 1975). 'Not for lesbians only'. In Bunch, Charlotte and Steinem, Gloria (eds), *Building Feminist Theory: Essays from Quest*. New York: Longman.

Burke, Caroline (1981). 'Irigaray through the looking glass'. *Feminist Studies*, 7, 2, 288–306.

Burton, Antoinette (1990). 'The white woman's burden: British feminists and the Indian Woman, 1865–1915'. *Women's Studies International Forum*, 13, 4, 295–308.

Busia, Abena (1993) 'Afer/words: and this is what we've decided to tell you after everything we've shared'. In James, Stanlie and Busia, Abena (eds) (1993).

Butler, Judith (1990). *Gender Trouble: Feminism and the Subversion of Identity*. New York and London: Routledge.

Butler, Judith (1991). 'Imitation and gender insubordination'. In Fuss, Diana (ed.), *Inside/Out: Lesbian Theories, Gay Theories*. London: Routledge.

Butler, Judith (1992). 'Contingent foundations: feminism and the question of "postmodernism"'. In Butler, Judith and Scott, Joan W. (1992).

Butler, Judith (1993). *Bodies That Matter*. New York and London: Routledge.

Butler, Judith, and Scott, Joan W. (eds) (1992). *Feminists Theorize the Political*. New York and London: Routledge.

Cain, Maureen (1990). 'Realist philosophy and standpoint epistemologies or feminist criminology as a successor science'. In Gelsthorpe, Lorraine and Morris, Allison (eds), *Feminist Perspectives in Criminology*. Milton Keynes: Open University Press.

Cain, Maureen (1993). 'Foucault, feminism and feeling: what Foucault can and cannot contribute to feminist epistemology'. In Ramazanoglu, Caroline. (ed.) (1993).

Callinicos, Alex (1989). *Against Postmodernism*. London: Polity.

Cameron, Deborah (1985). *Feminism and Linguistic Theory*. London: Macmillan.

Cameron, Deborah, and Frazer, Elizabeth (1987). *Lust to Kill*. Cambridge: Polity.

Cameron, Deborah, and Coates, Jennifer (eds) (1989). *Women in their Speech Communities: New Perspective on Language and Sex*. London: Longman.

Cameron, Ian (ed.) (1972). *Movie Reader*. London: November Books.

Campbell, Colin (1987). *The Romantic Ethic and the Spirit of Modern Consumerism*. Oxford: Blackwell.

Canaan, Joyce and Griffin, Christine (1990). 'The new men's studies: part of the problem or part of the solution?' In Hearn, Jeff and Morgan, David (eds), *Men, Masculinities and Social Theory*. London: Unwin Hyman.

Carby, Hazel (1982). 'White women listen: black feminism and the boundaries of sisterhood'. In Centre for Contemporary Cultural Studies (eds), *The Empire Strikes Back*. London: Hutchinson.

Carmody, Denise Lardner (1979). *Women and World Religions*. Nashville, TN: Abingdon.

Carter, Angela (1978). *The Bloddy Chamber*. New York: Harper & Row (Penguin edition, 1981).

Carter, Angela (1979). *The Sadeian Woman*. London: Virago.

Castle, Terry (1986). *Masquerade and Civilization*. London: Methuen.

Caute, David (1988). *Sixty-Eight: The Year of the Barricades*. London: Hamish Hamilton.

Cavarero, Adriana (1995). *In Spite of Plato: A Feminist Rewriting of Ancient Philosophy*. Trans. Serena Anderlini-D'Onofrio and Aine O'Healy. Cambridge: Polity Press.

Cavendish, Ruth (1982). *Women On the Line*. London: Routledge and Kegan Paul.

Centre for Contemporary Cultural Studies: Women' Studies Group (1978). *Woman Take Issue*. London: Hutchinson.

Chambers, Iain (1985). *Urban Rhythms: Pop Music and Popular Culture*. London: Macmillan.

Chapman, Rowena and Rutherford, Jonathon (eds) (1988). *Male Order: Unwrapping Masculinity*. London: Lawrence & Wishart.

Chaudhuri, Nupur and Strobel, Margaret (eds) (1992). *Western Women and Imperialism: Complicity and Resistance*. Bloomington: Indiana University Press.

Chicago, Judy (1993) (Originally published 1975). *Through the Flower: My struggles as a Woman Artist*. New York: Penguin.

Chodorow, Nancy (1978). *The Reproduction of Mothering*. Berkeley, CA: University of California Press.

Chowdhry, Geeta (1995). 'Engendering development: women in development (WID) in international development regimes'. In Marchand, Marianne and Parpart, Jane (eds) (1995).

Christ, Carol (1986). 'Why women need the Goddess: phenomenological, psychological, and political reflections'. In Pearsall, M. (ed.) (1986).

Christ, Carol, and Plaskow, J. (eds) (1979). *Womanspirit Rising: A Feminist Reader in Religion*. New York: Harper and Row.

Christian, Barbara (1985). *Black Feminist Criticism: Perspectives on Black Women Writers*. New York: Pergamon.

Christine de Pisan (1983). *Le Livre de la Cite des Dames [The Book of the City of Ladies]*. Trans. Earl Jeffrey Richards. London: Picador.

Cixous, Hélène (1976a). 'The laugh of the Medusa'. Trans. Keith Cohen and Paula Cohen, *Signs*, 1, 4, 875–93.

Cixous, Hélène (1976b). 'Fiction and its phantoms: a reading of Freud's *Das Unheimliche* ("the Uncanny")'. *New Literary History*, 525–48.

Cixous, Hélène (1981). 'Sorties'. In Marks, Elaine, and de Courtivron, Isabelle (eds) (1981).

Cixous, Hélène (1990). *The Body and the Text: Hélène Cixous, Reading, Writing and Teaching*. Ed. Helen Wilcox *et al.* New York and London: Harvester Wheatsheaf.

Cixous, Hélène, and Clément, Cathérine (1986). *The Newly Born Woman*. Trans. Betsy Wing. Minneapolis: University of Minnesota Press.

Clark, Alice (1992) (first published 1919). *Working Life of Women in the Seventeenth Century*. New edition with Introduction by Louise Erickson. London: Routledge.

Clark, Danae (1993). 'Commodity lesbianism'. In Abelove *et al.* (eds) (1993).

Clark, Vèvè *et al.* (eds) (1996). *Anti-feminism and the Academy*. New York and London: Routledge.

Clarke, John, Critcher, Chas, and Johnson, Richard (eds) (1979). *Working-Class Culture: Studies in History and Theory*. London: Hutchinson.

Clear, Catriona (1987). *Nuns in Nineteenth Century Ireland*. Dublin: Gill & Macmillan.

Cockburn, Cynthia (1983). *Brothers: Male Dominance and Technological Change*. London: Pluto.

Cockburn, Cynthia (1991). *In the Way of Women: Men's Resistance to Sex Equality in Organizations*. Basingstoke: Macmillan.

Cocks, Joan (1989). *The Oppositional Imagination: Feminism, Critique and Political Theory*. London and New York: Routledge.

Cohen, Anthony (1985). *The Symbolic Construction of Community*. London: Routledge.

Cohen, Robin (1987). *The New Helots: Migrants in the International Division of Labour*. Aldershot: Gower.

Cohn, Carol (1995) (first published 1987). 'Sex and death in the rational world of defense intellectuals'. In Lovell, Terry (ed.), *British Feminist Thought: A Reader*. Oxford: Blackwell, 1990.

Collins, Patricia Hill (1990). *Black Feminist Thought*. Boston and London: Unwin Hyman.

Collinson, David, and Hearn, Jeff (1994). 'Naming men as men: implications for work organisation and masculinity'. *Gender, Work and Organisation*, 1, 1, 2–22.

Combahee River Collective (1982) (first published 1977). 'A Black feminist statement'. In Hull, Gloria T., Scott, Patricia Bell, and Smith, Barbara (eds), *All the Women Are White, All the Blacks Are Men, But Some of Us Are Brave*. Old Westbury, NY: The Feminist Press.

Connolly, Clare (1991). 'Washing our linen: one year of women against fundamentalism'. *Feminist Review*, 37, 68–77.

Connolly, Clare (1993). 'Culture or citizenship? Notes from the gender and colonialism conference, Galway, Ireland, May 1992'. *Feminist Review*, 44, 104–11.

Coole, Diana (1996). 'Is class a difference that makes a difference?' *Radical Philosophy*, 77, May/June, 17–25.

Cooper, Davina (1995). *Power in Struggle: Feminism, Sexuality and the State*. Buckingham: Open University Press.

Coote, Anna, and Campbell, Beatrix (1982). *Sweet Freedom*. London: Pan Books.

Cornell, Druscilla L. (1992). 'Gender, sex, and equivalent rights'. In Butler, Judith, and Scott, Joan W. (eds) (1992).

Cornell, Druscilla, and Thurschwell, Adam (1987). 'Feminism, negativity, intersubjectivity'. In Benhabib, Seyla, and Cornell, Druscilla (eds) (1987).

Corrigan, Paul (1979). *Schooling The Smash Street Kids?* London: Macmillan.

Cott, Nancy (1977). *The Bonds of Womanhood: Woman's Sphere in New England, 1780–1835.* New Haven: Yale University Press.

Cott, Nancy (1979). 'Passionlessness: an interpretation of Victorian sexual ideology 1790–1850'. *Signs*, 4, 2, 219–36.

Coward, Rosalind (1983). *Patriarchal Precedents: Sexuality and Social Relations.* London: Routledge & Kegan Paul.

Coward, Rosalind (1985). *Female Desire: Women's Sexuality Today.* London: Paladin.

Cowie, Celia and Lees, Sue (1981). 'Slags or drags'. *Feminist Review*, 9, 17–31.

Cowie, Elizabeth (1984). 'Fantasia'. *m/f*, 9, 70–105.

Cranny-Francis, Anne (1990). *Feminist Fiction: Feminist Uses of Generic Fiction.* Oxford: Polity Press.

Cranny-Francis, Anne (1995). *The Body in the Text.* Carlton Smith, Victoria: Melbourne University Press.

Creed, Barbara (1993). *The Monstrous Feminine: Film, Feminism and Psychoanalysis.* London: Routledge.

Crowley, Helen and Himmelweit, Susan (1992). 'Discrimination, subordination and difference'. In Crowley, Helen and Himmelweit, Susan (eds), *Knowing Women: Feminism and Knowledge.* Cambridge: Polity, in association with the Open University.

Culler, Jonathan (1981). *In Pursuit of Signs: Semiotics, Literature, Deconstruction.* London: Routledge.

Culler, Jonathan (1982). *On Deconstruction: Theory and Criticism After Structuralism.* Ithaca, NY: Cornell University Press.

Dahelrup, D. (ed.) (1986). *The New Women's Movement.* London: Sage.

Dalla Costa, Mariosa, and James, Selma (1975). *The Power of Women and the Subversion of the Community.* Bristol: Falling Wall Press.

Daly, Mary (1974). *Beyond God the Father: Toward a Philosophy of Women's Liberation.* Boston: Beacon Press.

Daly, Mary (1984). *Pure Lust: Elemental Feminist Philosophy.* London: The Women's Press.

Daly, Mary (1991) (first published 1978). *Gyn/Ecology: The Metaethics of Radical Feminism.* Boston, MA: Beacon Press, and London: The Women's Press.

Daly, Mary, with Caputi, Jane (1987). *Webster's First Intergalactic Wickedary of the English Language.* Boston, MA: Beacon Press.

Davidoff, Leonore (1983). 'Class and gender in Victorian England'. In Newton, J.L., Ryan, M.P., and Walkowitz, J. (eds) (1983).

Davidoff, Leonore, and Hall, Catherine (1987). *Family Fortunes: Men and Women of the English Middle Class, 1780–1850*. London: Hutchinson.

Davis, Angela (1982) (first published 1981). *Women, Race and Class*. London: The Women's Press.

Davis, Natalie Zemon (1965). *Society and Culture in Early Modern France*. Stanford: Stanford University Press.

Dawson, Graham (1994). *Soldier Heroes: British Adventure, Empire and the Imagining of Masculinities*. London: Routledge.

De Beauvoir, Simone (1953) (first published 1949). *The Second Sex*. Trans. and ed. by H.M. Parshley. London: Picador.

De Groot, Joanna and Maynard, Mary (1993). 'Facing the 1990s'. In de Groot, Joanna and Maynard, Mary (eds).

De Lauretis, Teresa (1984). *Alice Doesn't: Feminism, Semiotics, Cinema*. Bloomington: Indiana University Press.

De Lauretis, Teresa (1987). *Technologies of Gender: Essays on Theory, Film, and Fiction*. Bloomington: Indiana University Press.

De Lauretis, Teresa (1989). 'The essence of the triangle, or taking the risk of essentialism seriously: feminist theory in Italy, the U.S. and Britain'. *Differences: A Journal of Feminist Cultural Studies*, 1, 2, 3–37. Reprinted in Schor, Naomi, and Weed, Elizabeth (eds) (1994).

De Lauretis, Teresa (1990a). 'Eccentric Subjects: Feminist Theory and Historical Consciousness'. *Feminist Studies*, 16, 1 (Spring), 115–50.

De Lauretis, Teresa (1991a). 'Film and the Visible'. In Bad Object Choices (eds) *How Do I Look? Queen Film and Video*. San Francisco: Bay Press.

De Lauretis, Teresa (1991b). 'Queer theory: lesbian and gay sexualities: an introduction'. *Differences: A Journal of Feminist Cultural Studies*, 3, 2.

De Lauretis, Teresa (ed.) (1986). *Feminist Studies/Critical Studies*. Bloomington: Indiana University Press.

De Lauretis, Teresa, and Heath, Stephen (eds) (1980). *The Cinematic Apparatus*. London: Macmillan.

Del Rosario, Virginia (1995). 'Mail-order brides: women in limbo'. Paper presented at the British Sociological Association Annual Conference, Contested Cities: Social Processes and Spatial Forms, 10–13 April, University of Leicester.

Deleuze, Gilles (1985) (first published 1973). 'Nomad thought'. In Allison, David B. (ed.), *The New Nietzsche: Contemporary Styles of Interpretation*. Cambridge, MA: MIT Press.

Deleuze, Gilles, and Guattari, Felix (1977) (first published 1972). *Anti-Oedipus: Capitalism and Schizophrenia*. New York: Viking Press.

Deleuze, Gilles and Guattari, Felix (1992) (first published 1987). *A Thousand Plateaus: Capitalism and Schizophrenia*. Trans. Brian Massumi. London: The Athlone Press.

Delphy, Christine (1984). *Close to Home: A Materialist Analysis of Women's Oppression*. London: Hutchinson.

Delphy, Christine and Leonard, Diana (1986). 'Class analysis, gender analysis and the family'. In Crompton, Rosemary and Mann, Michael (eds).

Delphy, Christine and Leonard, Diana (1992). *Familiar Exploitation: A New Analysis of Marriage in Contemporary Western Societies*. Cambridge: Polity, in association with Blackwell.

Derrida, Jacques (1974) (first published in French 1971). 'White mythology: metaphor in the text of philosophy'. Trans. F.C.T. Moore. *New Literary History*, 4, 1, 5–74.

Derrida, Jacques (1976). *Of Grammatology*. Baltimore and London: Johns Hopkins University Press.

Di Leonardo, Michaela (1987). 'The female world of cards and holidays: women, families and the work of kinship'. *Signs* 12, 3, 440–53.

Diamond, I. and Quimby, L. (eds) (1988). *Feminism and Foucault: Reflections on Resistance*. Boston: Northeaster University Press.

Diaz-Diocaretz, Myriam (1985). *Translation of Poetic Discourse: Questions on Feminist Strategies in Adrienne Rich*. Amsterdam and Philadelphia: Critical Theory Journal.

Dick, Leslie (1989). 'Feminism, writing, postmodernism'. In Carr, Helen (ed.) (1989).

Dickens, Linda (1994). 'The business case for women's equality: is the carrot better than the stick?' *Employee Relations*, 16, 8, 5–18.

Dinnerstein, Dorothy (1977). *The Mermaid and the Minotaur*. New York: Harper & Row.

Diprose, Ros (1994). *The Bodies of Women*. London and New York: Routledge.

Doane, Mary Ann (1987). *The Desire to Desire: Women's Film of the 1940s*. Bloomington: Indiana University Press.

Doane, Mary Ann, Mellencamp, Patricia, and Williams, L. (eds.) (1984). *Re-Vision: Essays in Feminist Film Criticism*. Los Angeles: American Film Institute.

Dodd, Kathyrn (1990). 'Cultural politics and women's historical writing: the case of Ray Stacey's *The Cause! Women's Studies International Forum*, 13, 1/2, 127–37. Reprinted in Lovell (1995).

Donald, James and Rattansie, Ali (eds) (1992). *'Race'. Culture and Difference*. London: Sage.

Donzelot, Jacques (1979). *The Policing of Families*. London: Hutchinson.

Douglas, Mary (1966). *Purity and Danger: An Analysis of the Concepts of Pollution and Taboo*. London: Routledge.

Douglas, Mary (1970). *Natural Symbols: Explorations in Cosmology*. New York: Pantheon.

Draper, Patricia (1975). !Kung women: contrasts in sexual equalitarianism in foraging and sedentary contexts. In Reiter, Rayna (ed.) *Toward an Anthropology of Women*. New York, London: Monthly Review Press.

Driver, Emily and Droisen, Audrey (eds) (1988). *Child Sexual Abuse: A Feminist Perspective*.

Dreyfus, Hubert and Rabinow, Paul (eds) (1983). *Michel Foucault: Beyond Structuralism and Hermeneutics.* Chicago: University of Chicago Press.

Dworkin, Andrea (1981). *Pornography: Men Possessing Women.* London: Women's Press.

Dyer, Richard (1981). 'Entertainment and utopia'. In Altman, Rick (ed.). *Genre: The Musical: A Reader.* London: Routledge and Kegan Paul.

Dyer, Richard (1983). 'Don't look now'. *Screen*, 23, 3/4, 61–73.

Dyer, Richard (1992). *Only Entertainment.* London: Routledge.

Dyer, Richard (1993). *The Matter of Images: Essays on Representation.* London and New York: Routledge.

Dyer, Richard. *White.* London: Routledge, forthcoming.

Dyer, Richard *et al.* (1980). *Coronation Street.* London: British Film Institute.

Eagleton, Mary (1996). 'Who's who and where's where: constructing feminist literary studies'. *Feminist Review*, 53, 1–23.

Eagleton, Terry (1984). *The Functions of Criticism: From the Spectator to Post-Structuralism.* London: Verso.

Eagleton, Terry (1994). 'Ideology and its vicissitudes in Western Marxism'. In Zizek (ed.) (1994).

Echols, Alice (1993). 'Cultural feminism and the anti-pornography movement'. *Social Text*, 7, 34–53.

Edwards, Anne (1996). 'Gendered sexuality and the social construction of rape and consensual sex: a study of process and outcome in six recent rape trials'. In Holland, Janet and Adkins, Lisa (eds).

Edwards, Jeanette *et al.* (1993). *Technologies of Procreator: Kinship in the Age of Assisted Conception.* Manchester: Manchester University Press.

Edwards, Richard *et al.* (1975). *Labor Market Segmentation.* Lexington, MA: D.C. Heath.

Ehrenreich, Barbara (1992). Life without father: reconsidering socialist-feminist theory. In McDowell, Linda and Pringle, Rosemary (eds), *Defining Women.* Cambridge: Polity.

Eisenstein, Zillah (1981). *The Radical Future of Liberal Feminism.* New York: Longman.

Ekins, Paul (1992). *A New World Order: Grassroots Movements for Global Change.* London: Routledge.

Elgin, Suzette Haden (1985). *Native Tongue.* London: Women's Press.

Elgin, Suzette (1988). *The Judas Rose (Native Tongue II).* London: Women's Press.

Elshtain, J.B. (1974). 'Moral woman and immoral man: a consideration of the public/private split and its political ramifications', *Politics and Society*, 4, 453–61.

Elshtain, J.B. (1987). *Women and War.* New York: Basic Books.

Elson, Diane and Pearson, Ruth (1981). 'Nimble fingers make cheap workers'. *Feminist Review*, 7, 87–107. Also in Young, Kate, McCullah, Roslyn and Wolkowitz, Carol (eds) (1987). *Of Marriage and the Market.* London: Routledge and Kegan Paul.

Encyclopaedia of Religion (1987). New York: Macmillan. London: Collier.

Engels, Friedrich (1972). *The Origins of the Familty, Private Property and the State*. First published 1884. London: Lawrence and Wishart.

Enloe, Cynthia (1983). *Does Khaki Become You?: The Militarisation of Women's Lives*. London: Pluto.

Enloe, Cynthia (1989). *Bananas, Beaches and Bases: Making Feminist Sense of International Politics*. London: Pandora.

Etienne, Mona and Leacock, Eleanor (eds) (1980). *Women and Colonization: Anthropological Perspectives*. New York: Praeger Publishers.

Evans, David (1993). *Sexual Citizenship: The Material Construction of Sexualities*. London: Routledge.

Evans, Mary (1982). 'In praise of theory: the case for women's studies'. *Feminist Review*,10, 61–71.

Faderman, Lillian (1981). *Surpassing the Love of Men*. London: Junction Books.

Fahey, Tony (1995). 'Privacy and the family: conceptual and empirical reflections'. *Sociology* 29,4, 687–702.

Faludi, Susan (1992). *Backlash: The Undeclared War against Women*. London: Virago.

Fanon, Frantz (1967). *The Wretched of the Earth*. Farrington, Constance (trans.). Harmondsworth: Penguin.

Fausto-Sterling, Anne (1985). *Myths of Gender: Biological Theories about Women and Men*. New York: Basic.

Felman, Shoshana (1982). 'Re-reading femininity'. *Yale French Studies, 62*, 19–24.

Felman, Shoshana (1993). *What does a woman want? Reading and sexual difference*. Baltimore: John Hopkins University Press.

Felski, Rita (1989a). *Beyond Feminist Aesthetics: Feminist Literature and Social Change*. London: Hutchinson Radius.

Felski, Rita (1989b). 'Feminism, postmodernism and the critique of modernity'. *Cultural Critique*, Fall 1989.

Felstead, Alan, and Jewson, Nick (with John Goodman) (1996). *Homeworkers in Britain*. Department of Trade and Industry/Department of Education and Employment, Research Studies RS1P. London: HMSO.

Ferguson, Margaret, and Wicke, Jennifer (eds) (1994). *Feminism and Postmodernism*. Durham and London: Duke University Press.

Ferguson, Moira *et al.* (1996). 'Feminism and anti-feminism: from civil rights to culture wars'. In Clark, Vèvè *et al.* (eds) (1996).

Fetterley, Judith (1978). *The Resisting Reader*. Bloomington, IN: Indiana, NC, and University Press.

Finch, Janet (1983). *Married to the Job*. London: Allen and Unwin.

Finch, Janet (1984). '"It's great to have someone to talk to": the ethics and politics of interviewing women'. In Bell, Colin and Roberts, Helen (eds), *Social Researching: Politics, Problems, Practice*. London: Routledge and Kegan Paul.

Fiorenza, Elisabeth Schüssler (1983). *In Memory of Her: A Feminist Theological Reconstruction of Christian Origins.* London: SCM Press.

Firestone, Shulamith (1971). *The Dialectics of Sex.* London: Jonathan Cape.

Fiske, John (1987). *Television Culture.* New York: Methuen.

Fiske, John (1989). *Reading the Popular.* Boston: Unwin Hyman.

Fletcher, John (1989). 'Freud and his uses: psychoanalysis and gay theory'. In Shepherd, Simon and Wallis, Nick (eds) (1989), *Coming On Strong: Gay Politics and Culture.* London: Unwin Hyman.

Forbes, Geraldine (1990). 'Caged tigers: "first wave" feminists in India'. *Women's Studies International Forum,* 5, 6, 525–36.

Forrest, Katherine V. (1986). *An Emergence of Green.* Talahasee: Naiad Press.

Foucault, Michel (1972). *The Archaeology of Knowledge.* Trans. A.M. Sheridan Smith. London: Tavistock.

Foucault, Michel (1977). *Discipline and Punish: The Birth of the Prison.* Trans. Alan Sheridan. London: Penguin.

Foucault, Michel (1980b). *The History of Sexuality* Vol. 1, Translated by Robert Hurley. New York: Vintage.

Foucault, Michel (1986). *The Care of the Self.* Trans. Robert Hurley. Harmondsworth: Penguin.

Foucault, Michel (1988). *Politics, Philosophy, Culture: Interviews and other Writings, 1977–1984.* London: Routledge.

Fowler, Bridget (1991). *The Alienated Reader: Women and Popular Romantic Literature in the Twentieth Century.* New York and London: Harvester Wheatsheaf.

Fowler, Bridget (1997). *Pierre Bourdieu and Cultural Theory: Critical Investigations.* London: Sage.

Frank, Andre Gunder (1978). *Dependent Accumulation and Underdevelopment.* London: Macmillan.

Frankenberg, Ruth (1993). *White Woman, Race Matters: The Social Construction of Whiteness.* Minneapolis: University of Minnesota Press, and London: Routledge.

Franklin, Sarah, and Stacey, Jackie (1988). 'Dyketactics for difficult times: A review of the "Homosexuality, Which Homosexuality?" conference'. *Feminist Review,* 29, 1383–150.

Fraser, Linda and Gordon, Linda (1994). 'A Genealogy of Dependency'. *Signs,* 19, 2, 309–36.

Fraser, Nancy (1989). *Unruly Practices: Power, Discourse and Gender in Contemporary Social Theory.* Minneapolis: University of Minnesota Press.

Fraser, Nancy (1995). 'From recognition to redistribution? Dilemmas of justice in a "post-socialist" age'. *New Left Review,* 212, 68–93.

Fraser, Nancy, and Nicholson, Linda (1990). 'Social criticism without philosophy: an encounter between feminism and postmodernism'. In Nicholson, Linda (ed.) (1990).

Frazer, J.G. (1963). *The Golden Bough: A Study in Magic and Religion.* London: Macmillan.

Freud, Sigmund (1900) *The Interpretation of Dreams.* Standard Edition, 4. London: Hogarth Press.

Freud, Sigmund (1905). *Three Essays on the Theory of Sexuality.* Standard Edition, 7. London: Hogarth Press.

Freud, Sigmund (1919). *Introductory Lecture on Psychoanalysis.* In *Standard Edition.* (1955).

Freud, Sigmund (1920). 'The psychogenesis of a case of homosexuality in a woman'. Standard Edition, 17. London: Hogarth Press.

Freud, Sigmund (1931). 'Female sexuality'. *Standard Edition,* 21. London: Hogarth Press.

Freud, Sigmund (1933) 'Femininity'. *Standard Edition,* 22. London: Hogarth Press.

Friedan, Betty (1963). *The Feminine Mystique.* New York: W. W. Norton.

Friedan, Betty (1981). *Second Stage.* New York: Summit Books.

Friedberg, Anne (1993). *Window Shopping: Cinema and the Postmodern.* Berkeley, CA and Oxford: University of California Press.

Frith, Gill (1991), 'Transforming features: double vision and the female reader'. *New Formations,* 15, Winter, 67–81. Reprinted in Lovell, Terry (ed.) (1995).

Frith, Simon (1981). *Sound Effects: Youth, Leisure, and the Politics of Rock 'n' Roll.* New York: Pantheon.

Fuentes, Annette, and Ehrenreich, Barbara (1982). *Women and the Global Factory.* New York: Institute for Communications.

Fuss, Diana (1989). *Essentially Speaking: Feminism, Nature and Difference.* New York and London: Routledge.

Fuss, Diana (1991). *Inside/Outside: Lesbian Theories.* London: Routledge.

Gadamer, Hans-Georg (1975). *Truth and Method.* Trans. William Glen-Doepel. London: Sheed & Ward.

Gagnon, John, and Parker, Richard (1995). 'Conceiving sexuality'. In Parker, Richard and Simon, John (eds), *Conceiving Sexuality: Approaches to Sex Research in a Postmodern World.* New York and London: Routledge.

Gamarnikow, E. (ed.) (1983). *The Public and the Private.* London: Heinemann.

Gamman, Lorraine and Makinen, M. (1994). *Female Fetishism.* London: Lawrence & Wishart.

Garber, Marjorie (1992). *Vested Interests: Cross-Dressing and Cultural Anxiety.* London: Routledge.

Garber, Marjorie (1996). *Vice Versa: Bisexuality and the Eroticism of Everyday Life.* London: Hamish Hamilton.

Garnham, Nicholas, and Williams, Raymond (1980). 'Pierre Bourdieu and the sociology of culture: an introduction'. *Media, Culture, and Society,* 2, 3, 208–23.

Gatens, Moira (1991). *Feminism and Philosophy: Perspectives on Difference and Equality.* Cambridge: Polity.

Gatens, Moira (1992). 'Power, bodies, difference'. In Barrett, Michèle, and Phillips, Anne (eds) (1992).

Gatens, Moira (1995). *Imaginary Bodies: Ethics, Power, and Corporeality.* London and New York: Routledge.

Gearhart, S. (1985). *The Wanderground: Stories of the Hill Women.* London: The Women's Press.

Genette, Gerard (1980). *Narrative Discourse.* Trans. Jane E. Lewin. Oxford: Blackwell.

Geraghty, Christine (1991). *Women and Soap Opera.* Cambridge: Polity Press.

Gershuny, Jonathan (1985). 'Economic development and change in the mode of provision of services'. In Redclift, Nannelea and Mingione, Enso (eds), *Beyond Employment: Household, Gender and Subsistence.* Oxford: Basil Blackwell.

Giddens, Anthony (1990). *The Consequences of Modernity.* Cambridge: Polity Press, in association with Blackwell.

Gilbert, Sandra M., and Gubar, Susan (1979). *The Madwoman in the Attic: The Woman Writer and the Nineteenth-Century Literary Imagination.* New Haven: Yale University Press.

Gilbert, Sandra M., and Gubar, Susan (1988). *No Man's Land: The Place of the Woman Writer in the Twentieth Century.* New Haven and London: Yale University Press.

Gilligan, Carol (1982). *In a Different Voice.* Cambridge, MA: Harvard University Press.

Gilman, Charlotte Perkins (1979) (first published 1915). *Herland.* New York: Pantheon.

Gilman, Charlotte Perkins (1981) (first published 1892). *The Yellow Wallpaper.* London: Virago.

Gilman, Sander L. (1988). *Disease and Representation: Images of Illness from Madness to Aids.* Ithaca, NY, and London: Cornell University Press.

Gilman, Sander S. (1985). *Difference and Pathology: Stereotypes of Sexuality, Race and Madness.* Ithaca, NY, and London: Cornell University Press.

Glasgow Media Group (1977). *Bad News.* London: Routledge & Kegan Paul.

Glasgow Media Group (1980). *More Bad News.* London: Routledge & Kegan Paul.

Glaser, B. and Strauss, A. (1967). *The Discovery of Grounded Theory: Strategies for Qualitative Research.* New York: Sociology Press.

Gledhill, Christine (1984). 'Recent developments in feminist film criticism'. In Doane, Mary Ann, Mellencamp, Patricia and Williams, Linda (eds) (1984).

Gledhill, Christine (1992). 'Pleasurable negotiations'. In Bonner, Frances, *et al.* (eds.), *Imagining Women: Cultural Representations and Gender.* Cambridge: Polity.

Gledhill, Christine (ed.) (1987). *Home is Where the Heart Is: Studies in Melodrama and the Woman's Film.* London: BFI Publishing.

Goffman, Erving (1976). *Gender Advertisements.* London: Macmillan.

Golding, Peter (1974). *The Mass Media.* London:

Goldmann, Emma (1970). The Traffic in Women and Other Essays on Feminism. Alix Shulman. Washington: Times Change Press.

Goldmann, Lucien (1964). *The Hidden God*. London: Routledge & Kegan Paul.

Goldstein, Laurence (ed.) (1993). 'The Male Body'. a special issue, *Michigan Quarterly Review*, 32, 4.

Gordon, Richard (1983). 'The computerization of daily life, the sexual division of labour and the homework economy'. Silicon Valley Workshop Conference, University of California at Santa Cruz.

Graham, Hilary (1991). 'The Concept of Caring in Feminist Research: The Case of Domestic Service'. *Sociology*, 25, 1, 61–78.

Graham, Hilary (1993). 'Social divisions in caring'. *Women's Studies International Forum*, 16, 5, 461–70.

Gramsci, Antonio (1971). *Prison Notebooks*. London: Lawrence & Wishart; New York: International Publishers.

Greed, Clara H. (1994). *Women and Planning: Creating Gendered Communities*. London: Routledge.

Greenblatt, Stephen (1980). *Self-fashioning from More to Shakespeare*. Chicago: University of Chicago Press.

Greenblatt, Stephen (1991). *Shakespearean Negotiations: The Circulation of Social Energy in Renaissance England*. Berkeley: California University Press.

Greer, Germaine (1971). *The Female Eunuch*. London: Paladin.

Greer, Germaine (1991). *The Change: Women, Aging and the Menopause*. London: Hamish Hamilton.

Gregson, Nicky, and Lowe, Michelle (1994). *Servicing the Middle Class*. London: Routledge.

Griffin, Gabriele (ed.) (1993). *Outwrite, Lesbianism and Popular Culture*. London: Pluto Press.

Griffin, Susan (1984). *The Roaring Inside Her*. London: Women's Press.

Grimshaw, Jean (1996). 'Philosophy, feminism and universalism'. *Radical Philosophy*, 76, March/April, 19–28.

Gross, Elizabeth (1987). 'What is feminist theory?' In Pateman, Carol, and Gross, Elizabeth (eds) (1987).

Grosz, Elizabeth (1989). *Sexual Subversions: Three French Feminists*. Sydney, London, Wellington, Boston: Allen and Unwin.

Grosz, Elizabeth (1990). *Jacques Lacan: A Feminist Introduction*. London: Routledge.

Grosz, Elizabeth (1994). *Volatile Bodies: Toward a Corporeal Feminism*. Bloomington and Indianapolis: Indiana University Press.

Grosz, Elizabeth (1995). *Space, Time and Perversion*. London: Routledge.

Guha, Ranajit (ed.) (1982). *Subaltern Studies I: Writing on South Asian History and Society*. New Delhi: Oxford University Press.

Gunew, Sneja (ed.) (1991). *A Reader in Feminist Knowledge*. London and New York: Routledge.

Haaken, Janet (1994). 'Sexual abuse, recovered memory, and therapeutic practice: a feminist-psychoanalytic perspective'. *Social Text*, 40, 115–45.

Haaken, Janet (1996). 'The recovery of memory, fantasy, and desire: feminist approaches to sexual abuse and psychic trauma'. *Signs*, 21, 4, 1069–94.

Habermas, Jurgen (1983). *The Theory of Communicative Action*. Boston: Beacon Press.

Habermas, Jurgen (1989). *The Structural Transformation of the Public Sphere*. Vol. II: 'Lifeworld and Systems: A Critique of Functionalist Reason'. Trans. Thomas McCarthy. Cambridge: Polity.

Hakim, Catherine (1979). *Occupational Segregation: A Comparative Study of the Degree and Pattern of the Differentiation between Men's and Women's work in Britain, the US and Other Countries*. London: Department of Employment.

Hall, Stuart (1980). 'Cultural studies: two paradigms'. *Media, Culture and Society*, 2, 1, 57–72.

Hall, Stuart (1992). 'New ethnicities'. In Donald, J., and Rattansi, A. (eds), *Race, Culture and Difference*. London: Sage.

Hall, Stuart (ed.) (1977). *On Ideology*. London: Hutchinson.

Hall, Stuart, and Jefferson, Tony (eds) (1976). *Resistance Through Rituals: Youth Subcultures in Post-War Britain*. London: Hutchinson.

Hall, Stuart, and Whannel, Paddy (1967). *The Popular Arts*. Boston: Beacon Press.

Hall, Stuart, Chritcher, Chas, Jefferson, Tony, Clarke, John, and Roberts, Brian (1978). *Policing the Crisis: Mugging, the State, and Law and Order*. London: Macmillan.

Hall, Stuart, Hobson, Dorothy, Lowe, Andrew, and Willis, Paul (eds) (1980). *Culture, Media, Language*. London: Hutchinson.

Hamer, Diane (1990). 'Significant others: lesbianism and psychoanalytic theory'. *Feminist Review*, 34 (Spring).

Hamner, Jalna, and Maynard, Mary (eds) (1987). *Women, Violence, and Social Control*. London: Macmillan.

Hanscombe, Gillian, and Smyers, Virginia (1987). *Writing for their Lives: The Modernist Women, 1910–40*. London: The Women's Press.

Haraway, Donna (1988). 'Situated knowledges: the science question in feminism and the privilege of the partial perspective'. *Feminist Studies*, 14, 3, 575–99.

Haraway, Donna (1991). *Simians, Cyborgs, and Women: The Reinvention of Nature*. London: Free Association Books.

Harding, Sandra (1987). 'Introduction'. In Harding, Sandra (ed.). *Feminism and Methodology*. Bloomington and Indiana: Indiana University Press, and Milton Keynes: Open University Press.

Harding, Sandra (1986). *The Science Question in Feminism*. Ithaca, NY: Cornell University Press.

Harding, Sandra (1990). 'Feminism, science, and the anti-Enlightenment critique'. In Nicholson, Linda (ed.) (1990).

Harding, Sandra (1993). 'Rethinking standpoint epistemology: what is strong objectivity?' In Alcoff, Linda and Potter, Elizabeth (eds) (1993).

Harré, Rom, and Krausz, Michael (1996). *Varieties of Relativism.* Oxford: Blackwell.

Harris, Jocelyn (1987). *Samuel Richardson.* Cambridge: Cambridge University Press.

Hartmann, Heidi (1979). 'Capitalism, patriarchy and job segregation'. In Eisenstein, Zillah (ed.), *Capitalism, Patriarchy and the Case for Socialist Feminism.* New York and London: Monthly Review Press.

Hartmann, Heidi (1981). 'The unhappy marriage of Marxism and feminism: towards a more progressive union'. In Sargent, Lydia (ed.) (1981).

Hartsock, Nancy (1981). *Money, Sex and Power: An Essay on Domination and Community.* New York: Longman.

Hartsock, Nancy (1983). 'The feminist standpoint: developing the ground for a specifically feminist historical materialism'. In Harding, Sandra and Hintikka, Merrill (eds) (1983). *Discovering Reality: Feminist Perspectives on Epistomology, Metaphysics and the Philosophy of Science.* Dordrecht: Reidel.

Hawthorn, Jeremy (1992). *A Glossary of Contemporary Literary Theory.* London: Edward Arnold.

Hayek, F.A. (1962) (first published 1944). Second edition. *The Road to Serfdom.* 2nd ed. London: Routledge & Kegan Paul.

Hearn, Jeff, *et al.* (eds) (1989). *The Sexuality of Organisation.* London: Sage.

Hebdige, Dick (1979). *Subcultures: The Meaning of Style.* London: Methuen.

Hebdige, Dick (1988). *Hiding in the Light: On Images and Things.* London: Routledge.

Hekman, Susan J. (1990). *Gender and Knowledge: Elements of a Postmodernist Feminism.* Oxford: Polity.

Hennessy, Rosemary (1993). *Materialist Feminism and the Politics of Discourse.* New York and London: Routledge.

Herman, Didi (1993). 'The politics of law reform: lesbian and gay rights struggles into the 1990s'. In Bristow, Joseph and Wilson, Angela (eds).

Herman, Didi, and Stychin, Carl (eds) (1995). *Legal Inversions: Lesbians, Gay Men, and the Politics of Law.* Philadelphia: Temple University Press.

Herrnstein, Richard and Murray, Charles (1994). *The Bell Curve: Intelligence and the Class Sructure in American Life.* New York: Free Press.

Hervey, David (1992). *The Creatures that Time Forgot: Photography and Disability Imagery.* London: Routledge.

Heyzer, Noeleen, *et al.* (1994). *The Trade in Domestic Workers.* London, Kualar Lumpur, Asian and Pacific Development Centre: Zed.

Hirsch, Marianne (1989). *The Mother/Daughter Plot: Narrative, Psychoanalysis, Feminism.* Bloomington: Indiana University Press.

Hirst, Paul Q. (1983). 'Ideology, culture and personality'. *Canadian Journal of Political and Social Theory*, 7, 1 and 2.

Hite, Shere (1988). *The Hite Report.* (First published as *Women in Love: A Cultural Revolution in Progress, The Hite Report,* 1987). London: Viking.

Hobson, Dorothy (1982). *Crossroads: The Drama of a Soap Opera.* London: Methuen.

Hochschild, Arlie (1983). *The Managed Heart: The Commercialization of Human Feeling.* Berkeley and London: University of California Press.

Hoggart, Richard (1958). *The Uses of Literacy.* Harmondsworth: Penguin.

Holden, Pat (ed.) (1983). *Women's Religious Experience: Cross-Cultural Perspectives.* London: Croom Helm,

Hollis, Patricia (ed.) (1979). *Women in Public: The Women's Movement, 1850–1900.* London: George Allen and Unwin.

Hollway, Wendy (1993). 'Theorising heterosexuality: a response'. *Feminism and Psychology: An International Journal*, 3, 3, 412–17.

Hollway, Wendy (1995). 'A second bite at the heterosexual cherry'. *Feminism and Psychology: An International Journal*, 5, 1, 126–30.

Homans, Margaret (1980). *Women Writers and Poetic Identity.* Princeton: Princeton University Press.

Home Net (The International Bulletin for Home-based workers, Leeds) (1996). The ILO Convention. 4, July.

hooks, bell (1982). *Ain't I a Woman?* London: Pluto.

hooks, bell (1984). *Feminist Theory: From Margins to Centre.* Boston, MA: South End Press.

hooks, bell (1989) (first published 1988). *Talking Back: Thinking Feminist, Thinking Black.* London: Sheba.

hooks, bell (1991). 'Postmodern blackness'. In hooks, bell, *Yearning: Race, Gender and Cultural Politics.* Boston: Turnaround.

Hughes, Donna and Foster, Kathleen (1996). 'War, nationalism and rape: women respond by opening a centre against sexual violence in Belgrade Serbia'. Women's Studies International Forum 19, 1/2, 183–184.

Humm, Maggie (1989). *The Dictionary of Feminist Theory.* New York and London: Harvester Wheatsheaf.

Humm, Maggie (1994). *A Reader's Guide to Contemporary Feminist Literary Criticism.* Hemel Hempstead: Prentice Hall/Harvester Wheatsheaf.

Humm, Maggie (1995). *Practising Feminist Criticism.* Hemel Hempstead: Prentice Hall/Harvester Wheatsheaf.

Hutcheon, Linda (1994). 'The post always rings twice: the postmodern and the post-colonial'. *Textual Practice*, 8, 2, 205–38.

Ignatieff, Michael (1994). *Blood and Belonging: Journeys into the New Nationalism.* London: Vintage.

Irigaray, Luce (1974). *Speculum of the Other Woman.* Trans. Gillian C. Gill. Ithaca, NY: Cornell University Press.

Irigaray, Luce (1981). 'When the goods get together'. Trans. Claudia Reeder. In Marks, Elaine and de Courtivron, Isabelle (eds) (1981).

Irigaray, Luce (1985a) (first published 1977). *This Sex Which Is Not One.* Trans. Catherine Porter with Carolyn Burke. Ithaca, NY: Cornell University Press.

Irigaray, Luce (1985b). *Parler n'est Jamais Neutre.* Paris: Minuit.

Irigaray, Luce (1986). 'Equal to whom?' In Schor, Naomi, and Weed, Elizabeth (eds) (1994).

Irigaray, Luce (1991). *The Irigaray Reader*. Edited and with an introduction by Margaret Whitford. Oxford: Blackwell.

Irigaray, Luce (1993). *An Ethic of Sexual Difference*. Trans. C. Burke and G.C. Gill. London: Athlone.

Iser, Wolfgang (1978). *The Act of Reading: A Theory of Aesthetic Response*. Baltimore: Johns Hopkins University Press.

Jackson, Cecile (1995). 'Radical environmental myths: a gender perspective'. *New Left Review*, 210, 124–140.

Jackson, Rosemary (1981). *Fantasy: A Literature of Subversion*. London: Methuen.

Jackson, Stevi, and Scott, Sue (1996). 'Sexual skirmishes and feminist factions: twenty-five years of debate on women and sexuality'. In Jackson, Stevi, and Scott, Sue (eds), *Feminism and Sexuality: A Reader*. Edinburgh: Edinburgh University Press.

Jacobus, Mary (1986). *Reading Women: Essays in Feminist Criticism*. London: Methuen.

Jakobson, Roman (1971) (first published 1956). 'Two aspects of language and aphasic disturbances'. In Jakobson, Roman, and Halle, Morris (eds), *Fundamentals of Language*. The Hague: Mouton.

James, Stanlie (1993). 'Mothering: a possible black feminist link to social transformation?' In James, Stanlie, and Busia, Abena (eds) (1993).

James, Stanlie, and Busia, Abena (eds), (1993). *Theorising Black Feminisms: The Visionary Pragmatism of Black Women*. London: Routledge.

Jameson, Frederic (1979). 'Reification and utopia in mass culture'. *Social Text*, 1, 130–48.

Jameson, Frederic (1991). *Postmodernism, or The Cultural Logic of Late Capitalism*. London: Verso.

Jardine, Alice (1985). *Gynesis: Configurations of Woman and Modernity*. Ithaca, NY: Cornell University Press.

Jauss, Hans R. (1982). *Toward an Aesthetic of Reception*. Trans. T. Bahti. Brighton: Harvester Press.

Jayawardena, Kumari (1986). *Feminism and Nationalism in the Third World*. London: Zed.

Jayawardena, Kumari (1995). *The White Woman's Other Burden: Western Women and South Asia during British Colonial Rule*. New York and London: Routledge.

Jeffreys, Sheila (1985). *The Spinster and her Enemies: Feminism and Sexuality 1880–1930*. London: Pandora.

Jeffreys, Sheila (1990). *Anticlimax: A Feminist Perspective on the Sexual Revolution*. London: The Women's Press.

Jelin, Elizabeth (ed.) (1990). *Women and Social Change in Latin America*. London: Zed.

Jenson, Jane, Hagen, Elizabeth, and Reddy, Ceallaigh (eds) (1988). *Feminisation of the Labour Force: Paradoxes and Promises.* Cambridge: Polity.

Jewson, Nick, and Mason, David (1992). 'The theory and practice of equal opportunities policies: liberal and radical approaches'. In Braham, Peter, Rattansi, Ali, and Skellington, Richard (eds), *Racism and Antiracism: Inequalities, Opportunities and Policies.* London: Sage.

Johnson, Barbara (1980). *The Critical Difference: Essays in the Contemporary Rhetoric of Reading.* Baltimore and London: Johns Hopkins University Press.

Johnson, Richard (1986–7). 'What is cultural studies anyway?' *Social Text,* 16.

Johnstone, Jill (1973). *Lesbian Nation: The Feminist Solution.* New York: Simon & Schuster.

Jones, Vivien (ed.) (1990). *Women in the Eighteenth Century: Constructions of Femininity.* London and New York: Routledge.

Jordanova, Ludmilla J. (1989). *Sexual Visions: Images of Gender in Science and Medicine Between the Eighteenth and Twentieth Centuries.* New York and London: Harvester Wheatsheaf.

Joreen (1974). 'The tyranny of structurelessness'. In Koedt, Anne, Levine, Ellen, and Rappone, Anits (eds) (1974).

Jung, Carl Gustav (1972). *Collected Writings.* Ed. Sir Herbert Read, trans. Michael Fordham, and Gerhard Adler. Princeton: Princeton University Press.

Junor, Beth (1996). *Greenham Common Women's Peace Camp: A History of Non-violent Resistance, 1984–1995.* London: GCWPC Books.

Kaplan, Cora (1986). *Sea Changes: Culture and Feminism.* London: Verso.

Kaplan, Cora (1993). 'Dirty Harriet/*Blue Steel*: feminist theory goes to Hollywood'. *Discourse,* 16: 1, 50–70.

Kappeler, Susan (1986). *The Pornography of Representation.* Cambridge: Polity Press.

Kay, Geoffrey (1975). *Development and Underdevelopment: A Marxist Analysis.* London: Macmillan.

Keller, Evelyn Fox (1985). *Reflections on Gender and Science.* New Haven: Yale University Press.

Keller, Evelyn Fox (1989). 'Holding the center of feminist theory', *Women's Studies International Forum,* 12, 3, 313–18.

Kelly, Liz. *et al.* (1994). 'Researching women's lives or studying women's oppression'. In Maynard, Mary, and Purvis, June (eds) (1994).

King, Ursula (1989). *Women and Spirituality: Voices of Protest and Promise.* London: Macmillan.

King, Ursula (1995). *Religion and Gender.* Oxford: Blackwell.

Kirkup, Gill, and Keller, Laurie Smith (eds) (1992). *Inventing Women: Science, Technology and Gender.* Cambridge: Polity/Open University Press.

Kishwar, Madhu (1990). 'Why I do not call myself a feminist'. *Manushi,* 61, 2–6.

Kittay, Eva Feder, and Meyers, Diana T. (eds) (1987). *Women and Moral Theory*. Savage, MD: Rowman and Littlefield.

Kitzinger, Celia (1987). *The Social Construction of Lesbianism*. Newbury Park, CA: Sage.

Kitzinger, Celia, and Wilkinson, Sue (1996). 'Deconstructing heterosexuality: a feminist social-constructionist analysis'. In Charles, Nickie, and Hughes-Freeland, Felicia (eds), *Practising Feminism: Identity, Difference, Power*. London: Routledge.

Klein, Melanie (1928). 'Early stages of the Oedipus conflict'. In *The Selected Melanie Klein*. Ed. Juliet Mitchell. Harmondsworth: Penguin.

Koedt, Anne, Levine, Ellen, and Rappone, Anita (eds) (1974). *Radical Feminism*. Quadrangle.

Kofman, Sarah (1985). *The Enigma of Woman: Woman in Freud's Writings*. Ithaca, NY and London: Cornell University Press.

Kollontai, Alexandra (1977). *Selected Writings of Alexandra Kollontai*. Translated with an introduction by Alix Holt. London: Allison and Busby.

Koltun, Elizabeth (ed.) (1978). *The Jewish Woman*. New York: Schocken Books.

Kristeva, Julia (1980). *Desire in Language: A Semiotic Approach to Literature and Art*. Ed. Leon S. Roudiez; trans. Thomas Gora, Alice Jardine and Leon S. Roudiez. Oxford: Blackwell.

Kristeva, Julia (1982). *The Powers of Horror: An Essay in Abjection*. Trans. Leon S. Roudiez. New York: Columbia University Press.

Kristeva, Julia (1984) (first published 1974). *The Revolution in Poetic Language*. Trans. Margaret Waller. New York: Columbia University Press.

Kristeva, Julia (1986). *The Kristeva Reader*. Ed. Toril Moi; trans. Seán Hand. Oxford: Blackwell.

Kristeva, Julia (1989) (first published 1981). 'Women's time'. In Belsey, Catherine and Moore, Jane (eds) (1989).

Kuhn, Annette (1982). *Women's Pictures: Feminism and Cinema*. London: Routledge & Kegan Paul.

Kuhn, Annette (1985). *The Power of the Image: Essays on Representation and Sexuality*. London: Routledge & Kegan Paul.

Kuhn, Annette and Wolpe, Anne-Marie (eds) (1978). *Feminism and Materialism: Women and Modes of Production*. London: Routledge.

Kuhn, Thomas (1970) (first published 1962). *The Structure of Scientific Revolutions*. Chicago: University of Chicago Press.

Kumar, Krishnan (1987). *Utopia and Anti-Utopia in Modern Times*. Oxford: Blackwell.

Kymlicka, Will (1989). *Liberalism, Community and Culture*. Oxford: Clarendon Press.

Lacan, Jacques (1975). *Seminaire I: Les Ecrits Techniques de Freud*. Paris: Seuil.

Laclau, Ernesto, and Mouffe, Chantal (1985). *Hegemony and Socialist Strategy*. London: Verso.

Lakoff, Robin (1975). *Language and Woman's Place*. New York: Harper & Row.

Landry, Donna, and MacLean, Gerald (1993). *Materialist Feminisms*. Oxford: Blackwell.

Laplanche, Jean, and Pontalis, Jean-Baptiste (1986). 'Fantasy and the origins of sexuality'. In Burgin, V., Donald, J., and Kaplan, C. (eds), *Formations of Fantasy*. London: Methuen.

Laqueur, Thomas (1990). *Making Sex: Body and Gender from the Greeks to Freud*. Cambridge MA: Harvard University Press.

Larrain, Jorge (1979). *The Concept of Ideology*. London: Hutchinson.

Larrington, Carolyne (ed.) (1992). *Feminist Companion to Mythology*. London: Pandora.

Lash, Scott (1993). 'Pierre Bourdieu: cultural economy and social change'. In Calhoun, Craig, LiPuma, Edward and Postone, Moishe (eds), *Bourdieu: Critical Perspectives*. Cambridge: Polity Press.

Lash, Scott, and Urry, John (1987). *The End of Organised Capitalism?* Cambridge: Polity.

Lash, Scott, and Urry, John (1994). *Economies of Time and Space*. London: Sage.

Lazreg, Marnia (1990). 'Feminism and difference: the perils of writing as a woman on women in Algeria'. In Hirsch, Marianne, and Keller, Evelyn Fox (eds) (1992). *Conflicts in Feminism*. New York and London: Routledge.

Le Doeuff, Michèle (1991). *Hyparchia's Choice: An Essay Concerning Women, Philosophy, Etc.* Oxford: Blackwell.

Leavis, F.R., and Thompson, Denys (1933). *Culture and Environment*. London: Chatto & Windus.

Leeds Revolutionary Feminist Group (1981). 'Political lesbianism: the case against heterosexuality'. In Onlywomen Press (ed.), *Love Your Enemy: The Debate between Heterosexual Feminism and Political Lesbianism*. London: Onlywomen Press.

Lees, Sue and Gregory, Jeanne (1994). 'In search of gender justice: sexual assault and the criminal justice system'. Feminist Review, 48, 80–93.

Lefanu, Sarah (1988). *In the Chinks of the World Machine: Feminism and Science Fiction*. London: The Women's Press.

Lefevère, Andre (1992). *Translating Literature: Practice and Theory in a Comparative Literature Context*. New York: MLA.

Leonard, Diana, and Adkins, Lisa (eds) (1996). *Sex in Question: French Materialist Feminism*. London: Taylor & Francis.

Lévi-Strauss, Claude (1966). *The Savage Mind*. Trans. George Weidenfeld and Nicolson. London: Weidenfeld and Nicolson.

Lévi-Strauss, Claude (1968). *The Raw and the Cooked: Introduction to a Science of Mythology*. London: Jonathan Cape.

Lévi-Strauss, Claude (1969). *Elementary Structures of Kinship*. London: Eyre & Spottiswood.

Leys, Colin (1996). *The Rise and Fall of Development Theory*. Nairobi: EAEP. Bloomington: Indiana University Press. London: James Currey.

Libreria delle Donne di Milano (1987). *Non Credere di Avere dei Diritti: La Generazione della Liberta Femminile nell'idea e nelle Vicende di un Gruppo di Donne*. Turin: Rosenberg.

Liddle, Joanna, and Joshi (1986). *Daughters of Independence: Gender, Caste and Class in India*. London: Zed.

Liff, Sonia (1993). 'From equality to diversity'. In Wajcman, Judy (ed.), *Organisation, Gender and Power: Papers from an IRRU Workshop*. Warwick Papers in Industrial Relations No. 48, December.

Light, Alison (1991). *Forever England: Femininity, Literature, and Conservatism Between the Wars*. London and New York: Routledge.

Lim, Linda (1990). 'Women's work in export factories'. In Tinker, Irene (ed.), *Persistent Inequalities*. New York and London: Oxford University Press.

Locke, John (1952). *Two Treatises on Government* (1689–90). Ed. Peter Laslett. Second edition. Cambridge: Cambridge University Press.

Lonsdale, Susan (1990). *Women and Disability: The Experience of Physical Disability Among Women*. London: Macmillan.

Lont, Cynthia M. (1995). *Women and the Media: Contributions and Criticism*. Belmont, CA: Wadsworth.

Loomba, Ania (1993). 'Overworlding the "Third World"'. In Williams, Patrick, and Chrisman, Laura (eds) (1993).

Lorde, Audre (1983). *Zami: A New Spelling of My Name*. Trumansberg, NY: Crossing Press.

Lorde, Audre (1984). *Sister Outsider*. Trumansberg, NY: Crossing Press.

Lovell, Terry (1980). *Pictures of Reality: Aesthetics, Politics and Pleasure*. London: British Film Institute.

Lovell, Terry (1987). *Consuming Fiction*. Oxford: Blackwell.

Lovell, Terry (ed.) (1990). *British Feminist Thought*. Oxford: Blackwell.

Lovell, Terry (ed.) (1995). *Feminist Cultural Studies*. 2 vols. Aldershot: Edward Elgar.

Lovibond, Sabina (1989). 'Feminism and postmodernism'. *New Left Review*, 178, 5–28.

Luddy, Maria and Murphy, Cliona (eds) (1989). *Women Surviving: Studies in Irish Women's History in the 19th and 20th Centuries*. Swords: Poolbeg.

Lukács, Georg (1970). *Writer and Critic*. London: Merlin Press.

Lukács, Georg (1971). *History and Class Consciousness*, London: Merlin Press.

Lyotard, Jean-François (1979). *The Postmodern Condition: A Report on Knowledge*. Trans. Geoff Bennington, and Geoff Massumi. Minneapolis: University of Minnesota Press.

MacCabe, Colin (1974). 'Realism and the cinema: notes on some Brechtian theses'. *Screen*, 15, 2, 7–27.

Macherey, Pierre (1978) (first published 1974). *A Theory of Literary Production*. Trans. Geoffrey Wall. London: Routledge.

MacKay, Jane, and Thane, Pat (1986). 'The Englishwoman'. In Colls, Robert, and Dodd, Phillip (eds) (1986).

MacKinnon, Catharine (1982). 'Feminism, Marxism, method and the state: an agenda for theory'. *Signs*, 7, 3, 515–44.

MacKinnon, Catharine (1987). *Feminism Unmodified: Discourses on Life and Law*. Cambridge MA: Harvard University Press.

MacKinnon, Catharine (1992). 'Does sexuality have a history?' In Stanton, Donna (ed.) *Discourses of Sexuality: From Aristotle to AIDS*. Ann Arbor: University of Michigan Press.

MacKinnon, Catharine (1994). *Only Words*. London: HarperCollins.

Maitland, Sara (1983). *A Map of the New Country: Women and Christianity*. London: Routledge and Kegan Paul.

Mangan, James and Walvin, James (eds) (1987). *Manliness and Morality*. Manchester: Manchester University Press.

Mani, Lata (1992). 'Multiple mediations: feminist scholarship in the age of multinational reception'. In Crowley, Helen, and Himmelweit, Susan (eds), *Knowing Women: Feminism and Knowledge*. Cambridge: Polity Press/The Open University.

Marchand, Marianne and Parpart, Jane (eds) (1995). *Feminism/Postmodernism/Development*. London: Routledge.

Marcus, Jane (ed.) (1981). *New Feminist Essays*. London: Macmillan.

Marcus, Jane (ed.) (1983). *Virginia Woolf: A Feminist Slant*. Nebraska: University of Nebraska Press.

Marcus, Sharon (1992). 'Fighting bodies, fighting words: a theory and politics of rape prevention'. In Butler, Judith and Scott, Joan W. (eds) (1992).

Marcuse, Herbert (1964). *One-Dimensional Man: The Ideology of Industrial Society*. London: Routledge and Kegan Paul.

Marks, Elaine, and de Courtivron, Isabelle (eds) (1981). *New French Feminisms*. Brighton: Harvester.

Marsden, Jill (1996). 'The philosophy of "cyberfeminism"'. *Radical Philosophy*, 78, July/Aug, 6–16.

Martin, Emily (1987). *The Woman in the Body*. Milton Keynes: Open University Press.

Martin, Emily (1994). *Flexible Bodies*. Boston: Beacon Press.

Marx, Karl (1970) (first published 1887). *Capital*. 3 vols. Trans. S. Moore and E. Aveling. London: Lawrence and Wishart.

Marx, Karl (1973) (first published 1939). *Grundrisse*. Trans. with an introduction by Martin Nicolaus. London: Penguin.

Marx, Karl and Engels, Frederick (1965) (first published 1888). *The German Ideology*. London: Lawrence and Wishart.

Marxist-Feminist Literary Collective (1978). 'Women writing: *Jane Eyre, Shirley, Villette, Aurora Leigh*'. *Ideology and Consciousness*, 1, 3, 27–48.

Mascia-Lees, Francess, Sharpe, Patricea and Cohen, Colleen (1989). 'The postmodern turn in anthropology: cautions from a feminist perspective'. *Signs*, 15, 1, 7–33.

Mason, Jennifer (1996). 'Gender, care and sensibility in family and kin relationships'. In Holland, Janet & Adkins, Lisa (eds), *Sex, Sensibility and the Gendered Body*. Basingstoke: Macmillan.

Masson, Jeffrey (1984). *The Assault on Truth*. New York: Farrar, Straus & Giroux.

Mathieson, Margaret (1975). *Preachers of Culture: A Study of English and its Teachers*. London: Allen & Unwin.

Matrix Group (1984). *Making Space: Women and the Man-Made Environment*. London and Sydney: Pluto.

Maynard, Mary (1994a). '"Race", gender and the concept of "difference" in feminist thought'. In Afshar, Haleh and Maynard, Mary, *The Dynamics of 'Race' and Gender: Some Feminist Interventions*. London: Taylor & Francis.

Maynard, Mary (1994b). 'Methods, practice and epistemology'. In Maynard, Mary, and Purvis, June (eds) (1994).

Mayne, Judith (1993). *Cinema and Spectatorship*. London and New York: Routledge.

Mbiliny, Margorie (1989). ' "I'd have rather been a man": politics and the labor process in producing personal narratives'. In Personal Narratives group (ed.).

McClintock, Anne (1993). 'Family feuds: gender, nationalism and the family'. *Feminist Review*, 44, 61–80.

McClintock, Anne (1995). *Imperial Leather: Race, Gender and Sexuality in the Imperial Context*. New York and London: Routledge.

McGuigan, Jim (1992). *Cultural Populism*. London and New York: Routledge.

McIntosh, Mary (1978). 'The state and the oppression of women'. In Kuhn, Annette and Wolpe, Anne Marie (eds) (1978).

McIntosh, Mary, and Segal, Lynne (eds) (1992). *Sex Exposed*. London: Virago.

McKendrick, Neil, Brewer, John, and Plumb, J.H. (1982). *The Birth of a Consumer Society: The Commercialization of 18th Century England*. London: Europa Publications.

McLennan, Gregor, Held, David and Hall, Stuart (eds)(1984). *State and Society in Contemporary Britain: A Critical Introduction*. Cambrdige: Polity.

McLennan, Gregor (1995). 'Feminism, epistemology and postmodernism: reflections on current ambivalence'. *Sociology*, 29, 3, 391–409.

McLuhan, Marshall (1964). *Understanding Media*. London: Routledge and Kegan Paul.

McNay, Lois (1992). *Foucault and Feminism*. Cambridge: Polity.

McPherson, C.B. (1962). *The Political Theory of Possessive Individualism*. Oxford: Oxford University Press.

McRobbie, Angela (1987). *Feminism and Youth Culture: From Jackie to Just Seventeen*. London: Macmillan.

McRobbie, Angela, and Nava, Mica (eds) (1984). *Gender and Generation*. London: Macmillan.

McWilliams, Sally (1991). 'Tsitsi Dangarembga's *Nervous Condition*: At the crossroads of feminism and post-colonialism'. *World Literature Written in English*, 31, 1, 103–12.

Mead, George Herbert (1955). *Mind, Self and Society*. Chicago: University of Chicago Press.

Mead, Margaret (1963) (first published 1935). *Sex and Temperament in Three Primitive Societies*. New York: William Morrow.

Meekosha, Helen and Dowse, Leanne (1996). 'Enabling citizenship: gender, disability and citizenship'. Unpublished paper prepared for the Women and Citizenship Conference, University of Greenwich, London, 16–18 July.

Menchu, Rigoberta (1984). *I, Rigoberta Menchu: An Indian Woman in Guatemala* (edited and introduced by Elisabeth, Burgos-Debray,). London: Verso.

Merchant, Carolyn (1992). *Radical Ecology: The Search for a Liveable World*. New York and London: Routledge.

Mernissi, Fatima (1994). *The Harem Within: Tales of a Moroccan Girlhood*. London: Bantam Books.

Merton, Robert (1968) (first published 1949). *Social Theory and Social Structure*. New York and London: The Free Press.

Metz, Christian (1983). *Psychoanalysis and Cinema: The Imaginary Signifier*. London: Macmillan.

Mies, Maria, and Shiva, Vandana (1993). *Ecofeminism*. London: Zed.

Miles, Robert (1989). *Racism*. London: Routledge.

Milkman, Ruth (1986). 'Women's history and the Sears case'. *Feminist Studies* 12, 394–95.

Miller, Jane (1990). *Seductions: Studies in Reading and Culture*. London: Virago.

Miller, Jane (1996). *School for Women*. London: Virago.

Millett, Kate (1971). *Sexual Politics*. London: Sphere.

Mills, Jane (1989). *Womanwords*. London: Longman.

Mills, Sara (1995). *Feminist Stylistics*. London: Routledge.

Minow-Pinkney, Makito (1987). *Virginia Wolfe and the Problem of the Subject*. Brighton: Harvester.

Mitchell, Juliet (1974). *Psychoanalysis and Feminism*. London: Allen Lane.

Modleski, Tania (1982). *Loving With a Vengeance: Mass-Produced Fantasies for Women*. New York: Methuen.

Modleski, Tania (1986). *Studies in Entertainment: Critical Approaches to Mass Culture*. Indiana University Press.

Modleski, Tania (1991). *Feminism Without Women: Culture and Criticism in a 'Postfeminist' Age*. New York and London: Routledge.

Moers, Ellen (1977). *Literary Women: The Great Writers*. London: The Women's Press.

Mohanty, Chandra Talpade (1992). 'Feminist encounters: locating the politics of experience'. In Barrett, Michèle, and Phillips, Anne (eds) (1992).

Mohanty, Chandra Talpade (1993) (first published 1985). 'Under western eyes: feminist scholarship and colonial discourse'. In Williams, Patrick, and Chrisman, Laura (eds.) (1993).

Moi, Toril (1985). *Sexual/Textual Politics: Feminist Literary Theory*. London and New York: Methuen.

Moi, Toril (1989). 'Feminist, female, feminine'. In Belsey, Catherine, and Moore, Jane (eds) (1989).

Moi, Toril (1991). 'Appropriating Bourdieu: feminist theory and Pierre Bourdieu's sociology of culture'. *New Literary History*, 22, 1017–49. Reprinted in Lovell (ed.) (1995).

Moi, Toril (1994). *Simone de Beauvoir: The Making of an Intellectual Woman*. Oxford: Blackwell.

Moi, Toril (ed.) (1987). *French Feminist Thought: A Reader*. Oxford: Blackwell.

Molyneux, Maxine (1995). 'Gendered transition in Eastern Europe'. *Feminist Studies*, 21, 3, 637–46.

Moraga, Cherrie (1983). *Loving in the War Years*. Boston, MA: South End Press.

Moraga, Cherríe, and Anzaldúa, Gloria (1981). *This Bridge Called My Back: Writings by Radical Women of Colour*. Watertown, MA: Persephone Press.

Morgan, David (1992). *Discovering Men*. London: Routledge.

Morgan, Robyn (1984). *Sisterhood is Global: The International Women's Movement Anthology*. Garden City, NY: Anchor Doubleday. Harmondsworth: Penguin.

Morgan, Robyn (ed.) (1970). *Sisterhood is Powerful*. New York: Vintage.

Morley, Dave, and Brunsdon, Charlotte (1978). *Everyday Television: Nationwide*. London: British Film Institute.

Morley, Louise and Walsh, Val (eds) (1995). *Feminist Academics: Creative Agents for Change*. London: Taylor & Francis.

Morris, Jenny (1991). *Pride Against Prejudice: Transforming Attitudes to Disability*. London: The Women's Press.

Morrison, Toni (1992). *Playing in the Dark: Whiteness and the Literary Imagination*. Cambridge, MA, and London: Harvard University Press.

Mouffe, Chantal (1992). 'Feminism, citizenship, and radical democratic politics'. In Butler, Judith and Scott, Joan W. (eds) (1992).

Mouffe, Chantal (1993). 'Liberal socialism and pluralism: which citizenship?' In Squire, J. (ed.). *Principled Positions*. London: Lawrence & Wishart.

Mukta, Parita (1994). *Upholding the Common Life: The Community of Mirabai*. Delhi: Oxford University Press.

Mulhern, Francis (1979). *The Moment of 'Scrutiny'*. London: Verso.

Mulvey, Laura (1989a) (first published 1975). 'Visual pleasure and narrative cinema'. In Mulvey, Laura (1989b).

Mulvey, Laura (1989b). *Visual and Other Pleasures*. Bloomington: Indiana University Press.

Munt, Sally (1994). *Murder By the Book? Feminism and the Crime Novel*. London: Routledge.

Narayan, Luma (1989). 'The project of feminist epistemology: perspectives from a nonwestern feminist'. In Jaggar, Alison and Bordo, Susan (eds) *Gender/Body/Knowledge*. New Brunswick and London: Rutgers University Press.

Nava, Mica (1992). *Changing Cultures: Feminism, Youth and Consumerism*. London: Sage.

Negt, Oskar and Kluge, Alexander (1993). *Public Sphere and Experience: Towards an Analysis of the Bourgeois and Proletarian Sphere*. Trans. P. Labanyi, J.O. Daniel and A. Oksiloff. Minneapolis and London: University of Minneapolis Press.

Neitz, Mary Jo (1993). 'Inequality and difference: feminist research in the sociology of religion'. In William H. Swatos Jr, *A Future for Religion? New Paradigms for Social Analysis*. London and New Delhi: Sage.

Nelson, Cary, and Grossberg, Lawrence (eds) (1988). *Marxism and the Interpretation of Culture*. Urbana: University of Illinois Press.

Nicholson, Linda (1987). 'Feminism and Marx: integrating kinship with the economic'. In Benhabib, Seyla, and Cornell, Druscilla (eds) (1987).

Nicholson, Linda (ed.) (1990). *Feminism/Postmodernism*. New York and London: Routledge.

Nochlin, Linda (1989). *Women, Art and Power and Other Essays*. London: Thames & Hudson.

Nussbaum, Martha, and Glover, Jonathan (1995). *Women, Culture and Development: A Study in Human Capabilities*. Oxford: Clarendon Press.

Nye, Andrea (1988). *Feminist Theory and the Philosophies of Man*. New York and London: Routledge.

O'Faolain, Julia, and Martines, Lauro (1979). *Not in God's Image: Women in History*. London: Virago.

Oakley, Ann (1972). *Sex, Gender and Society*. London: Temple-Smith.

Oakley, Ann (1974). *The Sociology of Housework*. Oxford: Martin Robertson.

Oakley, Ann (1976). *Housewife*. Harmondsworth: Penguin.

Oliver, Michael (1991). *The Politics of Disablement*. London: Macmillan.

Olson, Carl (ed.) (1983). *The Book of the Goddess: An Introduction to Her Religion*. New York: Crossroad.

Ortner, Sherry (1974). 'Is female to male as nature is to culture?'. In Rosaldo, Michelle Z., and Lamphere, Louise (eds) (1974).

Outhwaite, William, and Bottomore, Tom (eds) (1993). *The Blackwell Dictionary of Twentieth-Century Social Thought*. Oxford: Blackwell.

Pahl, Ray (1984). *Divisions of Labour*. Oxford: Blackwell.

Palmer, Paulina (1989). *Contemporary Women's Fiction: Narrative Practice and Feminist Theory*. New York and London: Harvester Wheatsheaf.

Parker, Rozsika (1984). *The Subversive Stitch: Embroidery and the Making of the Feminine*. London: The Women's Press.

Parker, Rozika and Pollock, Griselda (1981). *Old Mistresses: Women, Art and Ideology*. London and Henley: Routledge & Kegan Paul.

Parker, Rozika and Pollock, Griselda (1987). *Framing Feminism: Art and the Women's Movement, 1970–85.* London and New York: Pandora.

Parpart, Jane (1995). 'Deconstructing the development "expert": gender, development and the "vulnerable groups"'. In Marchand, Marianne and Parpart, Jane (eds) (1995).

Parry, Benita (1987). 'Problems in current theories of colonial discourse'. *Oxford Literary Review,* 9, 1/2, 27–59.

Parsons, Talcott (1951). *The Social System.* Glencoe IL: Free Press. London: Routledge & Kegan Paul.

Pateman, Carole (1988). *The Sexual Contract.* Cambridge: Polity.

Pateman, Carole and Gross, Elizabeth (eds) (1986). *Feminist Challenges: Social and Political Theory.* London: Allen & Unwin.

Pearce, Lynne (1994). *Reading Dialogics.* London: Edward Arnold.

Pearson, Ruth (1992). 'Gender issues in industrialisation'. In Hewitt, Tom *et al.* (eds), *Industrialisation and Development.* Oxford: Oxford University Press, in association with the Open University.

Penley, Constance (ed.) (1988). *Feminism and Film Theory.* New York and London: Routledge and BFI Publishing.

Perkins, T.E. (1979) 'Rethinking stereotypes'. In Barrett, M., Corrigan, P., Kuhn, A., and Wolff, J. (eds) (1979).

Peters, Julie, and Wolper, Andrea (eds) (1995). *Women's Rights, Human Rights: International Feminist Perspectives.* London and New York: Routledge.

Phillips, Anne (1992). 'Universal pretensions in political thought'. In Barrett, Michèle, and Phillips, Anne (eds) (1992).

Phillips, Anne (ed.) (1987). *Feminism and Equality.* Oxford: Blackwell.

Phillips, Anne and Barbara Taylor (1986). 'Sex and skill'. In *Feminist Review* (ed.).

Phizacklea, Annie (1983). *One-way Ticket.* London: Routledge & Kegan Paul.

Phizacklea, Annie (1990). *Unpacking the Fashion Industry.* London: Routledge.

Phizacklea, Annie (1996). 'Women, migration and the State'. In Rai, Shirin and Lievesly, Geraldine (eds) (1996).

Phizacklea, Annie, and Wolkowitz, Carol (1995). *Homeworking Women: Gender, Class and Racism at Work.* London: Sage.

Phoenix, Ann (1987). 'Theories of gender and black families'. In Weiner, G. and Arnot, M. (eds), *Gender Under Scrutiny.* London: Unwin Hyman.

Phoenix, Ann (1994). 'Practicing feminist research: the intersection of gender and "race" in the research process'. In Maynard, Mary and Purvis, June (eds) (1994).

Piercy, Marge (1979). *Bodies of Glass.* London: Michael Joseph.

Pietilä, Hilkka, and Vickers, Jeanne (1994) (first published 1990). *Making Women Matter: The Role of the United Nations.* London and New Jersey: Zed Books.

Plant, Sadie (1995). 'The future looms: weaving women and cybernetics'. *Body and Society,* Vol 1, 3–4, 45–64.

Plaza, Monique (1978). 'Phallomorphic powers and the psychology of "woman"'. *Ideology and Consciousness*, 4: 4–36.
Plotke, David (1995). 'So what's so new about social movements?' In Lyman, Stanford (ed.) (1995).
Plumwood, Val (1993). *Feminism and the Mastery of Nature*. London: Routledge.
Pollert, Anna (1981). *Girls, Wives, Factory Lives*. London: Macmillan.
Pollert, Anna (ed.) (1991). *Farewell to Flexibility?* Oxford: Basil Blackwell.
Pollock, Griselda (1985). *Vision and Difference: Femininity, Feminism and Histories of Art*. London: Routledge & Kegan Paul.
Poole, Roger (1978). *The Unknown Virginia Woolf*. Cambridge: Cambridge University Press.
Poovey, Mary (1984). *The Proper Lady and the Woman Writer: Ideology as Style in the Works of Mary Wollstonecraft, Mary Shelley, and Jane Austen*. Chicago and London: Chicago University Press.
Popper, Karl (1959). *The Logic of Scientific Discovery*. London; Hutchinson.
Popper, Karl (1966) (first published 1947). *The Open Society and its Enemies*. London: Routledge and Kegan Paul.
Porter, Elizabeth (1991). *Women and Moral Identity*. Sydney and London: Allen & Unwin.
Potts, Lydia (1990). *The World Labour Market: A History of Migration*. London: Zed.
Pratt, Annis (1982). *Archetypal Patterns in Women's Fiction*. Brighton: Harvester Press.
Pribram, E. Dierdre (1988). *Female Spectators: Looking at Film and Television*. London: Verso.
Prince, Gerald (1988). *A Dictionary of Narratology*. Aldershot: Scolar Press.
Pringle, Rosemary (1989). 'Bureaucracy, rationality and sexuality: the case of secretaries'. In Hearn, Jeff *et al.* (eds), *The Sexuality of Organization*. London: Sage.
Radford, Jill, *et al.* (eds), (1996). 'Introduction'. In Hester, Marianne, *et al.*, *Women, Violence and Male Power*. Buckingham: Open University.
Radicalesbians (1970). 'The woman-identified woman'. *The Ladder*, 14, 11/12, 6–8. Reprinted in Hoagland, Sarah Lucia, and Penelope, Julia (eds), *For Lesbians Only: A Separatist Anthology*. London: Onlywomen Press (1988).
Radway, Janice (1984). *Reading the Romance: Women, Patriarchy and Popular Culture*. Chapel Hill: University of North Carolina Press.
Rai, Shirin, and Geraldine Lievesey (eds) (1996). *Women and the State: International Perspectives*. London: Taylor & Francis.
Ramazanoglu, Caroline (1989). *Feminism and the Contradictions of Oppression*. London: Routledge.
Ramazanoglu, Caroline (ed.) (1993). *Up Against Foucault: Explorations of Some Tensions between Foucault and Feminism*. London: Routledge.
Ramazanoglu, Caroline, and Holland, Janet (1993). 'Women's sexuality and men's appropriation of desire'. In Ramazanoglu, Caroline (ed.) (1993).

Ramusack, Barbara (1990). 'Cultural missionaries, maternal imperialists, feminist allies: 'British women activists in India, 1865–1945'. *Women's Studies International Forum*, 13, 4, 309–21.

Randall, Vicki (1982). *Women and Politics*. London: Macmillan.

Ratcliffe, Peter (ed.) (1994). *'Race', Ethnicity and Nation*. London: UCL Press.

Rawls, John (1972). *A Theory of Justice*. Oxford: Oxford University Press.

Rendall, Jane (1985). *The origins of Modern Feminism: Women in Britain, France and the United States, 1780–1860*. Chicago: Lyceum Books.

Reskin, Barbara, and Roos, Patricia (1990). *Job Queues, Gender Queues: Explaining Women's Inroads into Male Occupations*. Philadelphia: Temple University Press.

Rich, Adrienne (1977). *Of Woman Born: Motherhood as Experience and Institution*. London: Virago.

Rich, Adrienne (1979) *On Lies, Secrets and Silence: Selected Prose, 1966–1978*. New York: WW Norton; London: Virago, 1980.

Rich, Adrienne (1980a). *Compulsory Heterosexuality and Lesbian Existence*. London: Onlywomen Press. Reprinted in Snitow, Ann, *et al.* (eds) (1984).

Rich, Adrienne (1980b). 'Towards a woman-centred university' In *Lies, Secrets, Silence: Selected Prose, 1966–1978*. London: Virago, 125–55.

Richardson, Diane (ed.) (1996). *Theorizing Heterosexuality*. Buckingham: Open University Press.

Richardson, Dorothy (1938). 'Foreword'. *Pilgrimage*. London: J.M. Dent and Cresset Press.

Richardson, Marilyn (1980). *Black Women and Religion: A Bibliography*. Boston: G.K. Hall.

Richardson, Samuel (1962). *Pamela* (1740). Ed. by M. Kinkead-Weekes. London: Dent.

Riley, Denise (1988). *'Am I That Name?': Feminism and the Category of 'Women' in History*. London: Macmillan.

Riviere, Joan (1929). 'Womanliness as a Masquerade'. *The International Journal of Psychoanalysis*, 10.

Robinson, Victoria (1996). 'Heterosexuality and masculinity: theorising male power or the male wounded psyche?' In Richardson, Diane (ed.), *Theorising Heterosexuality*. Buckingham: Open University Press.

Roof, Judith (1991). *A Lure of Knowledge: Lesbian Sexuality and Theory*. Columbia University Press.

Roper, Michael (1994). *Masculinity and the British Organization Man since 1945*. Oxford: Oxford University Press.

Rorty, Richard (1989). *Contingency, Irony, and Solidarity*. Cambridge: Cambridge University Press.

Rorty, Richard (1991). *Objectivity, Relativism, and Truth: Philosophical Papers, Vol I*. Cambridge: Cambridge University Press.

Rosaldo, Michelle Z. (1980). 'The use and abuse of anthropology: reflections on feminism and cross-cultural understanding'. *Signs*, 5, 31, 389–417

Rosaldo, Michelle Z., and Lamphere, Louise (eds) (1974). *Women, Culture and Society*. Stanford, CA: Stanford University Press.

Rose, Jacqueline (1986). *Sexuality in the Field of Vision*. London: Verso.

Rose, Jacqueline (1990) (first published 1983). 'Femininity and its discontents'. In Lovell, Terry (ed.) (1990).

Rose, Jacqueline (1991). *The Haunting of Sylvia Plath*. London: Virago.

Rosenberg, Caroll Smith (1985). *Disorderly Conduct: Visions of Gender in Victorian America*. New York and Oxford: Alfred A. Knopf.

Roseneil, Sasha (1995). *Disarming Patriarchy: Feminism and Political Action at Greenham*. Buckingham: Open University Press.

Roszak, Theodore (1969). *The Making of a Counter-Culture*. New York: Anchor.

Rowbotham, Sheila (1972). *Women, Resistance and Revolution*. London: Allen Lane, Penguin Press.

Rowbotham, Sheila (1973a). *Hidden From History*. London: Pluto.

Rowbotham, Sheila (1973b). *Women's Consciousness, Men's World*. Harmondsworth: Penguin.

Rowbotham, Sheila (1990). *The Past is Before Us: Feminism in Action Since the 1960s*. London: Penguin.

Rowbotham, Sheila (1992). *Women in Movement*. London: Routledge.

Rowbotham, Sheila, Segal, Lynne, and Wainwright, Hilary (1979). *Beyond the Fragments: Feminism and the Making of Socialism*. Newcastle Socialist Centre and Islington Community Press.

Rubin, Gayle (1975). 'The traffic in women: the "political economy" of sex'. In Reiter, Rayna (ed.) (1975).

Rudd, Inger Marie (1981). *Women's Status in the Muslim World: A Bibliographical Survey*. Cologne: Brill.

Ruddick, Sara (1990). *Maternal Thinking: Towards a Politics of Peace*. London: The Women's Press.

Ruether, Rosemary R. (ed.) (1974). *Religion and Sexism: Images of Women in the Jewish and Christian Traditions*. New York: Simon & Schuster.

Ruether, Rosemary (1986). *Women-Church: The Theology and Practice of Feminist Liturgical Communities*. New York: Harper and Row.

Rule, Jane (1986). *Desert of the Heart*. London: Pandora Press.

Rush, Florence (1984). 'The great freudian cover up'. *Trouble and Strife*, 4, 28–36.

Russ, Joanna (1985). *The Female Man*. London: The Women's Press.

Russell, Diana (1993). 'Introduction'. In Russell, Diana (ed.), *Making Violence Sexy: Feminist Views on Pornography* Buckingham: Open University Press.

Russo, Mary (1994). *The Female Grotesque: Risk, Excess and Modernity*. New York and London: Routledge.

Ryan, Joanna (1990) (first published 1983). 'Psychoanalysis and women loving women'. In Lovell, Terry (ed.) (1990).

Saghal, Gita (1989). 'Fundamentalism and the multi-cultural fallacy'. In Southall Black Sisters (eds) (1989).

Said, Edward (1978). *Orientalism*. London: Routledge & Kegan Paul.

Said, Edward (1983). *The World, the Text and the Critic*. London: Vintage.

Said, Edward (1993). *Culture and Imperialism*. London: Chatto & Windus.

Sargent, Lydia (ed.) (1981). *The Unhappy Marriage of Marxism and Feminism: A Debate on Class and Patriarchy*. London: Pluto.

Sartre, Jean-Paul. (1961) (first published 1945). *The Age of Reason*, trans. Eric Sutton. Harmondsworth: Penguin.

Sartre, Jean-Paul (1966) (first published 1943). *Being and Nothingness*. Trans. Hazel E. Barnes. New York: Washington Square Press.

Saussure, Ferdinand de (1974). *Course in General Linguistics*. London: Fontana.

Sawicki, Jana (1991). *Disciplining Foucault: Feminism, Power and the Body*. London: Routledge.

Sayers, Janet (1982). *Biological Politics*. London: Tavistock.

Sayers, Janet, Evans, Mary, and Redclift, Nanneke (eds) (1987). *Engels Revisited: New Feminist Essays*. London and New York: Tavistock.

Scarry, Elaine (1985). *The Body in Pain*. New York and Oxford: Oxford University Press.

Schor, Naomi (1987). *Reading in Detail: Aesthetics and the Feminine*. London: Methuen.

Schor, Naomi, and Weed, Elizabeth (eds) (1994). *The Essential Difference*. Bloomington and Indianapolis: Indiana University Press.

Schulman, Sarah (1984). *The Sophie Horowitz Story*. Tallahassee FL.

Schulman, Sarah (1993). *Empathy*. London: Sheba Press.

Schuurman, Frans (ed) (1993). *Beyond the Impasse: New Directions in Development Theory*. London: Zed Books.

Schwarzkopf, Jutta (1992). *Women in the Chartist Movement*. London: Macmillan.

Scott, Alison MacEwen (ed.) (1994). *Gender Segregation and Social Change: Men and Women in Changing Labour Markets*. Oxford: Oxford University Press.

Scott, Bonnie Kime (ed.) (1990). *The Gender of Modernism*. Bloomington: Indiana University Press.

Scott, Joan Wallach (1988). *Gender and the Politics of History*. New York: Columbia University Press.

Scott, Joan Wallach (1990). 'Deconstructing equality-versus-difference'. In Hirsch, Marianne, and Keller, Evelyn Fox (eds) (1990).

Scott, Sarah (1986) (first published 1762). *A Description of Millennium Hall*. New edition with introduction by Jane Spencer. London: Virago.

Sedgwick, Eve Kosofsky (1991). *The Epistemology of the Closet*. Hemel Hempstead: Harvester Wheatsheaf.

Sedgwick, Eve Kosofsky (1994). *Tendencies*. London: Routledge.

Sedgwick, Eve Kosofsky, and Parker, Andrew (eds) (1995). *Performance and Performativity*. London: Routledge.

Segal, Lynne (1987). *Is the Future Female? Troubled Thoughts on Contemporary Feminism.* London: Virago.

Segal, Lynne (1994). *Straight Sex.* London: Virago.

Segal, Lynne, and McIntosh, Mary (eds) (1992). *Sex Exposed: Sexuality and the Pornography Debate.* London: Virago.

Seidler, Victor (1989). *Rediscovering Masculinity.* London: Routledge.

Seidler, Victor (ed.) (1992). *Men, Sex and Relationships: Writings from Achilles Heel.* London: Routledge.

Seifert, Ruth (1996). 'The second front: the logic of sexual violence in wars'. *Women's Studies International Forum* 19, 1/2, 35–43.

Sen, Amartya, and Heyzer, Noleen (eds) (1995). *Gender, Economic Growth and Poverty.* Kali for Women.

Sen, Gita and Gvocon, Caven (Centre for Development Alternatives with Women for a New Era) (1988). *Development, Crises and Alternative Visions: Thrid world women's Perspectives.* London: Earthscan.

Sheridan, Alan (1980). *Michel Foucault: The Will to Truth.* London: Tavistock.

Shildrick, Margrit (1997). *Leaky Bodies and Boundaries.* London: Routledge (forthcoming).

Shiva, Vandana (1988). *Women, Ecology and Development.* London and Delhi: Zed Books and Kali for Women.

Shostak, Majorie (1989). '"What the wind won't take away": the genesis of *Nisa-The Life and words of a !Kung woman'.* In personal Narratives Group (ed.).

Showalter, Elaine (1978). *A Literature of their Own: British Women Novelists from Brontë to Lessing.* London: Virago.

Showalter, Elaine (1979). 'Toward a feminist poetics'. In Jacobus, Mary (ed.), *Women Writing and Writing about Women.* London: Croom Helm.

Showalter, Elaine (1992). *Sexual Anarchy: Gender and Culture at the Fin de Siècle.* London: Virago.

Silverman, Kaja (1988). 'Masochism and male subjectivity'. *Camera Obscura,* 17, 31–66.

Sinfield, Alan (ed.) (1983). *Society and Literature, 1945–1970,* New York: Holmes & Meier.

Sinha, Mrinilini (1987). 'Gender and imperialism'. In Kimmel, Michael (ed.), *Changing Men.* Newbury Park and London: Sage.

Sinha, Mrinilini (1995). *Colonial Masculinity: The 'Manly Englishman' and the 'Effeminate Bengali' in the Late Nineteenth Century.* Manchester: Manchester University Press.

Skinner, Jane (1988). 'Who's changing whom? Women, management and work reorganisation'. In Coyle, Angela, and Skinner, Jane (eds), *Women and Work: Positive Action for Change.* Basingstoke: Macmillan.

Sklair, Leslie (1995) (first published 1991). *Sociology of the Global System.* London: Prentice Hall.

Smart, Carol (1984). *The Ties that Bind: Law, Marriage, and the Reproduction of Patriarchal Relations.* London: Routledge and Kegan Paul.

Smart, Carol (1989). *Feminism and the Power of Law*. London: Routledge.

Smart, Carol (1995). *Law, Crime and Sexuality: Essays in Feminism*. London: Sage.

Smart, Carol (1996). 'Collusion, collaboration and confession: moving beyond the heterosexuality debate'. In Richardson, Diane (ed.) (1996).

Smith, Anthony (1986). *The Ethnic Origins of Nations*. Oxford: Blackwell.

Smith, Barbara (1985) (first published 1977). 'Towards a Black feminist criticism'. In Showalter, Elaine (ed.) (1985).

Smith, Dorothy (1988). *The Everyday World as Problematic*. Boston: North Eastern University Press.

Smith, Dorothy (1990). *The Conceptual Practice of Power: A Feminist Sociology of Knowledge*. Boston: North Eastern University Press.

Smith, Joan (1989). *Misogynies: Reflections on Myths and Malice*. London: Faber & Faber.

Smith, Valerie (1990). 'Split affinities: the case of interracial rape'. In Hirsch, Marianne and Keller, Evelyn Fox (eds) (1990).

Smith, Vicki, and Gottfried, Heidi (1996). 'Flexibility in work and employment: the impact on women'. Unpublished paper. Forthcoming in Birgit Pfau-Effinger *et al.* (eds), *Frauenforschung zur Sozio-okonomischen Theorieentwicklung* (Feminist Research on Labour Market Theories).

Snitow, Ann Barr (1984). 'Mass market romance: pornography for women is different'. In Snitow, Ann, Stansell, Christine, and Thompson, Sharon (eds) (1984).

Sommers, Christine Hoff (1994). *Who Stole Feminism: How Women have Betrayed Women*. New York and London: Simon & Schuster.

Soper, Kate (1986). *Humanism and Anti-Humanism*. London: Hutchinson.

Soper, Kate (1989). 'Feminism as critique'. *New Left Review*, 176, 91–112.

Soper, Kate (1990). *Troubled Pleasures: Writings on Politics, Gender and Hedonism*. London: Verso.

Southall Black Sisters (eds) (1989). *Against the Grain*. London: Southall Black Sisters Press.

Spacks, Patricia Meyer (1976) (First published 1975). *The Female Imagination. A Literary and Psychological Investigation of Women's Writing*. London: Allen and Unwin.

Spelman, Elizabeth V. (1990). *Inessential Woman*. London: The Women's Press.

Spencer, Jane (1986). *The Rise of the Woman Novelist: From Aphra Behn to Jane Austen*. Oxford: Blackwell.

Spender, Dale (1980). *Man Made Language*. London: Routledge and Kegan Paul.

Spender, Dale (1983). *Women of Ideas (and What Men Have Done to Them)*. London: Ark.

Spender, Dale (1986). *Mothers of the Novel: 100 Good Women Writers Before Jane Austen*. London: Pandora.

Spillers, Hortense (1984). 'Interstices: a small drama of words'. In Vance, Carol S. (ed.), *Pleasure and Danger*. London: Routledge & Kegan Paul.

Spivak, Gayatri Chakravorty (1987). *In Other Worlds*. London: Methuen.

Spivak, Gayatri Chakravorty (1989) (first published 1985). 'Three women's texts and a critique of imperialism'. In Belsey, Catherine, and Moore, Jane (eds) (1989).

Spivak, Gayatri Chakravorty (1990). *The Post-Colonial Critic: Interviews, Strategies, Dialogues*. London: Routledge.

Spivak, Gayatri Chakravorty (1993a) (first published 1988). 'Can the subaltern speak?'. In Williams, Patrick, and Chrisman, Laura (eds) (1993).

Spivak, Gayatri Chakravorty (1993b). *Outside the Teaching Machine*. London and New York: Routledge.

Stacey, Jackie (1988). 'Desperately seeking difference'. In Gamman, Lorraine, and Marshment, Margaret (eds), *The Female Gaze: Women as Viewers of Popular Culture*. London: The Women's Press.

Stacey, Jackie (1994b). *Star-Gazing: Hollywood Cinema and Female Spectatorship*. London and New York: Routledge.

Stacey, Judith (1987). 'Sexism by a subtler name? Post-industrial and postfeminist consciousness in the Silicon Valley'. *Socialist Review*, 96, 7–28.

Stacey, Judith (1990). *Brave New Families: Stories of Domestic Upheaval in Late Twentieth Century America*. New York: Basic Books.

Stacey, Judith (1991). 'Can there be a feminist ethnography'? In Gluck, Sherna Berger, and Patai, Daphne (eds) (1991).

Stacey, Margaret (1989). 'Older women and feminism: a note about my experience of the WLM'. *Feminist Review* 31, 140–42.

Stanley, Liz (ed.) (1984). *Hannah Cullwick's Diaries*. London: Virago.

Stanley, Liz (ed.) (1990). *Feminist Praxis: Research, Theory and Epistemology in Feminist Sociology*. London: Routledge.

Stanley, Liz ,and Morgan, David (1993). 'Editorial introduction'. *Sociology*, 27, 1, 1–4.

Stanley, Liz and Wise, Sue (1983). *Breaking Out: Feminist Consciousness and Feminist Research*. London: Routledge & Kegan Paul.

Stanton, Elizabeth Cady (1985) (first published 1898). *The Woman's Bible: The original Feminist attack on the Bible*. Edinburgh: Polygon Books.

Stanworth, Michelle (1987). *Reproductive Technologies, Gender, Motherhood and Medicine*. Cambridge: Polity.

Steedman, Carolyn (1982). *The Tidy House: Little Girls Writing*. London: Virago.

Stewart, Ann (1996). 'Should women give up on the state?: Africa experience'. In Rai, Shirin, and Lievesey, Geraldine (eds) (1996).

Stoller, Robert (1968). *Sex and Gender*. London: The Hogarth Press.

Strathern, Marilyn (1988). *The Gender of the Gift: Problems with Women and Problems with Society in Melanesia*. Berkeley and London: University of California Press.

Strossen, Nadine (1996). *Defending Pornography: Free Speech, Sex and the Fight for Women's Rights*. London: Abacus.

Studlar, Gaylyn (1988). *In the Realm of Pleasure: Von Sternberg, Deitrich, and the Masochistic Aesthetic*. Urbana: University of Illinois Press.

Suleri, Sara (1991). *Meatless Days*. London: Flamingo.

Suleri, Sara (1993). 'Woman skin deep: feminism and the post-colonial condition'. In Williams, Patrick, and Chrisman, Laura (eds) (1993).

Summerfield, Penny (1984). *Women Workers in the Second World War: Production and Patriarchy in Conflict*. London: Routledge.

Swain, John, *et al.* (1993). *Disabling Barriers, Enabling Environments*. London: Sage.

Swingewood, Alan (1977). *The Myth of Mass Culture*. London: Macmillan.

Tabet, Paola (1987). '*Du donn au tarif: Les relations sexuelles impliquant une compensation*'. *Les Temps Moderne*, 490, 1–53.

Tasker, Yvonne (1991). *Feminist Crime Writing: The Politics of Genre*. Sheffield: Pavic.

Taylor, Barbara (1983). *Eve and the New Jerusalem: Socialism and Feminism in the Nineteenth Century*. London; Virago.

Taylor, Charles (1989). *Sources of the Self*. Cambridge, MA, and London: Harvard University Press.

Taylor, Charles (1991). *The Ethics of Authenticity*. Cambridge, MA, and London: Harvard University Press.

Taylor, Helen (1989). *Scarlett's Women: Gone with the Wind and its Female Fans*. London: Virago.

Theweleit, Klaus (1993). 'The bomb's womb and the genders of war'. In Cooke, Miriam, and Woollacott, Angela (eds). *Gendering War Talk*. Princeton: Princeton University Press.

Taylor, Jenny Bourne (1990). 'Raymond Williams: gender and generation'. In Lovell, Terry (ed.) (1990).

Thompson, E.P. (1968). *The Making of the English Working Class*. Harmondsworth: Penguin.

Thompson, E.P. (1978). *The Poverty of Theory and Other Essays*. London: Merlin Press.

Thornton, Merle (1986). 'Sex equality is not enough for feminism'. In Pateman, Carole, and Gross, Elizabeth (eds) (1986).

Tickner, Lisa (1987). *The Spectacle of Women: Imagery of the Suffrage Campaign, 1907–14*. London: Chatter and Windus.

Tilly, Louise A., and Scott, Joan W. (1989) (first published 1978). *Women, Work and the Family*. London: Routledge.

Timpararo, Sebastiano (1975). *On Materialism*. London: New Left Books.

Todd, Jane Marie (1986). 'The veiled woman in Freud's *das unheimliche*'. *Signs*, 2/3, 519–28.

Todd, Janet (1993). *Gender, Art and Death*. Cambridge: Polity.

Todorov, Tzvetan (1973). *The Fantastic*, Ithica, NY: Cornell.

Tomasevski, Katarina (1993). *Women and Human Rights*. London and New Jersey: Zed Books.

Tompkins, Jane P. (ed.) (1980). *Reader-Response Criticism: From Formalism to Post-Structuralism*. Baltimore: Johns Hopkins University Press.

Tong, Rosemary (1989). *Feminist Thought: A Comprehensive Introduction*. London: Unwin Hyman.

Touraine, Alain (1995). 'Beyond social movements?' In Lyman, Stanford (ed.).

Trinh, T. Minh-Ha (1990). *Woman, Native, Other: Writing Post-Coloniality and Feminism*. Bloomington: Indiana University Press.

Trombley, Stephen (1981). *'All that Summer She Was Mad': Virginia Woolf and Her Doctors*. London: Junction Books.

Tuana, Nancy (ed.) (1989). *Feminism and Science*. Bloomington, IN: Indiana University Press.

Turner, Brian (1990). 'Outline of a theory of citizenship'. *Sociology*, 24, 2, 189–218.

Urmson, J.O., and Rée, Jonathan (eds) (1989). *The Concise Encyclopaedia of Western Philosophy and Philosophers*. New revised edition. London: Unwin Hyman.

Valenze, Deborah (1995). *The First Industrial Woman*. New York: Oxford University Press.

Vance, Carole (1984). *Pleasure and Danger: Exploring Female Sexuality*. London: Routledge.

Van Zoonen, E. (1993). *Feminist Media Studies*. London: Sage.

Vilar, Pierre (1973). 'Marxist history: a history in the making'. *New Left Review*, 80.

Visweswaran, Kamala (1994). *Fictions of Feminist Ethnography*. Minneapolis and London: University of Minnesota Press.

Volosinov, V.N. (1986). *Marxism and the Philosophy of Language*. Trans. Ladislav Matejka and I.R. Titunik. Cambridge, MA, and London: Harvard University Press.

Vygotsky, L.S. (1978). *Mind in Society*. Cambridge, MA: Harvard University Press.

Wadsworth, M.E.J. (1991). *The Imprint of Time: Childhood, History, and Adult Life*. Oxford: Clarendon Press.

Waites, Bernard, Bennett, Tony, and Martin, Graham (eds) (1982). *Popular Culture: Past and Present*. London: Croom Helm.

Wajcman, Judy (1991). *Feminism Confronts Technology*. Cambridge: Polity Press.

Wajcman, Judy (1996). 'Desperately seeking difference: is management style gendered'. *British Journal of Industrial Relations* September, 333–49.

Walby, Sylvia (1990). *Theorizing Patriarchy*. Oxford: Basil Blackwell.

Walker, Alice (1984a). *In Search of Our Mothers' Gardens*. London: The Women's Press.

Walker, Alice (1984b). *The Temple of My Familiar*. London: The Women's Press.

Walkowitz, Judith (1980). *Prostitution and Victorian Society: Women, Class and the State*. Cambridge: Cambridge University Press.

Wandor, Michelene (1990). *Once a Feminist: Stories of a Generation*. London: Virago.

Ward, Margaret (1983). *Unmanageable Revolutionaries: Women and Irish Nationalism*. London: Pluto.

Ware, Veronica (1992). *Beyond the Pale: White Women, Racism and History*. London: Verso.

Warner, Marina (1985). *Alone of All Her Sex: The Myth and Cult of the Virgin Mary*. London: Weidenfeld & Nicholson.

Warner, Marina (1995). *From the Beast to the Blonde: Fairy-Tales and their Tellers*. London: Vintage.

Warren, Bill (1980). *Imperialism: The Pioneer of Capitalism*. London: Verso.

Waters, Malcolm (1995). *Globalization*. London: Routledge.

Watson, Peggy (1993). 'The rise of masculinism in Eastern Europe'. *New Left Review*, 198, 71–82.

Watson, Sophie (ed.) (1992). '"Women's interests" and the post-structuralist state'. In Barrett, Michèle, and Phillips, Anne (eds) (1992).

Watt, Ian (1957). *The Rise of the Novel*. Harmondsworth: Penguin.

Webster, Alison (1995). *Found Wanting: Women, Christianity and Sexuality*. London: Cassell.

Webster, Paula (1975). 'Matriarchy: a vision of power'. In Reiter, Rayna (ed.).

Weedon, Chris (1987). *Feminist Practice and Poststructuralist Theory*. Oxford: Blackwell.

Weldon, Fay (1983). *The Lives and Loves of a She-Devil*. London: Hodder & Stoughton.

Wendell, Susan (1992). 'Toward a feminist theory of disability'. In Holmes, Helen Bequaert, and Purdy, Laura M. (eds) (1992).

Weston, Kath (1991). *Families We Choose: Lesbians, Gays, Kinship*. New York: Columbia University Press.

Westwood, Sallie (1984). *All Day Every Day: Factory and Family in the Making of Women's Lives*. London: Pluto.

Whitford, Margaret (1991). *Luce Irigaray: Philosophy in the Feminine*. London and New York: Routledge.

Williams, Linda (1990). *Hardcore*. London: Pandora.

Williams, Linda (1994). 'The pornographic subject: feminism and censorship in the 1990s'. In Ledger, Sally, *et al. Political Gender*. New York and London: Harvester Wheatsheaf.

Williams, Patrick, and Chrisman, Laura (eds) (1993). *Colonial Discourse and Post-Colonial Theory*. Hemel Hempstead: Harvester Wheatsheaf.

Williams, Raymond (1961). *The Long Revolution*. London: Chatto and Windus.

Williams, Raymond (1977a). *Marxism and Literature*. Oxford: Oxford University Press.

Williams, Raymond (1977b). 'Realism and non-naturalism'. In the 1977 Edinburgh International Television Festival Official Programme, *Broadcast.*

Williams, Raymond (1979). *Politics and Letters.* London: Verso.

Williams, Raymond (1980a) (first published 1973). 'Base and superstructure in Marxist cultural theory'. In Williams (1980b).

Williams, Raymond (1980b). *Problems in Materialism and Culture.* London: Verso.

Williams, Raymond (1983) (first published 1976). *Keywords.* London: Fontana.

Williams, Raymond (1987) (first published 1958). *Culture and Society: Coleridge to Orwell.* London: Hogarth Press.

Williams, Rosalind H. (1982). *Dream Worlds: Mass Consumption in Late Nineteenth-Century France.* Berkeley, Los Angeles and London: University of California Press.

Williamson, Judith (1978). *Decoding Advertisements: Ideology and Meaning in Advertising.* London: Marion Boyars.

Williamson, Judith (1986). 'The problem of being popular'. *New Socialist*, September.

Willis, Paul (1977). *Learning to Labour: How Working Class Kids Get Working Class Jobs.* London: Saxon House.

Willis, Paul (1978). *Profane Culture.* London: Routledge & Kegan Paul.

Wilson, Elizabeth (1985). *Adorned in Dreams: Fashion and Modernity.* London: Virago.

Wilson, Elizabeth (1990) (first published 1981). 'Psychoanalysis: psychic law and order?' *Feminist Review*, 8. Reprinted in Lovell, Terry (ed.) (1990).

Wilson, Elizabeth (1991). *The Sphinx in the City.* London: Virago.

Wilson, Elizabeth. (1977). *Women and the Welfare State.* London: Tavistock Publications.

Wings, Mary (1988). *She Came in a Flash.* London: Women's Press.

Winship, Janet (1987). *Inside Women's Magazines.* London and New York: Pandora.

Wittgenstein, Ludwig (1967). *Philosophical Investigations.* Oxford: Blackwell.

Wittig, Monique (1971) (first published in French 1969). *The Guérillères.* Trans. David Le Vay. London: Pan.

Wittig, Monique (1992). *The Straight Mind and Other Essays.* Hemel Hempstead: Harvester Wheatsheaf.

Wolff, Janet (1983). *Aesthetics and the Sociology of Art.* London: Macmillan.

Wolff, Janet (1985). 'The invisible flaneuse: women and the literature of modernity'. *Theory, Culture and Society*, special issue, 2, 3.

Wolff, Janet (1993). 'On the road again. Metaphors of travel in cultural criticism'. *Cultural Studies*, 7, 2, May, 224–39.

Wolkowitz, Carol (1987). 'Controlling women's access to political power'. In Afshar, Haleh (ed.), *Women, State and Ideology: Studies from Africa and Asia.* London: Macmillan.

Wollstonecraft, Mary (1982). *Vindication of the Rights of Woman*. Harmondsworth: Penguin.

Wollstonecraft, Mary (1987) (first published 1788 and 1798). *Mary* and *The Wrongs of Women*. Oxford: World's Classics.

Woolf, Virginia (1943). *Three Guineas*. London: Hogarth Press.

Woolf, Virginia (1977) (first published 1929). *A Room of One's Own*. London: Granada.

Woolf, Virginia (1979). *Women and Writing*. Ed. Michèle Barrett. London: The Women's Press.

Woolf, Virginia (1992) (first published 1928). *Orlando*. London: Hogarth Press.

Wright, Elizabeth (ed.) (1992). *Feminism and Psychoanalysis: A Critical Dictionary*. Oxford: Basil Blackwell.

Young, Iris Marion (1990a). 'The ideal of community and the politics of difference'. In Nicholson, Linda (ed.) (1990).

Young, Iris Marion (1990b). *Throwing Like a Girl and Other Essays in Feminist Philosophy and Social Theory*. Princeton: Princeton University Press.

Young, Kate (1993). *Planning Development with Women: Making a World of Difference*. London: Macmillan.

Young, Kate, McCullah, Roslyn and Wolkowitz, Carol (eds) (1987) (first published, 1981). *Of Marriage and the Market: Women's Subordination in International Perspective*. London: Routledge & Kegan Paul.

Yuval-Davis, Nira (1985). 'Front and rear: the sexual division of labour in the Israeli Army'. *Feminist Studies*, 2, 3, 649–76.

Yuval-Davis, Nira (1996). 'Women, citizenship and difference'. Unpublished Background Paper for the Conference on Women and Citizenship, University of Greenwich, London, 16–18 July.

Zizek, Slavoj (ed.) (1994). *Mapping Ideology*. London: Verso.